Macmillan/McGraw-Hill READING

Macmillan McGraw-Hill

New York   Farmington

Contributors

The Princeton Review, Time Magazine, Accelerated Reader

The Princeton Review is not
affiliated with Princeton
University or ETS.

learning through listening

Students with print disabilities may be eligible to obtain an accessible, audio version of the
pupil edition of this textbook. Please call Recording for the Blind & Dyslexic at 1-800-221-4792
for complete information.

Macmillan/McGraw-Hill

A Division of The McGraw·Hill Companies

Published by Macmillan/McGraw-Hill, a division of The McGraw-Hill Companies, Inc., Two Penn Plaza, NY, NY 10121

I, Bk.2

2 3 4 5 6 7 8 9 073/043 05 04 03 02

Macmillan/McGraw-Hill READING

Authors

James Flood

Jan E. Hasbrouck

James V. Hoffman

Diane Lapp

Donna Lubcker

Angela Shelf Medearis

Scott Paris

Steven Stahl

Josefina Villamil Tinajero

Karen D. Wood

Macmillan
McGraw-Hill

New York   Farmington

Managing the

Computer Center

Art Center

Working with Words Center

Phonics Center

Reading and Listening Center

Writing Center

cat
dog

Classroom

Math Center

1 2 3 4 5

Teacher Directed
Small Group Instruction

Sample Management Plan

Group 1	Group 2	Group 3	Group 4
With Teacher	Phonics Center or Word Center	Writing Center or Reading Center	Cross-Curricular Center
Phonics Center or Word Center	**With Teacher**	Cross-Curricular Center	Writing Center or Reading Center
Writing Center or Reading Center	Cross-Curricular Center	**With Teacher**	Phonics Center or Word Center
Cross-Curricular Center	Writing Center or Reading Center	Phonics Center or Word Center	**With Teacher**

Creating Centers

Establishing independent Centers and other independent activities is the key to helping you manage the classroom as you meet with small groups.

Reading and Listening

Set up a classroom library that includes Theme Big Books, Leveled Books, and other independent reading titles on each group's independent reading level. Also, see the Theme Bibliography on pages T98 and T99 for suggested titles.

Children can use the Reading Center for:

- Self-selected reading
- Paired reading
- Listening to selections on audiocassette

Phonics

Children can practice the phonics skills they are learning. Phonics Center activities may include:

- Using Word Building Manipulative Cards to build words
- Substituting letters to build words
- Using Phonics Picture Cards to identify words
- Identifying initial and final blends
- Classifying words by vowel sounds

TEACHING TIP

WORD WALLS Write each letter of the alphabet on an index card. Place the cards on a wall.

Allow space underneath the cards for adding cards for words that begin with that letter. Add new vocabulary words to the Word Wall.

Writing

Children can practice their fine motor, handwriting, and writing skills.

Children can use the Writing Center for:

- Writing/drawing about their own experiences
- Practicing forming letters
- Responding to literature
- Journal writing

Working with Words

Children can practice reading and identifying high-frequency words. Place Word Building Manipulative Cards for the words *ride, small, out, no, saw, two, very, want, away, put, into, good, about, again, around, use,* and *small* in the Center. Have pairs of children practice reading the words together.

Children can use the Working with Words Center for:

- Matching word cards
- Reading words
- Using words in sentences
- Playing word games

Cross-Curricular

CENTERS

Set up Cross-Curricular Centers to help extend selection concepts and ideas. Suggestions for Cross-Curricular Centers can be found throughout the unit.

Science

- Animal Posters, 8D
- Fish, 26
- Sink or Swim?, 48
- Rain, 74
- A to Z Bugs, 96D
- A Healthy Pet, 128

Math

- Add It!, 8D
- Pet Bar Graph, 28
- How Many in the Tub?, 46
- Word Problems, 82
- How Many Spots?, 106

Social Studies

- Weather Chart, 22
- Silk from China, 58
- Work Boots, 78
- Butterfly Migrations, 114
- A Veterinarian's Day, 124D

Art

- Feelings, 14
- Bug Bonanza, 36D
- Design a Toy, 54
- Torn Paper Mural, 66D
- Butterfly Pictures, 116

Additional Independent Activities

The following independent activities are offered as a means to practice and reinforce concepts and skills taught within the unit.

PUPIL EDITION: READER RESPONSE

Story Questions to monitor student comprehension of the selection. The questions are leveled, progressing from literal to more critical thinking questions.

Story Activities related to the selection. Four activities are always provided: one Writing activity, two Cross-Curricular activities, and a Research and Inquiry activity in the "Find Out More" project, which encourages students to use the Internet for research.

LEVELED PRACTICE

Each week, Reteach, Practice, and Extend pages are offered to address the individual needs of students as they learn and review skills.

McGraw-Hill Reading

Theme Chart

MULTI-AGE Classroom

Using the same global themes at each grade level facilitates the use of materials in multi-age classrooms.

GRADE LEVEL	Experience — Experiences can tell us about ourselves and our world.	Connections — Making connections develops new understandings.
Kindergarten	**My World** — We learn a lot from all the things we see and do at home and in school.	**All Kinds of Friends** — When we work and play together, we learn more about ourselves.
Subtheme 1	At Home	Working Together
Subtheme 2	School Days	Playing Together
1	**Day by Day** — Each day brings new experiences.	**Together Is Better** — We like to share ideas and experiences with others.
2	**What's New?** — With each day, we learn something new.	**Just Between Us** — Family and friends help us see the world in new ways.
3	**Great Adventures** — Life is made up of big and small experiences.	**Nature Links** — Nature can give us new ideas.
4	**Reflections** — Stories let us share the experiences of others.	**Something in Common** — Sharing ideas can lead to meaningful cooperation.
5	**Time of My Life** — We sometimes find memorable experiences in unexpected places.	**Building Bridges** — Knowing what we have in common helps us appreciate our differences.
6	**Pathways** — Reflecting on life's experiences can lead to new understandings.	**A Common Thread** — A look beneath the surface may uncover hidden connections.

Themes: Kindergarten – Grade 6

Six Units IN EVERY GRADE

Expression	Inquiry	Problem Solving	Making Decisions
There are many styles and forms for expressing ourselves.	By exploring and asking questions, we make discoveries.	Analyzing information can help us solve problems.	Using what we know helps us evaluate situations.
Time to Shine We can use our ideas and our imagination to do many wonderful things.	**I Wonder** We can make discoveries about the wonders of nature in our own backyard.	**Let's Work It Out** Working as part of a team can help me find a way to solve problems.	**Choices** We can make many good choices and decisions every day.
Great Ideas	In My Backyard	Try and Try Again	Good Choices
Let's Pretend	Wonders of Nature	Teamwork	Let's Decide
Stories to Tell Each one of us has a different story to tell.	**Let's Find Out!** Looking for answers is an adventure.	**Think About It!** It takes time to solve problems.	**Many Paths** Each decision opens the door to a new path.
Express Yourself We share our ideas in many ways.	**Look Around** There are surprises all around us.	**Figure It Out** We can solve problems by working together.	**Starting Now** Unexpected events can lead to new decisions.
Be Creative! We can all express ourselves in creative, wonderful ways.	**Tell Me More** Looking and listening closely will help us find out the facts.	**Think It Through** Solutions come in many shapes and sizes.	**Turning Points** We make new judgments based on our experiences.
Our Voices We can each use our talents to communicate ideas.	**Just Curious** We can find answers in surprising places.	**Make a Plan** Often we have to think carefully about a problem in order to solve it.	**Sorting It Out** We make decisions that can lead to new ideas and discoveries.
Imagine That The way we express our thoughts and feelings can take different forms.	**Investigate!** We never know where the search for answers might lead us.	**Bright Ideas** Some problems require unusual approaches.	**Crossroads** Decisions cause changes that can enrich our lives.
With Flying Colors Creative people help us see the world from different perspectives.	**Seek and Discover** To make new discoveries, we must observe and explore.	**Brainstorms** We can meet any challenge with determination and ingenuity.	**All Things Considered** Encountering new places and people can help us make decisions.

Together Is Better

We like to share ideas and experiences with others.

ONE GOOD PUP **8A**

written and illustrated by **Frank Asch**

S K I L L S			
Phonics	**Comprehension**	**Vocabulary**	**Study Skill**
• **Introduce/Apply** Short *u* • **Review** Short *u, i, a; sh, th*	• **Introduce** Story Elements	• **Introduce** Inflectional Ending *-ed*	• Maps

REALISTIC FICTION

THE BUG BATH **36A**

written by **Anne Miranda**
illustrated by **Bernard Adnet**

S K I L L S			
Phonics	**Comprehension**	**Vocabulary**	**Study Skill**
• **Introduce/Apply** Short *o* • **Review** Short *o, u, i, a; ck*	• **Review** Story Elements (Problem and Solution)	• **Review** Inflectional Ending *-ed*	• Maps

A FANTASY

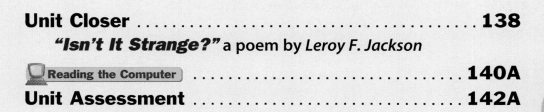
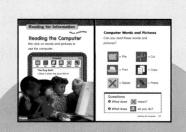

Unit Planner

	WEEK 1 One Good Pup	**WEEK 2** The Bug Bath
Leveled Books	**Easy:** *Cam and Luck* **Independent:** *The Pup and the Cat* **Challenge:** *Five Little Ducks*	**Easy:** *Big?* **Independent:** *The Big Sun* **Challenge:** *Whose Footprints?*
☑ **Tested Skills**	☑ **Phonics** Introduce Short *u*, 8I–8J Review Short *u*, 35E–35F Review Short *u, i, a; sh, th*, 35G–35H ☑ **Comprehension** Introduce Story Elements, 35I–35J ☑ **Vocabulary** Introduce Inflectional Ending *-ed*, 35K–35L ☑ **Study Skills** Maps, 34	☑ **Phonics** Introduce Short *o*, 36I–36J Review Short *o*, 65E–65F Review Short *o, u, i, a; ck*, 65G–65H ☑ **Comprehension** Review Story Elements (Problem and Solution), 65I–65J ☑ **Vocabulary** Review Inflectional Ending *-ed*, 65K–65L ☑ **Study Skills** Maps, 64
Minilessons	**Genre:** Story, 11 **Make Inferences,** 17 **/s/ *s* and /sh/ *sh*,** 19 **Context Clues,** 21 **High-Frequency Words,** 23 **Summarize,** 29	**Genre:** Story, 39 **Phonics and Decoding:** Digraphs, 45 **High-Frequency Words,** 47 **Make Inferences,** 51 **Context Clues,** 55 **Compare and Contrast,** 57 **Main Idea,** 59
Language Arts	**Writing:** Interactive Writing, 35M **Grammar:** Nouns, 35O **Spelling:** Words with Short *u*, 35Q	**Writing:** Interactive Writing, 65M **Grammar:** Plural Nouns, 65O **Spelling:** Words with Short *o*, 65Q

Activities

Curriculum Connections	**Read Aloud:** "The Emerald Tree," 8G
	
	Phonics Rhyme: "Tub Song," 8/9
	
	Art: Feelings, 14
	
	Social Studies: Weather Chart, 22
	
	Science: Animal Posters, 8D
	  Fish, 26
	
	Math: Add It, 8D
	  Pet Bar Graph, 28
		Read Aloud: "Hey Bug!" 36G
		
		Phonics Rhyme: "Jack-in-the-Box," 36/37
		
		Science: Alike and Different, 36D; Insects, Large and Small, 42; Sink or Swim? 48
		
		Math: How Many in the Tub? 46
		
		Art: Bug Bonanza, 36D
		  Design a Toy, 54
		
		Social Studies: Silk from China, 58

CULTURAL PERSPECTIVES	Dogs, 20	Beetlemania, 56

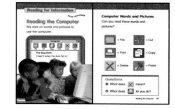

WEEK **3** Splash!	WEEK **4** What Bug Is It?	WEEK **5** A Vet	WEEK **6** Review, Writing, Reading Information, Assessment
Easy: *The Box* **Independent:** *A Big, Big Pig* **Challenge:** *Picnic Farm*	**Easy:** *Around Bug Town* **Independent:** *A Box of Bugs* **Challenge:** *Sitting in My Box*	Self-Selected Reading of Leveled Books	Self-Selected Reading

☑ **Phonics** Introduce Short *e*, 66I–66J Review Short *e*, 95E–95F Review Short *e, o, u, i, a; th,* 95G–95H	☑ **Phonics** Introduce Blends, 96I–96J Review Blends, 123E–123F Review Blends; Digraphs *sh, th, ck,* 123G–123H	☑ **Phonics** Review, Short a, e, i, o, u, 124I–124J	☑ **Assess Skills** Short *u* Short *o* Short *e* Blends Story Elements Main Idea Inflectional Ending -*ed* Context Clues Maps
☑ **Comprehension** Introduce Main Idea, 95I–95J (beginning, middle, end)	☑ **Comprehension** Review Main Idea and Supporting Details, 123I–123J	☑ **Comprehension** Review Story Elements, 137E–137F Review Main Idea, 137G–137H	
☑ **Vocabulary** Review Context Clues, 95K–95L	☑ **Vocabulary** Review Context Clues, 123K–123L	☑ **Vocabulary** Review Inflectional Ending -*ed*, 137I–137J Review Context Clues, 137K–137L	
☑ **Study Skills** Maps, 94	☑ **Study Skills** Maps, 122	☑ **Study Skills** Maps, 136	☑ **Assess Grammar and Spelling** Review Nouns, 142A Review Spelling Patterns, 142B
Genre: Story, 69 **Make Inferences,** 71 **Short *a*,** 75 **Sequence of Events,** 83 **Context Clues,** 87 **Main Ideas,** 89	**Genre:** Informational Story, 99 **Short *u*,** 105 **Context Clues,** 107 **Summarizing,** 111 **Make Inferences,** 117	**Genre:** Narrative Nonfiction, 127 **Fantasy and Reality,** 131	☑ **Unit Progress Assessment** ☑ **Standardized Test Preparation** **Reading the Computer**, 140A

Writing: Interactive Writing, 95M **Grammar:** Irregular Plural Nouns, 95O **Spelling:** Words with Short *e*, 95Q	**Writing:** Interactive Writing, 123M **Grammar:** Proper Nouns, 123O **Spelling:** Words with Blends, 123Q	**Writing:** Interactive Writing, 137M **Grammar:** Days, Months, and Holidays, 137O **Spelling:** Words from Social Studies, 137Q	

Read Aloud: "The Mitten," 66G	**Read Aloud:** "How Spiders Got Eight Legs," 96G	**Read Aloud:** "Your Friendly Vet," 124G	**Cooperative Theme Project Research and Inquiry:** Together is Better, 6J
Phonics Rhyme: "Pets," 66/67	**Phonics Rhyme:** "Snacks," 96/97	**Phonics Rhyme:** "At the Vet," 124/125	
Art: Torn Paper Mural, 66D	**Science:** A to Z Bugs Class Walk, 96D; Mighty Ants, 104; Ladybug Facts, 108	**Social Studies:** A Veterinarian's Day, 124D	
Science: Water, Water!, 66D Rain, 74	**Math:** How Many Spots?, 106	**Math:** Animal Word Patterns, 124D	
Language Arts: Sentences, 76	**Social Studies:** Butterfly Migrations, 114	**Science:** A Healthy Pet, 128	
Social Studies: Work Boots, 78	**Art:** Butterfly Pictures, 116		
Music: Let It Rain, 80			
Parts of the Body, 72	Anansi the Spider, 110		

Unit Resources

LITERATURE

LEVELED BOOKS

📖 **Easy:**
- *Cam and Luck*
- *Big?*
- *The Box*
- *Around Bug Town*

📖 **Independent:**
- *The Pup and the Cat*
- *The Big Sun*
- *A Big, Big Pig*
- *A Box of Bugs*

📖 **Challenge:**
- *Five Little Ducks*
- *Whose Footprints?*
- *Picnic Farm*
- *Sitting In My Box*

THEME BIG BOOK
Share *My River* to set up the unit theme and make content-area connections.

💿 📼 LISTENING LIBRARY
For student book selections and poetry. Available on **compact disc** and **audiocassette.**

Macmillan/McGraw-Hill
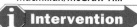
i Intervention ➡️
Skills Intervention Guide
Easy Leveled Books

SKILLS

LEVELED PRACTICE

Practice: Student practice for phonics, comprehension, vocabulary and study skills; plus practice for instructional vocabulary and story comprehension. Take-Home Story included for each lesson.

Reteach: Reteaching opportunities for students who need more help with each assessed skill.

Extend: Extension activities for vocabulary, comprehension, story and study skills.

TEACHING CHARTS
Instructional charts for vocabulary and tested skills. Also available as transparencies.

WORD BUILDING MANIPULATIVE CARDS
Letter and word cards to utilize phonics and build instructional vocabulary.

LANGUAGE SUPPORT BOOK
ESL Parallel lessons and practice for students needing language support.

PHONICS/PHONEMIC AWARENESS PRACTICE BOOK
Additional practice on key phonetic elements.

FLUENCY ASSESSMENT
Evaluation and practice for building reading fluency.

LANGUAGE ARTS

GRAMMAR PRACTICE BOOK
Provides practice for grammar and mechanics lessons.

SPELLING PRACTICE BOOK
Provides practice with the word list and spelling patterns. Includes home involvement activities.

DAILY LANGUAGE ACTIVITIES
Activities that provide reinforcement of grammar, mechanics, and usage skills. Available as blackline masters and transparencies.

HANDWRITING HANDBOOKS
Available for instruction and practice.

McGraw-Hill School
TECHNOLOGY

💿 **Phonics** CD-ROM
Provides phonics support.

*inter*NET **CONNECTION** Extends lesson activities through research and inquiry ideas. Visit **www.mhschool.com/reading.**

Handwriting CD-ROM
Provides practice activities.

Resources for Meeting Individual Needs

	EASY	**INDEPENDENT**	**CHALLENGE**	**LANGUAGE SUPPORT**

BOOK 2

One Good Pup

EASY
 **Leveled Book:** *Cam and Luck*
Reteach, 43–50
Alternate Teaching Strategies, T64–T76
Writing: Draw Pictures, 35M–35N
Phonics CD-ROM

INDEPENDENT
 **Leveled Book:** *The Pup and the Cat*
Practice, 43–50
Alternate Teaching Strategies, T64–T76
Writing: New Story Pages, 35M–35N
Phonics CD-ROM

CHALLENGE
 **Leveled Book:** *Five Little Ducks*
Extend, 43–50
Writing: Journal Entry, 35M–35N
Phonics CD-ROM

LANGUAGE SUPPORT
Teaching Strategies, 10A, 11, 13, 17, 21, 24, 29, 35N
Language Support, 46–54
Alternate Teaching Strategies, T64–T76
Writing: Write a Poem, 35M–35N
Phonics CD-ROM

The Bug Bath

EASY
 **Leveled Book:** *Big?*
Reteach, 51–58
Alternate Teaching Strategies, T64–T76
Writing: Draw Pictures, 65M–65N
Phonics CD-ROM

INDEPENDENT
 **Leveled Book:** *The Big Sun*
Practice, 51–58
Alternate Teaching Strategies, T64–T76
Writing: New Story Ending, 65M–65N
Phonics CD-ROM

CHALLENGE
 **Leveled Book:** *Whose Footprints?*
Extend, 51–58
Writing: Journal Entry, 65M–65N
Phonics CD-ROM

LANGUAGE SUPPORT
Teaching Strategies, 38A, 39, 41, 43, 51, 52, 65N
Language Support, 55–63
Alternate Teaching Strategies, T64–T76
Writing: Write a Guide, 65M–65N
Phonics CD-ROM

Splash!

EASY
 **Leveled Book:** *The Box*
Reteach, 59–66
Alternate Teaching Strategies, T64–T76
Writing: Draw Pictures, 95M–95N
Phonics CD-ROM

INDEPENDENT
 **Leveled Book:** *A Big, Big Pig*
Practice, 59–66
Alternate Teaching Strategies, T64–T76
Writing: Journal Entry, 95M–95N
Phonics CD-ROM

CHALLENGE
 **Leveled Book:** *Picnic Farm*
Extend, 59–66
Writing: New Story, 95M–95N
Phonics CD-ROM

LANGUAGE SUPPORT
Teaching Strategies, 68A, 69, 71, 82, 86, 95N
Language Support, 64–72
AlternateTeaching Strategies, T64–T76
Writing: Make a Weather Chart, 95M–95N
Phonics CD-ROM

What Bug Is It?

EASY
Leveled Book: *Around Bug Town*
Reteach, 67–74
Alternate Teaching Strategies, T64–T76
Writing: Draw Pictures, 123M–123N
Phonics CD-ROM

INDEPENDENT
Leveled Book: *A Box of Bugs*
Practice, 67–74
Alternate Teaching Strategies, T64–T76
Writing: New Story, 123M–123N
Phonics CD-ROM

CHALLENGE
Leveled Book: *Sitting In My Box*
Extend, 67–74
Writing: Journal Entry, 123M–123N
Phonics CD-ROM

LANGUAGE SUPPORT
Teaching Strategies, 98A, 99, 102, 105, 112, 123N
Language Support, 73–81
Alternate Teaching Strategies, T64–T76
Writing: Write an Article, 123M–123N
Phonics CD-ROM

A Vet

EASY
Review
Reteach, 75–82
Alternate Teaching Strategies, T64–T76
Writing: Draw Pictures, 137M–137N
Phonics CD-ROM

INDEPENDENT
Review
Practice, 75–82
Alternate Teaching Strategies, T64–T76
Writing: New Story, 137M–137N
Phonics CD-ROM

CHALLENGE
Review
Extend, 75–82
Writing: Journal Entry, 137M–137N
Phonics CD-ROM

LANGUAGE SUPPORT
Teaching Strategies, 126A, 127, 130, 137N
Language Support, 82–90
Alternate Teaching Strategies, T64–T76
Writing: Write a Class Story, 137M–137N
Phonics CD-ROM

INFORMAL

Informal Assessment

- Phonics, 8J, 31, 35F, 35H; 36J, 61, 65F, 65H; 66J, 91, 95F, 95H; 96J, 119, 123F, 123H; 124J, 133
- Comprehension, 30, 31, 35J; 60, 61, 65J; 90, 91, 95J; 118, 119, 123J; 132, 133, 137F, 137H
- Vocabulary, 35L, 65L, 95L, 123L, 137J, 137L

Performance Assessment

- Research and Inquiry, 6J, 139
- Listening, Speaking, Viewing Activities, 8G, 8H, 10A, 10–35, 35D, 35M–N; 36G, 38H, 38A, 38–65, 65D, 65M–N; 66G, 66H, 68A, 68–95, 95D, 95M–N; 96G, 96H, 98A, 98–123, 123D, 123M–N; 124G, 124H, 126A, 126–137, 133D, 133M–N
- Portfolio, 35N, 65N, 95N, 123N, 137N
- Writing, 35M–N, 65M–N, 95M–N, 123M–N, 137M–N
- Fluency, 30, 60, 90, 118, 132

Leveled Practice

Practice, Reteach, Extend

- **Phonics and Decoding**
  Short *u,* 43, 47, 48, 56, 64, 75
  Short *o,* 51, 55, 56, 64, 75
  Short *e,* 59, 63, 64, 75
  Blends, 67, 71, 72, 75
- **Comprehension**
  Story Elements, 49, 57, 79
  Main Idea, 65, 73, 80
- **Vocabulary Strategies**
  Inflectional Ending -*ed*, 50, 58, 81
  Context Clues, 66, 74, 82
- **Study Skills**
  Maps, 46, 54, 62, 70, 78

FORMAL

Selection Assessments

- **Skills and Vocabulary Words**
  One Good Pup, 21–24
  The Bug Bath, 25–28
  Splash! 29–32
  What Bug Is It? 33–36
  A Vet, 37–38

Unit 2 Test

- **Phonics and Decoding**
  Short *u*
  Short *o*
  Short *e*
  Blends
- **Comprehension**
  Story Elements
  Main Idea
- **Vocabulary Strategies**
  Inflectional Ending -*ed*
  Context Clues

Grammar and Spelling Assessment

- **Grammar**
  Nouns, 37, 43, 49, 55, 61, 63–64
- **Spelling**
  Unit 2 Assessment, 63–64

Fluency Assessment

- Fluency Passages, 10–13

Diagnostic/Placement Evaluation

- Phonemic Awareness Assessment
- Placement Tests
- Informal Reading Inventories
- Running Records

Test Preparation

- Test Power in Teacher's Edition, 35, 65, 95, 123, 137

💿 Reading Test Generator

- Assessment Software

Assessment Checklist

Student .... Grade ....

Teacher ....

	One Good Pup	The Bug Bath	Splash!	What Bug Is It?	A Vet	Assessment Summary
LISTENING/SPEAKING						
Participates in oral language experiences						
Listens and speaks to gain knowledge of culture						
Speaks appropriately to audiences for different purposes						
Communicates clearly						
READING						
Uses phonological awareness strategies, including:						
• Identifying, segmenting, and combining syllables						
• Producing rhyming words						
• Identifying and isolating initial and final sounds						
Uses a variety of word identification strategies:						
• Phonics and decoding: short *u*						
• Phonics and decoding: short *o*						
• Phonics and decoding: short *e*						
• Phonics and decoding: blends						
• Inflectional Ending *-ed*						
• Context Clues						
Reads with fluency and understanding						
Reads widely for different purposes in varied sources						
Develops an extensive vocabulary						
• **Uses Comprehension Strategies:** Main Idea						
Responds to various texts						
Analyzes the characteristics of various types of texts:						
• Story Elements (Character, Setting, Plot)						
Conducts research using various sources: • Maps						
Reads to increase knowledge						
WRITING						
Writes for a variety of audiences and purposes						
Composes original texts using the conventions of written language such as capitalization and penmanship						
Spells proficiently						
Composes texts applying knowledge of grammar and usage						
Uses writing processes						
Evaluates own writing and writing of others						

+ Observed   − Not Observed

Introduce the Theme

Together Is Better

We like to share ideas and experiences with others.

DISCUSS THE THEME Read the theme statement to the children. Ask them to talk about some of the things they do with friends. Encourage children to think about what it feels like to share things that happen to them with someone close to them. Ask:

- How do friends and family help you to understand things?
- Who do you like to talk to most? Why?

SHARE A STORY Have children preview the unit by reading the table of contents and paging through the selections. Use the Big Book *My River* to help establish the unit theme. Have children discuss how the story supports the idea that "Together Is Better." Ask children to tell why it is better for everyone in the book if they all share the river.

MY RIVER
by Shari Halpern

PREVIEW UNIT SELECTIONS Have children preview the unit by reading the selection titles and looking at the illustrations. Have children work in small groups to brainstorm a list of ways that the stories, poems, and the *Time for Kids* magazine article relate to the theme Together Is Better. Ask:

- How do these pieces relate to the Together Is Better theme?
- What are some ways these stories are alike?
- What are some ways these stories are different?
- Are any of these selections about real people and real events? How can you tell?

Have each group present their list to the class and then give the groups an opportunity to add any new ideas they heard to their lists.

THEME CONNECTIONS

Each of the five selections relates to the unit theme Together Is Better as well as to the global theme Connections. These thematic links will help children to make connections across texts.

One Good Pup On a rainy day, a boy and his pup do things together.

The Bug Bath Two dirty bugs share the experience of finding a bath just their size.

Splash! One rainy day, a girl and her pets help one another stay dry.

What Bug Is It? A teacher and her students share what they know about bugs.

A Vet A vet helps many animals stay healthy.

Research and Inquiry

Theme Project: Together with Pets Have children work in teams to brainstorm kinds of animals that people keep as pets. They will then choose one animal from the lists as the subject of a project that will tell all about that animal as a pet.

List What They Know Once children have chosen an animal, have them list what they already know about it.

Ask Questions and Identify Resources Next, ask children to brainstorm some questions they would need to answer in order to prepare their presentations. Have them list possible resources. Remind children to take notes about any important details.

Present Experiences When their research is complete, have children form groups again. Challenge them to note how their animals are similar to one another. Have groups make presentations. Encourage children to use visuals in their presentation.

QUESTIONS	POSSIBLE RESOURCES	ANSWERS
• What is it like to live with this pet? • How big is the pet? • What does it eat? • What makes the animal a good pet?	• library books • dictionary • talk with other people about their pets • the Internet	

See **Wrap Up the Theme**, page 140.

Research Strategies

Encourage children to make use of all published resources. Information on animals abounds. Encourage them to look in the following locations. Share these resource tips:

• Look at the table of contents and illustrations in library books to find information about your animal.

• Look in a dictionary to find an entry for your animal.

• Talk with other people about their pets.

• Use the Internet or a CD-ROM to find facts about your animal.

interNET CONNECTION Children can learn more about animal pets by visiting **www.mhschool.com/reading**

Poetry

Read the Poem

READ ALOUD Tell children that poems are often about someone important to the poet and that someone isn't always a person! Read aloud "Cat Kisses," by Bobbi Katz. Ask:

- What words describe what is happening in the poem?
- In the poem, how does each day begin?
- How does the cat help make the start of each day a good one?

LISTENING LIBRARY The poem is available on **audiocassette** and on **compact disc.**

ECHO READING Read the poem aloud in parts, having children repeat what you've read. Encourage children to continue tracking the words with their finger and focus on your emphasis and fluency.

Learn About Poetry

IMAGERY

Explain the following features of imagery:

- Poets often use *imagery,* or word pictures, to get their meaning across.
- The imagery in a poem is often about something you can imagine touching, feeling, hearing, or seeing.

6

MEET THE POET

ABOUT BOBBI KATZ Children may be interested in knowing that Bobbi Katz writes only for children. She writes poetry because she loves "the sound of the words and their taste on her tongue." Bobbi Katz has two children of her own—a boy named Joshua and a girl named Lori. Another poem by her that children might enjoy is "Things to Do If You Are a Subway."

Together Is Better

Cat Kisses

Sandpaper kisses
on a cheek or a chin—
that is the way
for a day to begin!

Sandpaper kisses—
a cuddle, a purr.
I have an alarm clock
that's covered with fur.

by Bobbi Katz

7

Poetry

CLOSE YOUR EYES AND IMAGINE
Read the title of the poem to children. Then read "Cat Kisses" aloud. Have children close their eyes and imagine what "sandpaper kisses" feel like. Also, ask them what "an alarm clock covered with fur" might feel like. Have volunteers who have cats as pets tell how the poem might relate to their own experiences.

Oral Response

SMALL-GROUP DISCUSSIONS Have children share personal responses to the poem and discuss these questions:

- Do you think the poet likes sandpaper kisses?
- Why does the poet call cat kisses "an alarm clock covered with fur"? Why an alarm clock? What is the cat doing?
- Where else can one get sandpaper kisses? Why doesn't the poet use *nose?* Why use *cheek* and *chin?*
- What words rhyme in this poem?

RESPONDING TO POETRY

Do any of the children have a pet? If so, what does this pet do that is special? Have children draw a real or imaginary pet doing something special—like the "cat kisses" described in the poem. Help them with suggestions, such as a dog carrying slippers or a bird sitting on its owner's shoulder.

7

Concept
• Pet Care

Comprehension
• Story Elements

Phonics
• Short *u*

Vocabulary
• no
• ride
• small
• out

Anthology

One Good Pup

Selection Summary A boy tries to plan things to do inside with his pup on a rainy day. But, his pup's idea of fun is still to go out and play.

Listening Library

Rhyme applies to Phonics

INSTRUCTIONAL pages 10–35

About the Author/Illustrator This is Frank Asch and his pup. As a

little boy, Mr. Asch spent a lot of time outdoors in a special tree that he called his "thinking tree." Mr. Asch started writing when he was in elementary school. Today he is the author and illustrator of many children's books. His books have been translated into many different languages.

Same Concept, Skills and Vocabulary!

Leveled Books

EASY
Lesson on pages 35A and 35D
`DECODABLE`

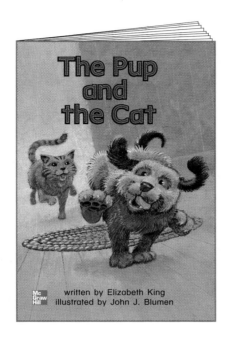

INDEPENDENT
Lesson on pages 35B and 35D

🏠 *Take-Home version available*

`DECODABLE`

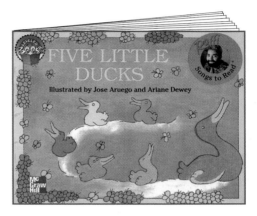

CHALLENGE
Lesson on pages 35C and 35D

Leveled Practice

EASY
Reteach, 43-50 Blackline masters with reteaching opportunities for each assessed skill

INDEPENDENT/ON-LEVEL
Practice, 43-50 Workbook with Take-Home Stories and practice opportunities for each assessed skill and story comprehension

CHALLENGE
Extend, 43-50 Blackline masters that offer challenge activities for each assessed skill

Quizzes Prepared by Accelerated Reader

Center Activities

Science	Animal Posters, *8D*
	Fish, *26*
Math	Add it!, *8D*
	Pet Bar Graph, *28*
Art	Feelings, *14*
Language Arts	Read Aloud, *8G*
Cultural Perspectives	Dogs, *20*
Writing	About Pup, *32*
Research and Inquiry	Find Out More, *33*
Internet Activities	www.mhschool.com/reading

Center Activities

Each of these activities takes 15-20 minutes.

Phonics

Build Short *u* Words

PARTNERS **Objective:** Generate words with short *u*.

◆ Have children write "___u___" on a large sheet of construction paper.

◆ Partners place consonant cards before and after the *u* to build words. Children then write the words that they built.

Writing

Rainy Day Sentences

ONE **Objective:** Write and illustrate sentences about a rainy day.

◆ Show children how to fold their sheet of paper in half.

◆ On one half, children draw themselves doing their favorite rainy day activities.

◆ On the other half, they can write sentences that tell about their pictures.

Reading and Listening

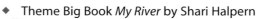

Independent/Self-Selected Reading

ONE **Objective:** Listen and use illustrations to understand a story.

Fill the Center with books and corresponding audiocassettes or CD-ROMs children have read or listened to this week. You can also include books from the Theme Bibliography on pages T98 and T99.

Leveled Readers

◆ *Cam and Luck* by Gary Apple
◆ *The Pup and the Cat* by Elizabeth King
◆ *Five Little Ducks* by José Aruego

◆ Theme Big Book *My River* by Shari Halpern
◆ *One Good Pup* by Frank Asch
◆ "Cat Kisses" by Bobbi Katz
◆ Phonics Practice Reader, Vol. 1

Working with Words

Word Search

Objective: Reinforce vocabulary
ONE words: *no, ride, small, out.*

◆ Provide children with a chart as shown.

◆ Have children search *One Good Pup* and find sentences that contain each vocabulary word.

◆ Children then fill in their charts.

MATERIALS
- *One Good Pup* from the Student Anthology
- Paper
- Pencil

Word	Page	Story Sentence
no	29	It is no fun for pup.
ride		
small		
out		

Science

Animal Posters

Objective: Plan and create
GROUP posters about a favorite animal.

◆ Have children think of an animal, where it lives, and what it does.

◆ They make a poster about the animal and use the story title as a model for the title of their posters.

MATERIALS
- Drawing paper
- Crayons or markers

One Good Penguin
Penguins like snow!
Penguins live in cold places.

Math 3+2

MATERIALS
- Construction paper
- Crayons

Add It!

Objective: Write and illustrate addition
ONE problems.

◆ Write several addition and subtraction problems on the chalkboard, leaving out the answer. For example, 5 + 3 = _____.

◆ Have children choose one of the problems and illustrate it with rainy-day art, such as raindrops, umbrellas, or clouds.

◆ Have children illustrate the answer, too!

◆ Encourage children to add other addition or subtraction problems to the chart.

One Good Pup
by Frank Asch

Suggested Lesson Planner

READING AND LANGUAGE ARTS	**DAY 1** Focus on Reading and Skills	**DAY 2** Read the Literature
● **Phonics Daily Routines**	Daily **Phonics** Routines: Segmenting, 8J **Phonics** CD-ROM	Daily **Phonics** Routine: Blending, 10A **Phonics** CD-ROM
● **Phonological Awareness** ● **Phonics** *Short u* ● **Comprehension** ● **Vocabulary** ● **Study Skills** ● **Listening, Speaking, Viewing, Representing**	**Read** **Read Aloud,** 8G "The Emerald Tree" ☑ **Develop Phonological Awareness,** 8H ☑ **Introduce Short *u*,** 8I–8J **Reteach, Practice, Extend,** 43 **Phonics/Phonemic Awareness Practice Book, 95–98** **Read** **Apply Short *u*,** 8/9 "Tub Song" ⓘ Intervention Program	**Build Background,** 10A Develop Oral Language **Vocabulary,** 10B–10C | no	ride
small	out	 **Word Building Manipulative Cards Teaching Chart 32** **Reteach, Practice, Extend,** 44 **Read** **Read the Selection,** 10–31 **Guided Instruction** ☑ Short *u* **Genre: Story,** 11 **Writer's Craft,** 13 **Cultural Perspectives,** 20 ⓘ Intervention Program
● **Curriculum Connections**	**Link** Language Arts, 8G	**Link** Social Studies/Science, 10A
● **Writing**	✎ **Writing Prompt:** Write about some things a pup might like to have.	✎ **Writing Prompt:** Write about the things that you and a pup could play with. 📓 **Journal Writing** Quick-Write, 31
● **Grammar**	**Introduce the Concept: Nouns,** 35O Daily Language Activity: Identify nouns. **Grammar Practice Book,** 33	**Teach the Concept: Nouns,** 35O Daily Language Activity: Identify nouns. **Grammar Practice Book,** 34
● **Spelling** *Short u*	**Introduce: Words with Short *u*,** 35Q **Spelling Practice Book,** 33–34	**Teach the Patterns: Words with Short *u*,** 35Q **Spelling Practice Book,** 35

Meeting Individual Needs

 = **Skill Assessed in Unit Test**

 Intervention Program Available

 **Read EVERY DAY**

DAY 3 Read the Literature	**DAY 4** Build Skills	**DAY 5** Build Skills
Daily  Routines: **Fluency, 33**  CD-ROM	Daily  Routines: **Build Words, 35F**  CD-ROM	Daily  Routines: **Writing, 35H**  CD-ROM

DAY 3 — Read the Literature

Rereading for Fluency, 30

Story Questions, 32
　Reteach, Practice, Extend, 45

Story Activities, 33

Study Skill, 34
　☑ Maps
　Teaching Chart 33
　Reteach, Practice, Extend, 46

Test Power, 35

 Read the Leveled Books, 35A–35D
　Guided Reading
　☑ Short *u*
　☑ High-Frequency Words

 Intervention Program

DAY 4 — Build Skills

 Read the Leveled Books and Self-Selected Books

☑ Review Short *u,* 35E–35F
　Teaching Chart 34
　Reteach, Practice, Extend, 47
　Language Support, 51
　Phonics/Phonemic Awareness
　Practice Book, 95–98

☑ Review Short *u, i, a; sh, th,* 35G–35H
　Teaching Chart 35
　Reteach, Practice, Extend, 48
　Language Support, 52
　Phonics/Phonemic Awareness
　Practice Book, 95–98

Minilessons, 17, 19, 21, 23, 29

Writer's Craft, 13

 Intervention Program

DAY 5 — Build Skills

 Read Self-Selected Books

☑ **Introduce Story Elements,** 35I–35J
　Teaching Chart 36
　Reteach, Practice, Extend, 49
　Language Support, 53

☑ **Introduce Inflectional Ending -*ed,*** 35K–35L
　Teaching Chart 37
　Reteach, Practice, Extend, 50
　Language Support, 54

Listening, Speaking, Viewing, Representing, 35N
　Sing a Silly Song
　Make a CD Box

Minilessons, 17, 19, 21, 23, 29

Intervention Program

 **Art,** 14

 **Science,** 8D, 26

 **Math,** 8D, 28

Writing Prompt: What in your house would you show to a new pup?

Journal Writing, 35D

Writing Prompt: Pretend you have One Good Duck. What things do you play with? Write a sentence about playing with your duck.

Interactive Writing: Write a Poem, 35M
　Prewrite, Draft

Meeting Individual Needs for Writing, 35N

Writing Prompt: You and your pup are going on a trip. Write about where you will go.

Interactive Writing: Write a Poem, 35M
　Revise, Publish

Practice and Write: Nouns, 35P
　Daily Language Activity: Create sentences.

Grammar Practice Book, 35

Practice and Write: Nouns, 35P
　Daily Language Activity: Create a word web.

Grammar Practice Book, 36

Assess and Reteach: Nouns, 35P
　Daily Language Activity: Indentify nouns.

Grammar Practice Book, 37–38

Practice and Extend: Words with Short *u*, 35R

Spelling Practice Book, 36

Practice and Write: Words with Short *u*, 35R

Spelling Practice Book, 37

Assess and Reteach: Words with Short *u*, 35R

Spelling Practice Book, 38

8F

Link
Language Arts

Read Aloud

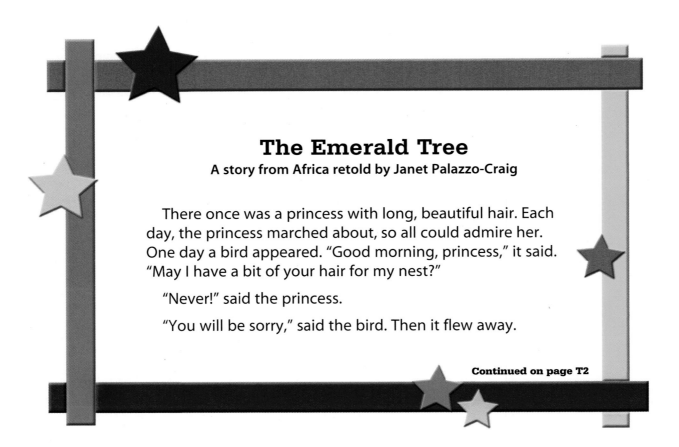

The Emerald Tree
A story from Africa retold by Janet Palazzo-Craig

There once was a princess with long, beautiful hair. Each day, the princess marched about, so all could admire her. One day a bird appeared. "Good morning, princess," it said. "May I have a bit of your hair for my nest?"

"Never!" said the princess.

"You will be sorry," said the bird. Then it flew away.

Continued on page T2

Oral Comprehension

LISTENING AND SPEAKING Motivate children to create a visual picture of the story in their heads as they listen. Ask children questions to encourage visualization such as: *What color hair do you think the Princess has? What does the bird look like?*

Activity Have children draw three beautiful trees Muoma found at the mountaintop. Remind children that one was gold, one was silver, and one was emerald. Explain that *emerald* is another word for green.

▶ **Auditory/Visual**

GENRE: LEGEND Explain to children that a legend is a story handed down from an earlier time that may or may not be true. Explain that legends are often based on people who did very good, brave, or amazing things. Ask children why they think someone created this legend about Muoma. What did he do?

Develop Phonological Awareness

MATERIALS
- puppet

Teach   Have children sit in a circle. Tell them the puppet will say a word. Have the puppet say: *Which of these words rhymes with* rug: bag, run, bug? *(bug)*

Practice   Go around the circle to each child, and have the puppet say the first word in each word set below. Have a child identify which of the three words in each set rhymes with the first word: *bun— run, jug, ban; duck—dock, dug, cluck; hush—hum, rash, rush; buck—back, luck, bat; yum—Sam, sum, fun.*

Blend Sounds · **Phonemic** Awareness

MATERIALS
- Phonics Picture Cards from Word Building Cards

Teach   Hold up the *mouse* picture card. Ask children to name the animal. Have them say the beginning sound of the animal's name. (/m/) Tell children you are going to say the /m/ sound and two more sounds. Ask them to listen carefully as you put the sounds together. Say: */m/-/u/-/g/—mug.* Have children repeat the three sounds separately and then blend them together to say the word.

Practice   Hold up another animal picture card. Ask children to say the beginning sound of the animal's name. Tell them you will say some more sounds. They will listen carefully, repeat each sound, and then blend them together to say each of the following words: /k/-/u/-/b/—*cub*; /k/-/u/-/t/—*cut*; /th/-/u/-/d/—*thud*; /d/-/u/-/k/—*duck*; /p/-/u/-/p/—*pup*; /r/-/u/-/sh/—*rush*.

Segment Sounds · **Phonemic** Awareness

MATERIALS
- Word Building Boxes

Teach   Say: *Bug—/b/-/u/-/g/.* As children say the word with you, sound by sound, point to a word box for each sound.

Practice   Say the following words. Have children say the words with you, sound by sound, pointing to a word box for each sound: *bus, tuck, thud, gum, luck, shut, jug, rush, nut, buck, yum.*

INFORMAL ASSESSMENT

Observe children as they identify rhyming words, blend sounds, and segment sounds. If children have difficulty, see Alternate Teaching Strategies on page T64.

Introduce Short *u*

Skills Finder

Short *u*	
Introduce	B2: 8I-J
Review	B2: 35E-F, 35G-H, 65G-H, 95G-H, 124I-J
Test	Book 2
Maintain	B4: 19, 105

SPELLING/PHONICS CONNECTIONS

Words with Short *u*: See the 5-Day Spelling Plan, pages 35Q–35R.

TEACH

Identify the Letter *u* as the Symbol for /u/

Let children know they will learn to read words with the letter *u*, which stands for the /u/ sound. Introduce the *u* letter card and the sound /u/.

- Display the *u* letter card and say /u/.

BLENDING Model and Guide Practice with Short *u* Words

- Have children repeat the sound /u/ after you as you point to the *u* card.

- Point to the *u* letter card and say /u/. Have children repeat after you.

- Place the *p* letter card after the *u* letter card.

- Blend the sounds together and have children repeat after you.

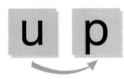

- Place another *p* letter card before the *u* letter card.

- Blend the sounds together and say *pup* and have children repeat after you.

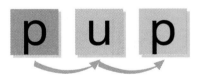

Use the Word in Context

- Use the word in context to reinforce its meaning. Example: *The pup sat on the mat.*

Repeat the Procedure

- Use the following words to continue modeling and guided practice with short *u*.

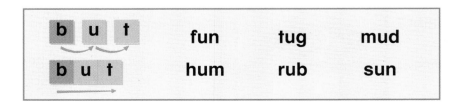

Daily Routines

PRACTICE

LETTER SUBSTITUTION
Build and Rhyme Short u Words

GROUP

Build the word *tub*, asking children to repeat it after you. Replace the *t* with an *r*. Have children repeat the new word: *rub*. Point out that *tub* and *rub* rhyme—they have the same ending sound. Replace the *r* with *c*. Have children identify the new word: *cub*. Repeat this process to form the following words: *rug, bug; cut, hut; fun, sun*. Identify which part of each word rhymes. ▶ **Visual/Kinesthetic**

r   t u b

ASSESS/CLOSE

Read and Write Short u Words

To assess children's ability to blend and read short *u* words, observe them as they build words in the Practice activity. Have children write a sentence using a short *u* word.

ADDITIONAL PHONICS RESOURCES

Phonics/Phonemic Awareness Practice Book,
pages 95–98

PHONICS KIT
Hands-on Activities and Practice

McGraw-Hill School TECHNOLOGY
Phonics CD-ROM
activities for practice with Blending and Building Words

DAY 1 **Segmenting** Distribute letter boxes. Say a short *u* word aloud. Have children write the spelling of each sound in the appropriate box. (Use *sun, fun, hum, mud, tub*.)

DAY 2 **Blending** Write the spelling of each sound in *but* as you say it. Have children repeat after you. Ask children to blend the sounds to read the word. Repeat with *bug, run*, and *tug*.

DAY 3 **Fluency** Build a list of short *u* words using the letter cards. Point to each word, asking volunteers to read each word as they blend the sounds.

DAY 4 **Build Words** Build the following words: *bud, mud, bug, dug, cut*. Have children use word cards and take turns building and reading each word.

DAY 5 **Writing** Have children draw a picture of something they like to do that is fun. Then have them complete and write the sentence ___ *is fun*.

Meeting Individual Needs for Phonics

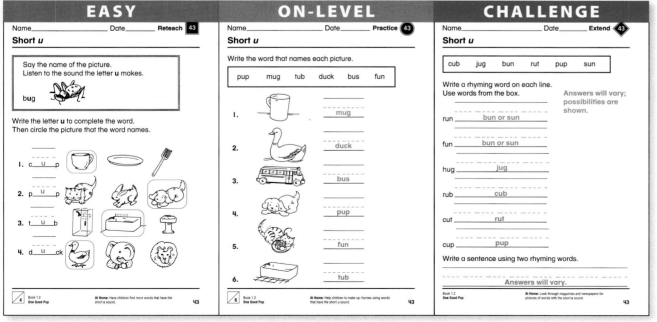

Reteach, 43   Practice, 43   Extend, 43

8J

TESTED OBJECTIVES

Children will read a poem with words containing short *u*.

Apply Short *u*

Tub Song

Rub, rub, rub-a-dub,
We are in the tub.
Hum, hum, we can sing.
We sing in the tub.
Fun, fun, we have fun.
A fun bath in the sun!

Anthology pages 8–9

Read and Build Fluency

READ THE POEM Tell children they will read a poem called "Tub Song." Model reading the lines rhythmically. Track the print by running your finger under each sentence. Ask children to read the poem with you.

REREAD FOR FLUENCY Have children work in small groups to reread the poem as a lively chant.

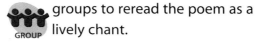

READ A DECODABLE STORY For additional practice reading and to develop fluency, have children read *Pup and Bug* from **Phonics Practice Reader, Vol. 1.**

Dictate and Spell

DICTATE WORDS Segment the word *tub* into its three individual sounds. Repeat the word aloud and use it in a sentence: *Two pups are in the tub.* Then have children say the word and write the letter that represents each sound until they make the entire word. Repeat with *rub, hum, fun,* and *sun* from the poem. Then repeat with short *u* words not from the poem, such as *duck, run, cut, jug, rush, tug,* and *yum.*

ⓘ Intervention **Skills Intervention Guide,** for direct instruction and extra practice in Short *u*

Build Background

Concept: Pet Care

Social Studies/Science

Evaluate Prior Knowledge

CONCEPT: PET CARE Show children a photograph of a pet dog. Ask children what they know about what a dog needs and wants. Use the following activities if children need more information about taking care of a dog.

CLASSIFY AND CATEGORIZE Distinguish   "wants" (what a dog would like to have) from "needs"

GROUP   WRITING

(what a dog must have to survive). Have children suggest things a dog may want and things a dog needs. Draw a two-column chart on the chalkboard. Guide children to place their suggestions in the appropriate column. ▶ **Logical/Linguistic**

Wants	Needs
toys	food
bones	water
petting	exercise
	sleep

MAKE A DOG BULLETIN-BOARD

  DISPLAY Give each child a

ONE   WRITING

piece of drawing paper. Ask children to draw a picture of themselves taking care of a pet dog. Have them write a sentence describing their picture. Post the photograph of the dog you showed earlier and have children place their drawings around it.

Develop Oral Language

CONNECT WORDS AND ACTIONS Set

ESL up an interview with children. Model the interview with one child.

T: Do you have a pet dog?

C: Yes.

T: What is your dog's name?

T: What color is it?

T: How do you take care of your dog?

T: Show me what you do.

Divide the class into pairs. Have them interview each other about their pets, which can be either real or imaginary. Make sure each child demonstrates an aspect of pet care by acting it out. ▶**Linguistic/Kinesthetic**

One Good Pup
by Frank Asch

FIVE LITTLE DUCKS
Illustrated by Jose Aruego and Ariane Dewey

The Pup and the Cat

Cam and Luck
by Gary Apple
Illustrated by Vickey Bolling

LANGUAGE SUPPORT

To build more background, see pages 46–49 in the **Language Support Book**.

DAILY Phonics ROUTINES

DAY 2 **Blending** Write the spelling of each sound in *but* as you say it. Have children repeat after you. Ask children to blend the sounds to read the word. Repeat with *bug, run,* and *tug*.

Phonics **CD-ROM**

10A

OBJECTIVES

Children will:

- identify high-frequency words *ride, small, out,* and *no.*

MATERIALS

- Teaching Chart 32
- Word Building Manipulative Cards *ride, small, out, no*

TEACHING TIP

The following chart indicates words from the upcoming story that children have learned to decode and high-frequency words taught in this lesson. As children read, observe any difficulties they may have in reading these words.

Decodable	High-Frequency
but	no
fun	out
pup	ride
tub	small
tug	

SPELLING/VOCABULARY CONNECTIONS

These words are Challenge Words. See page 35Q for Day 1 of the 5-Day Spelling Plan.

---

no
ride
out
small

Vocabulary
High-Frequency Words

Can My Pup Ride?

Can my pup <u>ride</u> on your bus?

"<u>No</u>, <u>no</u>," said the man to us.

Can my pup <u>ride</u> in your van?

"Go <u>out</u>!" said the moving man.

Can my pup <u>ride</u> this <u>small</u> ship?

"<u>No</u>," the man said. "Not on this trip."

Can my pup <u>ride</u> in your car?

"Yes," said Dad. "But not that far."

Teaching Chart 32

Auditory

LISTEN TO WORDS Ask children to imagine a pup—a dog they own, or one they've seen. Tell them you will read a poem about a pup, and ask them to picture the pup in the poem. Without displaying it, read aloud "Can My Pup Ride?" on **Teaching Chart 32**. After you've read the poem, have children talk about what they imagined.

PANTOMIME HIGH-FREQUENCY WORDS Have children aurally identify each high-frequency word using the following activity:

- Say aloud one of the words. Have children make a gesture for that word. Say the word again, using the gesture. Then read a line of the poem where the word appears. Repeat with each word.

- After you have gestures for all the high-frequency words, read the poem as children use gestures while saying the high-frequency words.

Visual

TEACH WORDS Display "Can My Pup Ride?" on **Teaching Chart 32**. Read the poem, tracking the print with your finger. Next, point to and say the word *ride*. Ask children to hold up the vocabulary card for *ride* and say the word. Repeat this procedure for *small, out,* and *no.*

Hold up vocabulary cards for *ride, small, out,* and *no* one at a time. Have volunteers read the words and then underline them on the chart.

no	small
ride	out

Word Building Manipulative Cards

PLAY "CAN MY PUP RIDE?" Have one group ask "Can my pup ride?" and complete the questions differently than the poem. (Example: *on your train?*) Have the other group answer with a high-frequency word. (Note: Questions and answers don't have to rhyme.)

Activities

Word Wall

Missing Word
Explain to children that you are going to say a sentence with a word missing. The missing word is on the Word Wall. When they decide which word from the sentence is missing, have children point to it.

> We have _____ school Saturday. (no)
> I _____ the bus to school. (ride)
> These shoes are too _____. (small)
> My job is to take the garbage _____. (out)

Snappy Spelling
Invite children to create a snappy rhythm to accompany the spelling of one of the Word wall words. Children can share their snappy spellings with the class.

Assess

Tell a Sentence
Observe children to see if they were able to identify and spell the high-frequency words in the Word Wall activity. Ask children to suggest a sentence using each word. Then have them orally spell the high-frequency word in each sentence.

LANGUAGE SUPPORT

To help children develop understanding and recognition of high-frequency words, see page 46 in the **Language Support Book.**

TEACHING TIP

PHONICS TEACHING TIP Explain that in some very short words that end with the letter *o*, the letter *o* says its name, /ō/. Write the words *no, so,* and *go* on the chalkboard. Read each word as you point to it, emphasizing the long *o* sound. Then read each word with children. Next, have children read the words on their own.

Meeting Individual Needs for Vocabulary

EASY	ON-LEVEL	ON-LEVEL	CHALLENGE

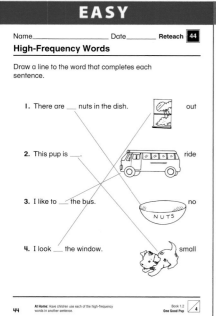

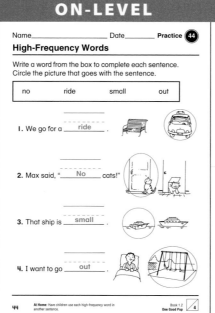

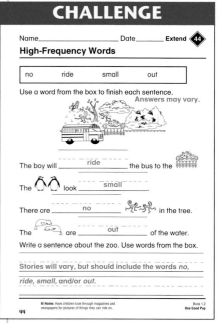

Reteach, 44

Practice, 44

Practice, 44a
Take-Home Story

Extend, 44

Comprehension

Prereading Strategies

PREVIEW AND PREDICT Point to and read aloud the title and the name of the author/illustrator. Discuss the role of the author/illustrator. Take a **picture walk** through the illustrations, looking for pictures that give strong clues about the setting and characters.

Ask children to make predictions about the story by asking questions, such as:

- What might be a problem for the boy and his pup?
- What do the pictures tell you about what the boy and his pup like to do?
- What will the story most likely be about?

Chart children's predictions about the story.

PREDICTIONS	WHAT HAPPENED
It is raining. A boy and his pup cannot go out.	
The pup wants to play.	

SET PURPOSES Ask children what they want to find out as they read the story.

- What games do the boy and the pup play?
- Why is the pup sad?

 Meet Frank Asch

 Frank Asch discovered his love of writing and drawing when he was a boy. He wrote poems, plays, cartoons, and greeting cards. "I remember when I was just 13 or 14 making my first children's book for my sister," he says. Asch is now the author and illustrator of many award-winning children's books.

10

Meeting Individual Needs • Grouping Suggestions for Strategic Reading

EASY

Shared Reading Read the story aloud as you track print and model directionality. Invite children to chime in with repetitive words and phrases as you read the story aloud. Model the strategy of paying attention to the plot to help understand what is happening in the story.

ON-LEVEL

Guided Instruction Ask children to read the story with you. Monitor any difficulties children may have in order to determine which prompts from the Comprehension section to emphasize. After reading the story, have children reread it. See rereading suggestions on page 30.

CHALLENGE

Independent Reading Have children preview the illustrations and come up with questions they would like to ask the boy in the story. After they have read the story, invite children to take turns being the boy and have the other children ask their questions.

One Good Pup ②

by Frank Asch

11

Comprehension

☑ **Phonics** Short *u*

☑ **Apply Analyze Character and Plot**

STRATEGIC READING Tell children that often it is helpful to take notes of events in the story as you read. This can be done in a Learning Log. Using these Learning Logs will help children remember all the events in the story so they can retell it.

① Point to the picture of the author/illustrator on page 10. His name is Frank Asch. How do you think he came up with the idea for this story? (Answers will vary.) Let's read what it says about the author. *Concept of a Book: Author/Illustrator*

② **Phonics** **SHORT *u*** Let's look at the title of this story. *"One Good . . ."* Let's blend the sounds of the next word together. P u p Pup *Graphophonic Cues*

LANGUAGE SUPPORT

A blackline master of the Learning Log can be found in the **Language Support Book.** Children can take notes of the story events in their logs to help them do story retelling later.

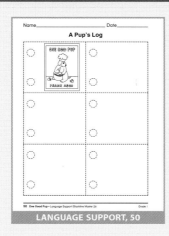

Name_____ Date_____
A Pup's Log

LANGUAGE SUPPORT, 50

Genre

Story

Explain that a story:

• is a fictional piece.

• focuses on a plot about one or more characters in a specific setting.

• presents a problem that must be solved.

Activity Ask children to identify the setting as a rainy day at home. Then ask them to share what they like to do on a rainy day. After reading the story, have children discuss which activities Pup and the boy do that they like to do as well.

Comprehension

3 Let's read the sentences on this page. Who is talking? (the boy) To whom is he talking? (his pup) *Use Illustrations/Make Inferences*

4 Imagine you are with the boy and the pup. Why are you inside? (It is raining.) What might you do inside with the dog? (play a game, pet the dog) *Analyze Plot/Character*

PHONOLOGICAL AWARENESS
Listen for the word that rhymes with *fish*. Clap each time you hear the word.

3 You wish to go out, Pup.
You wish and wish.

12

Fluency

PARTNER READING

PARTNERS Designate partners by reading ability. Model this activity for the class. Then monitor children as they work in pairs.

• Partner 1 reads a page of text. Partner 2 then reads the next page.

• Partners read both pages together in unison.

• If children have difficulty reading together, have them track print and read aloud together as they point to each word.

PREVENTION/INTERVENTION

PHONOLOGICAL AWARENESS
Have children listen for rhyming words. Remind children that words that rhyme end with the same sound. Read the sentences on page 12 aloud.

• Have children clap each time they hear a word that rhymes with *dish*.

• Tell them to name the rhyming word.

• Then encourage them to suggest other words that rhyme with *dish* and *wish*.

• Follow the same process and have children raise their hands when they hear a word that rhymes with *up*.

But it is wet out. **7**

It is so wet.

13

Comprehension

5 Does Pup like walks? (yes) How can you tell? (He is holding his leash. He is smiling and looks happy.) *Make Inferences*

6 Pup is holding his leash for a walk. Describe how the boy and Pup might get ready to go for a walk. *Sequence of Events*

7 The boy says, "But it is wet out." Why does he say this to his pup? (to let the pup know that it is raining and they can't go out) *Draw Conclusions*

Writer's Craft

REPETITION

Explain to children that a writer sometimes uses repeating words to give rhythm to the story. Repeating words can also emphasize important words or ideas.

Example: Look at the sentences on page 12. Ask children which words repeat in the sentence pair. By repeating the word *wish*, the writer wants to show how much Pup wishes to go outside.

GROUP Read page 13 together. Emphasize the rhythm of the repeating words. Ask: What words repeat? Why do you think the writer chose to repeat these words?

LANGUAGE SUPPORT

ESL The /sh/ sound may be difficult for some children to pronounce. Show children the position of your mouth as you say the /sh/ sound. Have the children join in. Show them the letters on page 12 that make this sound. Write *wash*, *fish, dish,* and *ship* on the board. Draw a quick sketch for each word. Have children say the words together; then ask for volunteers to say the words. Help with pronunciation as needed.

Comprehension

8 Listen as I read the first sentence on this page. Raise your hand when you hear a word in the sentence that rhymes with *cap*. (nap) **Nonverbal Response**

9 Look at the picture on page 15. What are the boy and the pup doing? (resting, napping) What do you like to do on a rainy day? (Accept all reasonable answers.) *Use Illustrations/Make Connections*

8 I wish to nap, Pup.
I can nap.

14

Activity

Cross Curricular: Art

FEELINGS Point out that the boy in the picture feels tired. Have children brainstorm other feelings they may have. (hunger, anger, happiness, sadness) Write them on chart paper.

Activity Have each child make a four-page book by folding a large sheet of plain paper in half. The cover should have the title *Feelings* and the owner's self-portrait. Have children label the other pages with feelings they select from the chart. Children can draw and write descriptions of why they feel that way.
▶ **Linguistic/Visual**

Can you nap?
Nap with me, Pup. ⑩

15

Comprehension

⑩ Let's read the first sentence on page 15 again. How does it end? (with a question mark) The question mark tells us to read the sentence as if we are expecting someone to answer us. Let's read the sentence again and raise our voice at the end. *Concepts of Print*

BLENDING WITH SHORT *a* Find the first word in the last sentence and point to it. Now read the word with me, using your finger to help you remember to blend the sounds of the letters together. n a p nap *Graphophonic Cues*

TEACHING TIP

PERIODS AND QUESTION MARKS
Point to each word as you reread the first sentence on page 15. Pause when you come to the question mark. Model moving your finger up as you lift your voice at the end of the sentence. Read the next sentence. Move your finger down to emphasize that your voice goes down when you say a sentence with a period. Read the sentences as you model them.

PREVENTION/INTERVENTION

BLENDING WITH SHORT *a* Write the letter *a* on a card and tape it to the board. Have children tell you what short sound the letter *a* makes. (/a/) Write the following letters on the board: *c, t, d, s*. Invite children to use any of the letters to build words with *a* in the middle. Prompt them by suggesting *cat*. Write each new word on the chalkboard. (*dad, sad, sat*) Then have children read the word with you as you run your hand underneath it. Repeat this activity with other consonants. *Graphophonic Cues*

Comprehension

(11) ANALYZE CHARACTER What does the pup wish to do? (go out) Does the pup wish to go out very strongly? (yes)

(p/i) CONCEPTS OF PRINT How many sentences do you see on this page? (two) Point to the first sentence. Now point to the second sentence. *Syntactic Cues*

TEACHING TIP

DIRECTIONALITY Ask children to point to the second sentence on the page. Explain that the second sentence is underneath the first sentence. Have children note that the sentences were written from top-to-bottom.

Together, think of a message to write to the boy in the story. As you write the message on chart paper, ask children to write the message on their own. Explain that you will start on the left side of the paper and move to the right. After you write a word, ask children to write the word. When you begin a new line, point out that the new line is written underneath the line above.

Reread the message, pointing out to children the directionality of left-to-right and top-to-bottom.

(11) You wish to go out, Pup.
You wish and wish.

16

(p/i) PREVENTION/INTERVENTION

CONCEPTS OF PRINT Remind children that a sentence is a group of words that tells an idea. Discuss the strategy of looking for a capital letter to determine where a sentence begins and a period to determine where a sentence ends. Then have children use a blank sentence strip to cover up the second sentence. Ask them to read the first sentence. After removing the sentence strip, have children read both sentences. Remind them to pause when they see the period at the end of the first sentence. *Syntactic Cues*

But it is wet out.
It is so wet.

17

Comprehension

12 Let's remember what has happened so far. What did the pup want to do? (go outside) What did the boy and the pup do instead? (took a nap) *Sequence of Events*

13 Look at the picture. Has the weather changed? (no) What might the boy do with his pup? (play inside, go out with an umbrella) *Make Predictions*

Minilesson

REVIEW/MAINTAIN

Make Inferences

Let children know that the words and pictures are descriptive. From them we can guess and conclude why the characters act or feel the way they do.

- Have children look carefully at the illustration on pages 16–17.
- Ask: Why is the boy on the floor? (He just woke up from a nap.)
- Then ask children why they think the pup is on top of the boy. (The pup is excited; the pup wants to get the boy's attention; the pup wants to go out.)

Activity Make a Venn diagram. Brainstorm feelings that the boy and the pup might have. Write those feelings in the appropriate parts of the diagram. Discuss feelings that the boy and pup might have in common.

LANGUAGE SUPPORT

ESL To make a Learning Log, give each child six index cards. Punch two holes through one edge and tie them together with string. Have children number each card. Tell children they will use their Learning Logs to record what happens in the story. Remind them to draw and write on each card every time the boy and the pup do something new.

17

Comprehension

(14) ANALYZE PLOT AND CHARACTER Let's think about what the boy and the pup have done so far. Draw a picture or write a sentence in your Learning Log to help you remember what has happened. *Graphic Organizer*

(15) What are the boy and the pup doing here? (sitting in a box) Why do you think they are doing that? (They are playing. The box is a ship.) *Make Inferences*

(p/i) CONCEPTS OF PRINT Look at the first sentence on this page. What kind of sentence is it? (a question) How do you know? (There is a question mark at the end.) *Syntactic Cues*

Can you sit in this small ship, Pup?
Sit in this small ship with me.

18

CONCEPTS OF PRINT Recall with children that a question asks something. Tell them to point to the question mark that ends the first sentence. As you read the question, model raising your voice at the end. Invite children to read the question aloud with you. Tell them to look for other questions in the story and use the proper intonation when they read them. *Syntactic Cues*

You wish to go out, Pup.
But it is wet out. **17**

19

Comprehension

16 Are the boy and the pup really sitting in a small ship? (no) What are they doing? (They are sitting in a box. The boy is pretending the box is a ship.) *Distinguish Between Fantasy and Reality*

17 **ANALYZE PLOT** What does the pup want to do? (go outside) Does the boy want to go outside? (no) Why not? (It is wet outside.)

Minilesson

REVIEW/MAINTAIN

/s/*s* and /sh/*sh*

Children may need practice pronouncing *s* and *sh*. Emphasize the beginning sound of the words *sit* and *ship* as you read page 18. Ask children to:

- find the words in the first sentence on page 18 that begin with the sounds /s/ and /sh/.
- name the words with those same sounds in the second sentence.

Activity Cut a small hole in an index card. Have the children slide the index card along each line of print to frame either /s/ or /sh/. Remove the card and say the word.

Phonics **CD-ROM** Have children use the interactive phonics activities for more reinforcement with initial consonants and digraphs.

Comprehension

18 What do you see the boy doing in the picture? (playing with the pup) Why do you think the boy is doing that? (The pup wants to play, but they can't go outdoors.)
Draw Conclusions

19 **Phonics** SHORT *u* *"I wish to play . . . "* Let's blend this word together; t u g tug. Now read the next sentence with me. *Graphophonic Cues*

20 Do you think that the boy is still tired? (no) Why? (He is playing with his pup.)
Draw Conclusions

SELF-MONITORING STRATEGY

ASK QUESTIONS Ask yourself questions to help you remember what has happened in the story so far.

• What do the boy and the pup want to do?
• What have they done so far?

19 I wish to play tug, Pup.
I can tug.

20

CULTURAL PERSPECTIVES

DOGS Ask children who know a second language to share the word for "dog" in that language. Write their responses on the board. Include *perro* (Spanish), *cane* (Italian), *chien* (French), *haushund* (German), and any others that children contribute. Pronounce the words in each language, noting similarities.

Activity Write each foreign word and the language it is in on a strip of paper. Ask children to draw or cut out a picture of a dog. Display these and the word strips on a bulletin board.

▶ **Visual/Linguistic**

Can you tug?

Play tug with me, Pup. **20**

21

Comprehension

21 **ANALYZE PLOT** What has the boy done since the beginning of the story? Let's look at our Learning Logs to recall what he has done. Has anything new happened that we might note in our Learning Logs? (The boy played with his pup in his ship; they played tug.) Let's take some time to add this to our Learning Logs. *Graphic Organizer*

22 Look carefully at the picture on this page. Is it still raining outside? (yes) *Use Illustrations*

Minilesson
REVIEW/MAINTAIN
Context Clues

Remind students that they can use words they know and pictures to help them read new words.

- Have children look at page 21. Point out the word *play*.
- Ask children to describe what the boy and the pup are doing.
- Invite a volunteer to read the word *play* and define what it means based on what the illustration shows.

Activity Ask pairs of children to pantomime being the boy and the pup playing together. Then have partners switch roles. Ask them to state what game they are playing.

Comprehension

23 What is the pup doing? (jumping in the air) Why do you think the pup is doing this? (The pup is excited; the pup wants to go outside.) *Make Inferences*

24 Have any of you ever been excited about something? Show me what you do when you get excited. *Nonverbal Response*

You wish to go out, Pup.
You wish and wish.

22

Activity

Cross Curricular: Social Studies

WEATHER CHART Make a class weather chart. List the days of the week down one side. Write the names of American cities at the top. Be sure to include your city. Draw a picture to represent what the weather is like (sun, cloud, rain, snow, or wind) each day. ▶ **Visual/Kinesthetic**

RESEARCH AND INQUIRY Have children choose a city and find a weather fact about it.

But it is wet out.
It is so wet.

23

Comprehension

25 What is the boy doing now? (He is holding the pup outside.) **Why is he doing this?** (to show the pup that it is still raining) *Draw Conclusions*

26 **ANALYZE PLOT** Let's review the story. **Has the weather changed?** (no) **What has the boy done?** (He took a nap; he played in his ship with his pup; he played tug.) Let's make some new notes or drawings in our Learning Logs. *Graphic Organizer*

BLENDING WITH SHORT *e* **Which word in the sentence describes rain?** (*wet*) Now read the word with me. Blend the sounds as you read. *Graphophonic Cues*

P/i PREVENTION/INTERVENTION

BLENDING WITH SHORT *e* Use three or four sets of the following letter cards: *w, t, r, d, h, n, p*. Give a blank card to each child and instruct children to write the letter *e* on their cards. Then divide the class into small groups and give one set of the consonant cards to each group. Have children lay out the cards and work together to build words with the letter *e* in the middle. Ask children to blend the letters together to read each word, pointing out that nonsense words don't count. Model the procedure as necessary with the word *wet*. Invite groups to call out the words they build and list them on the chalkboard. *Graphophonic Cues*

Comprehension

27 What is the boy doing now? (He is sitting and reading a book.) *Use Illustrations*

28 Are the boy and the pup inside or outside? (inside) *Analyze Setting*

TEACHING TIP

MANAGEMENT Colorful empty tissue boxes make great containers for index cards or other small pieces of paper. For activities that require children to pick out letter cards, word cards, or sentence strips, use oblong tissue boxes. Their top openings make it easy for small hands to reach inside.

Can you sit?
Sit with me, Pup.

24

ESL Invite the children to go on a word search. Have them find and say all the words on pages 24–25 that contain the letter *i*. (*sit, with, wish, it, is*) List these words on the board and ask volunteers to circle the letter *i* in each word.

Have children practice using these words in context by creating new sentences in a question–answer format. Model this activity for them by saying *Can you sit? Yes, I can sit.*

You wish to go out, Pup. (29)
But it is wet out.

25

Comprehension

(29) ANALYZE CHARACTER Let's read the sentences together. Why do you think the boy keeps telling the pup that it is wet out? (The pup still wants to go out.) How do you think the boy feels towards the pup? (He feels sorry that they can't go out.)

(30) What do you think the boy and his pup will do next? (Answers will vary.) Let's turn the page and find out. *Make Predictions*

 SOUND/SYMBOL RELATIONSHIP Point to the word *Pup*. Name the letter it begins with. (*P*) Now point to the word *But*. Name the letter it begins with. (*B*) As I write each word on the board, say the word with me and blend the sounds. *Graphophonic Cues*

P/i   PREVENTION/INTERVENTION

SOUND/SYMBOL RELATIONSHIP
Some children may confuse the initial sounds in *But* and *Pup*. To help children identify the initial consonant, have them frame the uppercase *P* in *Pup* and the *B* in *But* and then say each sound. Have them trace each letter with their fingers. *Graphophonic Cues*

Comprehension

31 Now what are the boy and the pup doing? (mixing, cooking) *Use Illustrations*

32 Are they inside or outside? (inside) Why are they inside? (It is still wet and raining outside.) *Cause and Effect*

TEACHING TIP

MANAGEMENT Keep a stack of index cards handy for children to practice decoding strategies. Write an easily decodable word on one side and a harder one that rhymes or has the same consonant construction on the other side. Children can use the recognized portion of the easy word to figure out the harder one.

Can you mix, Pup?
Help me mix this, Pup.

26

Activity

Cross Curricular: Science

FISH Draw a simple picture of a fish on the board. Have children call out the different parts of a fish and label them. Be sure to include the eyes, fins, tail, mouth, scales, and gills. Have children copy the drawing and labels onto a piece of drawing paper. Ask volunteers to describe different fish they have seen in the wild or in an aquarium. ▶ **Visual/Linguistic**

RESEARCH AND INQUIRY Have children find out about what types of fish people eat. Ask them to investigate which fish can be caught in their area and which types are available in their local markets.

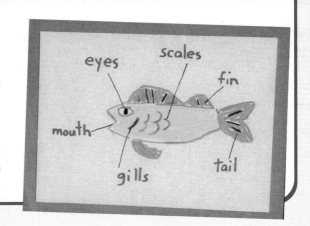

Can you fish, Pup?

We can fish in the tub, Pup. **34**

27

Comprehension

33 What is the boy doing in this picture? (He is fishing.) Do you think he will catch a real fish? (no) Would you describe what he is doing as real or make-believe? (make-believe) *Distinguish Between Fantasy and Reality*

34 **Phonics** **SHORT** *u* Listen as I read the final sentence again. Raise your hands when you hear the words with short *u*. (*tub, Pup*) Now point to these words on the page. *Nonverbal Response*

35 What have the boy and the pup done so far in the story? Let's make a list on the board. (They took a nap; sat in a small ship; played tug; read a book; mixed a cake; fished in a tub.) *Sequence of Events*

36 **ANALYZE PLOT AND CHARACTER** How do you think the pup feels? (Answers will vary.) Use your Learning Logs to add any new events to help you remember what happened in the story. Make sure you show how the boy and the pup feel. *Graphic Organizer*

Comprehension

37 Where is the pup now? (in a wagon) What is the boy doing? (pulling the wagon and giving the pup a ride) *Use Illustrations*

38 **Phonics** **SHORT** *u* Look at the third word on page 29. "This is . . ." Let's blend these sounds together to read this word. f̲ u̲ n̲ fun̲ *Graphophonic Cues*

TEACHING TIP

CHARACTER MOTIVES Tell children that sometimes they may not know or remember why a character says or does something. They may have to reread or look back at preceding pages. Make sure that children ask to look at previous pages if they do not understand why a character is saying or doing something.

Can you ride, Pup?
Take a little ride, Pup.

28

Activity

Cross Curricular: Math

PET BAR GRAPH Ask children to bring in pictures of pets. List the types of pets on chart paper. Then invite children to vote on their favorite pets. Each represents one vote. Have volunteers count and color the correct number of boxes for each pet. ▶ **Logical/Visual**

RESEARCH AND INQUIRY Have children find out how to take care of pets from local animal shelters.

*inter***NET** **CONNECTION** To find various sites about animals and household pets, go to **www.mhschool.com/reading**.

This is fun for me.
It is boxed:no fun for Pup.

29

Comprehension

39 **ANALYZE CHARACTER** Think about how the boy and the pup have felt throughout the story. Have their feelings changed? (no)

40 What do you think would make the pup feel better? (Going outside would make the pup feel happier.) *Cause and Effect*

Minilesson

REVIEW/MAINTAIN

Summarize

Explain to children that when they summarize a story, they tell only the main parts. Elicit their summarizing statements by asking:

- What does the pup want to do?
- How does the weather outside affect what happens in the story?
- What are some of the things the pup and boy do together?
- How does the story end?

Activity Have each child draw a simple comic strip of some of the events in the story. Use long strips of paper. Remind children to draw expressions on the characters' faces to show how they feel. Make sure the final panel of each comic strip shows how the story ends.

LANGUAGE SUPPORT

ESL Reread the story to children acquiring English. Before reading each page, ask children to tell what is happening in each picture. Then, encourage them to read the text with you. Involve all children in the rereading by encouraging those children at the beginning stages of English acquisition to either point to the illustrations or provide one- or two-word responses. Observe attempts carefully, then use the child's response to model complete thoughts.

Comprehension

41 Listen as I read the first sentence: *You are sad.* What does *sad* mean? Show me with your faces. *Nonverbal Response*

42 Why is the pup a good pup? (Answers will vary. Accept appropriate responses.) *Draw Conclusions*

43 **ANALYZE PLOT AND CHARACTER** How does the pup look now? (happy) Why is the pup happy? (The pup got to go outside.) Put this information in your Learning Logs at the end. *Graphic Organizer*

PARTNERS **RETELL THE STORY** Ask children to work with a partner to retell the story. Encourage them to refer to their Learning Logs and other summarizing aids you have created. In each pair, ask one child to take the role of the boy and one the role of the pup, and act out the story. *Summarize/Story Props*

STUDENT SELF-ASSESSMENT

Have children ask themselves the following questions to assess how they are reading:

- How did I use what I feel about rainy days to understand the characters and events in the story?

- How did I use what I know about pet dogs to understand why the pup was sad?

- How did I use the pictures and the letters and sounds I know to help me learn new words in the story?

TRANSFERRING THE STRATEGIES

- How can I use these strategies to help me read other stories?

41 You are sad.
But you are not bad.

30

REREADING FOR *Fluency*

PARTNERS Children who need fluency practice can read aloud with a partner or older student.

READING RATE When you evaluate reading rate, have children read aloud from the story for one minute. Place a stick-on note after the last word read. Count words read. To evaluate children's performance, see the Running Record in the **Fluency Assessment** book.

i Intervention For leveled fluency lessons, passages, and norms charts, see **Skills Intervention Guide**, Part 5, Fluency.

43

You are one good Pup!

31

Comprehension

Return to Predictions and Purposes

Reread children's predictions about the story. Discuss their predictions, noting whether any needed to be revised. Then ask children if the story answered the questions they had before they read.

PREDICTIONS	WHAT HAPPENED
It is raining. A boy and his pup cannot go out.	The boy tried to play indoors with his pup.
The pup wants to play.	They played inside. They went outside.

Have children talk about the strategies they used to remember events in the story. Did using their Learning Logs help them understand and remember the story events?

SSESSMENT

HOW TO ASSESS

Phonics **SHORT *u*** On page 21, have children point to and read the word *tug*. Repeat with *Pup*.

ANALYZE CHARACTER AND PLOT Ask children to fold a piece of paper down the center. Title one side *Boy* and the other side *Pup*. Have them draw and write one thing the boy did and one thing he felt. Do the same for the pup.

FOLLOW UP

Phonics **SHORT *u*** Continue to model blending sounds in short *u* words for children who are having difficulty.

ANALYZE CHARACTER AND PLOT Children who are having difficulty can use illustrations from the story, their Learning Logs, and any other summarizing aids the class has created to remind them of what the boy and pup did and felt.

LITERARY RESPONSE

QUICK-WRITE Have children draw a picture of the boy and the pup in their journals. Ask children to write what other things they could do together on a rainy day.

ORAL RESPONSE Have children use their journal entries to discuss these questions:

• Who would you rather play with, the boy or the pup?

• Could you do the same things with a pup as you could with your human friends?

SENTENCE STRIPS Children can use strips 1–39 to retell *One Good Pup*.

1
You wish to go out, Pup.

2
You wish and wish.

Story Questions

Tell children that now they will read some questions about the story. Help children read the questions. Discuss possible answers.

Answers:

1. Answers will vary. Accept appropriate responses, such as: naps; plays in pretend ship; plays tug; mixes cakes; fishes; plays with wagon. *Literal/Plot*

2. It is wet outside. *Inferential/Make Inferences*

3. Answers will vary. *Inferential/Draw Conclusions*

4. Answers will vary. *Summarize/Main Idea*

5. Answers will vary. *Critical/Reading Across Texts*

Write About Pup Help children read the directions in their anthologies. You may want to have volunteers share their pictures. Help children write sentences about their pictures as necessary.

Story Questions & Activities

READ TOGETHER

❶ What does the boy do with his pup?

❷ Why doesn't he take the pup out?

❸ What did you learn about pets?

❹ Make up another title for the story.

❺ Do you like Max or Pup better?

Write About Pup

Pretend Pup is yours.
Draw a picture.
Show you and Pup playing.
Write a sentence about your picture.

Meeting Individual Needs

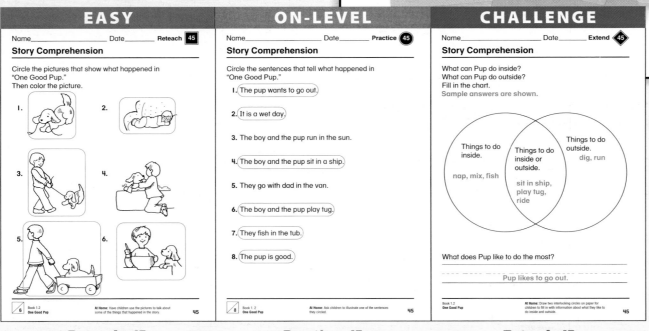

EASY	ON-LEVEL	CHALLENGE
Reteach, 45	Practice, 45	Extend, 45

Make Raindrops

Draw a big raindrop.

Cut it out.

Draw something else the boy and Pup can do.

Find Out More

Find out more about dogs.

What do they eat?

How do you teach a dog?

Share what you learn.

33

DAILY **Phonics** ROUTINES

DAY 3 Fluency Build a list of short *u* words using the letter cards. Point to each word, asking volunteers to read each word as they blend the sounds.

Phonics CD-ROM

Story Activities

Make Raindrops

Materials: blue construction paper, scissors, drawing paper, marking pens, crayons

 Read the directions aloud. Brainstorm with the class what they can do with a pup inside the house on a rainy day and outside on a sunny day. List these on the chalkboard. Children may work together in pairs to create drawings. Encourage them to make as many drawings on their raindrops as they wish, using the list for ideas.

Find Out More

Brainstorm a list of different types of dogs. Ask children to tell which dog they would like to own. Have children vote on their favorites. Keep a tally of votes. Then ask volunteers to explain why they voted as they did.

RESEARCH AND INQUIRY Have children interview people who own dogs. **GROUP** Prepare the children by creating interview questions, using the two that are suggested here. Have children work in groups to discuss what they learned. Then have groups present their findings to the class.

*inter***NET** CONNECTION Have children log on to ***www.mhschool.com/reading*** where they can access sites about dogs.

FORMAL ASSESSMENT

After page 33, see Selection Assessment.

33

Study Skills

MAPS

OBJECTIVES

Children will:

- learn to read a picture map.
- understand direction words.

Remind children that in the story they just read, the boy and the pup stayed inside until the very end. Tell children that now they will finally see the backyard where the boy and Pup play. Display **Teaching Chart 33.** Have them look at the picture map.

Invite children to close their eyes and pretend they are a bird looking down at their own backyard. Invite volunteers to tell what they see as you draw it on chart paper. Review *right, left, up,* and *down*. Use the direction words to locate things in Pup's backyard. Encourage children to point to and trace directions on the map. Then have children answer the questions under the map.

Answers: 1. bushes **2.** apples

A Picture Map

This is a picture map.

It shows Pup's back yard.

Look at the Map

1 What is next to the pool?

2 What is on the tree?

Meeting Individual Needs

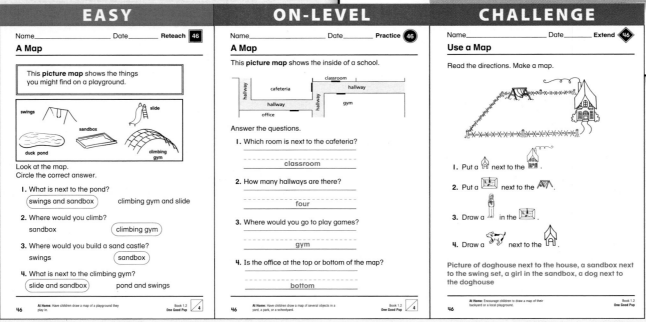

EASY	ON-LEVEL	CHALLENGE
Reteach, 46	Practice, 46	Extend, 46

Sara and Her Pup

Sara has a new pup.

His name is Pal.

Sara likes Pal.

Sara shows Pal to her friends.

They like to play with Pal.

They think that Pal is fun.

How does Sara feel about Pal?

○ Sara thinks Pal is ugly.

● Sara likes Pal.

What does the story tell you about feelings?

35

Test Power

THE PRINCETON REVIEW

Read the Page

Explain to children that you will be reading this story as a group. You will read the story, and they will follow in their books.

Request that children put pens, pencils, and markers away, since they will not be writing in their books.

Discuss the Question

Remind children about words that convey feelings. Have them look back to the story for words that describe feelings of like or dislike. Ask them what words they found, and what they mean.

Test-Tip

To answer a question about feelings, look for words that describe feelings.

Leveled Books

Cam and Luck

by Gary Apple
illustrated by Vickey Bolling

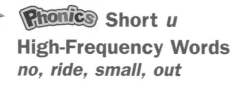
EASY

Cam and Luck

☑ **Phonics** Short *u*

High-Frequency Words
no, ride, small, out

Answers to Story Questions

1. a bat
2. Cam and Luck are thirsty.
3. Yes. Luck looks wet.
4. Cam and Luck go out, tug the bat, get a drink, ride, run, play in the mud, and take a bath.
5. There are a dog and a boy in both stories.

The Story Questions and Activity below appear in the Easy Book.

Story Questions and Activity

1. What do Cam and Luck tug?
2. Why do Cam and Luck stop for water?
3. Did Luck get a bath? How do you know?
4. Name the things Cam and Luck do.
5. How is this story like *One Good Pup?*

Draw a Picture

Think of a game you could play with a pet.
Draw a picture about it.
Write about your picture.

Guided Reading

PREVIEW AND PREDICT Take a **picture walk** and have children predict what the story is about. Chart their ideas.

SET PURPOSES Have children write or draw why they want to read *Cam and Luck.*

READ THE BOOK Use questions like the following to guide children's reading or after they have read **independently**.

Pages 2–3: *MODEL:* "Cam and"... I'm not sure what this word is, but I can blend the sounds of the letters together to read it. L u ck Luck. The word is *Luck,* the dog's name. Now look at the mark after the word *out* in this sentence. What does that mark tell me to do? (pause) Let's read the sentence again, pausing before the word *too.* *Phonics and Decoding, Track Print*

Pages 4–5: Who sees a vocabulary word we just learned on page 5? *(small)* What happened before Cam and Luck had something to drink? (Luck jumped on Cam.) *High-Frequency Words, Sequence of Events*

Pages 6–7: I see four short *u* words on page 7. Who can find and read them? *(Luck, run, mud, fun)* What happens to Cam and Luck? (They get dirty.) Why? (They ride and run through mud.) *Phonics and Decoding, Cause and Effect*

Page 8: Why is the tub no fun? (Possible answer: Cam wants to play instead.) *Make Inferences*

RETURN TO PREDICTIONS AND PURPOSES Discuss children's predictions. Ask which were close to the story and why. Have children review their purposes for reading.

LITERARY RESPONSE Focus children's responses by asking:

• Do you like to play with your pet? Why?

• Do you ever get in trouble when you play? Tell about it.

Also see the story questions and activity in *Cam and Luck.*

See the **Phonics** **CD-ROM** for practice using short *u* words.

Leveled Books

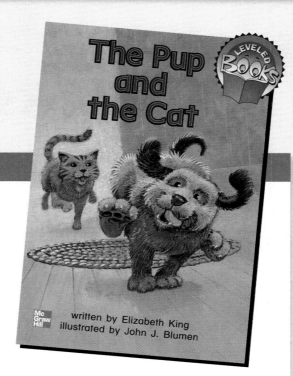

INDEPENDENT

The Pup and the Cat

☑  **Short *u***

High-Frequency Words:
no, ride, small, out

The Pup and the Cat
Leveled Books
written by Elizabeth King
illustrated by John J. Blumen

Guided Reading

PREVIEW AND PREDICT Take a **picture walk**, and have children predict what the story is about. Chart their ideas.

SET PURPOSES Have children write or draw why they want to read *The Pup and the Cat*.

READ THE BOOK Use questions like the following to guide children's reading or after they have read **independently**.

Pages 2–3: Point to the first word in the second sentence and read it with me, blending the sounds of the letters together. H u sh Hush Who sees some more short *u* words on these pages? *(rug, pup, fun)* Look at the pictures. What do you think the cat will do? (wake the pup) *Phonics and Decoding*

Pages 4–5: Let's read these pages together. Look at the pictures and tell what is happening. (The cat wakes up the pup.) Then what happens? (The pup gets mad. The cat runs out.) *Use Illustrations/Confirm Predictions/Cause and Effect*

Pages 6–7: Who sees some vocabulary words we just learned? *(no, rides)* What is the punctuation mark at the end of the second sentence on page 7 called? (exclamation mark) Let's read that sentence again, using a lot of expression. *High-Frequency Words/ Concepts of Print*

Page 8: What does it mean to "make up"? (stop fighting and be friends again) How is this picture like the one on page 2? (The pup is sleeping in both.) *Unfamiliar Words/Compare and Contrast*

RETURN TO PREDICTIONS AND PURPOSES Discuss children's predictions. Ask which were close to the story and why. Have children review their purposes for reading.

LITERARY RESPONSE Focus children's responses by asking:

- Does the girl in the story want her pets to fight?

- Have you ever fought and made up with someone? Tell about it.

Also see the story questions and activity in *The Pup and the Cat*.

See the **Phonics CD-ROM** for practice using short *u* words.

Answers to Story Questions

1. the cat
2. The cat ran away because the pup was mad at the cat.
3. Yes, because the pup looks for the cat.
4. The pup takes a nap. The cat wants to have fun. The cat wakes the pup. The pup is mad. The cat runs out. The pup looks for the cat. The pup and the cat make up. The pup and the cat take a nap.
5. They both take naps.

The Story Questions and Activity below appear in the Independent Book.

Story Questions and Activity

1. Who woke the pup?
2. Why did the cat run away?
3. Did the pup miss the cat? Tell why.
4. Tell the story in your own words.
5. How is the cat in this story like the cat in *Max, the Cat*?

Draw Pet Pals

Think of two pets that could be pals. Draw a picture of them. Write about your picture.

from The Pup and the Cat

Leveled Books

CHALLENGE

Five Little Ducks

☑  **Phonics** Short *u*

Guided Reading

PREVIEW AND PREDICT Take a **picture walk**, and have children predict what the story is about. Chart their ideas.

SET PURPOSES Have children write or draw why they want to read *Five Little Ducks*. For example: *I want to find out where the little ducks went.*

READ THE BOOK Use questions like the following to guide children's reading or after they have read **independently**.

Pages 3–11: *MODEL:* "Five little …" I'm not sure what this word is, but I can blend the sounds of the letters together to read it. d u ck s ducks. The word is *ducks*. Let's look at the pictures and read these pages together. What is happening? (The little ducks are leaving one by one.) *Phonics and Decoding/Use Illustrations/Draw Conclusions*

Pages 12–23: Let's read these pages together. How does the mother duck look on page 12? (happy) Now look at her on the next pages. What is happening? (She is getting sad because her ducks are leaving.) What happens then? (None of the ducks came back.) *Sequence of Events*

Pages 24–31: Look at pages 24 and 25. What is happening here? (The seasons are changing. Mother duck is very sad and lonely.) What happens at the end of the story? How does the mother duck look now? (happy, all of her ducks came home) *Use Illustrations/Make Inferences*

RETURN TO PREDICTIONS AND PURPOSES Discuss children's predictions. Ask which were close to the story and why. Have children review their purposes for reading. Did they find out what happened to the five little ducks?

LITERARY RESPONSE Focus children's responses by asking:

- Where do you think the little ducks went?

- Have you ever been lonely when someone went away? Tell about it.

Also see the story questions and activity at the far left.

See the **Phonics** **CD-ROM** for practice using short *u* words.

Answers to Story Questions

1. their mother
2. All of the little ducks are gone.
3. To have families of their own.
4. One by one, five little ducks leave their mother. Then they all come back with their new families.
5. Both stories have animals following a leader.

Story Questions and Activity

1. Who calls the little ducks back?
2. Why is the mother duck sad?
3. Why do you think the baby ducks went away?
4. What is this story about?
5. How is this story like *I Went Walking*?

What Do You See?

Pretend you are one of the little ducks.

What do you see over the hills?

Draw a picture.

Write a sentence.

from *Five Little Ducks*

Activities

Bringing Groups Together

Anthology and Leveled Books

Connecting Texts

PET CARE Write the story titles on a chart. Discuss with children how the children took care of their pets in each book. Call on volunteers from each reading level and write their suggestions on the chart.

Use the chart to talk about pet animals.

One Good Pup	Cam and Luck	The Pup and the Cat	Five Little Ducks
• Pup wants to go out in the rain, but the boy wants to play indoors. • Finally, they have fun together.	• Cam and Luck play together. • Cam and Luck have something to drink. • Luck gets a bath.	• The cat wants to play, but the pup is sleeping. • The little girl helps the pup find the cat.	• A mother duck's ducklings keep leaving. • Mother Duck takes care of her ducks.

Viewing/Representing

GROUP PRESENTATIONS Divide the class into groups, one for each of the four books. (For *One Good Pup*, combine children of different reading levels.) Have each group draw pictures of the main events and orally summarize the book. Have each group present its pictures and summary.

AUDIENCE RESPONSE Ask children to pay attention to each group's presentation. Allow time for questions after each group presents.

Research and Inquiry

MORE ABOUT PET CARE Have children ask themselves: What else would I like to know about taking care of my pets? Then invite them to do the following:

- Bring in pictures of different pets from home.

- Talk to the class about their pets and how they play with them and care for them.

- Ask a local veterinarian to come in and speak to the class about healthy pets.

inter NET CONNECTION Have children log on to **www.mhschool.com/reading** for more information about pets.

 Children can draw pictures representing what they learned in their journals.

JOURNAL

OBJECTIVES

Children will:
- identify /u/*u*.
- blend and read short *u* words.
- review /b/*b*, /t/*t*, /f/*f*, /m/*m*, /n/*n*, /g/*g*, /r/*r*, /s/*s*.

MATERIALS
- **Teaching Chart 34**
- letter cards from the **Word Building Manipulative Cards**

Skills Finder

Short *u*	
Introduce	B2: 8I-J
Review	B2: 35E-F, 35G-H, 65G-H, 95G-H, 124I-J
Test	Book 2
Maintain	B4: 19, 105

ALTERNATE TEACHING STRATEGY

SHORT *u*

For a different approach to teaching this skill, see pages T64 and T65.

Review Short *u*

> **PREPARE**

Listen for Short *u*   Read the following sentences aloud and have children tap the top of their heads when they hear a short *u* sound.

- The <u>puppy</u> is <u>fun</u>. She <u>runs</u> <u>under</u> the <u>rug</u>. She <u>runs</u> <u>under</u> the <u>tub</u>.

> **TEACH**

Review the Letter *u* as the Symbol for /u/
- Tell children that they will review the letter *u* and its sound.
- Say /u/. Tell children to write the letter that stands for /u/ as they say it.

Teaching Chart 34

BLENDING Model and Guide Practice with Short *u* Words
- Display **Teaching Chart 34.** Run your finger under the letters *t* and *u* and blend the sounds. t   u   tu
- Repeat, having children blend the sounds with you.
- Write the letter *g* in the blank space.
- Run your finger under the letters again, blending them to read the word tug. t   u   g   tug
- Repeat, having children read the word with you.

Use the Word in Context   Invite volunteers to use the word in a sentence to reinforce its meaning. Example: *I gave the rope a tug.*

Repeat the Procedure
- Continue until the chart is complete. Ask volunteers to complete each word and blend the sounds together.

PRACTICE

**BLENDING
Build Short *u*
Words with Letter
Cards**

PARTNERS

Distribute letter cards. Blend and say the word *tug*. Have children work with a partner to build the word with letter cards. Then say *rug*. Ask children to explain how they change *tug* into *rug*, guiding them to see that only the onset sound changes. Repeat with these words: *mug, dug; nut, hut, but; sun, run, fun*. Have children group words together by the same ending sounds. ▶ **Kinesthetic/Linguistic**

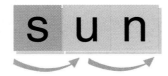

ASSESS/CLOSE

**Build and Read
Short *u* Words**

To assess children's mastery of blending and reading short *u* words, observe children as they build and read words in the Practice activity.

ADDITIONAL PHONICS RESOURCES

**Phonics/Phonemic Awareness
Practice Book,**
pages 95–98

PHONICS KIT
Hands-on Activities and Practice

McGraw-Hill School
TECHNOLOGY
 CD-ROM

activities for practice with
Blending and Building Words

DAY **4** **Build Words** Build the following words: *bud, mud, bug, dug, cut*. Have children use word cards and take turns building and reading each word.

 CD-ROM

SPELLING/PHONICS CONNECTIONS

Words with short *u*: See the 5-Day Spelling Plan, pages 35Q–35R.

i **Intervention** ▶ **Skills Intervention Guide,** for direct instruction and extra practice in Short *u*

Meeting Individual Needs for Phonics

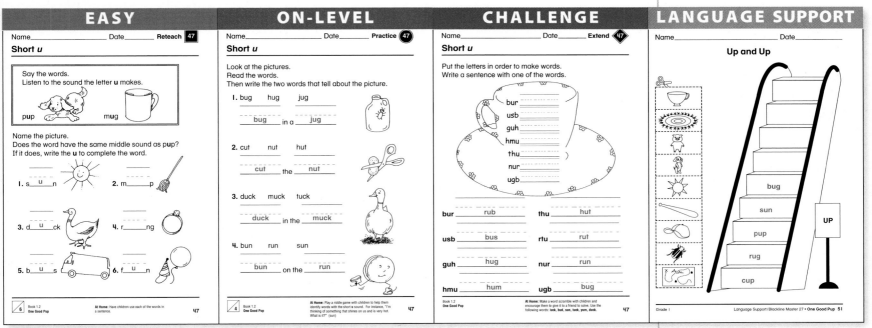

EASY	ON-LEVEL	CHALLENGE	LANGUAGE SUPPORT
Reteach, 47	Practice, 47	Extend, 47	Language Support, 51

35F

OBJECTIVES

Children will:

- review /a/ *a*, /i/ *i*, /u/ *u*, /sh/ *sh*, /th/ *th*.

- blend and read words with short *a, i, u; sh, th*.

- cumulative review: /b/*b*, /c/*c*, /d/*d*, /f/*f*, /m/*m*, /p/*p*, /w/*w*, /r/*r*.

....

MATERIALS

- **Teaching Chart 35**

- **Phonics Practice Reader, Volume 1**

- **Letter boxes from the Word Building Manipulative Cards**

Skills Finder

Short *u*	
Introduce	B2: 8I-J
Review	B2: 35E-F, 35G-H, 65G-H, 95G-H, 124I-J
Test	Book 2
Maintain	B4: 19, 105

ALTERNATE TEACHING STRATEGY
....

SHORT *u*

For a different approach to teaching this skill, see pages T64 and 65.

Review Short *u, i, a; sh, th*

PREPARE

Identify the Letters *sh* and *th* as the Symbols for /sh/ and /th/

Write the following words on the chalkboard: *with, ship, wish, this, push, that*. Have volunteers say each word and circle *sh* or *th* in it.

Discriminate Between /a/*a*, /i/*i*, and /u/*u*

Read the following words: *bath, wish, mush, this, that*. Have children raise their hands when they hear the sound /a/. Repeat with /u/ and /i/.

TEACH

BLENDING Model and Guide Practice with Short *a, i,* and *u* Words

- Display **Teaching Chart 35**. Explain to children that either one or both of the two letters will make a word when added to the blank space.

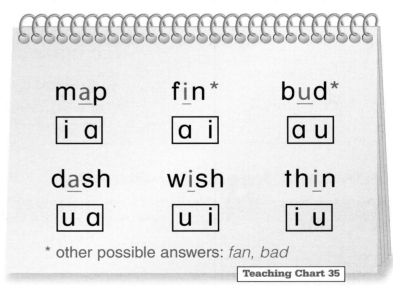

* other possible answers: *fan, bad*

Teaching Chart 35

- Blend the first example on the chart with children. m i p   mip
  m a p   map
- Ask children which word is the real word (map) and have a volunteer write the letter *a* in the blank space.

Use the Word in Context

Invite a volunteer to use the word in a sentence to reinforce its meaning. Example: *You use a map to find your way around*.

Repeat the Procedure

Have volunteers continue with each word on **Teaching Chart 35**. Have children blend the sounds as they say the words.

PRACTICE

BLENDING Build Short *a*, *i*, and *u* Words with Letter Banks

PARTNERS

Write the following letter banks on chart paper and display.

c	m	sh
b	r	p

	i	
	a	
	u	

b		th
p		sh

Have a volunteer choose a letter from the first bank. Write it on the chart paper. Have another child choose a letter from the second and third word banks to form a word. Ask children to read the word. Have pairs repeat the activity, keeping a list of words. ▶ **Spatial**

ASSESS/CLOSE

Segment and Read Words with Short *a*, *i*, *u* and *th*, *sh*

To assess children's mastery of short *a*, *i*, and *u* words, observe them in the Practice activity. Distribute letter boxes. Say *fish* and *math*. Have children write the spelling of each sound in the right box.

Read a Decodable Story

For additional practice reading words with short *u* and to develop fluency, direct children to read the story *Bud Has Six Pups* from the **Phonics Practice Reader, Volume 1.**

ADDITIONAL PHONICS RESOURCES

Phonics/Phonemic Awareness Practice Book, pages 95–98

PHONICS KIT
Hands-on Activities and Practice

McGraw-Hill School
TECHNOLOGY

Phonics **CD-ROM**

activities for practice with Blending and Building Words

DAILY Phonics ROUTINES

DAY 5

Writing Have children draw a picture of something they like to do that is fun. Then have them complete and write the sentence ___ *is fun.*

Phonics **CD-ROM**

ℹ **Intervention** ▶ **Skills Intervention Guide,** for direct instruction and extra practice in Short *u*

Meeting Individual Needs for Phonics

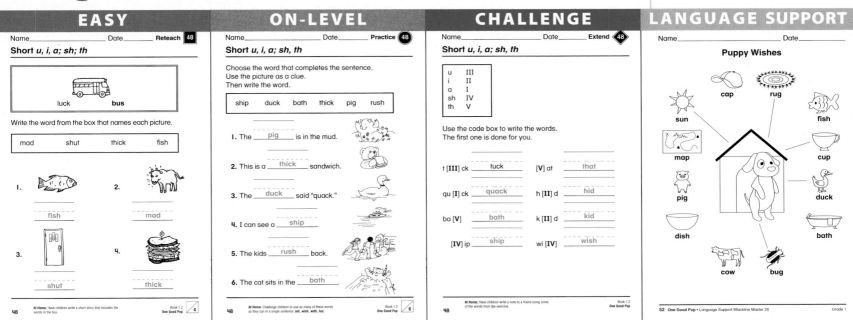

EASY

Name_____ Date_____ Reteach **48**

Short *u*, *i*, *a*; *sh*; *th*

luck   **bus**

Write the word from the box that names each picture.

| mad | shut | thick | fish |

1. fish
2. mad
3. shut
4. thick

48

At Home: Have children write a short story that includes the words in the box.

Book 1.2
One Good Pup 4

ON-LEVEL

Name_____ Date_____ Practice **48**

Short *u*, *i*, *a*; *sh*; *th*

Choose the word that completes the sentence. Use the picture as a clue. Then write the word.

| ship | duck | bath | thick | pig | rush |

1. The ___ pig ___ is in the mud.
2. This is a ___ thick ___ sandwich.
3. The ___ duck ___ said "quack."
4. I can see a ___ ship ___
5. The kids ___ rush ___ back.
6. The cat sits in the ___ bath ___

48

At Home: Challenge children to use as many of these words as they can in a single sentence: ant, wish, with, fast.

Book 1.2
One Good Pup 6

CHALLENGE

Name_____ Date_____ Extend **48**

Short *u*, *i*, *a*; *sh*; *th*

u	III
i	II
a	I
sh	IV
th	V

Use the code box to write the words. The first one is done for you.

t [III] ck ___ tuck ___   [V] at ___ that ___

qu [I] ck ___ quack ___   h [II] d ___ hid ___

ba [V] ___ bath ___   k [II] d ___ kid ___

[IV] ip ___ ship ___   wi [IV] ___ wish ___

48

At Home: Have children write a note to a friend using some of the words from the exercise.

Book 1.2
One Good Pup

LANGUAGE SUPPORT

Name_____ Date_____

Puppy Wishes

cap   rug

sun   fish

map   cup

pig   duck

dish   bath

cow   bug

52 One Good Pup • Language Support/Blackline Master 28   Grade 1

Reteach, 48   Practice, 48   Extend, 48   Language Support, 52

35H

OBJECTIVES

Children will learn to analyze character and plot.

....

MATERIALS
• Teaching Chart 36

Skills Finder

Story Elements

▶ Introduce	B2: 35I-J
▶ Review	B2: 65I-J, 137E-F; B3: 37I-J, 139G-H
▶ Test	Book 2, Book 3
▶ Maintain	B3: 89; B4: 25, B5: 39

TEACHING TIP

ANALYZE CHARACTER AND PLOT In order to analyze characters and plot, have children pantomime situations in the Teach and Practice activities and have the other children guess what they did and why. This will help children understand what happens in the story.

SELF-SELECTED Reading

....

Children may choose from the following titles.

ANTHOLOGY

• *One Good Pup*

LEVELED BOOKS

• *Cam and Luck*

• *The Pup and the Cat*

• *Five Little Ducks*

Bibliography, pages T98–T99

Introduce Story Elements

PREPARE

Introduce Analyzing Character and Plot

Tell children that the characters in a story are who the story is about. What happens to the characters in the story is called the plot.

TEACH

Identify Characters and Plot

Display **Teaching Chart 36.** Invite children to comment on the picture. Then read the chart aloud. Ask: *Who are the characters in this short story? What is happening in this story?*

Dog and Cat

Dog and Cat run a race.
They both try hard.
Cat runs fast.
Who wins the race?

Teaching Chart 36

MODEL Hmm . . . I wonder what this story is about. If I look at the picture I see a dog and a cat running. Let me read the first sentence. It says *Dog and Cat run a race.* So the characters in the story, or who the story tells about, are Dog and Cat. If I keep reading, it says *Cat runs fast.* So what happened in the story—the plot—is that Dog and Cat run a race and Cat wins.

Ask children to circle the winner of the race on **Teaching Chart 36.** Invite children to think of another character, and add to the story on the chart. Then read the "new" story aloud. For example: *Dog, Cat, and Horse run a race.*

Analyze Character and Plot Divide the class into small groups. Have them look back at *One Good Pup*. Have each group list the characters and analyze the characters' feelings, thoughts, and actions. ▶ **Linguistic**

GROUP

ASSESS/CLOSE

Make a Story Have groups of children write their own story. Provide them with a short list of characters and plots by writing the following on the chalkboard:

Character	Plot
—Tells Who	—Tells What
Pam the Pig	makes a friend
Rick the Duck	goes on a trip
Sam the Cat	takes a bath

Have children choose one plot and one or two characters to write their story. Remind them to include a problem that will need to be solved. Invite them to share their stories with the class.

ALTERNATE TEACHING STRATEGY

STORY ELEMENTS
For a different approach to teaching this skill, see page T67.

Intervention **Skills**

Intervention Guide, for direct instruction and extra practice in Story Elements.

Meeting Individual Needs for Comprehension

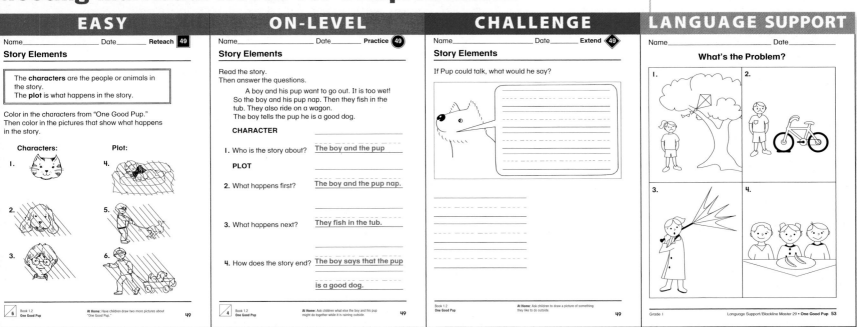

Reteach, 49   Practice, 49   Extend, 49   Language Support, 53

OBJECTIVES

Children will:

• read words with the inflectional ending *-ed.*

. . . .

MATERIALS

• **Teaching Chart 37**

• cards with the inflectional ending *-ed* from the **Word Building Manipulative Cards**

• index cards

Skills Finder

Inflectional Ending *-ed*

Introduce	B2: 35K-L
Review	B2: 65K-L, 137I-J; B4: 65K-L
Test	Book 2, Book 4

TEACHING TIP

DECODING-*ed* Tell children that the sound of the ending *ed* can stand for the sounds /t/ or /d/. Write the words *wished* and *hugged* on the chalkboard. Point to each word and read it, emphasizing the sound of *ed*. Then have children read the words with you. Explain that when *-ed* is added to the end of a word that ends in *t* or *d,* the sound of *ed* changes to /əd/. Say *landed* and clap the syllables. Have children repeat after you. Explain that the word has two parts or syllables—*land* and *ed.* Write *landed* on the chalkboard. Cover the *ed* and read *land* together. Then uncover *ed.* Have children blend the sounds and read the word.

Introduce Inflectional Ending -ed

PREPARE

Act It Out Write the word *quack* on the chalkboard. Have children stand up and quack. Then ask them to sit down and tell what they just did. As they say the word *quacked*, add *-ed*. Explain that we often add *-ed* to words to show that something has already happened.

TEACH

Identify Root Words Track the first sentence on **Teaching Chart 37** as you read it with children. Then point to the word *wished*. Ask children if they recognize part of the word. *(wish)* Model for children how understanding inflectional endings can help them read.

The girl wished for a puppy.

Dad packed his bag.

The boy fished in the pond.

Teaching Chart 37

MODEL I can use what I already know to help me read words I don't recognize. I know the word *wish*. I can see that the last two letters of the word are *–ed*. I know that sometimes when these two letters appear together at the end of a word, it means that someone did something in the past. The word is *wished*.

Repeat for the other two sentences. Then call on children to come up and draw a line under the root word in each sentence.

PRACTICE

Add -ed

PARTNERS

Distribute index cards to children. Then write *wished*, *packed*, *mixed*, and *fished* on the chalkboard. Have children read each word, identifying the part of the word that they know first. Then have partners write each word on an index card. Direct them to turn the card over and write the word without the *–ed* ending. Have partners practice reading the words. ▶ **Kinesthetic/Linguistic**

ASSESS/CLOSE

Show Past and Present

Invite children to use their index cards from the Practice activity. Say some sentences aloud, repeating the verb after each sentence is read. Tell children to hold up the side of the index card that has the verb used in the sentence. Use the following sentences:

- Sam mixed the batter. (mixed)
- We fish in the lake. (fish)
- I pack my lunch. (pack)
- Sue wished on a star. (wished)

ALTERNATE TEACHING STRATEGY

....

INFLECTIONAL ENDING
-ed

For a different approach to teaching this skill, see page T68.

i **Intervention** ▶ **Skills Intervention Guide,** for direct instruction and extra practice in Inflectional Ending *-ed*

Meeting Individual Needs for Vocabulary

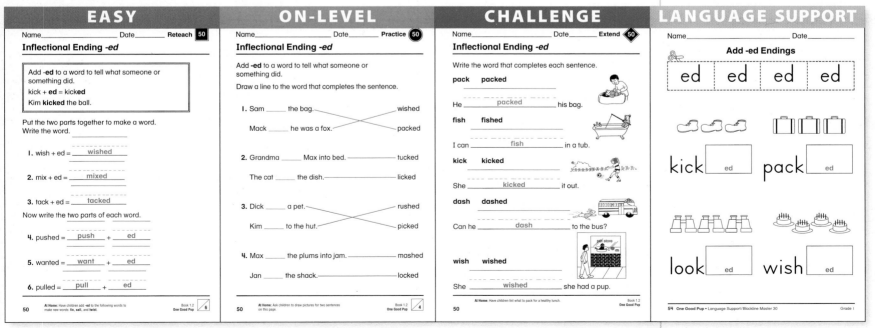

Reteach, 50	Practice, 50	Extend, 50	Language Support, 54

Handwriting CD-ROM

GRAMMAR/SPELLING
CONNECTIONS

Nouns: See Grammar and Usage lessons, pages 350–35P.

Words with Short *u*: See Spelling Lessons, pages 35Q–35R.

Interactive Writing
Write a Poem

Prewrite

LOOK AT THE STORY WORDS Have children revisit *One Good Pup* and guide them to notice again the important words in the story. Then tell them that the class will create a poem about the story. The poem will give ideas about how to spend a rainy day with a pet. Maybe the children would like to explain how to make a boat out of a box, or how to get ready for a nap (example: *Lie on the rug. Get really snug.*). Ask children to find specific words they would like to use in the story (Examples: *wet, rain, bake, nap*). Make a list of these words on the chalkboard. Can they think of any rhymes for these words? (examples: *pet, pain, cake, map*) List rhyming words next to the words with which they rhyme.

Draft

WRITE RHYMING COUPLETS Help children come up with complete rhyming sentences that help to tell the story in a poem.

- Begin by saying, for example, *It is wet. What rhymes with wet? Pet. How about writing It is wet, wet, wet. I can't take out my pet.* As you say words with familiar sounds and patterns, challenge children to come up and write them on the chalkboard. Write all unfamiliar words yourself.

- Encourage children to come up with pairs of sentences that rhyme. Ignore metrics.

Continue this process, having children write two rhyming lines at a time, until a sequence of events has been told in the poem.

Revise

CHECK NOUNS Ask children to reread two rhyming lines at a time to check and see if each group of sentences contains a noun. After they read the lines, have children point out the nouns in the sentences. Ask children why it is important that each sentence has a noun (*so we know who is doing the action in the sentence; so the sentence tells a complete thought*).

Publish

CREATE THE POEM Reread the pairs of rhyming lines. Help children decide in what order they should be placed in the poem. Have children create illustrations for each couplet, then copy the appropriate text onto their drawings.

TEACHING TIP

Technology
Remind children who use the computer to key a space between words. If they forget a space, it may be inserted later by placing the cursor where the space belongs, then hitting the space bar once.

Handwriting
Remind children to keep both feet flat on the floor when they write. See page T78 for illustrations of proper sitting positions.

Presentation Ideas

SING A SILLY SONG Encourage pairs of children to make up silly songs about a puppy on a rainy day. They can use a tune they know, or make up their own. Encourage them to listen for opportunities to make rhymes. Then have them sing their song and act it out for the rest of the class.

▶ **Listening/Representing**

MAKE A CD BOX Invite children to create art for a CD cover that features the silly songs they created. They may choose their own song, or someone else's. Allow them to use any combination of crayons, pencils, and felt-tipped markers. Then have them display their art and explain how they created it, or why they decided to include what they did in their pictures. ▶ **Speaking/Viewing**

Meeting Individual Needs for Writing

EASY	ON-LEVEL	CHALLENGE
Draw Pictures Children can draw pictures of another pet and the boy. Have them write captions for their pictures, using the word *We* and a simple verb, such as *We tug* or *We fish*.	**New Story Pages** Children can work in pairs to write new pages for *One Good Pup*. Ask them to think of other things they can do on a rainy day. Have them follow the language patterns from *One Good Pup* as they write their new pages.	**Journal Entry** Children can write a journal entry about how they might spend a sunny day with a pet, either real or imaginary. Invite them to use descriptive words and unusual ideas for activities.

5 Day Grammar and Usage Plan

DAY 1 Introduce the Concept

Oral Warm-Up Say the following sentence aloud: *This is my hat.* Ask children to find the word that names something. (*hat*)

Introduce Nouns Remind children that a sentence is a group of words. These words have special names. One kind of word is called a *noun.* Discuss with children:

> ### Nouns
>
> A **noun** is a word that names a person, place, or thing.

Daily Language Activity Say the following sentence: *Look at the ship.* Ask children which word names a thing. (*ship*) Say the following: *There is the man.* Ask which word names a person. (*man*) Say: *We go to the town.* Ask which word names a place. (*town*)

 WRITING Assign daily Writing Prompt on page 8E.

GRAMMAR PRACTICE BOOK, PAGE 33

DAY 2 Teach the Concept

Review Nouns Remind children that yesterday they learned about nouns. Write the following sentence on the chalkboard: *The mat is in the shack.* Read it aloud, asking children to read with you. Ask children to find the nouns in this sentence. (*mat, shack*)

Daily Language Activity Write the following sentence on the chalkboard: *My dad has a hat.* Read it aloud, asking children to read with you. Have them identify the nouns. (*dad, hat*) Ask students whether each noun names a person, a place, or a thing. (*dad,* person; *hat,* thing)

 WRITING Assign the daily Writing Prompt on page 8E.

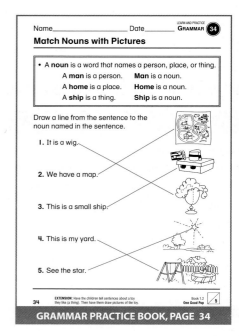

GRAMMAR PRACTICE BOOK, PAGE 34

Nouns

Learn from the Literature Review with children the three kinds of nouns. Write the following sentence from *One Good Pup* on the chalkboard:

Sit in this small ship with me.

Ask children to find the noun in the sentence. Does it name a person, a place, or a thing? (a thing)

Daily Language Activity Have children brainstorm nouns from the story. Then have them write a sentence containing a noun from *One Good Pup*.

 Assign the daily Writing Prompt on page 8F.

Review Nouns Write this sentence on the chalkboard: *The man has a van.* Ask children if the sentence has any nouns. (yes, two) What are they and what do they name? (*man,* person; *van,* thing)

Daily Language Activity Ask children to create a word web about toys, and put it on the chalkboard. Then have children pick nouns and make up sentences orally.

Mechanics and Usage Before children begin the daily Writing Prompt on page 8F, review and discuss sentence punctuation.

> **Sentence Punctuation**
> - Begin every sentence with a capital letter.
> - End a statement with a period.

 Assign the daily Writing Prompt on page 8F.

Daily Language Activity Write these sentences on the chalkboard. Read them with children. Have children identify the nouns in each sentence, telling whether they name persons, places, or things.

1. Put down the mug. *mug,* thing
2. Max likes the bus. *Max,* person; *bus,* thing
3. Kim can go to the city. *Kim,* person; *city,* place

Assess Use page 37 of the **Grammar Practice Book** for assessment.

Reteach Prepare word cards for each sentence presented on Days 1 through 5. Give each group one set. First have them identify the nouns and then whether they are persons, places, or things.

Use page 38 of the **Grammar Practice Book** for additional reteaching.

 Assign the daily Writing Prompt on page 8F.

Name_____ Date_____ PRACTICE AND WRITE GRAMMAR **35**

Nouns in Sentences

> - A **noun** is a word that names a person, place, or thing.
> - A **noun** can name a place.
>   I will play at **home**.

Write the name of a place from the word box in the sentence.

| home | sky | hill | bank | yard |

1. I go _____ home _____ after school.
2. The _____ sky _____ is blue.
3. The tree is on top of a _____ hill _____.
4. I plant flowers in our _____ yard _____.
5. I keep money in a _____ bank _____.

Book 1.2 *One Good Pup* EXTENSION: Have the students tell sentences that are about a place. Then have them draw pictures to show the place they told about. **35**

GRAMMAR PRACTICE BOOK, PAGE 35

Name_____ Date_____ MECHANICS GRAMMAR **36**

Sentences

> - Begin each sentence with a capital letter.
> - End every sentence with a special mark.

Circle the sentences that are correct.

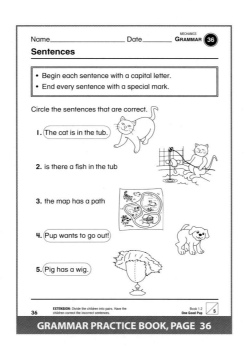

1. The cat is in the tub.
2. is there a fish in the tub
3. the map has a path
4. Pup wants to go out!
5. Pig has a wig.

EXTENSION: Divide the children into pairs. Have the children correct the incorrect sentences. Book 1.2 *One Good Pup* **36**

GRAMMAR PRACTICE BOOK, PAGE 36

Name_____ Date_____ TEST GRAMMAR **37**

Nouns

Circle each noun that names the picture.

1. The dog is playing.
2. A girl is reading.
3. The owl hoots.
4. The kite flies.
5. Go to the top of the hill.
6. It is a big house.

Book 1.2 *One Good Pup* **37**

GRAMMAR PRACTICE BOOK, PAGE 37

5 Day Spelling Plan

LANGUAGE SUPPORT

ESL In Spanish the sound represented by *u* sounds like the English /ü/as in *moon*. Help children to pronounce the short /u/ sound by providing opportunities for frequent practice in chanting and/or reading selections containing the sound.

Three Bear Cubs

Rub-a-dub-dub!

Three bear cubs

All together

In a big bathtub

One starts to run

Out into the sun

Soaking wet,

And having fun!

DAY 1 — Introduce Spelling Words

Assess Prior Knowledge Write the Spelling Words on the chalkboard. Read them aloud and invite children to repeat them after you. Ask children to make the sound they hear that is the same in all the words. Ask children what letter spells this sound.

Write the Challenge Words on the chalkboard. Read them aloud and have children repeat. Invite volunteers to use the words in sentences.

Word Study On page 34 of the **Spelling Practice Book** are word study steps and an at-home activity.

Spelling Words		Challenge Words	
1. but	4. cut	7. **no**	9. **small**
2. tug	5. buck	8. **ride**	10. **out**
3. rug	6. duck		

*Note: Words in **dark type** are from the story.*

Words with Short *u*

Complete each word by writing the letter that spells the short *u* sound.

1. b**u**t
2. t___u___g
3. d___u___ck
4. r___u___g
5. c___u___t
6. b___u___ck

Directions (to teacher)
Review the short *u* sound by explaining that the letter *u* stands for /u/ as in the word *but*. Write *but* on the chalkboard or form the word with letter cards. Say the word aloud and have children repeat it. Then have children look at the first example on the page. Point out that the letter *u* has been filled in.

Write the words *cut, tug, rug, duck,* and *buck* on the chalkboard. Read each word aloud and have children repeat it. Have them listen for the short *u* sound in each word. Then have them complete each word in the blank provided.

Book 1.2
Good Pup   33

SPELLING PRACTICE BOOK, PAGE 33
WORD STUDY STEPS AND ACTIVITY, PAGE 34

DAY 2 — Teach the Pattern

Find the Matching Word Write the word *buck* on the chalkboard. Say the word, repeating the final *-uck* sound. Have children identify which other word ends with *-uck*. Repeat for word pairs ending with *-ut* and *-ug*.

To extend the activity, write the words *nut, luck* and *dug* on the chalkboard. Read the words aloud, repeating the final sounds. Ask children to name the Spelling Words that rhyme with each word.

Words with Short *u*

Complete the spelling words inside each dog bone. Put the words with the same endings in the same box.

but tug duck rug cut buck

Words that end with **ut**
1. b___ut___   2. c___ut___

Words that end with **ug**
3. t___ug___   4. r___ug___

Words that end with **uck**
5. d___uck___   6. b___uck___

Book 1.2
Good Pup   35

SPELLING PRACTICE BOOK, PAGE 35

35Q *One Good Pup*

Words with Short *u*

Word Meaning: Synonyms Write the word *rug* on the chalkboard and tell children what the word means. Explain that they have already learned a synonym for *rug*—a different word that means the same thing. Guide them to recall the word *mat*, or write the word on the chalkboard and ask them what it means.

Tell children they can find synonyms in their Glossary. Ask them to look up the words *boy* and *nap* and find a synonym for each.

Identify Spelling Patterns Write this sentence on the chalkboard: *She gave a tug on the small rug.* Have a volunteer read it aloud. Ask children to tell which words have the sound /u/ and which word is the Challenge Word. Have volunteers make sentences that contain Spelling Words and Challenge Words.

Write Sentences Write all the spelling words in one column on the chalkboard, and all the Challenge Words in another. Draw a line between *duck* and *small*. Ask volunteers to make up sentences using both words; write some on the chalkboard. Then move the line to connect *tug* and *small*; ask children which sentences on the board will still make sense if *duck* is replaced by *tug*. Continue with different combinations.

WRITING Have children use as many spelling words as possible in the daily Writing Prompt on page 8F. Remind them to check their writing for errors in spelling, grammar, and punctuation.

Optional Spelling Test You may wish to give children a spelling test. You may administer the test in the following manner: (1) Read the word. (2) Give a simple sentence containing the word. (3) Say the word again. Or you may use page 38 of the **Spelling Practice Book** for the posttest. If you wish, you may create additional sentences for the Challenge Words.

Personal Word List Have children write **JOURNAL** any words they find difficult on their personal "troublesome word" list in their journals. For each word, have children find two sentences in the story or in classwork exercises that contain it, and review the sentences' meanings.

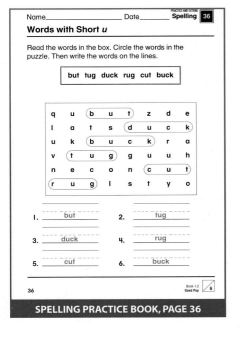

SPELLING PRACTICE BOOK, PAGE 36

Name_____ Date_____ **Spelling 36**
Words with Short *u*

Read the words in the box. Circle the words in the puzzle. Then write the words on the lines.

| but | tug | duck | rug | cut | buck |

1. but   2. tug
3. duck 4. rug
5. cut   6. buck

SPELLING PRACTICE BOOK, PAGE 37

Name_____ Date_____ **Spelling 37**
Words with Short *u*

Look at the picture. Complete each sentence with a spelling word.

1. Do not ____cut____ your hand!
2. The cat sits on the ____rug____.
3. The ____duck____ said, "Quack."
4. Do not ____tug____ the pup!
5. The ____buck____ ran up the path.
6. I wish to go out, ____but____ it is so wet!

SPELLING PRACTICE BOOK, PAGE 38

Name_____ Date_____ **Spelling 38**
Words with Short *u*

Look at the words in each set. One word in each set is spelled correctly. Use a pencil to color in the circle in front of that word. Before you begin, look at the sample sets of words. Sample A has been done for you. Do Sample B by yourself. When you are sure you know what to do, you may go on with the rest of the page.

Sample A
(A) bug
(B) bugg
(C) buug

Sample B
(D) diss
(E) dish
(F) dihs

1. (A) rugg
   (B) rug
   (C) ruug
2. (D) buck
   (E) buk
   (F) buc
3. (A) cut
   (B) kut
   (C) kutt
4. (D) dukk
   (E) duc
   (F) duck
5. (A) bot
   (B) buut
   (C) but
6. (D) tugg
   (E) tug
   (F) tuug

Concept
• Perspective

Comprehension
• Story Elements

Phonics
• Short *o*

Vocabulary
• saw
• very
• want
• two

Reaching All Learners

Anthology

The Bug Bath

Selection Summary Two bugs who want to take a bath find that things are not what they seem. After a big adventure, the bugs learn that it is better to take a bath closer to home.

Listening Library

INSTRUCTIONAL pages 38–65

Jack-in-the-Box
Dot the Bug can hop, hop, hop.
She can hop to the bottom.
She can hop to the top.
She hops to the box.
The box goes POP!
Dot the Bug takes
a very big hop!

Rhyme applies to Phonics

by Anne Miranda
illustrated by Bernard Adnet

About the Author As a child, Anne Miranda dreamed of becoming an artist. When she grew up, Ms. Miranda began writing stories. She says, "I found writing another way to put the pictures in my head down on paper, with words instead of color."

About the Illustrator Bernard Adnet grew up in France. "I drew for many of my nieces and nephews when they were children," he says. Today he lives in New York and illustrates children's books.

Same Concept, Skills and Vocabulary!

Leveled Books

EASY
Lesson on pages 65A and 65D
`DECODABLE`

INDEPENDENT
Lesson on pages 65B and 65D

🏠 *Take-Home version available*
`DECODABLE`

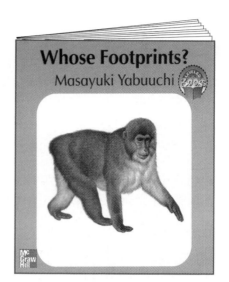

CHALLENGE
Lesson on pages 65C and 65D

Leveled Practice

EASY
Reteach, 51-58 Blackline masters with reteaching opportunities for each assessed skill

INDEPENDENT/ON-LEVEL
Practice, 51-58 Workbook with Take-Home Stories and practice opportunities for each assessed skill and story comprehension

CHALLENGE
Extend, 51–58 Blackline masters that offer challenge activities for each assessed skill

Quizzes Prepared by  Accelerated Reader®

Social Studies . . .	Silk From China, *58*	
Science	Insects: Large and Small, *42*	
	Sink or Swim, *48*	
Math	How Many in the Tub, *46*	
Language Arts . .	Read Aloud, *36G*	
Cultural Perspectives	Beetlemania, *56*	
Writing	A Skit, *62*	
Research and Inquiry	Find Out More, *63*	
💻 **Internet Activities**	www.mhschool.com/reading	

CENTER Activities

Each of these activities takes 15-20 minutes.

Phonics

Word Families

 Objective: Use letter substitution to build short *o* words.

- Write _op, _ock, _ox.

- Have children copy the word families across the top of their paper.

- Children place consonants at the beginning of each to build words, and list them in the appropriate column.

MATERIALS
- Letter cards (consonants) from the Word Building Manipulative Cards
- Paper
- Pencil

Writing

It's a Bug's Life

PARTNERS **Objective:** Write a story about two bug characters.

- Have partners use the pattern in *The Bug Bath* to write and illustrate a story about Al and Bob in another setting, such as a pond or a playground.

- Challenge children to use as many short *o* words as possible.

MATERIALS
- Paper
- Pencil
- Crayons

Reading and Listening

Independent/Self-Selected Reading

 Objective: Listen and use illustrations to understand a story.

Fill the Center with books and corresponding audiocassettes or CD-ROMs children have read or listened to this week. You can also include books from the Theme Bibliography on pages T98 and T99.

Leveled Readers

- *Big?* by Rachel Lear
- *The Big Sun* by Michael Maia
- *Whose Footprints?* by Masayuki Yabuuchi

- Theme Big Book *My River* by Shari Halpern
- *The Bug Bath* by Anne Miranda
- "Cat Kisses" by Bobbi Katz
- Phonics Practice Reader, Vol. 1

Science

Alike and Different

 PARTNERS **Objective:** Use a Venn diagram to compare and contrast two story animals.

MATERIALS
- Construction paper
- Crayons

- Have pairs of children draw two large, overlapping circles.

- Above each circle, children write the name of a story animal.

- Children write how the animals are alike and different on the diagram.

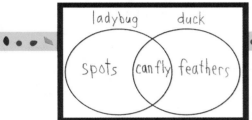

ladybug   duck

spots (can fly) feathers

Art

Bug Bonanza

 ONE **Objective:** Develop fine-motor skills.

MATERIALS
- Construction paper
- Scissors
- Glue
- Crayons
- Art materials (such as felt, yarn)

- Provide children with a variety of art materials.

- Have children create colorful bugs.

- For added fun, children can give their bugs short *o* names and introduce their bug creations to the class.

Working with Words

can big red

Bug Sentences

PARTNERS **Objective:** Reinforce vocabulary words: *saw, very, want, two.*

MATERIALS
- *The Bug Bath* from the Student Anthology
- Paper
- Pencil

The two bugs got in.

- Have partners find sentences in *The Bug Bath* that contain vocabulary words.

- Partners read aloud each sentence.

- Then they work together to write another "bug sentence" for each word.

- Suggest that children use the story illustrations for sentence ideas.

Suggested Lesson Planner

READING AND LANGUAGE ARTS	DAY 1 — Focus on Reading and Skills	DAY 2 — Read the Literature
Phonics Daily Routines	Daily **Phonics** Routine: Listening, 36J **Phonics** CD-ROM	Daily **Phonics** Routine: Segmenting, 38A **Phonics** CD-ROM
Phonological Awareness **Phonics** *Short o* **Comprehension** **Vocabulary** **Study Skills** **Listening, Speaking, Viewing, Representing**	**Read** **Read Aloud,** 36G "Hey Bug!" ☑ **Develop Phonological Awareness,** 36H ☑ **Introduce Short o,** 36I–36J **Reteach, Practice, Extend,** 51 **Phonics/Phonemic Awareness Practice Book,** 99–102 **Read** **Apply Short o,** 36/37 "Jack-in-the-Box" **Intervention Program**	**Build Background,** 38A Develop Oral Language **Vocabulary,** 38B-38C saw very want two **Word Building Manipulative Cards** **Teaching Chart 38** **Reteach, Practice, Extend,** 52 **Read** **Read the Selection,** 38–61 **Guided Instruction** ☑ Short o ☑ Story Elements **Genre: Story,** 39 **Cultural Perspectives,** 56
Curriculum Connections	**Link** Language Arts, 36G	**Link** Math, 38A
Writing	**Writing Prompt:** Write a sentence about two dogs in a bath.	**Writing Prompt:** Imagine that two bugs are taking a bath with toys. Write a list of the toys they have. **Journal Writing** Quick-Write, 61
Grammar	**Introduce the Concept: Plural Nouns,** 65O Daily Language Activity: Add *s* to nouns. **Grammar Practice Book,** 39	**Teach the Concept: Plural Nouns,** 65O Daily Language Activity: Add *es* to nouns. **Grammar Practice Book,** 40
Spelling *Short o*	**Introduce: Words with Short o,** 65Q **Spelling Practice Book,** 39–40	**Teach the Patterns: Words with Short o,** 65Q **Spelling Practice Book,** 41

Meeting Individual Needs

 = Skill Assessed in Unit Test

 Intervention Program Available

DAY 3 — Read the Literature

Daily **Phonics** Routine:
Blending, 63

Phonics CD-ROM

Reread for Fluency, 60

Story Questions, 62
Reteach, Practice, Extend, 53

Story Activities, 63

Study Skill, 64
☑ Maps
Teaching Chart 39
Reteach, Practice, Extend, 54

Test Power, 65

 Read the Leveled Books, 65A–65D
Guided Reading
☑ Short *o*
☑ Story Elements
☑ High-Frequency Words

 Intervention Program

 Activity Science, 42; Math, 46

 Writing Prompt: Think of your favorite toy to take in the bath. Write a sentence telling what you would do if you had ten of them instead of just one.

Journal Writing, 65D

Practice and Write: Plural Nouns, 65P
Daily Language Activity: Create sentences.

Grammar Practice Book, 41

Practice and Extend: Words with Short *o*, 65R

Spelling Practice Book, 42

DAY 4 — Build Skills

Daily **Phonics** Routine:
Writing, 65F

Phonics CD-ROM

 Read the Leveled Books and Self-Selected Books

☑ **Review Short *o*,** 65E–65F
Teaching Chart 40
Reteach, Practice, Extend, 55
Language Support, 60
Phonics/Phonemic Awareness
Practice Book, 99–102

☑ **Review Short *o*, *u*, *i*, *a*; *ck*,** 65G–65H
Teaching Chart 41
Reteach, Practice, Extend, 56
Language Support, 61
Phonics/Phonemic Awareness
Practice Book, 99–102

Minilessons, 45, 47, 51, 55, 57, 59

 Intervention Program

Activity Science, 36D, 48

Writing Prompt: What would happen if two ducks met two bugs? Write what the ducks and the bugs would say to each other.

Interactive Writing: Make a Guide, 65M
Prewrite, Draft

Meeting Individual Needs for Writing, 65N

Practice and Write: Plural Nouns, 65P
Daily Language Activity: Make nouns plural.

Grammar Practice Book, 42

Practice and Write: Words with Short *o*, 65R

Spelling Practice Book, 43

DAY 5 — Build Skills

Daily **Phonics** Routine:
Fluency, 65H

Phonics CD-ROM

 Read Self-Selected Books

☑ **Review Story Elements,** 65I–65J
Teaching Chart 42
Reteach, Practice, Extend, 57
Language Support, 62

☑ **Review Inflectional Ending -*ed*,** 65K–65L
Teaching Chart 43
Reteach, Practice, Extend, 58
Language Support, 63

Listening, Speaking, Viewing, Representing, 65N
Make a Bug
Improvise a Bug Story

Minilessons, 45, 47, 51, 55, 57, 59

Intervention Program

Activity Art, 36D, 54; Social Studies, 58

Writing Prompt: Imagine two bugs are friends. Write about what kind of bugs they are.

Interactive Writing: Make a Guide, 65M
Revise, Publish

Assess and Reteach: Plural Nouns, 65P
Daily Language Activity: Identify and make nouns plural.

Grammar Practice Book, 43–44

Assess and Reteach: Words with Short *o*, 65R

Spelling Practice Book, 44

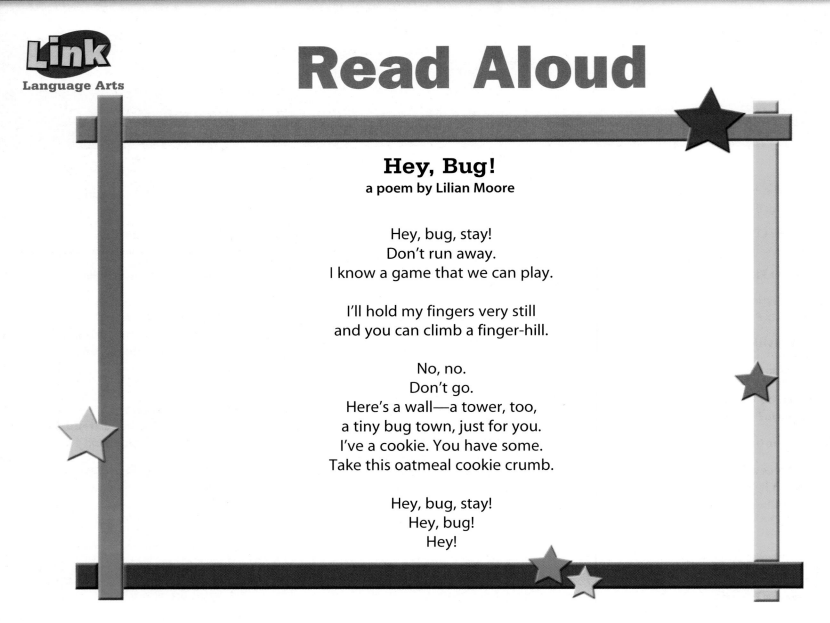

Read Aloud

Hey, Bug!
a poem by Lilian Moore

Hey, bug, stay!
Don't run away.
I know a game that we can play.

I'll hold my fingers very still
and you can climb a finger-hill.

No, no.
Don't go.
Here's a wall—a tower, too,
a tiny bug town, just for you.
I've a cookie. You have some.
Take this oatmeal cookie crumb.

Hey, bug, stay!
Hey, bug!
Hey!

Oral Comprehension

LISTENING AND SPEAKING Motivate children to think about character by reading them this poem. Have children think about the person who is talking in the poem. When you are done, ask children, "Do you think the person in the poem has a good imagination? Why?" You may also wish to focus on rhyme by rereading the poem and having children listen for and identify pairs of rhyming words.

Activity Have children work in small groups to draw pictures of the situations described in "Hey, Bug!" Each child can draw a picture that shows a different situation, such as the bug climbing the finger hill, or the tiny bug town. ▶ **Visual**

GENRE: POEM Tell children that many poems have rhyming words. Point out that many poems also describe things in new or imaginative ways. Discuss with children some of the features of the poem *Hey, Bug!* Ask children to find rhyming words in set of lines. Have children explain what they think the wall and the tower really are in the poem. Ask children why the poet used these words instead of the words "hand" and "fingers."

Develop Phonological Awareness

Blend Onsets and Rimes
Phonological Awareness

MATERIALS
- puppet

Teach Have the puppet say: */r/-/ok/. Listen as I say the sounds together. What word did I say?* (rock) Tell children the puppet will say the same beginning sound but will change the end sound. Have the puppet say: */r/-/od/. Listen as I say the sounds together. What word did I say?* (rod)

Practice Separate the onset and rime for each of the following word sets. Have children blend the sounds with you and then say the words: *dock, dog; fog, fox; hop, hot; lock, log; pot, pod.*

Blend Sounds
Phonemic Awareness

MATERIALS
- Phonics Picture Cards

Teach Place the Phonics Picture Card for *pot* behind your back. You will say the beginning and end sounds. Children will put the short *o* sound in the middle and then blend the sounds together to say the word. Say: */p/. . ./t/.* Children should respond: *pot.* Repeat with the card for *box.*

Practice Tell children you will think of words that have the sound */o/.* You will say the beginning and end sounds in the word. Children will tell you the word by saying the */o/* sound in the middle of the word. Use the following words: *rock, cob, dog, got, job, jog.*

Segment Sounds
Phonemic Awareness

MATERIALS
- colored blocks or felt squares (four per child)

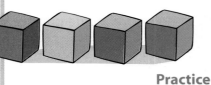

Teach Tell children you will say a word with three sounds. Have children say the separate sounds slowly, holding up a colored block for each sound. Model for children: *I say* log, *you say* /l/-/o/-/g/ as you hold up a colored block for each sound. Have children repeat the word and the sounds with you.

Practice Have children segment the sounds in the following words, holding up a colored block or felt square for each sound they say: *bob, clock, dot, fox, hog, shock, jot, not, on, pod.*

INFORMAL ASSESSMENT Observe children as they blend onsets and rimes, blend sounds, and segment sounds. If children have difficulty, see Alternate Teaching Strategies on page T69.

OBJECTIVES
Children will:
- identify /o/o.
- blend and read short *o* words.
- review: /b/b, /g/g, /h/h, /m/m, /n/n, /p/p, /r/r, /t/t, /ks/x, and /k/ck.

MATERIALS
- letter cards from the **Word Building Manipulative Cards**

Skills Finder

Short *o*	
Introduce	B2: 36I-J
Review	B2: 65E-F, 65G-H, 95G-H, 124I-J
Test	Book 2
Maintain	B4: 19

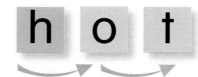

SPELLING/PHONICS CONNECTIONS
Words with short *o*: See the 5-Day Spelling Plan, pages 65Q–65R.

Introduce Short *o*

TEACH

Identify the Letter *o* as the Symbol for /o/ Explain to children that they will learn to read words with the letter *o*, which stands for the /o/ sound.

- Display the *o* letter card and make the /o/ sound.

BLENDING Model and Guide Practice with Words with Short *o*
- Have children repeat the /o/ sound as you point to the *o* letter card.
- Place the *t* letter card after the *o* letter card.
- Blend the sounds together and have children repeat after you.

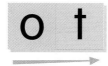

- Use the *h* letter card to form the word *hot*.

- Blend the sounds together to read *hot* and have children repeat after you.

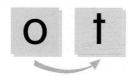

Use the Word in Context
- Use the word in context to reinforce its meaning. Example: *The sun is hot.*

Repeat the Procedure
- Use the following words to model and guide practice with short *o*.

top	mop	got	Bob
not	rock	box	on

PRACTICE

BLENDING
Build Short *o*
Words with
Letter Cards

PARTNERS

Use letter cards to build the word *pop*. Blend the sounds together and have children repeat after you. Ask them: *What can pop?* Then have pairs build and write the following words: *jog, mop, nod, rock,* and *sob*. Have children act out the meanings of the words.

▶ **Linguistic/ Kinesthetic**

ASSESS/CLOSE

Build and Read
Words with the
Short *o* Sound

To assess children's ability to blend and read words with the short *o* sound, observe them as they build words in the Practice activity. Have children tell a sentence using each word they built.

ADDITIONAL PHONICS RESOURCES

Phonics/Phonemic Awareness
Practice Book,
pages 99–102

PHONICS KIT
Hands-on Activities and Practice

McGraw-Hill School
TECHNOLOGY

Phonics **CD-ROM**
activities for practice with
Blending and Segmenting

Meeting Individual Needs for Phonics

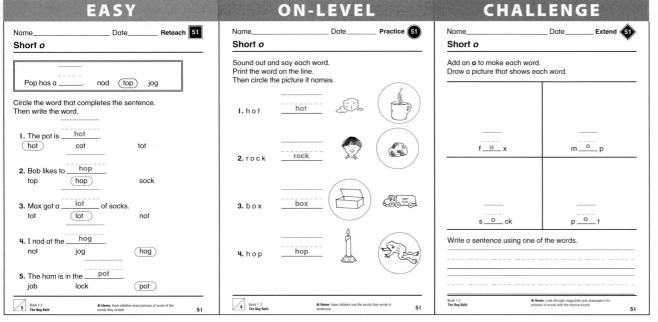

EASY	ON-LEVEL	CHALLENGE
Reteach, 51	Practice, 51	Extend, 51

Daily Routines

DAY 1
Listening Read the following list of words. When children hear a word with the short *o* sound, have them make the shape of an *o* with their fingers: *job, clap, nod, jump, mop, sit.*

DAY 2
Segmenting Distribute letter boxes. Say a word with short *o* aloud. Ask children to write the spelling of each sound in the appropriate box. Use *lock, box, sock, got,* and *not.*

DAY 3
Blending Have pairs work with letter cards to build short *o* words. One child builds a word and the other reads it. Have children take turns.

DAY 4
Writing Have children choose two words with short *o* and create a rhyming couplet with the words. Encourage children to illustrate their rhymes.

DAY 5
Fluency Write a list of words with the short *o* sound. Have children work in pairs, taking turns reading the words.

^{TESTED} OBJECTIVES

Children will read a poem with words containing short *o*.

Apply Short *o*

Jack-in-the-Box

Dot the Bug can hop, hop, hop.
She can hop to the bottom.
She can hop to the top.
She hops to the box.
The box goes POP!
Dot the Bug takes
   a very big hop!

36   37

Anthology pages 36-37

Read and Build Fluency

READ THE POEM Tell children they will read a poem called "Jack-in-the-Box." Provide auditory modeling as you read the poem expressively. Have children practice fluency as they read the poem along with you.

REREAD FOR FLUENCY Have children work in pairs to alternate reading lines of the poem. Encourage them to jump up when they say *pop!*

READ A DECODABLE STORY For additional practice reading and to develop fluency, direct children to read *Dot in Pop's Shop* from **Phonics Practice Reader, Vol. 1.**

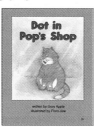

Dictate and Spell

DICTATE WORDS Segment the word *hop* into its three individual sounds. Repeat the word aloud and use it in a sentence: *Dot can hop and hop.* Then have children say the word and write the letter that represents each sound until they make the entire word. Repeat with *top, box, Dot,* and *pop* from the poem. Then repeat with short *o* words not from the poem, such as *cob, dock, hot, jog, shot, tock, mop, rock,* and *shock.*

Intervention Skills Intervention Guide, for direct instruction and extra practice in Short *o*

Build Background

Math

Concept: Perspective

Anthology and Leveled Books

Evaluate Prior Knowledge

CONCEPT: PERSPECTIVE Ask children whether they think they are big or little. Then ask them to name things that they consider large and others they find small. Use the following activities if children need help understanding that different people and animals have different perspectives on the world.

CLASSIFY AND CATEGORIZE Draw a line on the chalkboard, with one end labeled "Big" and the other "Small." Name a variety of animals (elephant, tiger, dog, mosquito) and ask children where they would place each animal on the line. Draw or write children's suggestions on the chalkboard. To reinforce the concept of perspective, discuss the size chart from the perspective of one of the animals on the line, for example, a cat.

▶ **Visual/Spatial**

  DRAW A PICTURE Invite children to choose two animals, one large and one small, and show those animals doing something together. Encourage children to be creative and humorous. Help them to write a sentence describing their pictures.

PARTNERS   **WRITING**

Develop Oral Language

CONNECT WORDS AND ACTIONS

ESL Tell children you want to play a game with them called "How Big? How Small?" Show them pictures of an elephant and a bug.

- Ask which is bigger and which is smaller.
- Ask them to show you with their hands how much bigger and how much smaller.
- Now ask them to show how much bigger these two creatures are compared to themselves.
- Try this game with other pictures of animals.

▶ **Visual/Kinesthetic**

DAILY Phonics ROUTINES

DAY 2 **Segmenting** Distribute letter boxes. Say a word with short *o* aloud. Ask children to write the spelling of each sound in the appropriate box. Use *lock, box, sock, got,* and *not.*

 Phonics **CD-ROM**

LANGUAGE SUPPORT

To build more background, see pages 55–58 in the **Language Support Book.**

Children will:

• identify high-frequency words *saw, two, very,* and *want*.

MATERIALS

• Teaching Chart 38

• Word Building Manipulative Cards *saw, two, very, want*

TEACHING TIP

The following chart indicates words from the upcoming story that children have learned to decode and high-frequency words taught in this lesson. Observe any difficulties children may have in reading these words.

Decodable		High-Frequency
Bob	on	saw
got	top	very
hot		want
not		two

SPELLING/VOCABULARY CONNECTIONS

These words are Challenge Words. See page 65Q for Day 1 of the 5-Day Spelling Plan.

---

saw

two

very

want

Vocabulary
High-Frequency Words

Bugs in a Tub

One small dog was on a rug.
(Two) small bugs sat in a tub.
One small dog was (very) hot.
And he (saw) the bugs were not.
One small dog said, "Do you (want) my rug?"
(Two) small bugs said, "No, we like our tub."

Teaching Chart 38

Auditory

LISTEN TO WORDS Without displaying it, read aloud "Bugs in a Tub" on **Teaching Chart 38**. Ask children to imagine how the bugs felt and how the dog felt.

CLAP SYLLABLES OF HIGH-FREQUENCY WORDS Have children aurally identify each high-frequency word using the following activity:

• Say aloud one of the high-frequency words. Read a line of the poem where the word appears.

• Before you read the line again, ask children to say the word and clap the syllables when you come to it. Then read the line again, pausing at the word.

• Repeat this activity for each of the high-frequency words.

Visual

TEACH WORDS Display "Bugs in a Tub" on **Teaching Chart 38**. Read the poem, tracking the print with your finger. Next, point to the word *saw*. Tell children that this is the word *saw*. Have them say the word with you. Ask them to hold up the vocabulary card for *saw* and say the word. Repeat this procedure for *two, very,* and *want*.

Hold up vocabulary cards for *saw, two, very,* and *want* one at a time. Have volunteers read the words and then circle them on the chart.

saw very
want two

Word Building Manipulative Cards

PLAY "GUESS THE WORD" Number the lines on the Chart, 1–6. Have one child pick a high-frequency word and write it. The other child tells which line the word is in. Once the child says the line, he or she names the high-frequency word. Have children switch roles. ▶ **Visual/Linguistic**

Word Wall

Fact Finders
Give information about one of the word wall words, such as the word *saw*.

> The word **saw** has three letters.
> The word **saw** has one vowel.
> The word **saw** rhymes with **raw**.

Ask children to continue giving information about other word wall words.

Say Spell Say
As a new chant, have children say, spell, then say the word again. For example, *want w-a-n-t want*.

LANGUAGE SUPPORT

To help children develop understanding and recognition of high-frequency words, see page 55 in the **Language Support Book**.

Assess

Write Words
Tell children that they will be writing the spelling words on a piece of paper. You will help them by giving them the first letter of the word. Children should determine which word to write. For example, "This word starts with the letter *s*." Children should write *saw*.

TEACHING TIP
PHONICS TEACHING TIP Explain that sometimes, when the letter *a* follows the letter *w*, the sound *a* changes to /o/, as in *want* and *wash*. Write the words on the chalkboard. Read each word as you point to it, emphasizing the sound of the letter *a*. Then read the words with children. Next, have children read the words on their own.

Meeting Individual Needs for Vocabulary

EASY	ON-LEVEL	ON-LEVEL	CHALLENGE

EASY — Reteach 52

Name_____ Date_____ Reteach **52**
High-Frequency Words

Choose a word to complete each sentence. Then write the words in the boxes.

| saw | two | very | want |

1. The sun is __very__ hot. | v e r y |
2. Do you __want__ a nut? | w a n t |
3. I __saw__ you on the bus. | s a w |
4. There were __two__ bugs. | t w o |

At Home: Have children make up another sentence using one of these words.
52   Book 1.2 The Bug Bath 4

ON-LEVEL — Practice 52

Name_____ Date_____ Practice **52**
High-Frequency Words

Write a word from the box to complete each sentence.

| want | saw | two | very |

1. The bugs __saw__ the tub.
2. The water was __very__ hot.
3. "We __want__ a bath," said the bugs.
4. The __two__ bugs got in.

At Home: Ask children to make up a sentence using each of the vocabulary words.
52   Book 1.2 The Bug Bath 4

ON-LEVEL — Practice 52a / Take-Home Story

Hot Pot

The hogs ran and got the pot. "Owl" said the hogs. "This pot is very hot!" Now the hogs did not like the pot. So they gave the pot back to the dog.

At Home: Encourage children to talk about a time they thought they wanted something and then changed their minds once they had it.

52a

CHALLENGE — Extend 52

Name_____ Date_____ Extend **52**
High-Frequency Words

| saw | very | want | two |

Complete each sentence. Use words from the box.

The bug is __very__ small.

The pups do not __want__ a bath.

There are __two__ socks on the rug.

They __saw__ a pig in the mud.

Write a sentence with one of the words.

__Answers will vary.__

At Home: Ask children to write a sentence about something they saw. Encourage them to draw a picture to go with their sentence.
52   Book 1.2 The Bug Bath

Reteach, 52   Practice, 52   Practice, 52a Take-Home Story   Extend, 52

Comprehension

Prereading Strategies

PREVIEW AND PREDICT Read aloud the title of the book and the names of the author and illustrator. Then take a **picture walk** through the illustrations up to page 51. Talk about the illustrations using some of the words from the story.

Use the following questions to preview the story and help children make predictions:

- Who are the main characters in the story?
- What do you think happens?
- Do you think this story could really happen?

Record children's predictions about the story.

PREDICTIONS	WHAT HAPPENED
The bugs try to take a bath in a real house.	
The main characters are two ladybugs.	

SET PURPOSES What do children want to find out by reading the story? For example:

- What does the boy do?
- What happens to the bugs?

READ TOGETHER

Meet Anne Miranda

As a child, Anne Miranda dreamed of becoming an artist. When she grew up, Miranda began writing stories. She says, "I found writing another way to put the pictures in my head down on paper, with words instead of color."

Meet Bernard Adnet

Bernard Adnet grew up in France. "I drew for many of my nieces and nephews when we were children," he says. Today he lives in New York and illustrates ① children's books.

38

Meeting Individual Needs • Grouping Suggestions for Strategic Reading

EASY

Shared Reading Read the story aloud, running your finger below the words to show that we read from left to right. Use an expressive voice to emphasize how the characters feel. Discuss the plot of the story, page by page. Have children make predictions throughout the story.

ON-LEVEL

Guided Instruction Read the selection with children, using the numbered prompts from the Comprehension section. Monitor any difficulties in reading or comprehension that children may have to determine which prompts to emphasize. After reading the story with children, have children reread it, using the rereading suggestions on page 60.

CHALLENGE

Independent Reading Have children set purposes before they read. Remind them to think about the characters as they read the story. You may wish to have children read in pairs, each taking the part of one of the bugs.

by Anne Miranda
illustrated by Bernard Adnet

39

Comprehension

☑ **Phonics** Apply Short *o*

☑ Apply Analyze Character and Plot

STRATEGIC READING Explain to children that thinking about plot and characters will help them understand the story. Have children use their Character/Plot charts to write their first impressions of each character, based on the **picture walk.** Have them update their charts as they read.

CHARACTERS	WHAT THEY LOOK LIKE	WHAT THEY DO
Al	ladybug small, purple	
Bob	ladybug small, blue	
Fish	big	
Duck	bigger	
Boy	biggest	

1 Let's look at the picture at the top of the page. It shows the author, Anne Miranda. Now look at the picture of the illustrator, Bernard Adnet. Let's read to find out about them. *Concept of a Book: Author/Illustrator*

Genre

Story

Explain that a story:

• is a fictional piece about something that is not real.

• focuses on characters in a setting.

• presents a problem that must be solved.

Activity Explain that *The Bug Bath* has two main characters with a common problem: they are dirty and they need a bath. Discuss with children the other problems Al and Bob face as they try to take a bath. Ask children to explain how their problem is finally solved in the end.

LANGUAGE SUPPORT

A blackline master for making the Character/Plot chart can be found in the **Language Support Book.** Model for children how to fill in the chart as the story progresses. Children use the chart to write or draw details about each character and how each character advances the plot of the story.

Name_____ Date_____
Character Chart

Characters	What They Look Like	What They Do
Al		
Bob		
Fish		
Duck		
Boy		

Grade 1   Language Support/Blackline Master 1c • The Bug Bath 59

LANGUAGE SUPPORT, 59

Comprehension

TRACKING PRINT Point to the word in the first sentence where we will begin reading. Let's read the sentence together. *Syntactic Cues*

② **Phonics** **SHORT** *o* Let's read the second sentence, "'I want a bath,' said . . ." hmm, I'm not sure what this bug's name is. Let's blend the sounds of the letters together to read it. B   o   b Bob
Graphophonic Cues

③ **ANALYZE CHARACTER AND PLOT** Look at the characters on page 40. What have they been doing? (working) How can you tell? (They are dirty. They have hard hats and lunchboxes such as those that people use for work.)

② "We are very dirty," said Al.
③ "I want a bath," said Bob.

40

Fluency

GROUP READING

 Model tracking print and rereading to achieve fluency.

- Point to the first word in a sentence and read it aloud.
- Run your finger under each word as you read the rest of the sentence.
- Then ask children to repeat this process, pointing to each word as they read. Repeat until children have achieved fluency.

PREVENTION/INTERVENTION

TRACKING PRINT Have pairs of children help each other find the correct starting point on the page. Help children identify the first sentence on the page and the first word in that sentence. Ask children to mark the first word with a self-stick note or self-adhesive dot. If a child is having difficulty finding the first word in the sentence, remind him or her to look for a capital letter.
Syntactic Cues

Al and Bob saw a big tub.
The two bugs got in.

41

Comprehension

4 What are the bugs doing in this picture? Use one of the following words to tell me about the picture: *saw, very, want, two.* *Use Illustrations/High Frequency Words*

5 **ANALYZE PLOT** How does this story begin? What characters have we seen so far? (Al and Bob) Let's write what they have done on our Character/Plot chart. *Graphic Organizer*

CHARACTERS	WHAT THEY LOOK LIKE	WHAT THEY DO
Al	ladybug small, purple	Saw a bath. Got in the bath.
Bob	ladybug small, blue	Saw a bath. Got in the bath.
Fish	big	
Duck	bigger	
Boy	biggest	

6 How do you think the bugs are feeling? Why? (They seem surprised and excited to see the tub. They want a bath and here is a tub of water!) *Make Inferences*

7 Sometimes clues in the picture can help us make a prediction. Look at the picture. What do you think might happen next? (The bugs will land in the bubble bath.) What clues in the picture did you use to help you decide? (The bath is full of water and bubbles. The bugs have set down their things. They are diving.) *Make Predictions*

LANGUAGE SUPPORT

ESL Help children acquiring English fill in the Character/Plot chart. To make sure they understand the words you are writing, draw a quick sketch to illustrate the meaning of each entry. Stop frequently and ask questions to ensure the children comprehend the ideas.

Comprehension

8 **Phonics** **SHORT** *o* Point to the last word in the first sentence. Let's blend the sounds together to read the word. h o t hot *Graphophonic Cues*

9 How can you tell that Bob and Al are having fun? (They look happy. Bob is swimming around and Al is singing.) *Make Inferences/Use Picture Clues*

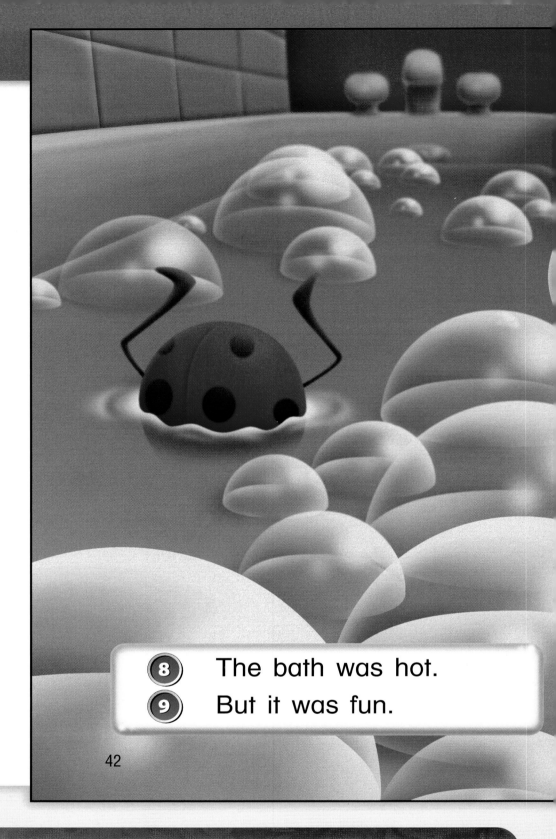

8 The bath was hot.
9 But it was fun.

42

Cross Curricular: Science

INSECTS: LARGE AND SMALL
Explain to children that insects can be as small as a fairy fly (one-hundredth of an inch long) or as large as an Atlas moth (wingspan of up to ten inches).

RESEARCH AND INQUIRY Invite children to look in fiction and nonfiction books to find insects of various sizes and make drawings of them.
▶ **Logical/Visual**

inter NET
CONNECTION For links to information about insects, help children log on to **www.mhschool. com/reading**.

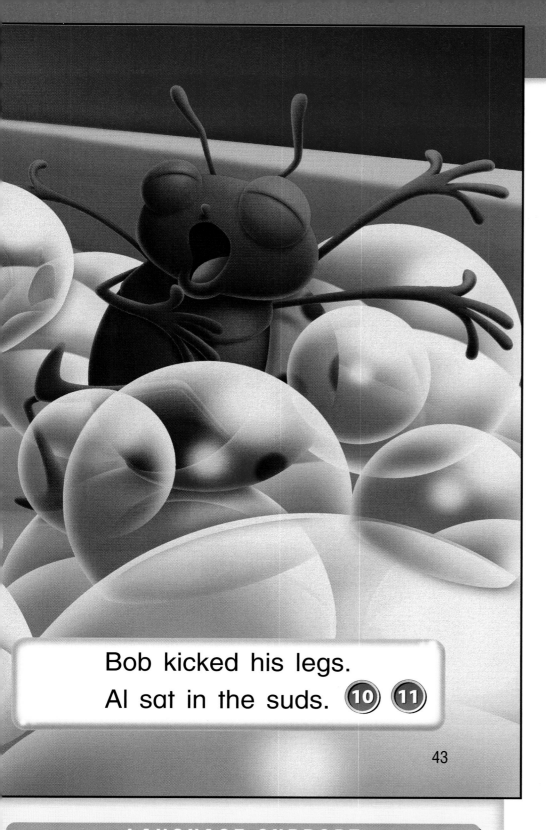

Bob kicked his legs.
Al sat in the suds. **10** **11**

43

LANGUAGE SUPPORT

ESL Have children role-play the different ways Bob moved in the tub. Have them point to the word *kicked*. Then have them demonstrate what Al did. Have them point to the word *sat*. Again, have them demonstrate what Al did.

Comprehension

10 What is the last word on this page? *(suds)* How can we use the picture and the other words to figure the word out? (The bugs are in a bath; the picture shows Al sitting on a bubble. The author states, "Al sat in the suds.") What is another word that means the same as suds? *(bubbles)* **Context Clues**

11 **ANALYZE CHARACTER** Think about what has happened in the story so far. What do you know about Al and Bob? Write what you learned on your Character/Plot chart. *Graphic Organizer*

CHARACTERS	WHAT THEY LOOK LIKE	WHAT THEY DO
Al	ladybug small, purple	Saw a bath. Got in the bath. Had fun in the bath.
Bob	ladybug small, blue	Saw a bath. Got in the bath. Had fun in the bath.
Fish	big	
Duck	bigger	
Boy	biggest	

TEACHING TIP

CHARACTER ANALYSIS Some children may need help in analyzing the story characters and their motives. Ask questions such as:

• How do Al and Bob look when you first see them? What does that tell you about them?

• What do you think Al and Bob do during the day? Why do you think they do what they do?

• The bugs are having fun in the tub. Do you think they like to play? How do you know?

You may wish to have children work in pairs to discuss the characters and fill in the chart.

43

Comprehension

 PHONOLOGICAL AWARENESS
Listen as I read this sentence: *A fish fell in the tub.* What two words begin with the same sound? (*fish, fell*)

A fish fell in the tub.
It got Bob and Al wet.

44

PREVENTION/INTERVENTION

Fluency

READ WITH EXPRESSION

ONE Model how to change your voice to add more expression to your reading.

- Read the sentences on page 45 several times. Change the speed and tone of your voice during each reading to express different feelings (surprise, fear, annoyance).
- Have the child repeat the process, experimenting with different ways to read the sentences.

PHONOLOGICAL AWARENESS
Make the /f/ sound for children, then say the following words: *fog, fox, fit, fun.* Ask children to think of other words that begin with the /f/ sound. Finally, read several sentences aloud to children, and ask them to raise their hands when they hear the /f/ sound. Example: *The fox can find food in the forest.*

44   *The Bug Bath*

"We saw that," said Bob. ⑫
"You got us wet," said Al. ⑬
⑭

45

Comprehension

⑫ What marks do you see before the word *we* and after the word *that*? (quotation marks) What do quotation marks tell you? (Someone is speaking.) Who speaks first on this page? (Bob) Who speaks next? (Al) **Concepts of Print**

⑬ Do you think the bugs thought the fish was real? Why or why not? (Answers will vary.) **Make Inferences**

⑭ "We …" hmm, I think we've seen that word before. What is it? *(saw)* Where have we already seen it? (page 41) **Unfamiliar Words**

Minilesson

REVIEW/MAINTAIN

Digraphs *sh* and *th*

Remind children that the digraphs *sh* and *th* make /sh/ and /th/, respectively. Write each digraph on the chalkboard, and make each sound for children. Ask children to:

• find the words on pages 44 and 45 that contain the digraphs. *(fish, the, that)*

• name other words that contain the digraphs.

Activity Invite volunteers to write a word with *sh* or *th* on the chalkboard and read it aloud.

Phonics **CD-ROM** Have children use the interactive phonics activities for more reinforcement with digraphs.

Comprehension

15 Why doesn't the fish swim? (It isn't real; it's a bathtub toy.) *Use Picture Clues/Distinguish Between Fantasy and Reality*

16 What do you think will happen next? *Make Predictions*

15 But the fish did not swim.
16 It just sat in the tub.

46

Cross Curricular: Math

HOW MANY IN THE TUB? Draw two ladybugs on the chalkboard, then write 1 + 1 = ? below the bugs. Model the addition fact for children. Draw two bugs together and one fish, and write 2 + 1 = ? below them. Model the second addition fact.

Activity Have children work in pairs to create pictures of animals in a bath. Suggest that children use groups of animals such as two ducks and three cats. Ask children to write the appropriate addition fact below their picture.

▶ **Visual/Auditory**

A big duck fell in the tub. 17
It landed on top of the bugs.

47

Comprehension

17 I wonder why things keep falling in the tub. This time it's a duck. It couldn't have fallen in by itself. (Someone dropped it in.) **Make Inferences**

18 What did the bugs do when they saw the duck? (They tried to get away.) Why? (They were scared.) **Use Illustrations/ Identify Cause and Effect**

BLENDING WITH SHORT *u* Find the third word in the first sentence and point to it with your finger. Now read the word with me, using your finger to help you remember to blend the sounds of the letters together. d u c k duck

Find two other words on this page that have the letter *u*. (tub, bugs) What sound does the letter *u* make? (/u/) **Graphophonic Cues**

Minilesson
REVIEW/MAINTAIN
High-Frequency Words

Tell children that they see certain words so often that they can recognize the words immediately.

- Write the following kindergarten high-frequency words on index cards: *a, of, the.*
- Have children read the words.
- Then have children find the same words on page 47.

Activity Review with children some more high-frequency words that appear in the story. Write *are, they, said, was,* and *we* on the chalkboard. Ask children to look through the story to find the words listed on the chalkboard. Have children take turns reading sentences from the story that contain the high-frequency words.

PREVENTION/INTERVENTION

BLENDING WITH SHORT *u* Write the following words on chart paper: *tug, rug, but, pup,* and *fun.* Ask volunteers to blend the sounds of the letters of each word together to read the word. Ask children what sound the letter *u* makes in each word. (/u/) **Graphophonic Cues**

Comprehension

(19) **ANALYZE PLOT** What has happened in the story so far? (Two dirty bugs decided to take a bath in a tub. A toy fish and a toy duck fell into the tub.) Let's add these events to our Character/Plot charts.
Graphic Organizer

CHARACTERS	WHAT THEY LOOK LIKE	WHAT THEY DO
Al	ladybug small, purple	Saw a bath. Got in bath. Had fun in bath.
Bob	ladybug small, blue	Saw a bath. Got in bath. Had fun in bath.
Fish	big	Fell in the tub. Got Al and Bob wet.
Duck	bigger	Landed on top of Al and Bob.
Boy	biggest	

"We saw that," said Bob.
(19) "You landed on us," said Al.

48

Cross Curricular: Science

SINK OR SWIM? Collect some small objects, such as a pencil, a penny, a small balloon with air in it, and a pencil eraser. Ask children to predict which ones will sink (penny, eraser) and which ones will float (pencil, balloon). Then fill a bowl with water and test. Make a class chart to show the results.
► **Visual/Logical**

RESEARCH AND INQUIRY Have children test other classroom objects to see if they will float.

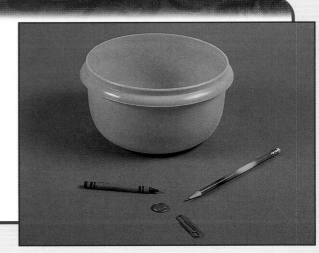

But the duck did not quack.
It just sat in the tub.

49

Comprehension

 PHONOLOGICAL AWARENESS
Listen as I read this sentence: *"You landed on us," said Al.* Which word in the sentence has two syllables? *(landed)*

Ⓢ ELF-MONITORING STRATEGY

ASK FOR HELP If you have questions about the story, you can ask a friend or your teacher for help.

MODEL I don't understand why Al and Bob keep talking to the animals in the tub. It doesn't make sense to me, so I can ask my friend about it. Then I can understand the story.

ⓟ/ᵢ PREVENTION/INTERVENTION

PHONOLOGICAL AWARENESS
Demonstrate how to clap out syllables in words.

- Say the word *duck* and clap as you say it. Ask children how many syllables are in the word.

- Repeat with the word *landed.*

- Continue with the words *dirty, quack, away,* and *boy.*

Comprehension

BLENDING WITH DIGRAPHS "A big ..." I remember that *t* and *h* together sound like /th/. I'll blend the sounds to read the word. th u d thud *Graphophonic Cues*

20 What do you think the bugs' voices sounded like when they asked the question? (scared, surprised) Let's read the sentence with that type of voice. *Fluency*

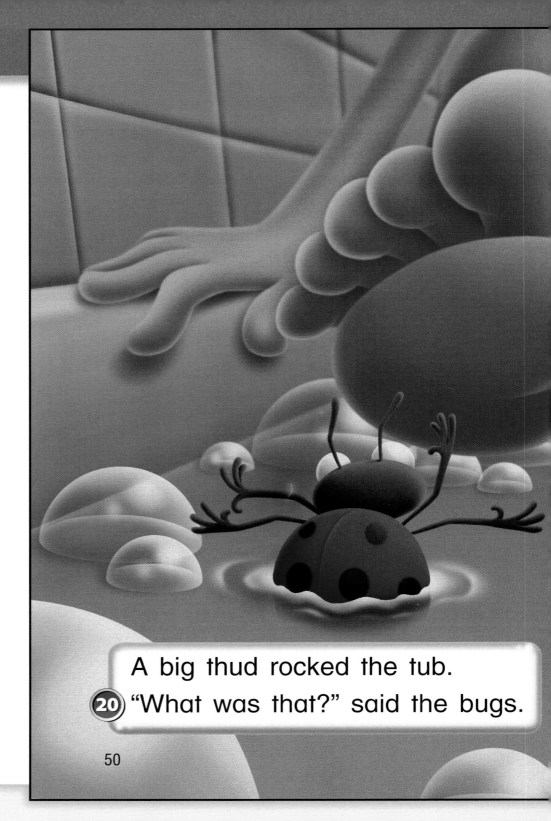

A big thud rocked the tub.
20 "What was that?" said the bugs.

50

Visual Literacy

VIEWING AND REPRESENTING

Discuss the illustration on pages 50–51. Whose point of view is the illustrator representing? Explain. (The illustrator has presented Al and Bob's view of the child and how enormous he seems to them.)

Ask children to look again at the pictures on the pages they have read so far. What other pictures show how small the bugs are? (Page 45 with the fish; pages 48 and 49 with the duck) How do the pictures help you understand the story and what Al and Bob feel?

PREVENTION/INTERVENTION

BLENDING WITH DIGRAPHS
Write the words *thud* and *that* on cards, several times for each word. Distribute the cards to children. Then read the sentences on this page, tracking each word with your finger.

Ask children to raise their cards when you read the matching word. Then ask children to say the word with you, blending the sounds together to read the word. *Graphophonic Cues*

"I see a leg," said Al.

"I see two legs," said Bob. **21**

51

Comprehension

21 Who do you think is getting into the tub now? (an adult or a child) **How can you tell?** (It looks like a person's legs; it's someone much bigger than the bugs.)
Use Illustrations/Make Inferences

Minilesson

REVIEW/MAINTAIN

Make Inferences

Explain to children that the author can use illustrations to show how characters are feeling and thinking.

- Ask children to describe the illustration on page 51. Talk about how the bugs' faces look.

- Have children describe how the bugs might be feeling and why.

- Have children close their eyes as you reread the text on page 51. Talk about how the illustration adds to the story.

Activity Have children look at the illustration on page 47. Brainstorm with children a list of words that tell how the bugs might be feeling. Write children's responses on the chalkboard.

LANGUAGE SUPPORT

ESL Point to the word *thud* in the first sentence on page 50 and then drop a textbook on a desk. Say the word and have children repeat after you. Ask children to stand and stomp their feet on the floor, alternating their right and left feet. Have children say *thud* each time they stomp a foot on the floor.
Fluency/Semantic Cues

51

Comprehension

22 What mark do you see after the word *it?* (question mark) What does it tell you? (Someone is asking a question.) Who is asking the question? (Bob) What mark do you see after the word *boy?* (exclamation mark) What does it tell you? (The character is frightened or excited.) *Concepts of Print*

23 What do you think will happen next? *Make Predictions*

TEACHING **TIP**

MANAGEMENT Combine native speakers and second-language learners in small groups for the Language Support activity. Ask children to work together to practice their intonation.

22 "What is it?" said Bob.
23 "It is a boy!" said Al.

52

LANGUAGE SUPPORT

ESL As you read pages 52 and 53, use intonation to model the difference between a question and an exclamation. Invite children to read these pages with you to practice their own intonation.
Fluency

"I want to get out!" said Bob.
"I want to run away!" said Al. **24**
26

53

Comprehension

24 What does Al want to do? (run away)
Show me how Al might move. *Role-Play*

25 How do you think Al and Bob are feeling now? (afraid) How can you tell?
(They look frightened in the illustrations.
They both want to get out of the tub.) *Use Picture Clues/Make Inferences*

26 **ANALYZE PLOT AND CHARACTER**
What has happened in the story so far? (Bob and Al wanted to take a bath. Then a fish and a duck fell into the tub. Then a boy got in the tub, and the bugs were afraid.) What does this tell you about the characters Al and Bob? (Responses will vary.)
Let's write our ideas on our Character/Plot charts. *Graphic Organizer*

CHARACTERS	WHAT THEY LOOK LIKE	WHAT THEY DO
Al	ladybug small, purple	Saw a bath. Got in the bath. Had fun in the bath.
Bob	ladybug small, blue	Saw a bath. Got in the bath. Had fun in the bath.
Fish	big	Fell in the tub. Got Al and Bob wet.
Duck	bigger	Landed on top of Al and Bob.
Boy	biggest	Got in the tub with a thud. Scared Al and Bob.

Comprehension

27 What are Bob and Al doing? (trying to swim away) *Use Illustrations*

28 **Phonics** SHORT *o* Let's look at page 55. Remember that the letter *o* makes the short *o* sound (/o/). What words on this page have a short *o*? *(Bob, got, on, top)*

"Bugs!" said the boy.
Bob and Al dashed away.

54

Activity

Cross Curricular: Art

DESIGN A TOY Talk about toys that children enjoy playing with in tubs and pools. Discuss the materials these toys are made from.

Activity Invite children to design and draw a water toy that they would

like to have. Ask them to name their toys. ▶ **Visual/Linguistic**

RESEARCH AND INQUIRY Have children ask some adults what kinds of toys they played with as children.

Dragon King

Bob got on top of the fish. **28**
The boy picked it up. **29**

55

USE ILLUSTRATIONS Have children look at the bugs on pages 46 and 47.

- How do they look in the first picture? (They look happy. They are having a good time.)

- How do they look in the second picture? (They look scared. They are trying to get away from the big duck.)

Have children look at pictures of Al and Bob on other pages in the story and use the illustrations to tell how they look in each one.

Comprehension

29 What is the boy doing? (lifting the fish out of the water and looking at the bug) *Use Illustrations*

USE ILLUSTRATIONS How many characters are in this picture? (3) Who are they? (Bob, the boy, the fish) Whose eye is Bob looking into? (the boy's) Who does the other eye belong to? (the fish) What part of the boy's hand can you see? (his fingers)

Minilesson

REVIEW

Use Context Clues

Remind children that they can find clues in words and pictures to understand unfamiliar words.

- Ask children to reread the second sentence on page 54.

- Discuss the meaning of the word *dashed*. Talk about how Bob and Al want to get away and how they are moving in the picture.

- Invite children to think of other words that could be used in the sentence, such as *hurried, scurried,* and *rushed*.

Activity Invite children to look through magazines or books to find pictures that illustrate the word *dash*. Ask children to use the word in a sentence to describe the action. For example: *The people had to dash to the train.*

55

Comprehension

(30) Where does Bob want to go?
(Responses will vary, but may include:
away from the boy, back outside) *Make
Predictions*

TEACHING TIP

SENTENCE PUNCTUATION Reread the
sentences on page 56, tracking each word. Pause
when you come to the comma in the first sentence
and the exclamation mark in the second sentence.
Model not lifting your finger to emphasize the
pause. Ask children to read the sentences aloud,
tracking each word and pausing at the appropriate
places. Encourage children to read the sentences
with expression.

"A bug," he said.
(30) "Let go!" said Bob.

56

CULTURAL PERSPECTIVES

BEETLEMANIA Tell children that bugs
are important in some cultures.

- Ancient Egyptians believed that a bee-
  tle's life was like the cycles of nature,
  such as the rising and setting of the
  sun.

RESEARCH AND INQUIRY Have the
librarian help children find pictures of
Egyptian drawings of beetles (or
scarabs).

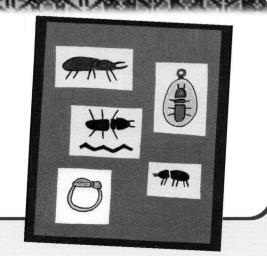

AI got on top of the duck.
The boy picked it up. (31)

57

Comprehension

CONCEPTS OF PRINT How many words do you see in the first sentence? (7) Let's read it together and count the words. Use your fingers to count the number of words. *Syntactic Cues*

(31) Where is AI now? (on top of the duck) What is the boy doing? (picking up the duck) *Use Illustrations*

PREVENTION/INTERVENTION

CONCEPTS OF PRINT Write the sentence *The boy picked it up.* on the chalkboard and read it with children. Elicit from them that this is a sentence. Remind children that words make up sentences, and that words have spaces between them. Ask volunteers to frame each word in the sentence with their index fingers. Then have children count the number of words in the sentence. (5) *Syntactic Cues*

Minilesson

REVIEW/MAINTAIN

Compare and Contrast

Tell children that by comparing and contrasting parts of a story they will:

• learn more about characters.

• better understand the plot.

Help children compare and contrast the different reactions of the boy and the bugs when they discover each other. Have them:

• reread pages 55–57, look at punctuation, and notice all the exclamation marks.

• think about whether the bugs and the boy are scared or happy.

Activity Create two word webs, one for AI and Bob and another for the boy. First, have children describe how the bugs react to the boy. Then ask them to describe the boy's reaction to AI and Bob.

Comprehension

32 **What did Al do?** (jumped from the duck and landed on the windowsill)
Use Illustrations

33 **ANALYZE CHARACTER** Think about what has happened in the story. What do you know about Bob and Al? Would you like to have them as friends? (Answers will vary. Possible answer: Al and Bob would be good friends to have because they like to have fun.)

TEACHING TIP

ANALYZE CHARACTERS' MOTIVES
Continue to ask questions to help children focus on the characters and the motives for their actions:

- Are Bob and Al brave? Why or why not?

- Do Bob and Al like to try new things? How do you know?

"A bug," he said.
33 "Let go!" said Al.

58

Cross Curricular: Social Studies

SILK FROM CHINA Tell children that some insects help make clothes.

- About 5,000 years ago, the Chinese began making silk from the cocoons of caterpillars called silkworms.

Show children where China is on a map.

RESEARCH AND INQUIRY Have children find other places where silk is made.

▶ Spatial

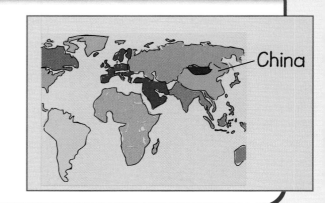

Al and Bob ran away.
They got very dirty. **35**

59

Comprehension

34 How did Bob and Al get dirty again?
(They ran through the grass and in the
dirt.) **Do you think this is funny?** (Yes,
because they just had a bath.) *Use Illustrations/
Make Inferences*

35 **Phonics** SHORT *o* **What word on**
this page rhymes with hot? *(got)* Point
to it with your finger and read it for me.
Graphophonic Cues

Minilesson

REVIEW/MAINTAIN

Main Idea

Explain to children that the main idea of a
story tells what the story is about. Write the
following sentences on chart paper. Read
them aloud. Have children choose the sentence that gives the main idea of the story.

- Bob got on the fish.
- A boy took a bath.
- Two bugs took a bath in a bathtub.

Activity Work with children to write a
summary of the story. Help them distinguish between important and unimportant
story details. Then have children dictate the
main idea, the important events in the
story, and how the story ends. Write the
sentences on chart paper. Invite children to
illustrate their favorite parts of the story.

Comprehension

36 **ANALYZE PLOT** How does the story end? (Bob and Al use a flower for a bathtub and take another bath.) Let's add this to our Character/Plot charts. *Graphic Organizer*

37 What do you think Al meant when he said, "We fit!"? (The flower bathtub was the right size for them.) *Make Inferences*

RETELL THE STORY Have pairs of children work together to retell the story. Children can role-play being Bob and Al. Encourage children to use their Character/Plot charts to help them remember plot and character details. You may also wish to use sentence strips to help children recall the sequence of events. *Summarize/Role-Play*

STUDENT SELF-ASSESSMENT

Have children ask themselves the following questions to assess how they are reading:

- How did I use what I know about bugs and baths to help me understand the story?
- How did I use pictures and what the characters said to help me understand the characters and the plot?
- How did I use the pictures and the letters and sounds I know to help me read the words?

TRANSFERRING THE STRATEGIES
- How can I use these strategies to help me read other stories?

"I see a bath," said Bob.
The bugs got in.

60

REREADING FOR *Fluency*

PARTNERS Have partners reread the story, alternating pages or reading as Al and Bob. Encourage them to read with expression and excitement.

READING RATE When you evaluate reading rate, have children read aloud from the story for one minute. Place a stick-on note after the last word read. Count words read. To evaluate children's performance, see the Running Record in the **Fluency Assessment** book**.**

i **Intervention** For leveled fluency lessons, passages, and norms charts, see **Skills Intervention Guide**, Part 5, Fluency.

"We fit!" said Al. **37**
"What a good bath for bugs!"
they said.

61

LITERARY RESPONSE

QUICK-WRITE Ask children to think of another place where Al and Bob could take a bath. Have them draw a picture and write a question about something in their picture or in the story that they would like to know more about.

ORAL RESPONSE Have children use their journal entries to discuss these questions:

- Do you think the bugs should have gotten into the bathtub?
- If you were the boy, what would you have said to the bugs?

SENTENCE STRIPS Children can use strips 1–44 to retell *The Bug Bath*.

> 1
> "We are very dirty," said Al.

> 2
> "I want a bath," said Bob.

Comprehension

Return to Predictions and Purposes

Reread children's predictions about the story. Discuss the predictions, noting which ones needed to be revised. Then ask children if the story answered all of their questions.

PREDICTIONS	WHAT HAPPENED
The bugs try to take a bath in a real house.	The bugs are frightened by a toy fish and a toy duck; then a boy scares them away. They take a bath in a flower bathtub.
The main characters are two bugs.	The main characters in the story are Al and Bob, two bugs.

Have children discuss the strategy of creating a Character/Plot chart. Did the chart help children remember details about each character and understand the plot of the story? How?

 **ASSESSMENT**

HOW TO ASSESS

Phonics SHORT *o* Have children turn to pages 46–47. Ask them to read the words with the short *o* sound.

ANALYZE CHARACTER AND PLOT Have children make a list of words that describe Al and Bob. Then ask children to write two sentences about the story's plot.

FOLLOW UP

Phonics SHORT *o* Use letter cards for blending with short *o* for children who are having difficulty.

ANALYZE CHARACTER AND PLOT Invite children to take a **picture walk** through the book to recall the main events. Have them summarize the plot and make a list of characters.

61

Story Questions

Tell children that now they will read some questions about the story. Help children read the questions. Discuss possible answers.

Answers:

1. a fish and a duck *Literal/Sequence of Events*

2. The boy threw them in. *Make Inferences*

3. Answers will vary. (Possible answer: Boys are much bigger than bugs.) *Inferential/Make Inferences*

4. Answers will vary. Accept appropriate examples. *Critical/Summarize*

5. Answers will vary. *Critical/Reading Across Texts*

Write a Skit Help children read the directions. Show them the mechanics of writing dialogue: a word (or picture) naming the character, followed by a colon, followed by what the character says.

Story Questions & Activities
READ TOGETHER

1. What fell in the tub?

2. What made them fall in the tub?

3. Why were the bugs afraid of the boy?

4. Tell the story's funny parts.

5. Have you read another story about bugs?

Write a Skit

Choose two bugs.
Write about what they say.

You can't catch
Buzz! Buzz

Just wait and
My web will trap

Meeting Individual Needs

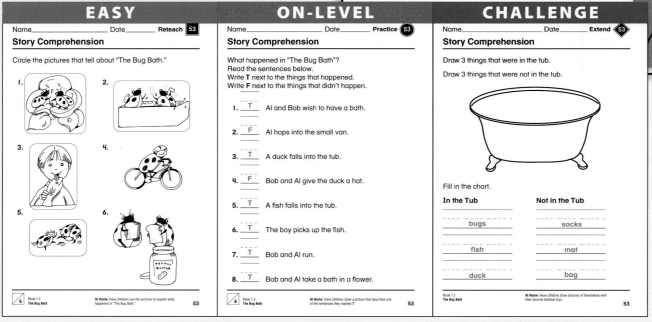

EASY	ON-LEVEL	CHALLENGE
Reteach, 53	Practice, 53	Extend, 53

EASY

Name_____ Date_____ Reteach 53

Story Comprehension

Circle the pictures that tell about "The Bug Bath."

1. 2.

3. 4.

5. 6.

Book 1.2
The Bug Bath   At Home: Have children use the pictures to explain what happened in "The Bug Bath."   53

ON-LEVEL

Name_____ Date_____ Practice 53

Story Comprehension

What happened in "The Bug Bath"?
Read the sentences below.
Write **T** next to the things that happened.
Write **F** next to the things that didn't happen.

1. __T__ Al and Bob wish to have a bath.

2. __F__ Al hops into the small van.

3. __T__ A duck falls into the tub.

4. __F__ Bob and Al give the duck a hat.

5. __T__ A fish falls into the tub.

6. __T__ The boy picks up the fish.

7. __T__ Bob and Al run.

8. __T__ Bob and Al take a bath in a flower.

Book 1.2
The Bug Bath   At Home: Have children draw a picture that describes one of the sentences they marked T.   53

CHALLENGE

Name_____ Date_____ Extend 53

Story Comprehension

Draw 3 things that were in the tub.

Draw 3 things that were not in the tub.

Fill in the chart.

In the Tub	Not in the Tub
bugs	socks
fish	mat
duck	bag

Book 1.2
The Bug Bath   At Home: Have children draw pictures of themselves with their favorite bathtub toys.   53

Make a Bug Puzzle

Draw a big bug on paper.

Cut it into small parts.

Ask a friend to put the parts together.

Find Out More

What is a spider?

Find out.

Share what you learn.

63

Story Activities

Make a Bug Puzzle

Materials: sheets of paper, crayons or felt-tipped markers, scissors

Read the directions aloud. Help children who have questions. Remind them that a puzzle is easier to put together if the parts are different shapes.

GROUP After the children have drawn and put together their puzzles, you may wish to have them create a mural of bug puzzle parts. They can place the completed puzzle on the mural.

Find Out More

RESEARCH AND INQUIRY Again, read the directions aloud, and help children **PARTNERS** who have questions. Then have them work in pairs.

Tell children that there are many different kinds of spiders. Use pictures to give examples: *The tarantula is the world's largest spider; water spiders can breathe underwater.* Have pairs write down common characteristics of spiders: They have eight legs; they have fangs; they are helpful to people because they eat harmful insects.

*inter*NET **CONNECTION** Have children log on to ***www.mhschool.com/reading***, where they can access links about bugs.

DAILY **Phonics** ROUTINES

DAY 3 **Blending** Have pairs work with letter cards to build short *o* words. One child builds a word and the other reads it. Have children take turns.

Phonics CD-ROM

FORMAL **ASSESSMENT**

See the Selection Assessment Test for Book 2.

Study Skills

MAPS

OBJECTIVES

Children will learn to read a map to gather information.

Remind children that they have just read a story about different creatures taking a bath. Tell them that now they will read a map of the bathtub.

Display **Teaching Chart 39.** Have children look at the map and bath toys. Then invite them to describe what they see. Have them trace the lines with their fingers. Point to the bath toys and ask children to name them. Then help children read the questions below the map, encouraging them to "hop" with their fingers as they answer each question.

Meeting Individual Needs

STUDY SKILLS

READ TOGETHER

A Hippity-Hop Map

Maps tell how far apart things are.

Look at the Map

❶ Start at the duck. How many hops to the boat?

❷ Start at the boat. How many hops to the fish?

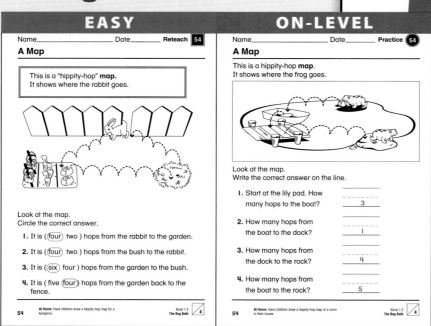

EASY	ON-LEVEL	CHALLENGE
Reteach, 54	Practice, 54	Extend, 54

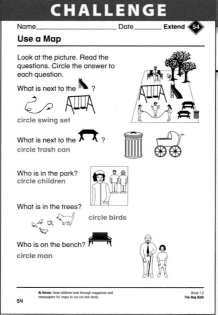

TEST POWER

October 20

Dear Grandma,

Thank you for the new bath toys.

I like the duck and the fish.

They were very nice birthday gifts.

Thanks for coming to my party.

You are the best grandma!

Love, Ken

Ken's gifts make him feel –

⬤ happy

◯ sad

What words in the story help you answer the question?

65

Test Power

THE PRINCETON REVIEW

Read the Page

Explain to children that you will be reading this story as a group. You will read the story, and they will follow in their books.

Request that children put pens, pencils, and markers away, since they will not be writing in their books.

Discuss the Question

Remind children about words that convey feelings. Have them look back to the story for words that describe feelings of like or dislike. Ask them what words they found and what they mean.

Test-Tip

To answer a question about feelings, look for words that describe feelings.

Leveled Books

EASY

Big?

☑ **Phonics** Short *o*

☑ **Analyze Character and Plot**
High-Frequency Words:
saw, very, want, two

by Rachel Lear
illustrated by Daniel Dumont

Answers to Story Questions

1. Mick ran when he saw Jan's eyes.
2. Mick's tub was a cup.
3. Answers will vary: A giant might think a sink looked like a little cup.
4. Mick the bug was taking a bath in the cup. Jan picked up the cup. Mick hopped out of the cup. Mick ran when he saw Jan. Jan caught Mick and looked at his small size.
5. They take baths.

The Story Questions and Activity below appear in the Easy Book.

Story Questions and Activity

1. When did Mick run fast?
2. What was Mick's tub?
3. Who might think your sink looked like a little cup?
4. Tell the story in your own words.
5. What is the same about Mick and the bugs in *The Bug Bath?*

Create a Bug

Draw a bug.
Give your bug a name.
Write a sentence that tells about your bug.

from Big?

Guided Reading

PREVIEW AND PREDICT Discuss each illustration up to page 5, using the high-frequency words. As you take the **picture walk**, have children predict what the story is about. Chart their ideas.

SET PURPOSES Have children write or draw why they want to read *Big?* For example: *I want to know what happens to Mick the bug.*

READ THE BOOK Use questions like the following to guide children's reading or after they have read the story independently.

Page 3: Who sees a vocabulary word we just learned? *(very)* Why is the tub big for Mick? *High-Frequency Words, Analyze Character*

Page 4: I can blend the sounds in a word together to read the word. The sounds /h/, /o/, /p/ blend together as: h o p hop. The word is *hop. Phonics and Decoding*

Page 7: Why does Mick crawl into Jan's hand? (He's not afraid anymore. She doesn't want to hurt him.) What makes

Mick big in the picture on page 7? (a magnifying glass) *Analyze Character and Plot*

Page 8: Who is bigger than Mick? (Jan and Dad) Who is bigger than Jan? (Dad) *Compare and Contrast*

RETURN TO PREDICTIONS AND PURPOSES Discuss children's predictions. Ask which were close to the story and why. Have children review their purposes for reading the story. Did they find out what happened to Mick the bug?

LITERARY RESPONSE The following questions will help focus children's responses:

- What things are smaller than you?
- What things are bigger than you?

Also see the story questions and activity in *Big?*

See the **Phonics** CD-ROM for practice with short *o.*

Leveled Books

INDEPENDENT

The Big Sun

- ☑  Short *o*
- ☑ Analyze Character and Plot

High-Frequency Words:
saw, very, want, two

written by Michael Maia
illustrated by Fran Lee

Guided Reading

PREVIEW AND PREDICT Discuss each illustration up to page 5, using the high-frequency words. As you take the **picture walk**, have children predict what the story is about. Chart their ideas.

SET PURPOSES Have children write or draw why they want to read *The Big Sun*. For example: *I want to find out why the sun is big but looks small.*

READ THE BOOK Use questions like the following as children read or after they have read independently.

Page 2: MODEL: I'm not sure what this word is, but I can blend the letters together to read it: h o t hot. The word is *hot*. *Phonics and Decoding*

Pages 4–5: Look at the pictures and tell what is happening. Where is the boy when the path looks small? (far away in a plane) Where is he when the path looks big? (standing right on it) *Analyze Plot/Use Illustrations*

Page 6: Now look at the punctuation mark at the end of each sentence. What is it called

and what does it tell you? (Question mark; the sentences are questions.) *Track Print*

Page 8: Who sees a vocabulary word we just learned? (*two, want*) *High-Frequency Words*

RETURN TO PREDICTIONS AND PURPOSES Discuss children's predictions. Ask which were close to the story and why. Ask them to review their purposes for reading. Did they find out why the sun is big but looks small?

LITERARY RESPONSE The following questions will help focus children's responses:

- Who is big or small compared to you?
- Have you ever been kind to someone smaller than you? Has someone big ever been kind to you? Tell about it.

Also see the story questions and activity in *The Big Sun*.

See the **Phonics CD-ROM** for practice with short *o*.

Answers to Story Questions

1. The path looks small.
2. When you are far away from the path, it looks small. When you are close to the path, it looks big.
3. Possible answers: the sun, people, trees, and houses are big things that look small sometimes.
4. The story is about how different things seem to change in size.
5. The bugs see things that are small as big, just as the boy does.

The Story Questions and Activity below appear in the Independent Book.

Story Questions and Activity

1. How does the path look to the boy when he is up?
2. Why does the path seem to change size?
3. What are some big things that look small sometimes?
4. Tell what the story is about.
5. How is this story like *The Bug Bath*?

Big and Small

Make something that looks small to you.

Think of how it would look to a bug.

Draw a picture of yourself with this thing.

Draw a picture of a bug with this thing.

from The Big Sun

65B

Leveled Books

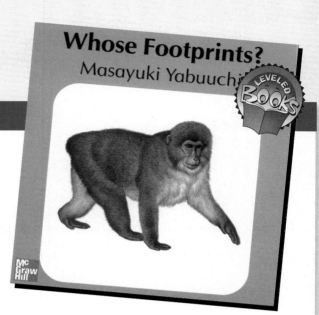

Whose Footprints?
Masayuki Yabuuchi

CHALLENGE

Whose Footprints?

- ☑ **Phonics** Short *o*
- ☑ **Analyze Character and Plot**

Guided Reading

PREVIEW AND PREDICT Have volunteers read the title. Take a **picture walk** through the illustrations up to page 11. Discuss children's predictions about the story.

SET PURPOSES Have children discuss why they want to read the story. List their purposes on the chalkboard.

READ THE BOOK Use the following prompts while children are reading or after they have read the story independently:

Pages 8–9: Does a duck have fur or feathers? (feathers) Describe the duck you see here. *Use Illustrations*

Pages 10–11: How many toes does a cat have? (four) *Story Details*

Pages 12–13: How many footprints would a cat make? (four) How can you tell? (The cat has four legs.) *Use Illustrations*

Pages 14–17: How is a goat different from a duck? (It has fur, not feathers like a duck. It has four feet, not two like a duck.) *Use Illustrations*

Pages 20–21: Is the horse walking slowly or is it running? (running) How can you

tell? (Its tail and mane are flying behind it.) *Use Illustrations*

Pages 22–23: Which word has the /o/ sound? *(on)* Let's blend the sounds together. o n on *Phonics and Decoding*

Pages 24–25: What words would you use to describe the bear? (big, strong) *Use Illustrations*

Pages 26–27: Why do you think the footprint belongs to a large, heavy animal? (It's very big.) *Use Illustrations*

RETURN TO PREDICTIONS AND PURPOSES Have children talk about their predictions and purposes for reading.

LITERARY RESPONSE Have children discuss questions like the following:

- Have you ever seen an animal's footprints? Where?

Also see the story questions and activity in *Whose Footprints?*

See the **Phonics** **CD-ROM** for practice with short *o*.

Answers to Story Questions

1. a duck
2. Both are hoofprints.
3. Answers will vary. Hippo.
4. One was made by webbed feet. One had toes and a pad. Two were made by hooves. One had claws. One was very big!
5. duck, cat, horse

The Story Questions and Activity below appear in the Challenge Book.

Story Questions and Activity

1. Who has webbed footprints?
2. How are the horse and goat footprints alike?
3. What other animals have big footprints?
4. Tell about the footprints you saw.
5. What animals are in this story and in *I Went Walking*?

Put Your Best Foot Forward

Draw an animal.
Draw its footprints.
Write about the footprints.

from *Whose Footprints?*

Bringing Groups Together

Anthology and Leveled Books

Connecting Texts

PERCEPTION

Lead a discussion about the concept of big and small with children, as it was presented in each story. Call on volunteers from each reading level to talk about the big and small characters in each book.

Have children create a web to compare the big and small characters from the stories.

The Bug Bath
The bugs look small in the boy's bathtub.

Big?
Mick and Jan are small, but Dad is big.

Perception

The Big Sun
The sun is very big, but it looks small because it is very far from us.

Whose Footprints?
Some animals have big footprints and some animals have small footprints.

Viewing/Representing

GROUP PRESENTATIONS Divide the class into groups, one for each of the four books. (For *The Bug Bath*, combine children of different reading levels.) Have each group pick characters from their book and draw pictures of them. Have each group present its pictures and retell the stories and make up further adventures for the characters.

AUDIENCE RESPONSE

Ask children to pay attention to each group's presentation. Allow time for questions after each group presents.

Research and Inquiry

MORE ABOUT PERSPECTIVE Have children ask themselves: What else would I like to know about the size of things? Then invite them to do the following:

- Bring in pictures of different-sized things: dinosaurs and bugs, for example.

- Talk to the class about how things appear to get bigger or smaller.

interNET CONNECTION Have children visit *www.mhschool.com/reading* for links to Web pages about perspective.

Children can draw pictures representing what they have learned in their journals.

Review **Short *o***

OBJECTIVES

Children will:

- identify /o/o.
- blend and read short *o*, CVC words.
- review initial/final consonants: *d, t, s, l, p, g, r, n, c, h, j, g.*
- review digraph *ck.*

....

MATERIALS

- word cards from the **Word Building Manipulative Cards**
- **Teaching Chart 40**

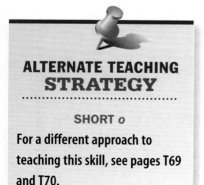

Skills Finder	
Short *o*	
Introduce	B2: 36I-J
Review	B2: 65E-F, 65G-H, 95G-H, 124I-J
Test	Book 2
Maintain	B4: 19

ALTERNATE TEACHING STRATEGY

....

SHORT *o*

For a different approach to teaching this skill, see pages T69 and T70.

| **PREPARE** |

Listen for Short *o*   Read the following sentences aloud. Have children raise their hands when they hear a word with short *o*.

- The <u>fox</u> <u>got</u> <u>on</u> a <u>box</u>.
- He <u>hopped</u> to the <u>top</u>.

| **TEACH** |

Review the Letter *o* as the Symbol for /o/

- Explain to children that they will review the letter *o* and the sound it makes.
- Say /o/. Have children write the letter that stands for /o/ as they make the sound.

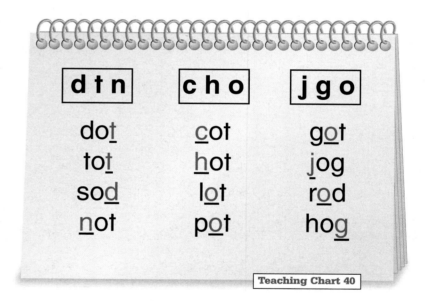

| d t n | c h o | j g o |

dot	cot	got
tot	hot	jog
sod	lot	rod
not	pot	hog

Teaching Chart 40

BLENDING Model and Guide Practice with Short *o* Words

- Display **Teaching Chart 40**. Tell children that they will make words with short *o*.
- Point to the letters *d* and *o* and blend the sounds. Repeat and have children blend the sounds with you.
- Choose the letter *t* from the box at the top of the column and write it in the blank space.
- Point to the letters again, and have children blend the sounds to read the word. d o t, dot

Use the Word in Context

- Have volunteers use the word in sentences to reinforce its meaning. Example: *Put a dot at the end of a sentence.*

Repeat the Procedure

- Select a letter from the box to make a real word. Make sure that children understand the meaning of the word.
- Continue the activity, asking children to choose letters and blend sounds together.

PRACTICE

Read and Sort Short o Words

GROUP

Write the following words on word cards: *dog, dock, hot, hog, nod, sock, sod, not,* and *nod.* Distribute the cards and ask a child to display his or her card. As a group, blend the sounds together and say each word. Then hold up all the word cards. Have children identify words that belong in the same word family. For example: *not, hot, dot, cot.*

▶**Visual/Linguistic**

dog   hot   sock   nod

ASSESS/CLOSE

Blend and Read Words with Short o

To assess children's mastery of blending and reading words with short *o*, observe them as they read words during the Practice activity.

ADDITIONAL PHONICS RESOURCES

Phonics/Phonemic Awareness Practice Book, pages 99–102

PHONICS KIT Hands-on Activities and Practice

McGraw-Hill School **TECHNOLOGY** **Phonics CD-ROM**

activities for practice with **Blending and Building Words**

DAILY Phonics ROUTINES

DAY 4

Writing Help children choose two words with short *o* and create a rhyming couplet with the words. Encourage children to illustrate their rhymes.

Phonics CD-ROM

SPELLING/PHONICS CONNECTIONS

Words with short *o*: See the 5-Day Spelling Plan, pages 65Q–65R.

i Intervention ▶ **Skills Intervention Guide,** for direct instruction and extra practice in Short *o*

Meeting Individual Needs for Phonics

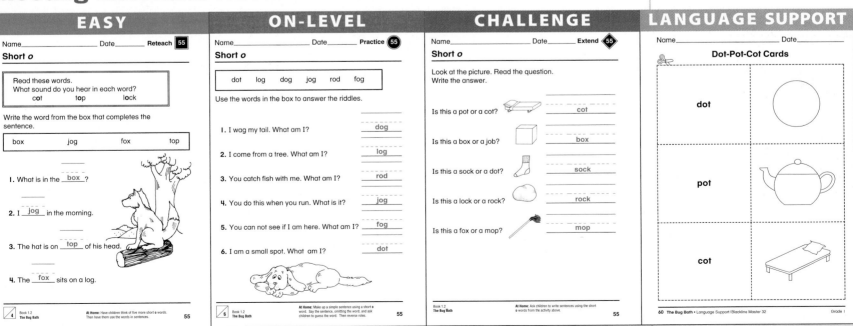

EASY	ON-LEVEL	CHALLENGE	LANGUAGE SUPPORT
Reteach, 55	Practice, 55	Extend, 55	Language Support, 60

OBJECTIVES

Children will:

- review /o/o, /a/a, /i/i, /u/u, and *ck*.

- blend and read words with short *o, a, i,* and *u,* and *ck*

- cumulative review: initial/final consonants: *c, d, h, l, m, n, p, s, t.*

....

MATERIALS

- letter cards from the **Word Building Manipulative Cards**

- **Teaching Chart 41**

- **Phonics Practice Reader, Volume 1**

Skills Finder

Short *o*	
Introduce	B2: 36I–J
Review	B2: 65E–F, 65G–H, 95G–H, 124I–J
Test	Book 2
Maintain	B4: 19

ALTERNATE TEACHING STRATEGY

....

SHORT *o, u*

For a different approach to teaching this skill, see pages T64, T65, T69 and and T70.

Review Short *o, u, i, a; ck*

PREPARE

Identify Letters and Symbols
- Remind children that the letter *o* stands for the /o/ sound. Write the letter *o* on the chalkboard and say the sound. Continue with the letters *u, i,* and *e.*

- Write the digraph *ck* on the chalkboard. Ask volunteers to say words that end with *ck.*

TEACH

BLENDING Model and Guide Practice with Short Vowels and *ck*
- Display **Teaching Chart 41**. Demonstrate how to build and blend words by choosing a letter from the box and writing it in the blank.

- Blend the first example with children.

h o t   hot

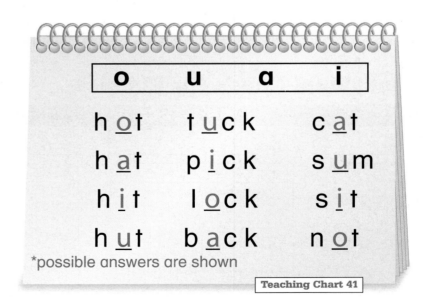

*possible answers are shown

Teaching Chart 41

Repeat the Procedure
- Continue with **Teaching Chart 41**. Have volunteers write letters to form words. Have them blend and read the words.

Use the Words in Context
- Ask volunteers to choose words and use them in sentences to reinforce their meanings. Challenge children to use two words in one sentence. Example: *The hat is on the cat.*

PRACTICE

BLENDING
Read Words with
Short *o, a, i, u* and
Digraph *ck*

GROUP

Have children work in small groups. Distribute letter cards for short *o, a, i, u*; the consonants *m, p, t, l*; and the digraph *ck*. Have children use the letter cards to make words that rhyme. Each group should share the words they created. ▶**Visual/Linguistic**

ASSESS/CLOSE

Read and Write
Words with Short
Vowel Sounds in
Sentences

Use your observations from the Practice activity to determine whether children need more reinforcement with short vowel sounds and the digraph *ck*. Invite children to write one or more short vowel words, read them, and use them in sentences.

Read a Decodable
Story

For additional practice reading words with short *o* and to develop fluency, direct children to read the story *Bob Bug* from the **Phonics Practice Reader, Volume 1.**

ADDITIONAL PHONICS RESOURCES

Phonics/Phonemic Awareness
Practice Book,
pages 99–102

PHONICS KIT
Hands-on Activities and Practice

McGraw-Hill School
TECHNOLOGY

Phonics CD-ROM

activities for practice with
Blending and Building Words

DAY 5 **Fluency** Write a list of words with the short *o* sound. Have children work in pairs, taking turns reading the words.

Phonics CD-ROM

i Intervention ▶ **Skills**
Intervention Guide, for direct instruction and extra practice in Short *o* and *u*

Meeting Individual Needs for Phonics

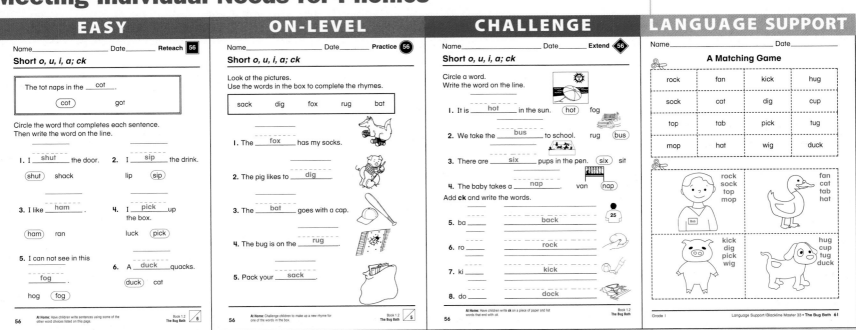

Reteach, 56   Practice, 56   Extend, 56   Language Support, 61

OBJECTIVES

Children will:

- review how to analyze character and plot.
- identify problem and solution.

MATERIALS

- **Teaching Chart 42**

Skills Finder

Story Elements

Introduce	B2: 35I-J
Review	B2: 65I-J, 137E-F; B3: 37I-J, 139G-H
Test	Book 2, Book 3
Maintain	B3: 89; B4: 107, 109

TEACHING TIP

MOTIVE Encourage children to think about the motives of the characters in the stories they read. Why do the characters do what they do? Why do they think and feel the way they do? Thinking about motive will help children understand better the stories they read.

SELECTION Connection

Children may choose from the following titles:

ANTHOLOGY

- *The Bug Bath*

LEVELED BOOKS

- *Big?*
- *The Big Sun*
- *Whose Footprints?*

Bibliography, pages T98–T99

Review **Story Elements**

PREPARE

Review the Concept
Remind children that when they read a story, they should think about who the characters are and what they do, say, and feel. Understanding the characters can help them better understand the plot, or what happens in a story.

TEACH

Analyze Characters and Plot
Display **Teaching Chart 42**. Tell children to think about who the story is about (the characters) and what the story is about (the plot). Then read it aloud with children.

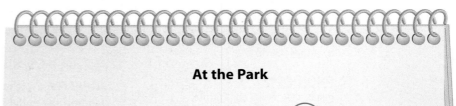

At the Park

"I want to hit a ball," said Nan.
Jack threw the ball.
Nan missed.
She frowned.
Jack threw the ball again.
Crack! The ball was in the sky.
"I can do it!" said Nan.

Teaching Chart 42

Identify Problem and Solution
MODEL I read that Nan wants to hit the ball, but she misses. This is the problem. She is frowning, which means she is unhappy. Nan tries again. Perhaps she is really keeping her eye on the ball this time. This time she hits the ball. The problem is solved. She must be proud of herself. She says, "I can do it!".

Have volunteers circle the names of the characters in the story on the chart. Ask children to retell the story, naming the problem and its solution.

PRACTICE

Expand on the Story

PARTNERS

Have children work in pairs and brainstorm possible continuations for the story. What other kinds of problems might a ball player have? Distribute paper, pencil, crayons, or markers. Have children draw a picture showing the plot and a problem the character is facing. Then encourage them to tell the solution to the problem.

▶ **Visual/Linguistic**

ASSESS/CLOSE

Compare Story Endings

Have children share and describe their drawings with the class. Tell children to compare their story expansions with others. Point out that a story can have many different actions, characters, and endings.

ALTERNATE TEACHING STRATEGY

Story Elements

For a different approach to teaching this skill, see page T66.

i **Intervention** ▶ **Skills**
Intervention Guide, for direct instruction and extra practice in Story Elements

Meeting Individual Needs for Comprehension

EASY	ON-LEVEL	CHALLENGE	LANGUAGE SUPPORT

EASY

Name_____ Date_____ Reteach **57**

Story Elements

The **characters** are the people or animals in a story.
The **plot** is what happens.

Read the story. Then complete the chart.

Jan likes to run. She runs with her dog, Lulu. They run down the path. They run to the park. Then they sit down and look at the sky. Jan looks at Lulu. She is asleep!

They run down the ___ path
They run to the ___ park
Jan and ___ Lulu
They look at the ___ sky
Lulu ___ falls asleep.

Book 1.2
The Bug Bath

At Home: Have children identify the main characters and the plot of a familiar story.

57

ON-LEVEL

Name_____ Date_____ Practice **57**

Story Elements

The **characters** are the people or animals a story is about.
The **plot** is what happens.
Read the story, then circle the answer to each question.

Max and Bob go out. It is very wet. Max hears a sob. What is it? Max and Bob look. Then they see a pup. The pup sits in the mud. Bob and Max take him home. They give him ham. Bob and Max call the pup "Lucky."

1. Who are the characters?
   Max, the pup
   Bob, Max
   (Max, Bob, the pup)

2. What do Max and Bob find?
   a cat
   (a pup)
   a hog

3. What do Max and Bob do?
   (take the pup home)
   pat the pup
   jog with the pup

4. What do they give the pup?
   (ham)
   nuts
   fish

Book 1.2
The Bug Bath

At Home: Ask children to think of three more things that Max, Bob and Lucky can do together. Then have them draw pictures showing one of these things.

57

CHALLENGE

Name_____ Date_____ Extend **57**

Story Elements

Read about the bugs Bob and Al. Circle the answer that tells about them.

Al and Bob saw a big tub. The two bugs got in. Why did they get in the tub?

Bob and Al were dirty.
Bob and Al were hungry.   circle the first choice
Bob and Al were wet.

A big duck fell in the tub. It landed on top of the bugs. Did the duck quack? No. Why not?
                        circle the second choice
The duck was big.
The duck was a toy.
The duck was bad.

Write what Bob and Al do when they get out of the tub.

_____

_____

Answers will vary.

Book 1.2
The Bug Bath

At Home: Ask children to tell a story from an insect's point of view.

57

LANGUAGE SUPPORT

Name_____ Date_____

Who and What?

Al	Bob	boy

Al   Bob

boy

62 The Bug Bath • Language Support/Blackline Master 34   Grade 1

Reteach, 57   **Practice, 57**   **Extend, 57**   **Language Support, 62**

OBJECTIVES

Children will review reading words with inflectional ending *-ed*.

MATERIALS
- **Teaching Chart 43**
- index cards

Skills Finder

Inflectional Ending *-ed*

Introduce	B2: 35K-L
Review	B2: 65K-L, 137I-J; B4: 65K-L
Test	Book 2, Book 4

TEACHING TIP

VERB TENSES Most first graders will have a well-developed ability to distinguish between present and past. It will still be helpful to emphasize all past-tense verbs and indicators. For example, point out things that you or the class are doing: We *look* at books. Then talk about what was done in the past: Yesterday, we *played* games.

ALTERNATE TEACHING STRATEGY

INFLECTIONAL ENDING -ed

For a different approach to teaching this skill see page T68.

65K *The Bug Bath*

Review Inflectional Ending -ed

PREPARE

Act It Out   Write the word *kick* on the chalkboard. Have children stand up and pantomime kicking a ball, as they say: *We kick.* When they sit down, ask: *What did we just do?* (We kicked.) Add *-ed* to *kick*. Explain that we often add *-ed* to words to show that something has happened.

TEACH

Identify Root Words   Track the first sentence on **Teaching Chart 43** as you read it with children. Point to the word *dashed*. Model for children how understanding inflectional endings can help them read.

1. The bug dashed to the rug.

2. The thud rocked the ship.

3. The man picked up a cup.

Teaching Chart 43

MODEL   I can use what I already know to help me read words I don't know. I know the word *dash*. I see that the last two letters of the word are *-ed*. I know that *-ed* at the end of a word sometimes means that somebody did something in the past. The word is *dashed*.

Have a volunteer underline the root word *dash*. Model the second and third sentences, and call on children to come up and draw a line under the root word in each.

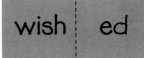

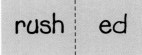

PRACTICE

Add -ed

PARTNERS

Distribute index cards to children. Then write the following sentences on the chalkboard:

1. I <u>kick</u> the can.
2. I <u>rush</u> to the bus.
3. I <u>pack</u> my bag.
4. I <u>wish</u> for a dog.

Ask children to read each sentence and write the underlined verb on the left half of an index card. Then add -ed to the verb in each sentence. Have children read each sentence again and write the -ed ending so that it appears after a dotted line. Have partners practice reading the words aloud. ▶ **Kinesthetic/Linguistic**

ASSESS/CLOSE

Show Past and Present

Show children how their cards can be folded and unfolded to make present-tense and past-tense verbs. Then tell them you will read some sentences. They should hold up their cards either folded or unfolded to show a word you read.

• Pat wished she had a big pig. *(wished)*

• Mack rushed with his dog. *(rushed)*

• I like to kick the ball. *(kick)*

• Nell can pack her own lunch. *(pack)*

ⓘ **Intervention** ▶ **Skills**

Intervention Guide, for direct instruction and extra practice of Inflectional Ending *-ed*

Meeting Individual Needs for Vocabulary

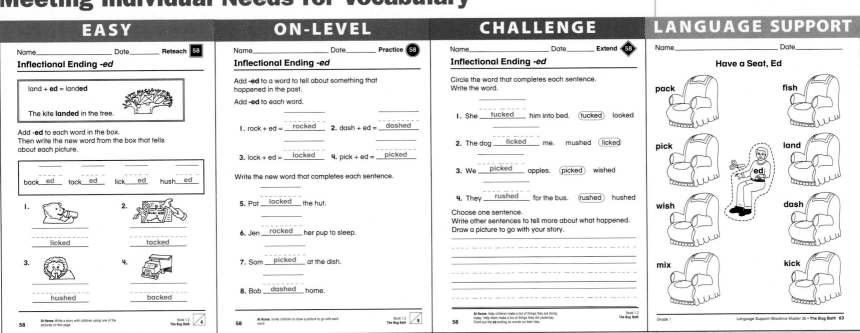

Reteach, 58   Practice, 58   Extend, 58   Language Support, 63

65L

Handwriting CD-ROM

GRAMMAR/SPELLING CONNECTIONS

Plural Nouns: See Grammar and Usage lessons, pages 650–65P.

Words with Short *o*: See Spelling lessons, pages 65Q–65R.

TEACHING TIP

Technology
After each sentence, children should hit the space bar twice to type two spaces. If they hit the space bar too many times, they can delete a space by hitting the backspace key.

Organization
Encourage children to make lists before they begin to write. It will help them remember everything they want to include in their writing.

Interactive Writing
Write a Guide

Prewrite

LOOK AT THE STORY ENDING Have children revisit *The Bug Bath,* paying careful attention to its ending. Then tell them that the class will write a guide to different places where ladybugs can bathe. The guide will have pictures and sentences. Then work with children to make a list of places where ladybugs might like to take a bath (Examples: pond, birdbath, puddle, rain bucket, and so on). Have children explain why each place would be a fun spot for bugs to bathe.

Draft

WRITE ABOUT EACH PLACE Help children write sentences explaining why each place they picked would be a good site for a bug bath. Guide children to use words they already know or can decode.

- Begin by saying: *Why is a pond a good place for bugs to take a bath? A pond is in the sun, right? And a pond is not too hot.* As you say a word with familiar sounds and patterns, challenge children to write the word. Write all unfamiliar words yourself.

- Let children explain why they think each place they suggested is a good place for a bug bath.

Revise

PLURAL NOUNS Invite children to reread their sentences. Have children check to see that any nouns that are plural have the appropriate -*s* or -*es* at the end. Have children point out each noun. If it is a plural noun, ask: *Should this have an -s or an -es at the end?*

Publish

CREATE THE GUIDE Reread the sentences together. Then help children assemble the sentences into a book. Discuss different ways of illustrating it. Should it be from a bug's-eye view or a child's-eye view? Have children create illustrations, then have them copy the appropriate text onto each page.

Presentation Ideas

MAKE A BUG Invite children to draw a bug on construction paper, cardboard, or oaktag, and cut it out. Help children decide what kinds of bugs to make, and what those bugs might look like. Ask: *What kinds of bugs have you seen? Which one do you want to draw? What do you find interesting about the way it looks?* ▶ **Representing/Viewing**

IMPROVISE A BUG STORY Encourage groups of children to tell a story about a bug. Have one child in the group make up one or two things about what the bug does. Then have the next child take up the story where the first child left off. Continue throughout the group. Encourage children to use gestures and movements to help them tell their story. ▶ **Speaking/Listening**

Listening and Viewing

LISTENING STRATEGIES
Encourage members of each group to listen carefully to the child who is speaking. Do they get any good ideas by listening to the speaker?

VIEWING STRATEGIES
Remind children that the bugs are not necessarily realistic. The artist may not have created a bug that looks exactly like a real bug, but the artist should have tried to capture the bug's most important features. Ask children: Do the bugs look real? Why or why not?

LANGUAGE SUPPORT

ESL Children acquiring English can participate in the activities with some support. Draw sketches of the places bugs could bathe. As you probe for why the places are good, use gestures, facial expressions, or sketches to ensure comprehension. Model how to draw an illustration to go with a sentence.

PORTFOLIO Invite children to include their guides or another writing project in their portfolio.

Meeting Individual Needs for Writing

EASY	ON-LEVEL	CHALLENGE
Draw Pictures Children can draw pictures of toys they play with in the bath. Have them label each picture with words that the bugs might say in the story. (Example: Let's take a ride on that boat.)	**New Story Pages** Have children choose one spot in the story where a toy goes into the tub. They can rewrite and illustrate the pages having the toys do the talking. Children should follow the language pattern of *The Bug Bath*.	**Journal Entry** Children can pretend they're one of the bugs from the story, and write a journal entry telling how they feel about their bath. Encourage them to use descriptive words to tell their stories well.

5 Day Grammar and Usage Plan

DAY 1 — Introduce the Concept

Oral Warm-Up Say the following: *A bug sat in the tub.* Ask children which words name things. (*bug, tub*)

Introduce Plural Nouns Review the definition of a noun. Then discuss:

Plural Nouns

- Some nouns name more than one person, place, or thing.
- This kind of noun is called a **plural noun**.
- Add *–s* to make most nouns name more than one.
- Add *–es* to form the plural of nouns that end with *s, sh, ch,* or *x.*

Daily Language Activity Say the following: *See the duck. See the ducks.* Ask which word names one thing and which names more than one. (*duck, ducks*) Ask how *duck* was changed to *ducks.* (add *-s*)

WRITING Assign daily Writing Prompt on page 36E.

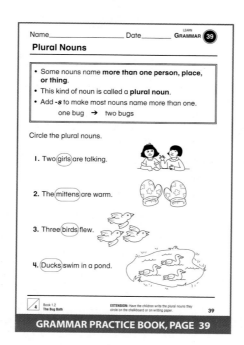

GRAMMAR PRACTICE BOOK, PAGE 39

DAY 2 — Teach the Concept

Review Plural Nouns Remind children that yesterday they learned about adding *-s* to make a noun name more than one person, place, or thing. Write these sentences on the chalkboard: *I see the bus. I see the buses.* Read the sentences aloud with children. Underline the root word *bus* in *buses.* Ask children if *buses* means more than one *bus.* (yes) How can we make the word *bus* tell about more than one bus? (add *-es*) Tell children that we add *-es* to nouns that end with *s, sh, ch,* or *x.*

Daily Language Activity Write the following on the chalkboard: *I can make a wish.* Ask children how they would write *wish* to show that there is more than one in this sentence: *I can make three wish___.* (add *-es*) Why? (*Wish* ends in *sh,* so we add *-es.*)

WRITING Assign the daily Writing Prompt on page 36E.

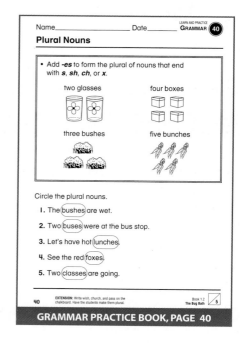

GRAMMAR PRACTICE BOOK, PAGE 40

Plural Nouns

DAY 3 — Review and Practice

Learn from the Literature Review with children what plural nouns are and how they are formed. Read the following sentences from *The Bug Bath*:

> "I see a leg," said Al.
>
> "I see two legs," said Bob.

Write on the chalkboard: *I see a leg. I see two legs.* Ask children which noun names one thing. (*leg*) Which noun names two things? (*legs*)

Daily Language Activity Have children brainstorm nouns from the story. Then help them write a sentence containing a plural noun from *The Bug Bath*.

 Assign the daily Writing Prompt on page 36F.

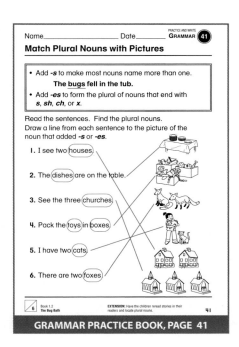

GRAMMAR PRACTICE BOOK, PAGE 41

DAY 4 — Review and Practice

Review Plural Nouns Write the following sentence on the chalkboard: *I see the fox.* Ask children to tell how to write the sentence if you saw more than one fox. (*I see the foxes.*) How did you make *fox* mean more than one? (added *-es*)

Daily Language Activity Ask children to orally form the plural of the following nouns: pup (*pups*), ship (*ships*), box (*boxes*), wish (*wishes*). Then have children use the nouns to form sentences orally.

Mechanics and Usage Before children begin the daily Writing Prompt on page 36F, review capitalization and punctuation of questions. Display and discuss:

> **Sentence Punctuation**
> • Begin every sentence with a capital letter.
> • End a question with a question mark.

 Assign the daily Writing Prompt on page 36F.

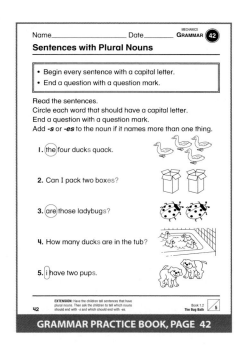

GRAMMAR PRACTICE BOOK, PAGE 42

DAY 5 — Assess and Reteach

Daily Language Activity Write these sentences on the chalkboard. Read them with children. Have children identify the nouns in each sentence, telling how to form more than one.

1. The big duck came back. (*ducks*)

2. The bug sat over there. (*bugs*)

3. I can pick up the dish. (*dishes*)

Assess Use page 43 of the **Grammar Practice Book** for assessment.

Reteach Prepare a word card for each singular noun from the sentences presented on Days 1 through 5. Also prepare several cards with *s* or *es* on them. Give each group one set. Have them pick a noun card and match it with an ending card to form the plurals.

 Assign the daily Writing Prompt on page 36F.

Use page 44 of the **Grammar Practice Book** for additional reteaching.

GRAMMAR PRACTICE BOOK, PAGE 43

GRAMMAR PRACTICE BOOK, PAGE 44

65P

5 Day Spelling Plan

LANGUAGE SUPPORT

ESL Children learning English may have difficulty differentiating between the vowel sounds in *hot, hit,* and *hut.* Write the following words on the board: *sock, sit, sun* and *top, tip, tug.* Say each group of words, stressing each vowel sound and have students repeat. Ask volunteers to underline the letter that spells the vowel sound in each word.

DAY 1 Introduce Spelling Words

Assess Prior Knowledge Write the Spelling Words on the board and read aloud with children. Ask children what vowel sound they hear in each word. (/o/) Ask what letter spells this sound. (o) Have volunteers underline the letter *o* in each word.

Write the Challenge Words on the board and read them aloud. Use the words in context and ask children to clap their hands when they hear a Challenge Word. Example: *Do not sit on a very hot rock.*

Spelling Words		Challenge Words	
1. **hot**	4. lock	7. **saw**	9. **want**
2. **top**	5. hop	8. **very**	10. **two**
3. **not**	6. rock		

*Note: Words in **dark type** are from the story.*

Word Study On page 40 of the **Spelling Practice Book** are word study steps and an at-home activity.

SPELLING PRACTICE BOOK, PAGE 39

WORD STUDY STEPS AND ACTIVITY, PAGE 40

DAY 2 Teach the Pattern

Build a Word Write the Spelling Words on the chalkboard. Ask children to read the words aloud. Write three columns labeled *-ot, -op,* and *-ock* on the chalkboard. Say each phonogram. Then say the word *hot* and ask students which sound it ends with. Write it under the heading *-ot.* Ask children which other Spelling Word ends with the same sound. (*not*) Repeat with pairs of words ending with *-op* and *-ock.*

To extend the activity, ask children what other words they could make by adding the letters *h, m, s, c,* and *r* to the phonograms.

SPELLING PRACTICE BOOK, PAGE 41

Words with Short *o*

DAY 3 — Practice and Extend

Word Meanings: Endings Write the words *lock* and *locked* on the chalkboard. Read the words aloud and ask children to repeat them. Write and say the following sentences: *I lock the door. Yesterday I locked the door.* Ask how the second sentence is different. (tells what happened yesterday) Circle the *-ed* ending and explain that this makes the word *lock* tell about the past. Write and say: *They rock the baby.* Ask children to say the sentence again, beginning with *Yesterday*. Ask how the word *rock* changed. (added *-ed*) Write *rocked* and circle *-ed*.

Identify Spelling Patterns Write the following sentences on the chalkboard and read them aloud as you track print:

> **I saw a top I want very much. It does not cost a lot. My sister got two.**

Ask children to raise their hands when they recognize a word that has the spelling pattern *-ot* or *-op* and to clap when they recognize a Challenge Word.

SPELLING PRACTICE BOOK, PAGE 42

DAY 4 — Practice and Write

Complete the Word Write incomplete spelling words on the chalkboard and ask children to tell what letter to write in the blank space. For example: *l_ck, ro_k, no_, h_p*. Invite children to use each word in a sentence. Some children may wish to make up a story that includes more than one Spelling Word.

 WRITING Have children use as many Spelling Words as possible in the daily Writing Prompt on page 36F. Remind them to check their writing for errors in spelling, grammar, and punctuation.

SPELLING PRACTICE BOOK, PAGE 43

DAY 5 — Assess and Reteach

Optional Spelling Test You may wish to give children a spelling test. You may administer the test in the following manner: (1) Read the word. (2) Give a simple sentence containing the word. (3) Say the word again. Or you may use page 44 of the **Spelling Practice Book** for the posttest. If you wish, you may create additional sentences for the Challenge Words.

JOURNAL **Personal Word List** Have children include any words they still find difficult in their personal "troublesome words" lists in their journals. Then ask them to draw pictures that tell about the words. They can write a label for each picture. Children should refer to the list during later writing activities.

SPELLING PRACTICE BOOK, PAGE 44

65R

Reaching All Learners

Concept
• Helping Out
Comprehension
• Story Elements
Phonics
• Short *e*
Vocabulary
• away
• good
• into
• put

Anthology

Splash!

Selection Summary A girl gets some much needed help from her pets on a very rainy day. But once she is warm and dry, the girl realizes that her animal friends need her help, too.

by Jessica Clerk
illustrated by Ken Spengler

Listening Library

Rhyme applies to Phonics

> **Pets**
> Jack has a duck and Meg
> has a cat.
> Jim has a pup that he calls Pat.
> Ken has a fish that swims
> in the tub.
> And there is one small pig
> in this club.
> Big and small, pets are fun.
> Pets, pets, pets for everyone.

INSTRUCTIONAL pages 68-95

About the Author Jessica Clerk wanted to be a pirate when she grew up. She had learned about pirates in one of her favorite places—the library. Today, Ms. Clerk is a children's book author and illustrator. She lives with a cat who does not like fish and a dog who does.

About the Illustrator Ken Spengler has illustrated everything from children's books to advertisements. "I always liked art, and I studied it a lot in school," he says. He likes to make people see simple things in new and different ways.

Same Concept, Skills and Vocabulary!

Leveled Books

EASY
Lesson on pages 95A and 95D
DECODABLE

INDEPENDENT
Lesson on pages 95B and 95D

🏠 *Take-Home version available*

DECODABLE

CHALLENGE
Lesson on pages 95C and 95D

Leveled Practice

EASY
Reteach, 59-66 Blackline masters with reteaching opportunities for each assessed skill

INDEPENDENT/ON-LEVEL
Practice, 59-66 Workbook with Take-Home Stories and practice opportunities for each assessed skill and story comprehension

CHALLENGE
Extend, 59–66 Blackline masters that offer challenge activities for each assessed skill

Quizzes Prepared by 📘 **Accelerated Reader**

Center Activities

Social Studies ... Work Boots, *78*

Science .... Rain, *74*

Math .... Word Problems, *82*

Music .... Let it Rain, *80*

Language Arts .. Read Aloud, *66G, 76*

Cultural Perspectives ..... Parts of the Body, *72*

Research and Inquiry ...... Find Out More, *93*

 Internet Activities .... www.mhschool.com/reading

CENTER Activities

Each of these activities takes 15-20 minutes.

Phonics

Short *e* Flashcards

PARTNERS **Objective:** Identify and write short *e* picture names

◆ Have partners place the Picture Cards in a pile.

◆ Partner 1 shows a card to Partner 2.

◆ Partner 2 says the picture name and writes it on an index card. Partners switch roles.

MATERIALS
- Phonics Picture Cards
- Large index cards
- Markers

n e t

Writing

Rain Words

ONE **Objective:** Write words about rain.

◆ Demonstrate how to trace and cut out a large raindrop from light blue construction paper.

◆ Have children write words related to rain on their raindrops and decorate them with glitter.

◆ Hang the raindrops from the ceiling.

MATERIALS
- Large outline of a raindrop
- Construction paper
- Scissors
- Silver glitter
- Glue

Reading and Listening

Independent/Self-Selected Reading

ONE **Objective:** Listen and use illustrations to understand a story.

Fill the Center with books and corresponding audiocassettes or CD-ROMs children have read or listened to this week. You can also include books from the Theme Bibliography on pages T98 or T99.

Leveled Readers

◆ *The Box* by Constance Andrea Keremes
◆ *A Big, Big Pig* by Andrea Katz
◆ *Picnic Farm* by Christine Morton and Sarah Barringer

◆ Theme Big Book *My River* by Shari Halpern

◆ *Splash* by Jessica Clerk

◆ "Cat Kisses" by Bobbi Katz

◆ Phonics Practice Reader, Vol. 1

Working with Words

Word Puzzles

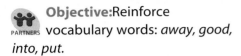**Objective:** Reinforce vocabulary words: *away, good, into, put.*

MATERIALS
- Large index cards
- Crayons or markers
- Scissors
- Envelopes

◆ Have children write a word on each card.

◆ Children cut each card into three pieces, place them in an envelope, and label the envelope "[name]'s Word Puzzle."

◆ Partners exchange and solve puzzles.

Art

Torn Paper Mural

Objective: Create a mural about rain.

MATERIALS
- Mural paper
- Construction paper
- Glue

◆ Have children brainstorm things that are helped by rain (plants, animals, people).

◆ Suggest that children draw one thing and cut it out.

◆ Children create a mural by gluing the cutouts on a large sheet of mural paper.

Science

Water, Water!

Objective: Conduct an experiment.

MATERIALS
- Two-column chart with heads *Object* and *What I Saw*
- Bowl of water
- Eye dropper or spoon
- Paper towel
- Sponge
- Coin
- Cloth towel

◆ Children place a drop of water on each of the following objects: paper towel, sponge, coin, cloth towel.

◆ Children observe what happens and write or draw it on their chart.

◆ Have children share their observations.

Object	What I saw
paper towel	
sponge	
coin	
towel	

Suggested
Lesson Planner

READING AND LANGUAGE ARTS	DAY 1 — Focus on Reading and Skills	DAY 2 — Read the Literature
Phonics Daily Routines	Daily **Phonics** Routine: Segmenting, 66J **Phonics** CD-ROM	Daily **Phonics** Routine: Blending, 68A **Phonics** CD-ROM
Phonological Awareness **Phonics** *Short e* **Comprehension** **Vocabulary** **Study Skills** **Listening, Speaking, Viewing, Representing**	**Read** **Read Aloud,** 66G "The Mitten" ☑ **Develop Phonological Awareness,** 66H ☑ **Introduce Short e,** 66I–66J Reteach, Practice, Extend, 59 Phonics/Phonemic Awareness Practice Book, **103–106** **Read** **Apply Short e,** 66/67 "Pets" ⓘ Intervention Program	**Build Background,** 68A Develop Oral Language **Vocabulary,** 68B–68C *away* *good* *into* *put* **Word Building Manipulative Cards Teaching Chart 44** Reteach, Practice, Extend, 60 **Read** **Read the Selection,** 68–91 **Guided Instruction** ☑ Short e ☑ Story Elements **Genre: Story,** 69 **Cultural Perspectives,** 72 ⓘ Intervention Program
Curriculum Connections	**Link** Language Arts, 66G	**Link** Social Studies, 68A
Writing	✏ **Writing Prompt:** Have you ever gotten caught in the rain? How did it happen? What did you do?	✏ **Writing Prompt:** Write about two hens that get caught in the rain. Would they be mad? What do they do? 📓 **Journal Writing** Quick-Write, 91
Grammar	**Introduce the Concept: Irregular Plural Nouns,** 95O Daily Language Activity: Identify irregular plural nouns. **Grammar Practice Book,** 45	**Teach the Concept: Irregular Plural Nouns,** 95O Daily Language Activity: Identify irregular plural nouns. **Grammar Practice Book,** 46
Spelling *Short e*	**Introduce: Words with Short e,** 95Q **Spelling Practice Book,** 45–46	**Teach the Patterns: Words with Short e,** 95Q **Spelling Practice Book,** 47

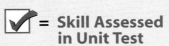

 = **Skill Assessed in Unit Test**

 Intervention Program Available

 **Read EVERY DAY**

DAY 3 — Read the Literature

Daily  Routine:
Fluency, 93

 CD-ROM

Rereading for Fluency, 90

Story Questions, 92
Reteach, Practice, Extend, 61

Story Activities, 93

Study Skill, 94
☑ Maps
Teaching Chart 45
Reteach, Practice, Extend, 62

Test Power, 95

 Read the Leveled Books, 95A–95D
Guided Reading
☑ Short e
☑ Story Elements
☑ High-Frequency Words

 Intervention Program

 Science, 66D, 74;
Language Arts, 76

✏ **Writing Prompt:** What do you wear on a rainy day? Write about getting ready for the rain.

Practice and Write: Irregular Plural Nouns, 95P
Daily Language Activity: Use irregular plural nouns

Grammar Practice Book, 47

Practice and Extend: Words with Short e, 95R

Spelling Practice Book, 48

DAY 4 — Build Skills

Daily Routine:
Writing, 95F

 CD-ROM

 Read the Leveled Books and Self-Selected Books

☑ Review Short e, 95E–95F
Teaching Chart 46
Reteach, Practice, Extend, 63
Language Support, 69
Phonics/Phonemic Awareness
Practice Book, 103–106

☑ Review Short e, o, u, i, a; th, 95G–95H
Teaching Chart 47
Reteach, Practice, Extend, 64
Language Support, 70
Phonics/Phonemic Awareness
Practice Book, 103–106

Minilessons, 71, 75, 83, 87, 89

Intervention Program

Social Studies, 78

✏ **Writing Prompt:** Write about finding two wet birds in your house. What do you do?

Interactive Writing: Make a Weather Chart, 95M
Prewrite, Draft

Meeting Individual Needs for Writing, 95N

Practice and Write: Irregular Plural Nouns, 95P
Daily Language Activity: Use irregular plural nouns.

Grammar Practice Book, 48

Practice and Write: Words with Short e, 95R

Spelling Practice Book, 49

DAY 5 — Build Skills

Daily Routine:
Letter Substitution, 95H

 CD-ROM

 Read Self-Selected Books

☑ Introduce Main Idea, 95I–95J
Teaching Chart 48
Reteach, Practice, Extend, 65
Language Support, 71

☑ Review Context Clues, 95K–95L
Teaching Chart 49
Reteach, Practice, Extend, 66
Language Support, 72

Listening, Speaking, Viewing, Representing, 95N
Draw an Outfit
Put on Imaginary Clothing

Minilessons, 71, 75, 83, 87, 89

 Intervention Program

Music, 80; **Art,** 66D

✏ **Writing Prompt:** Does it ever rain when you want to play outside? Write about what you do when you can't go out.

Interactive Writing: Make a Weather Chart, 95M
Revise, Publish

Assess and Reteach: Irregular Plural Nouns, 95P
Daily Language Activity: Identify irregular plural nouns.

Grammar Practice Book, 49–50

Assess and Reteach: Words with Short e, 95R

Spelling Practice Book, 50

Read Aloud

The Mitten
a story by Alvin Tresselt

It was the coldest day of the winter, and a little boy was trudging through the forest gathering firewood for his grandmother.

"Bring back all you can find," the old woman had said as she sat knitting a pair of mittens. "The north wind blows cold, and we must have a good fire to keep us warm."

All morning the boy worked, picking up sticks, until his sled was well loaded. Then a very strange thing happened. Just as he picked up the last stick, he dropped one of his mittens in the snow.

Now, how a boy could do this on the coldest day of winter I'll never know, but that's the way my grandfather tells the story.

Off he went with his load of wood, and the mitten was left lying on a snowdrift.

As soon as he was out of sight a little mouse came scurrying through the woods. She was very cold, and when she spied the little boy's mitten with its feathery fur cuff, she popped right in to get warm. It was just the right size for a tiny mouse.

Continued on page T3

Oral Comprehension

LISTENING AND SPEAKING Motivate children to think about character and plot by reading them this story about what happens when a generous mouse shares her home with other animals. Have children think about what the mouse is like, and what happens during the story. When you are done reading, ask, "What happens each time an animal comes by the mitten?" Then ask, "What words would you use to describe the mouse? Why?"

Activity Have children act out the story of "The Mitten." Get children started by helping them identify the different parts to be played. You may wish to have each child draw an animal mask that corresponds to the role that he or she plays.

▶ **Kinesthetic/Auditory/Linguistic**

GENRE: STORY Tell children that a story focuses on characters that have a problem to solve. A story ends when a solution to the problem is found. A story can be real or make-believe. After you read *The Mitten*, ask children the following questions: *What parts of this story could be real? What parts are make-believe? What problem does the boy face? How is it solved? What problems do the animals face?*

Develop Phonological Awareness

Blend Sounds
Phonemic Awareness

MATERIALS
- Phonics Picture Cards from Word Building Cards

Teach   Hold up the *bed* picture card. Say: /b/-/e/-/d/. Have children blend the sounds with you and identify the middle sound. (/e/) Then hold up the *sled* picture card. Have children repeat blending the sounds and identify the middle sound.

Practice   Tell children to blend the sounds you say together to say the word. Use the following words: *beg, deck, get, dock, hen, jet, tug, men, neck, pit, peg, then, shed, them, thin, vet, wet.*

Segment Sounds
Phonemic Awareness

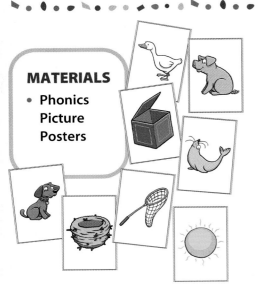

MATERIALS
- Phonics Picture Posters

Teach   Display the Phonics Picture Poster (picture side only) for *net.* Tell children to listen as you count the number of sounds you hear in the picture name. Say each sound and hold up a finger for each sound. Say: /n/-/e/-/t/; *net. I hear three sounds in the word* net. Ask children to slowly repeat the word, sound by sound, and explain that slowing down can help them hear each sound.

Practice   Display the following Phonics Picture Posters and have children count the sounds in each picture name. Use these posters: *egg* (2 sounds); *seal* (3); *dog* (3); *duck* (3), *nest* (4); *box* (3), *pig* (3) and *sun* (3).

Delete Sounds
Phonemic Awareness

MATERIALS
- puppet

Teach   Tell children that the puppet will say a word. They will repeat the word without the beginning sound. Have the puppet say: *What does the word* pet *sound like without the beginning sound? Listen as I say the word:* pet. (/et/)

Practice   Say the following words and have children repeat them without the beginning sound(s): *bet, fed, hem, leg, neck, pets, shed, yet.*

Informal ASSESSMENT   Observe children as they blend sounds, segment sounds, and delete initial sounds. If children have difficulty, see Alternate Teaching Strategies on page T71.

OBJECTIVES

Children will:

- identify /e/e.
- blend and read short e words.
- review: initial and final consonants; digraph *sh*

MATERIALS

- letter cards from the **Word Building Manipulative Cards**

Skills Finder

Short *e*	
Introduce	B2: 66I-J
Review	B2: 95E-F, 95G-H, 124I-J
Test	Book 2
Maintain	B4: 105

SPELLING/PHONICS CONNECTIONS

Words with short *e*: See the 5-day Spelling Plan, pages 95Q–95R

TEACHING TIP

SHORT *e* WORDS The following short e words from the story are decodable: *hen, legs, Meg, red, shed, wet*. Have children make up several sentences using these decodable words. This will help children remember the words by reinforcing their meanings.

Introduce Short *e*

> **TEACH**

Identify the Letter *e* as the Symbol for the Sound /e/

Let children know they will learn to read words with the letter *e,* which stands for the /e/ sound. Introduce the *e* letter card and the sound /e/.

- Display the *e* letter card and say /e/.

BLENDING Model and Guide Practice with Short *e* Words

- Have children repeat the sound /e/ after you as you point to the *e* letter card.
- Point to the *e* letter card and say /e/. Have children repeat after you.
- Place the *t* letter card after the *e* letter card.
- Blend the sounds together and have children repeat after you.

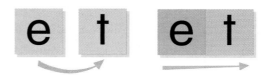

- Place the *p* letter card before the *e* letter card.
- Blend the sounds together and say *pet*. Have children repeat after you.

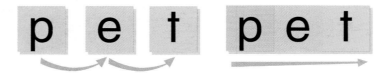

Use the Word in Context

- Use the word in context to reinforce its meaning. Example: *I have a pet cat.*

Repeat the Procedure

- Use the following words to continue modeling and guided practice with short *e*.

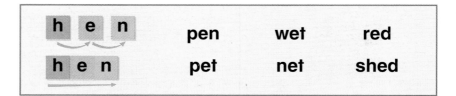

PRACTICE

LETTER SUBSTITUTION Build Short *e* Words with Letter Cards

Build the word *wet*, asking children to repeat each sound after you. Change the word to *set* by replacing the *w* with *s*. Next, ask children to work in small groups to build and write the following words, substituting the appropriate letter: met⟶men⟶pen⟶pet⟶bet⟶ bed⟶shed. ▶ **Kinesthetic/Linguistic/Spatial**

ASSESS/CLOSE

Build, Read, and Write Short *e* words

To assess children's ability to blend and read short *e* words, observe children as they build words in the Practice activity. Have them make a list of the short *e* words they formed. Tell them to read their list.

ADDITIONAL PHONICS RESOURCES

Phonics/Phonemic Awareness Practice Book, pages 103–106

PHONICS KIT
Hands-on Activities and Practice

McGraw-Hill School
TECHNOLOGY

Phonics **CD-ROM**

activities for practice with **Blending and Segmenting**

Meeting Individual Needs for Phonics

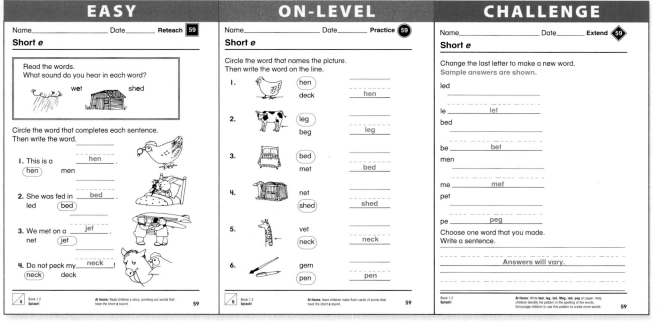

Reteach, 59   Practice, 59   Extend, 59

 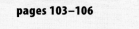 

Daily Routines

DAY 1 **Segmenting** Distribute letter boxes. Say a short *e* word aloud. Have children write the spelling of each sound in the appropriate box. Use *get, bed, hen, shed.*

DAY 2 **Blending** Write the spelling of each sound in *pet* as you say it. Then ask children to blend the sounds to read the word. Repeat with *leg* and *wet.*

DAY 3 **Fluency** Write a list of short *e* words. Point to each word, asking children to blend the sounds silently. Ask a volunteer to read each word.

DAY 4 **Writing** Have children choose two short *e* words and create a rhyming couplet with the words. Children can illustrate their rhymes.

DAY 5 **Letter Substitution** Using the CVC flip chart, have pairs of children build *hen*. Taking turns, one child is to change a letter to build a new word, asking the partner to read it.

66J

OBJECTIVES

Children will read a poem with words containing short *e*.

Apply Short e

Pets

Jack has a duck and Meg
    has a cat.
Jim has a pup that he calls Pat.
Ken has a fish that swims
    in the tub.
And there is one small pig
    in this club.
Big and small, pets are fun.
Pets, pets, pets for everyone.

66   67

Anthology pages 66–67

Read and Build Fluency

READ THE POEM Tell children they will read a poem called "Pets." Have children listen for words with short *e* as you read the poem aloud. Use your finger to model tracking print. Have children read along with you.

REREAD FOR FLUENCY Have children work in pairs and take turns rereading the poem. One child **PARTNERS** reads the poem, while the other tracks the print with his or her finger.

READ A DECODABLE STORY For additional practice reading and to develop fluency, ask children to read *Wet Pets!* from **Phonics Practice Reader, Vol. 1.**

Dictate and Spell

DICTATE WORDS Segment the word *Meg* into its three individual sounds. Repeat the word aloud **JOURNAL** and use it in a sentence: *Meg has a very soft cat.* Then have children say the word and write the letter that represents each sound until they make the entire word. Repeat with *pets* and *Ken* from the poem. Then repeat with other short *e* words such as *beg, deck, hem, peck, red, shed, them,* and *ten.*

i Intervention ➤ **Skills Intervention Guide,** for direct instruction and extra practice in Short *e*

Build Background

ial Studies

Concept: Helping Out

Evaluate Prior Knowledge

CONCEPT: HELPING OUT Ask children to share what they think about helping others. Use the following questions to encourage the discussion:

• Do you like it if someone helps you out when you need help?

• How does helping others make things better?

MAKE A HELPING-OUT LIST Work with children to create a list of things they might do to help other people. Have volunteers suggest ideas to add to the list. ▶ **Linguistic**

I HELP OUT WITH ...

• doing dishes

• baking a cake

• taking care of my baby sister

• putting toys away

DRAW A SCENE WITH YOU AND A FAMILY MEMBER Encourage children to draw a scene in which they help another family member. Suggest that children refer to the list they helped create. Have children write a sentence about the scene. (Example: *Dad and I wash the car.*)

Develop Oral Language

CONNECT WORDS AND ACTIONS Have   partners mimic helping each other out with a simple task, such as:

• *Setting a table.*

• *Carrying something heavy.*

• *Looking for lost keys.*

Prompt children to say how they feel about helping each other out by asking:

• *Why did you decide to work together?*

• *Is this easier to do because you're working together?*

• *How do you divide up the work to get the job done together?* ▶**Kinesthetic/Linguistic**

DAILY  **ROUTINES**

DAY 2 **Blending** Write the spelling of each sound in *pet* as you say it. Have children repeat after you. Ask children to blend the sounds to read the word. Repeat with *leg* and *wet*.

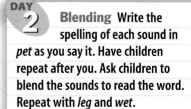 **CD-ROM**

OBJECTIVES

Children will:

- identify high-frequency words *away, put, into,* and *good.*

MATERIALS

- Teaching Chart 44
- Word Building Manipulative Cards *away, put, into, good*

TEACHING TIP

The following chart indicates words from the upcoming story that children have learned to decode and high-frequency words taught in this lesson. Observe any difficulties children may have in reading the words.

Decodable		High-Frequency
hen	shed	away
legs	wet	good
Meg	red	into
them	then	put
	pets	

SPELLING/VOCABULARY CONNECTIONS

These words are Challenge Words. See page 95Q for Day 1 of the 5-Day Spelling Plan.

---

away

into

put

good

Vocabulary

High-Frequency Words

Wet

It can be (good) to (put) your leg (into) the wet, wet pool.
It is good to wet your back and be very cool.
But, if the rain could go (away)
And I could see the sun,
Then ten of my pals and I
Could have lots of fun, fun, fun!

Teaching Chart 44

Auditory

LISTEN TO WORDS Without displaying it, read aloud "Wet" on **Teaching Chart 44**. After you've read the poem, have children pantomime how they think the child in the poem felt.

IDENTIFY HIGH-FREQUENCY WORDS Have children aurally identify each high-frequency word using the following activity:

- Divide the class into groups. Say one of the high-frequency words.
- Ask groups to make up a sentence using that word. The sentence should be about things to do on a rainy day. (Example: *I read a good book.*)
- Repeat this activity with each of the high-frequency words.

Visual

TEACH WORDS Display "Wet" on **Teaching Chart 44**. Read the poem, tracking the print with your finger. Next, point to the word *away*. Tell children that this is the word *away*. Have them say the word with you. Ask them to hold up the vocabulary card for *away* and say the word. Repeat this procedure for *put, into,* and *good*.

Hold up vocabulary cards for *away, put, into,* and *good* one at a time. Have volunteers read the words and then circle them on the chart.

away into
good put

Word Building Manipulative Cards

WRITE SENTENCES Hold up one of the vocabulary cards, and say the word with children. Then have groups race to write a sentence using that word. Have children read their sentences aloud.

Word Wall

Order Up! Ask children to sing the alphabet song. Then ask them to look at this week's word wall words. Have them write the word that starts with a letter that comes first in the alphabet. Continue with this week's other words until they are in ABC order.

Word Wall Chant Give a child a pointer and tell them to point to the word wall word of their choice. Lead them in this chant:

Where's the word? You can find it!
There it is! Now let's spell it!
(The class spells the word the child points to.)

Assess

Silent Spelling Encourage children to silently "mouth" the spelling of each of the words in order to practice. When you have the opportunity and the children are ready, have them individually spell the words for you in a quiet voice.

TEACHING TIP

PHONICS TEACHING TIP Point to the word *good*, emphasizing the sound /ù/. Explain that sometimes *oo* stands for the sound /ù/. Write the words *good, look,* and *took* on the chalkboard. Read each word as you point to it emphasizing the sound /ù/. Then read the words with children. Ask them to say the sound that is in each word. (/ù/) Then have them name the letters that make the sound /ù/. *(oo)*

Meeting Individual Needs for Vocabulary

EASY	ON-LEVEL	ON-LEVEL	CHALLENGE

EASY

Name_____ Date_____ Reteach **60**

High-Frequency Words

Fill in the word that completes the sentence.

into	good	away	put

1. Bob did a ___good___ job.

2. The duck swam ___away___ .

3. I ___put___ the doll in my bag.

4. Pat went ___into___ the house.

At Home: Have children write a sentence using one of the words above.

60   Book 1.2 Splash! 4

ON-LEVEL

Name_____ Date_____ Practice **60**

High-Frequency Words

good	into	put	away

Write the word from the box that completes each sentence.

1. That dish was ___good___ !

2. Sam went far ___away___ .

3. The dog ran ___into___ the shed.

4. She ___put___ the hat in a box.

At Home: Ask children to make up sentences using each of these four words.

60   Book 1.2 Splash! 4

ON-LEVEL

Ben the Gem

Ben's red rag is wet. What is this? There is a gem in the hem. It is good the man did not get the gem. It is good I have my pet. Ben is my gem.

At Home: Invite children to talk about what they would do if they lost a pet or something else of value to them.

60a

CHALLENGE

Name_____ Date_____ Extend **60**

High-Frequency Words

away	good	into	put

Write a word from the box to complete each sentence.
Draw a line to the picture that goes with the sentence.

1. The bear got ___into___ Bed.

2. She ___put___ the hen in a pen.

3. The dog ran ___away___ .

4. Sam was a ___good___ pup.

Choose a picture and write another sentence about it.

_____

At Home: Ask children to discuss something that they are good at.

60   Book 1.2 Splash!

Comprehension

Prereading Strategies

PREVIEW AND PREDICT Read aloud the names of the author and the illustrator. Then take a **picture walk** through the illustrations, stopping at page 86. Using words from the story, talk about the details of each illustration.

- What characters do you see?
- Where does this story take place?
- What do you think this story is about?
- Why do you think this story is called *Splash!*?

Have children predict what they think will happen in this story. Write all children's predictions on a chart and read them aloud.

PREDICTIONS	WHAT HAPPENED
The girl gets wet in the rain.	
A cat and dog help the girl stay dry.	

SET PURPOSES What do children want to find out by reading this book? For example:

- How will the animals get dry?
- Will the bus come?

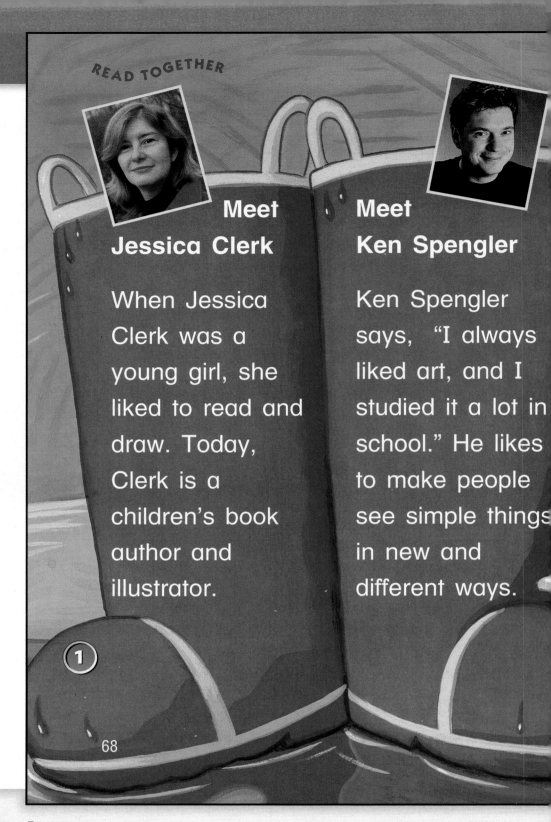

READ TOGETHER

Meet Jessica Clerk

When Jessica Clerk was a young girl, she liked to read and draw. Today, Clerk is a children's book author and illustrator.

Meet Ken Spengler

Ken Spengler says, "I always liked art, and I studied it a lot in school." He likes to make people see simple things in new and different ways.

①

68

Meeting Individual Needs • Grouping Suggestions for Strategic Reading

EASY

Shared Reading Read the story aloud as you track print and model directionality. Invite children to chime in with repetitive words and phrases as you read the story aloud. As you read, model the strategy of paying attention to the characters and the plot to help children understand what is happening.

ON-LEVEL

Guided Instruction Ask children to read the story with you. Monitor any difficulties that children may have in order to determine which numbered prompts from the Comprehension section to use. After reading the story with children, have children reread it, using the rereading suggestions on page 90.

CHALLENGE

Independent Reading Have children set purposes before they read. Remind them that as they read, visualizing the sequence of events can help them link the story ideas together. After reading, have children retell what they learned. Children can also use the questions on page 92 for a group discussion.

Splash!

by Jessica Clerk

illustrated by Ken Spengler

69

②

Comprehension

☑ **Phonics** Short *e*

☑ **Apply Analyze Character and Plot**

STRATEGIC READING Explain to children that paying attention to the characters and plot in *Splash!* is a strategy that will help them understand the story.

① We are going to read *Splash!* Let's make sure we have our story cutouts ready to help us as we read. *Story Props*

Point to the left-hand picture on page 68. This is Jessica Clerk. Let's read about her. When did she start writing? Now point to the picture on the right. This is Ken Spengler. When did he learn about art? *Concept of a Book: Author/Illustrator*

② I see a frog, an umbrella, and a puddle in this picture. What do you think the story will be about? (Answers will vary.) What clues from the picture make you think that? *Make Predictions/Use Illustrations*

Genre

Story

Remind students that a story:

• focuses on made-up characters facing a problem.

• shows what happens as the characters try to solve the problem.

In this story, Meg and her pets are trying to solve the problem of keeping dry on a very rainy day.

Activity Meg, the character in the story, has to go to school on a wet rainy day. Discuss with children what a very rainy day is like. Ask children to share how they prepare for stormy weather when they get ready for school. After reading the story, ask children to compare their preparations to Meg's preparations.

LANGUAGE SUPPORT

A blackline master of the patterns for making story cutouts can be found in the **Language Support Book.** Before reading, have children cut out a happy Meg and a sad Meg and paste them both on either side of a piece of construction paper. Then paste on each article of clothing as it is brought by her pets. Direct children to hold up the side that shows how Meg is feeling.

LANGUAGE SUPPORT, 68

Comprehension

③ Let's take a look at the picture on these pages. Who do you think this story will be about? (a little girl) What is the girl doing? (waiting for the school bus) What does the picture tell us about the weather? (It's raining.) *Make Predictions*

TRACKING PRINT Point to the word in the sentence where we will start reading. Now point to the punctuation mark that shows where the sentence ends. How many sentences are on this page? (one) Now let's read the sentence together. *Syntactic Cues*

④ **Phonics** SHORT *e* "*It rained on the . . .*" hmmm, I'm not sure what this word is. Let's blend the sounds of the letters together to read it. sh e d, shed

Let's finish reading the sentence, ". . .*and the big. . .*" Maybe I could sound this word out like the last one. Let's try it. r e d, red
Graphophonic Cues

Fluency

GROUP READING

 Model tracking print and rereading to achieve fluency.

- Point to and read aloud each word in the sentence.
- Have children repeat this process, pointing to each word as they read, until they can do this easily.
- Run your finger under each word as you read aloud the complete sentence without pausing.
- Have children read the complete sentence without pausing, running their fingers under each word. Repeat this process until fluency is achieved.

③
④ It rained on the shed and the big red barn.

70

P/i PREVENTION/INTERVENTION

TRACKING PRINT Children may think there are two sentences on this page because there are two lines of text. Encourage children to look for the capital letter to begin this sentence and a period to end this sentence. Have children use self-stick notes or self-adhesive dots to mark the first word in each sentence in their books. Tell them to look for capital letters to find the starting place for each sentence. Invite children to run their fingers under each word as you read it aloud. Demonstrate return sweep when you come to the end of the first line. Read without pausing until you come to the period. *Syntactic Cues*

Meg was wet, wet, wet. **5**

6

71

ESL Children may not know that when a word in a story is written more than once in a row, the author is making that word special, and wants the reader to take notice. Invite volunteers to demonstrate the use of the word *wet* three times in the sentence in humorous ways, first making their voices become louder with each successive *wet*, then making their voices go down in pitch with each successive *wet*. *Fluency*

Comprehension

5 **Phonics** SHORT *e* Hmmm . . . I don't think I know the first word in this sentence. Let's blend the sounds of letters together to figure it out. M e g, Meg Oh, it's *Meg*. That must be the little girl's name. *Graphophonic Cues*

6 **ANALYZE CHARACTER AND PLOT** Look at the expression on Meg's face in the picture on this page. How do you think she feels? (sad, upset, annoyed) How do you think she feels about getting wet? Show me with the story cutout. (She's not happy.) *Story Props*

Minilesson

REVIEW/MAINTAIN

Make Inferences

Remind children that they can often tell how a story character feels about something by looking at the pictures and imagining how they might feel in the same situation.

- Have children look at page 71.
- Invite them to explain why Meg looks unhappy. (She doesn't like being wet.)
- Ask what might make Meg happy. (a raincoat and umbrella)

Activity Invite children to make a drawing of the time they were surprised by a sudden change in the weather. Have them show their drawings to the class and share how they felt when the weather changed.

Comprehension

7 **Phonics** **SHORT** *e* This sentence has some short *e* words. Let's blend the ones we already know before we read the entire sentence. l e g s, legs. w e t, wet. *Graphophonic Cues*

8 Now let's look at the picture on this page and read the whole sentence aloud, pointing to each part of Meg's body that we can see. What part can't we see? (her back) **Why not?** (The picture shows the front of Meg.) *Use Illustrations/Draw Conclusions*

7

8

Her head, back, and legs were wet.

72

CULTURAL PERSPECTIVES

PARTS OF THE BODY Ask bilingual children to share the word for head in their first language. Include *cabeza* (Spanish), *tête* (French), *testa* (Italian), and *kopf* (German). Write their responses on the chalkboard and have them repeat the words after you.

Activity Have children make a giant construction-paper cutout of Meg. Ask pairs to label Meg's head, back, legs, hands, feet, and torso using another language.
▶ **Kinesthetic/Visual**

"It is not fun to be wet," said Meg. **9**
"Not fun at all." **10**

73

Comprehension

9 Look at the marks at the beginning and end of what Meg says on this page. These marks are called *quotation marks*. Quotation marks tell you that the words are spoken by one of the characters in the story. Let's read the sentences.

Who is saying the sentences we have read? (Meg) Now underline the words *said Meg* with your finger. Yes, Meg is the person who is saying the words in quotation marks. *Concepts of Print*

10 **ANALYZE CHARACTER AND PLOT** What do Meg's words tell us about her? (She is upset about getting wet.) Did we already think that she did not like being wet? (yes) Why? (Meg looks unhappy in the pictures.)

P/i **PRINT AWARENESS** Point to the words you see more than once on this page. *(not, fun)* Use your fingers to count the number of times you see each word. (2)

P/i **PREVENTION/INTERVENTION**

PRINT AWARENESS Have children turn back to page 71. Ask them how many times the word *wet* is used in that sentence. (3) Then have children go back to the beginning of the story on page 69 and count how many times the word *wet* has appeared so far up to this page in the story. (5) Repeat with the words *and* (2) and *fun* (2).

Comprehension

11 Then her cat ran up the path with her hat.

12

11 **ANALYZE CHARACTER AND PLOT**
Who is the new character who just entered the story? (a cat) What does the cat have in its mouth? (Meg's yellow hat) Where does the cat go? (up the path) Hold up the story cutout that shows how Meg will feel when she sees her cat. *Story Props*

12 What do you think will happen next? (Meg will wear the hat on her head.) How do you think Meg will feel about the cat running up the path with her hat? (happy) *Make Predictions*

TEACHING TIP

ACTION WORDS Remind children that the cat ran up the path. Ask what other ways the cat might move up the path. (walk, hop, crawl) Have children repeat each word. Invite volunteers to come to the front of the room and mimic ways the cat might have moved. Let other children guess what movement it is. To avoid accidents, clear the space of desks and children.

Cross Curricular: Science

RAIN Tell children that rain can sometimes be annoying, but it's necessary for Earth and every living thing on it.

- Rain gives us drinking water.
- Plants we eat need rain to grow.
- Birds and animals need rain as well.

RESEARCH AND INQUIRY Invite children to share what they know about rain.

interNET CONNECTION Have children log on to **www.mhschool.com/reading**, where they can access links to various weather sites.

"Good cat!" said Meg,
as she put on her hat.

75

Comprehension

13 The cat brought Meg her hat. Which part of Meg's body is not going to be wet any more? (her head) *Make Inferences*

14 **ANALYZE CHARACTER AND PLOT** Let's move the hat cutout. Where should it go now? (The hat is on Meg's head.) *Story Props*

15 Look closely at Meg's face. How does Meg feel about getting her hat? (happy) **How do you know?** (She is smiling. She says, "Good cat!") *Use Picture Clues/Make Inferences*

Minilesson

REVIEW/MAINTAIN

Short *a*

Remind children that they have already learned many short *a* words. Ask:

This page has a few short *a* words. What are they? *(cat, as, hat)*

Ask children to write a sentence using two short *a* words. Have them select from the short *a* words on this page or from memory.

Phonics CD-ROM Have children use the interactive phonics activities for more reinforcement with short *a* .

Comprehension

(16) **ANALYZE CHARACTER AND PLOT**
Some characters, like Meg, have a very big part in a story, and other characters do not. There is a very small character on this page who doesn't have a very big part. Who is it? (cat)

(17) Which parts of Meg's body are still wet? (her back and legs) Can you guess what might happen next? (Another character might bring her something to cover her back or her legs.) *Make Predictions*

(16) "But my back and legs are wet," said Meg.

(17)

76

Activity

Cross Curricular: Language Arts

Have children read the first sentence on page 77. On the chalkboard write, "*It is not fun to be* ____," said ____. Ask children to volunteer words for things that are not fun (*cold, sick, sad*) to complete the first sentence. Then have the class recite the sentence again, using a volunteer's word in the first blank and his or her name in the second blank. Example: "*It is not fun to be cold,*" *said Sue.*
▶ **Linguistic/Visual**

"It is not fun to be wet," said Meg. (18)
"Not fun at all."

77

Comprehension

(18) **ANALYZE CHARACTER AND PLOT**
Let's look at the picture on this page.
Is Meg happy now that she has her hat? (no)
Why not? (She looks sad because she is still wet.) *Use Illustrations*

SELF-MONITORING STRATEGY

ASK QUESTIONS Ask yourself questions to help you remember what has happened so far.

- What kind of day is it?
- When Meg first went to the bus stop, what parts of her body were wet?
- What did the cat do?
- Why isn't Meg happy yet?

Comprehension

(19) Phonics SHORT *e* There are three short *e* words on this page (*then, hen, red*). Let's blend the sound of the letters together to read them. th e n, then. Now let's do the same with the next word. h e n, hen. Now sound out the last word. r e d, red. *Graphophonic Cues*

(20) ANALYZE CHARACTER AND PLOT A new character appears on this page. Who is it? (the hen) What did it do? (It ran up the path with Meg's red boots.)

TEACHING TIP

PHONEMIC AWARENESS Distinguishing the correct sound of *e* in words can be a challenge for many children. Some children might think that *her* is a short *e* word, but it doesn't sound the same. Have them say the words *hen, then, red,* and *her*. Ask children if the *e* sound is the same.

---

(19) Then her hen ran up the path with her red boots.

(20)

78

---

78 *Splash!*

Activity

Cross Curricular: Social Studies

WORK BOOTS Boots keep our legs and feet dry when it rains. Some boots work harder and they are called *work boots*.

- Boots protect firemen from heat and fire.
- Boots offer mountain climbers and forest rangers secure footing.

- *Waders,* or long boots, keep fisherman dry.

Activity Have children draw themselves wearing boots. ▶ **Visual**

"Good hen!" said Meg,
as she put them on.

79

Comprehension

21 **ANALYZE CHARACTER AND PLOT**
Where are the hen and the boots now?
(The hen is on the fence; the boots are on
Meg's feet.) Let's use our story cutouts and
put the boots on Meg. *Story Props*

22 Is Meg happy again in this picture?
(yes) Why? (The hen brought her
boots.) Turn back to page 75 to see that Meg
was happy there, too. Now turn forward to
pages 76 and 77. Did Meg stay happy? (no)
Why? (Her back and legs were still wet.) Now
return to page 79. Do you think she will stay
happy now? (no) Why? (Her back is wet; a hat
and boots won't cover her back.) *Identify
Sequence of Events/Make Predictions*

23 **ANALYZE CHARACTER AND PLOT**
Look at the picture on this page. How
many characters can we see? (4) Who are
they? (Meg, her cat, her hen, and the frog) *Use
Illustrations*

Comprehension

24 How many times has Meg been helped out so far? (twice) Did anybody on this page help Meg? (yes) Who are they? (the hen and the cat) How did they help Meg? (The cat brought Meg a hat; the hen brought Meg her boots.) *Summarize*

25 Looking for clues can help you understand what will happen in the story. Let's remember what always happens right after Meg says, *"It is not fun to be wet. Not fun at all."* (An animal brings Meg something to keep her dry.) *Make Predictions*

TEACHING **TIP**

MANAGEMENT Before you ask children to mimic crawling like a spider or dancing in a puddle, have them move away from their chairs and space themselves an arm's length away from each other to avoid collision.

24
25 "But my back is wet, wet, wet," said Meg.

80

Cross Curricular: Music

LET IT RAIN Rain has inspired many song writers. Children can mimic a spider crawling or dancing in a puddle as they listen to a recording of:

- "Raindrops Keep Fallin' on My Head"
- "Walkin' in the Rain"

- "The Itsy Bitsy Spider"
- "Singin' in the Rain"
- "Rain, Rain, Go Away"

▶ **Auditory/Kinesthetic**

"It is not fun to be wet," said Meg. (26)
"Not fun at all."

81

Comprehension

(26) Let's look at the picture on this page. Who is Meg talking to? (the frog) Can you think of someone who listens to you when you need to talk? *Make Connections*

BLENDING WITH SHORT *u* Find the word *fun* and point to it with your finger. Now read the word with me, using your finger to help you remember to blend the sounds of the letters together. f u n, fun *Graphophonic Cues*

PREVENTION/INTERVENTION

BLENDING WITH SHORT *u* Write the following words on chart paper: *fun, pup, duck*, and *tub*. Ask volunteers to blend the sounds of the letters of each word together to read the word. Have children tell you what sound the letter *u* makes. (/u/) *Graphophonic Cues*

Comprehension

(27) **ANALYZE CHARACTER AND PLOT**
Let's look at this page. Here's a new character. Who is it? (a dog) What's he doing? (running with Meg's coat) What cutout should we prepare? *Story Props*

(28) It looks like our prediction was right. Let's see if the dog brings the coat to Meg. Peek ahead to the picture on the next page. Were we correct? *Confirming Predictions*

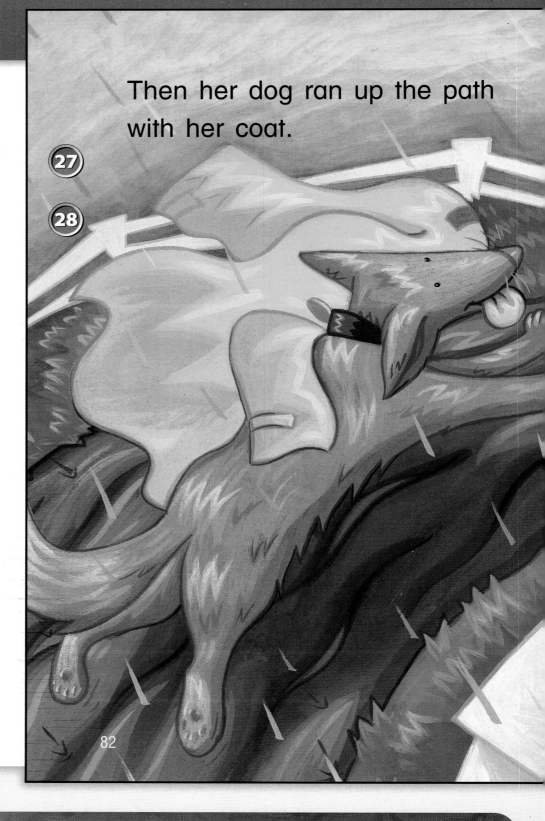

Then her dog ran up the path with her coat.

(27)

(28)

82

Cross Curricular: Math

WORD PROBLEMS Tell children that they can get good ideas for math word problems by reading a story. Here is one from this story:

• The cat brought Meg one hat. The hen brought Meg two boots. The dog brought Meg one coat. 1 + 2 + 1 = 4

Altogether Meg received four pieces of clothing.
▶ Logistical/Linguistic

RESEARCH AND INQUIRY Have pairs of children count things in other books.

"Good dog!" said Meg,
as she put it on.

29

30

83

Comprehension

29 **ANALYZE CHARACTER AND PLOT**
What did the dog do in this story? (It brought Meg her coat.) **Put the coat cutout on Meg.** *Story Props*

30 **ANALYZE CHARACTER AND PLOT**
In this story the characters help Meg. Who are they and what do they do to help her? (The cat brings her hat, the hen brings her boots, the dog brings her coat, and the frog is a good listener.) *Summarize*

Minilesson
REVIEW/MAINTAIN

Sequence of Events

Remind children that at the beginning of the story Meg's head, back, and legs were wet. Then have them look at the illustration on page 83.

• Is her head wet now? Why not?

• Are her legs wet now? Why not?

• Is her back wet now? Why not?

Activity Invite children to think of how else they can get wet, aside from the rain. (swimming pool, bath tub, ocean) Have them illustrate one of these scenes.

Comprehension

ANALYZE CHARACTER AND PLOT
(31) Let's look at the picture of Meg on this page. What is she doing? (smiling, dancing in a puddle) Why do you think she's happy? (She's not wet anymore.)
Use Illustrations/Draw Conclusions

Visual Literacy

VIEWING AND REPRESENTING

The author doesn't tell us how Meg feels now that she's not wet. But the illustrator lets us know in the picture. How? (She's smiling and dancing.) Let's compare this picture to the one on page 73. How does Meg look in this picture? (She's sad; she's frowning.)

(31) "I am not wet," said Meg. "Not wet at all!"

84

LANGUAGE SUPPORT

ESL Conduct an oral Cloze activity. As you read, pause instead of reading the word *wet*. Encourage children acquiring English to say the word. Use this technique for other familiar words from the story.

Focus on making sure children acquiring English understand the words that describe how Meg is feeling and what she is doing throughout the story. If needed, act out the story using gestures and vocal intonations to ensure comprehension. *Semantic Cues*

It rained on Meg and on her pets.

(32)

85

Comprehension

MAKE PREDICTIONS We can see that Meg is dry now. Do you think she will go to school now? (Accept appropriate responses.) Will she leave her pets behind in the rain? (Accept appropriate responses.)

(32) **ANALYZE CHARACTER AND PLOT** Let's look at the picture on this page. Is it still raining? (yes) Do you think Meg's pets are getting wet? (yes) *Use Illustrations*

PREVENTION/INTERVENTION

MAKE PREDICTIONS It might be difficult for some children to imagine the ending of a story. To help them predict what might happen next, go back through the story to talk about what has happened so far. Make a story line on the chalkboard to help children remember the sequence of events:

Meg was wet.

She did not like to be wet.

The cat brought Meg her hat.

The hen brought her boots.

The dog brought her coat.

Meg was not wet anymore.

It rained on Meg's pets.

Comprehension

33 **Phonics** **SHORT** *e* This page has three different short *e* words. What are they? (Meg, pets, wet) Let's read the words out loud. One of the short *e* words is repeated three times. What is it? (wet) Let's say this word together three times. *Graphophonic Cues*

34 Now let's try to remember back in the story. What does Meg always say after a page that has *wet, wet, wet*? ("It is not fun to be wet. Not fun at all.") So what do you think she will say on the next page? *Make Predictions*

TEACHING TIP

PHONEMIC AWARENESS Some children might think that *were* is a short *e* word. Just as you did with *her* on page 78, have children say the sounds of *Meg, pets,* and *wet* aloud. Then ask them if the *e* in *were* sounds the same.

33 Meg looked at her pets. They were wet, wet, wet.

86

ESL For children who are still having difficulty distinguishing between short *e* words and short *a* words, have them repeat after you slowly: *I pat the pet*. Then have them repeat: *The cat is wet*. Then, have them repeat: *Meg has a red hat*.

Provide more practice by using poems from the Teaching Charts and have children listen for and mark words with short *e* and short *a* sounds.

"It is not fun to be wet," said Meg. **34**
"Not fun at all."

35

87

Comprehension

35 Look at Meg's pets in the picture on this page. Raise your hand if you think they look happy. Raise your hand if you think they look sad. *Nonverbal Response*

Minilesson

REVIEW/MAINTAIN

Use Context Clues

Explain that children can remind themselves of the meanings of some words by looking at the pictures. Have children look at the rain on the animals and on Meg and then repeat the story pattern after you: "*It is not fun to be wet. Not fun at all.*"

- Ask children what the opposite of *wet* is. *(dry)* Write both words on the board.

- Make sure children have a clear understanding of the word *wet*. Ask them to give you examples of other things that are wet, besides rain. (a bathing suit after you've gone swimming, a towel after you've taken a bath, and so on)

Activity Ask children to use the words *wet* and *dry* in sentences. Have them write their sentences in their journals.

Comprehension

36 Let's look at the picture on this page. Can anybody guess where Meg is going? (home) Why do you think she's going there? (Accept appropriate responses.) *Make Predictions*

37 Let's remember that Meg's pets helped her stay dry in the rain. Has anyone ever helped them when they were in the cold or the rain? Did someone button up their coat? Give them an umbrella? *Make Connections*

 MULTIPLE-MEANING WORDS
Sometimes a word has two different meanings. Notice that the word *back* is used on this page. Look at page 80. Do you see the word *back* also? Does *back* on this page mean the same thing that it means on page 80? On this page, it means returning to the same place. When Meg says, "*I will be back*," she means that she is going to return to the same place. On page 80, what does *back* mean? (part of Meg's body) *Semantic Cues*

"I will be back," said Meg, as she ran away down the path.

36

37

88

 PREVENTION/INTERVENTION

MULTIPLE-MEANING WORDS
Explain to children that some words have more than one meaning. Remind children to use context clues to figure out which meaning the word that they are reading has. Write the following sentences on the chalkboard:

• *I feel the sun on my back.*
• *I will come back to see you.*
Ask children to explain the meaning of the word *back* in each sentence. Then ask volunteers to make up their own sentence pairs that use the two meanings of *back*. *Semantic Cues*

Meg went into the shed.
Then she went back to her pets.

89

Comprehension

38 **ANALYZE CHARACTER AND PLOT** Where has Meg gone now? (to the shed) What did she do next? (She went back to her pets.)

39 We know that Meg got something in the shed. The author tells us that, and the picture shows Meg going into the shed. What do you think Meg got in the shed? (Accept appropriate responses.) *Make Predictions*

p/i **BLENDING WITH *sh*** Find the last word in the first sentence and point to it. Now read the word with me, using your finger to help you remember to blend the sounds of the letters together. sh e d,   shed *Graphophonic Cues*

Minilesson

REVIEW/MAINTAIN

Main Ideas

Remind children that the main idea

- tells what the story is about, and
- can be told in one or two sentences.

Work with children to write a sentence that tells the main idea of this story. Have them

- reread the title of the story.
- look through the story, and notice how often they see the word *wet*.
- think about what else they see Meg doing in the pictures.

Activity Write the main idea of the story within an outline of a rain cloud on poster board. Have children suggest supporting details and copy them down inside giant rain drops.

p/i **PREVENTION/INTERVENTION**

BLENDING WITH *sh* For some children, the /sh/ sound may be difficult to pronounce or to distinguish from /s/. If you notice children having problems pronouncing this sound, hold your finger to your lips and say "Shhhh." Have the children repeat the action and the sound. Then have children model saying the following sentence after you: *She went into the shed.* *Graphophonic Cues*

Comprehension

40 **ANALYZE CHARACTER AND PLOT**
Let's look at the picture on this page.
What did Meg get in the shed? (an umbrella)
Use Illustrations

41 Who's dry now? (Meg, the cat, the hen, the dog) Where's our friend the frog? (on top of the umbrella) Why doesn't the frog need to be under the umbrella? (Frogs live near water; they like to get wet.) *Make Inferences*

RETELL THE STORY Divide the class into groups of three to retell the story. After children decide on what they will say on their retelling, have them choose roles. One child should retell the story as the other two use the story cutouts of Meg to act out the story. *Summarize/ Story Props*

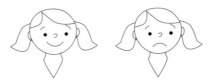

 STUDENT SELF-ASSESSMENT

Have children ask themselves the following questions to assess how they are reading:

• How did I use what I know about helping out to help me read the story?

• How did I use what I knew about the characters and plot to help me read and understand what was going to happen?

• How did I use the pictures to help me enjoy the story even more?

TRANSFERRING THE STRATEGIES

• How can I use these strategies to help me learn from other books?

40
41 When the bus came, there were Meg and her pets.

90

REREADING FOR *Fluency*

 GROUP Children who need fluency practice can read along silently or aloud as they listen to the story on the recording.

READING RATE When you evaluate reading rate, have children read aloud from the story for one minute. Place a stick-on note after the last word read. Count words read. To evaluate children's performance, see the Running Record in the **Fluency Assessment** book.

i Intervention For leveled fluency lessons, passages, and norm charts, see **Skills Intervention Guide**, Part 5, Fluency.

And they were not wet at all!

91

Comprehension

Return to Predictions and Purposes

Reread children's predictions about the book. Discuss their original predictions and the predictions they made along the way, noting which needed to be revised. Then ask children if the book answered the questions they had before they began reading.

PREDICTIONS	WHAT HAPPENED
The girl gets wet in the rain.	Meg forgot her rain clothes at home, so she got wet.
A cat and dog help the girl stay dry.	Meg's pets brought her a hat, a coat, and boots so she could stay dry.

INFORMAL ASSESSMENT

HOW TO ASSESS

Phonics SHORT *e* Have children read to page 78 and point to the short *e* words.

ANALYZE CHARACTER AND PLOT Ask children if they know what each character did to move the story along. Have volunteers name each character.

FOLLOW UP

Phonics SHORT *e* Continue to model the blending of sounds in short *e* words for children who are having difficulty.

ANALYZE CHARACTER AND PLOT Children who are having difficulty should reread the book, stopping to explain what the characters do on each page.

LITERARY RESPONSE

QUICK–WRITE Have children draw pictures of Meg and her pets in their journals, and write what they liked or didn't like about the story.

ORAL RESPONSE Have children use their journal entries to discuss these questions:

• What do you think the frog would have said if he could talk?

• Were you surprised when the animals in the story brought Meg clothing?

SENTENCE STRIPS Children can use strips 1–32 to retell *Splash!*

> 1
> It rained on the shed and the big red barn.

> 2
> Meg was wet, wet, wet.

Story Questions

Tell children that now they will read some questions about the story. Help children read the questions. Discuss possible answers.

Answers:

1. because she is wet *Literal/Details*

2. Answers will vary. (one possible answer: to school) *Inferential/Make Inferences*

3. Accept appropriate answers that show affection, loyalty, and so on. (One answer might be: They like her.) *Inferential/Make Inferences*

4. Accept appropriate summaries. *Critical/Summarize*

5. Answers will vary. (One possible answer: It is raining in both stories.) *Critical/Reading Across Texts*

Draw a Picture Help children read the directions in their anthologies. Discuss what it feels like to walk in the rain. What might you wear?

Story Questions & Activities

READ TOGETHER

1. Why do Meg's pets help her?

2. Where is Meg going?

3. How do Meg's pets feel about her?

4. What is this story about?

5. How is "Splash!" like "One Good Pup"?

Draw a Picture

Draw a picture.
Show yourself walking in the rain.
What will you wear?

Meeting Individual Needs

EASY	ON-LEVEL	CHALLENGE
Name_____ Date_____ Reteach **61**	Name_____ Date_____ Practice **61**	Name_____ Date_____ Extend **61**
Story Comprehension	**Story Comprehension**	**Story Comprehension**
Circle the pictures that tell about "Splash!"	Read these sentences. Circle the sentences that describe what happened in "Splash!"	
1. [girl with dog] 2. [person with duck]	1. (Meg puts on her hat.)	[umbrella drawing with figure]
3. [girl with dog] 4. [girl in rain]	2. (The hen gets the boots.)	
5. [person with dog] 6. [person with umbrella and pets]	3. The cat gets a box.	Draw the animals from "Splash!" Children will draw a cat, hen, dog, and possibly a frog. Write what Meg may say to the animals.
	4. The pets sit in the shed.	
	5. (Meg puts on her coat.)	_____ Thank you. _____
	6. (Meg sees her wet pets.)	
	7. Meg runs away.	_____ Now we will all stay dry! _____
	8. (The bus comes.)	
6 Book 1.2 Splash! At Home: Have children tell the story, "Splash!" by using the pictures. 61	8 Book 1.2 Splash! At Home: Have children draw a picture that illustrates one of the sentences they circled. 61	Book 1.2 Splash! At Home: Have children draw a picture of themselves dressed for rain and write a sentence about it. 61

Reteach, 61   Practice, 61   Extend, 61

Make a Weather Calendar

Make a picture for the rain.

Make a picture for the sun.

Make a picture for the clouds.

Draw the pictures on a calendar.

Sunday	Monday	Tuesday	Wednesday	Thursday	Friday	Saturday

Find Out More

Find out how birds keep dry in the rain.

93

Story Activities

Make a Weather Calendar

Materials: paper, crayons or markers, one large sheet of paper for class calendar

GROUP Read the directions aloud. Help children who have questions. Have the class discuss what symbols they could use for rain, sun, snow, clouds, wind.

Find Out More

RESEARCH AND INQUIRY Tell children that all birds try to keep dry in a rainstorm. Ask pairs to look at photos of birds in books or magazines. Ask them to find out how birds stay dry in the rain. (Possible responses: They find shelter, their feathers protect them.) Ask pairs to choose a bird to research. Have them write two or three sentences about their birds and present them to class.

 Have children log on to **www.mhschool.com/reading**, where they can access sites about birds.

FORMAL ASSESSMENT

See the Progress Assessment Test for Book 1.2.

DAILY Phonics ROUTINES

DAY 3 **Fluency** Write a list of short *e* words. Point to each word, asking children to blend the sounds silently. Ask a volunteer to read each word.

Phonics CD-ROM

Study Skills

MAPS

OBJECTIVES

Children will learn to read a map to gather information.

Remind children that Meg followed a path back into the shed to get something for her pets. Tell them that sometimes people use a map to help them follow paths. Now they will look at a map to learn more about getting to and from places.

Display **Teaching Chart 45**. Have children look at the map and read the title with you. Then invite children to describe what they notice on the map. Ask children what they think Meg is trying to find. Have children trace their fingers over the path that Meg takes in the house. Ask children to name each place Meg enters and leaves. Then help children read the questions below the map, encouraging them to identify the places on the map that answer each question.

STUDY SKILLS

READ TOGETHER

Meg's Footprint Map

Look at the Map

It shows the path Meg used to get her bag.

❶ Did Meg go in and out the same door?

❷ Where was her bag?

Meeting Individual Needs

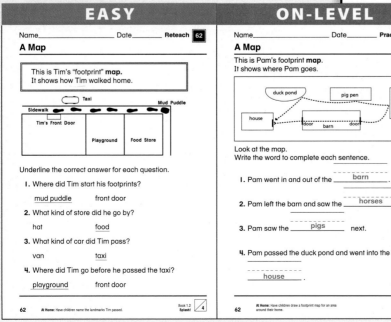

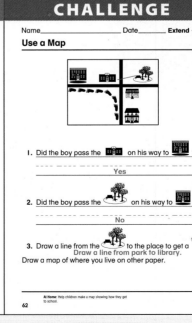

EASY	ON-LEVEL	CHALLENGE
Reteach, 62	Practice, 62	Extend, 62

This Rain Hat

This is a rain hat.

This rain hat is a black hat.

It is on a rack.

Oh, no! It fell off the rack.

Now it is a flat hat.

It is a flat, black, rain hat.

What is this story about?

⬤ A hat that falls off the rack

◯ A hat that a boy wears

Tell yourself the story in your own words.

95

Test Power

THE PRINCETON REVIEW

Read the Page

Explain to children that you will be reading this story as a group. You will read the story, and they will follow in their books.

Request that children put pens, pencils, and markers away, since they will not be writing in their books.

Discuss the Question

Have children read the answer choices, and then carefully reread the story, looking for clues as to which one is better. Is the story about a hat that falls off a rack or a hat that a boy wears? Since there is no mention of a boy, it must be the former.

Test-Tip

Try to put the main idea in your own words to help you answer the question.

Leveled Books

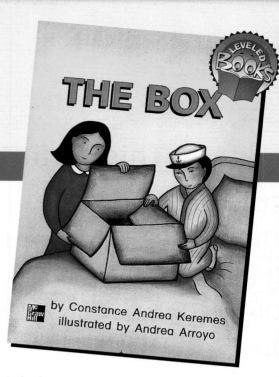

THE BOX

by Constance Andrea Keremes
illustrated by Andrea Arroyo

EASY

The Box

☑  Short *e*

☑ **Analyze Character and Plot**

High-Frequency Words:
away, good, into, put

Answers to Story Questions

1. They pretend the box is a ship.
2. Ken is sad because he is sick and has to get in bed.
3. The big box could be used as a pen for a hen and as a jet.
4. Ken is sick. He has to get in bed. Meg tries to cheer up Ken with a box. They pretend the box is a ship, a pen for a pet hen, and a jet.
5. Answers will vary.

The Story Questions and Activity below appear in the Easy Book.

Story Questions and Activity

1. What is the first thing that Ken and Meg pretend the box is?
2. Why is Ken sad?
3. What are other ways to use the big box?
4. Tell the story in your own words.
5. Name another story where someone helps out.

Your Box

Pretend you have a big box. How would you have fun with it? Draw a picture. Write a sentence about your picture.

from The Box

Guided Reading

PREVIEW AND PREDICT Take a **picture walk** to page 4, using the high-frequency words to discuss illustrations. Have children chart their predictions about the story.

SET PURPOSES Have children write or draw why they want to read *The Box*. For example: *I want to find out what else Meg and Ken do with that box.*

READ THE BOOK The following questions can be used to guide children's reading.

Page 2: What does Ken have to do? (get into bed) Which word did we just learn that helps you understand this? *(into) High-Frequency Words*

Pages 4–5: What can you tell about Meg? Is she helpful and friendly, or is she unhelpful and unfriendly? (helpful and friendly) How do you know? (She helps Ken not to feel sad.) *Analyze Character and Plot*

Page 6: Model: Let's blend the letters together to sound out the word after *good*. The first letter is *p*, which stands for /p/. The second letter is *e*, which makes the /e/ sound. The last letter is *n*, which is the /n/

sound. Let's blend the sounds together. The word is *pen. Phonics and Decoding*

Page 8: Can you act out what Ken is doing that shows he is learning to use his imagination the way Meg has been using hers? *Analyze Character and Plot/Role-Play*

RETURN TO PREDICTIONS AND PURPOSES Ask children which of their predictions were close to the story. Have them review their purposes for reading.

LITERARY RESPONSE The following questions will help focus children's responses:

- Have you ever been kind to someone who was sick? Tell about it.

- Has someone ever been kind to you when you were sick? Tell about it.

- What else can you use to play pretend? Tell about it.

Also see the story questions and activity in *The Box*.

See the **Phonics CD-ROM** for practice with short *e*.

Leveled Books

by Andrea Katz
illustrated by John Wallner

INDEPENDENT

A Big, Big Pig

☑  Short *e*

☑ **Analyze Character and Plot**
High-Frequency Words:
away, good, into, put

Guided Reading

PREVIEW AND PREDICT Conduct a **picture walk** to page 5, discussing illustrations using the high-frequency words. Have children chart predictions about the story.

SET PURPOSES Have children write about why they want to read *A Big, Big Pig*. For example, they may want to know how else Ned helps his father.

READ THE BOOK Use the following prompts while children are reading or to discuss after they have read independently.

Page 3: What does Ned have to do with his cup? (put it away) Which of the words we just learned helps you to understand this? (*put* and *away*) *High-Frequency Words*

Pages 4–5: Do you think Ned likes to help out? (yes) How do you know? (He says it is fun to mop, and he is very cheerful while he feeds the hens.) *Analyze Character and Plot*

Page 7: Model: The sounds /sh/ /e/ /d/ blend together as shed. The word is *shed*. *Phonics and Decoding*

Page 8: Can you show me how Ned feels when his Dad praises him? *Analyze Character and Plot/Pantomime*

RETURN TO PREDICTIONS AND PURPOSES Discuss children's predictions. Ask which were close to the story and why. Have children review their purposes for reading. Did they learn how Ned helps out?

LITERARY RESPONSE Have children discuss questions like the following:

• Have you ever helped with a grown-up job? What was that like?

• How does it feel when someone is proud of you?

Also see the story questions and activity in *A Big, Big Pig*.

See the  **CD-ROM** for practice with short *e*.

Answers to Story Questions

1. Ned pets the pup.
2. Yes, the hens are hungry because they peck.
3. A birthday is a special day because you become one year older.
4. On his birthday, Ned gets to help his dad by doing many new things like mop, feed the hens and the duck, and put the pup in the shed.
5. Answers will vary. *What Does Pig Do?* is also about a pig.

The Story Questions and Activity below appear in the Independent Book.

Story Questions and Activity
1. Who does Ned pet?
2. Are the hens hungry? How can you tell?
3. Why is a birthday a special day?
4. Tell the story in your own words.
5. What other story is about a pig?

Draw a Barn
On a piece of paper, draw a barn.
Put farm animals in it.
Draw yourself helping in the barn.
Color your picture.
Write a sentence about your picture.

from A Big, Big Pig

Leveled Books

CHALLENGE

Picnic Farm

☑  Short *e*

☑ **Analyze Character and Plot**

Guided Reading

PREVIEW AND PREDICT Discuss the title and each illustration up to page 13. As you take the **picture walk**, have children chart their predictions about the story.

SET PURPOSES Have children write down their purpose for reading *Picnic Farm*. For example, they may want to find out how the farm helps make the picnic.

READ THE BOOK Use the following prompts to guide children's reading or to discuss after they have read the story independently.

Pages 4–5: Which word has the short *e* sound, *sheep* or *hen*? Model: I will say each of these words very slowly so I can hear the *e* sounds: /sh/ /ē/ /p/. That *e* does not sound like short *e*: /h/ /e/ /n/. *Hen* has the short *e* sound. *Phonics and Decoding/Discriminating*

Pages 12–13: What are some of the characters doing that tells you something about them? What does it tell you? (They are all bringing food to share for the picnic. They are all glad to help out.) *Analyze Character and Plot/Use Illustrations*

Pages 14–21: Do you think that helping out on a farm makes a better picnic? (yes) How do you know? (All the things brought to the picnic come from the farm.) *Analyze Character and Plot/Draw Conclusions*

Pages 24–25: Why do you think everybody is so tired? (They worked hard to make their picnic, and then they ate a lot of food.) *Analyze Character and Plot*

RETURN TO PREDICTIONS AND PURPOSES Have children talk about their predictions and purposes for reading.

LITERARY RESPONSE Have children discuss questions like the following:

* Would you like to help out on a farm? Why?

* What would you bring to a picnic?

Also see the story questions and activity in *Picnic Farm*.

See the 💿 **Phonics CD-ROM** for practice with short *e*.

Answers to Story Questions

1. a sheep, a hen, grass
2. They have seen many things! They have had a lot to eat!
3. Answers will vary.
4. Children who visit a farm.
5. Goat

The Story Questions and Activity below appear in the Challenge Book.

Story Questions and Activity

1. Name three things the children see.
2. Why do the children fall asleep?
3. What foods come from farm animals?
4. What is this story about?
5. What animal from *Whose Footprints?* might be in *Picnic Farm*?

Plan a Picnic!

List things to bring.
Where will the picnic be?
Draw a picture of the picnic.
Write about it.

from *Picnic Farm*

Bringing Groups Together

Anthology and Leveled Books

Connecting Texts

HELPING OUT
Write the concept of Helping Out in the center circle of a Frayer Model chart. Then write the story titles in the surrounding boxes, leaving room for more writing. Discuss with children how the concept of Helping Out was used in each story. Call on volunteers from each reading level and write their suggestions on the chart.

Use the chart to talk about Helping Out.

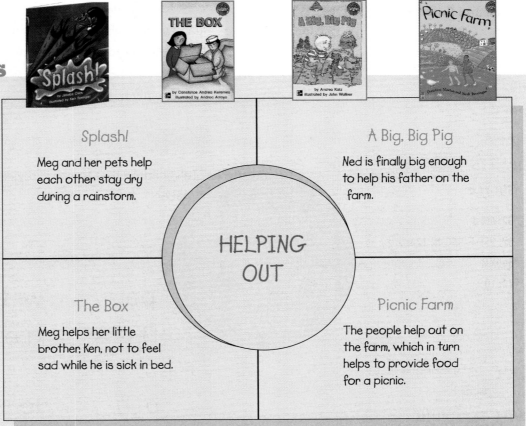

Splash!
Meg and her pets help each other stay dry during a rainstorm.

A Big, Big Pig
Ned is finally big enough to help his father on the farm.

HELPING OUT

The Box
Meg helps her little brother, Ken, not to feel sad while he is sick in bed.

Picnic Farm
The people help out on the farm, which in turn helps to provide food for a picnic.

Viewing/Representing

GROUP PRESENTATIONS Have groups draw and present a poster of the way the characters in each story would help out in the following scenarios:

- *Splash!* It is a very, very hot day.

- *The Box* Meg is sick in bed.

- *A Big, Big Pig* Dad is cooking dinner.

- *Picnic Farm* It hasn't rained in a long time.

AUDIENCE RESPONSE
Encourage children to ask questions after each group presents its poster.

Research and Inquiry

MORE ABOUT HELPING OUT Have children ask themselves: What else would I like to know about how to help on a farm? Then invite them to do the following:

- bring in pictures of different food items that come from a farm.

- ask an adult who works on a farm or a person who works in a food-related industry to speak with the class.

inter NET CONNECTION Have children visit **www.mhschool.com/reading** for links to Web pages about farm products.

Review Short e

OBJECTIVES

Children will:

- identify /e/e.
- blend and read short *e* words.
- review initial and final consonants.

....

MATERIALS
- **Teaching Chart 46**

Skills Finder

	Short e
Introduce	B2: 66I-J
Review	B2: 95E-F, 95G-H, 124I-J
Test	Book 2
Maintain	B4: 105

ALTERNATE TEACHING STRATEGY

REVIEW SHORT *e*

For a different approach to teaching this skill, see pages T71 and T72.

PREPARE

Listen for Short *e* Read the following sentences aloud and have children clap whenever they hear a word with the short *e* sound:

- We have a <u>hen</u> for a <u>pet</u>. She runs to the <u>shed</u> <u>when</u> it rains. She really hates to <u>get</u> <u>wet</u>.

TEACH

Review the Letter *e* as the Symbol for /e/

- Tell children that they will review the letter *e* and the /e/ sound it makes.

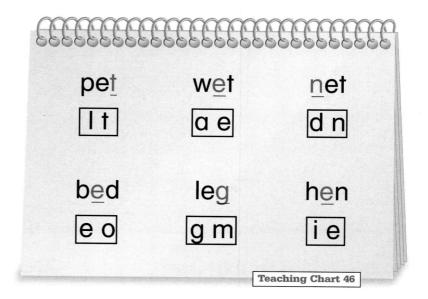

Teaching Chart 46

BLENDING Model and Guide Practice with Short *e* Words

- Display **Teaching Chart 46**. Explain to children that they can make words by writing one of the two letters in the blank space. Tell children that the other letter will not make a real word.

- Run your hand under the letters *p* and *e* and blend the first example on the chart with children. p e l pel p e t pet

- Ask children which word is the real word. *(pet)*

- Have a volunteer write the letter *t* in the blank and read the word.

Use the Word in Context

- Have volunteers use the word in a sentence to reinforce its meaning. Example: *My dog is a good pet.*

Repeat the Procedure

- Continue the activity until the chart is complete. Ask volunteers to choose letters and blend the sounds together to form real words.

PRACTICE

LETTER SUBSTITUTION
Build New Short e Words with a Letter List

GROUP

Have children use the following letters to form other words with the word family *et* as in *pet*.

pet   b   n   m   s   g   j   w

Have children work in small groups. Ask a volunteer from each group to write *pet* on a sheet of paper. The next group member crosses out the p and replaces it with another letter to form a new word; for example, *bet*. Ask children to write the new word below the word *pet*. Continue until children have used all of the letters.

ASSESS/CLOSE

Build and Read Short e Words

To assess children's mastery of blending and reading short *e* words, observe them as they form and read words in the Practice activity.

ADDITIONAL PHONICS RESOURCES

Phonics/Phonemic Awareness Practice Book, pages 103–106

PHONICS KIT
Hands-on Activities and Practice

McGraw-Hill School
TECHNOLOGY
 CD-ROM
activities for practice with **Blending and Segmenting**

DAILY Phonics ROUTINES

DAY 4
Writing Have children choose two short *e* words and create a rhyming couplet with the words. Children can illustrate their rhymes.

Phonics CD-ROM

SPELLING/PHONICS CONNECTIONS

Words with Short e: See the 5-Day Spelling Plan, pages 95Q–95R.

i Intervention Skills Intervention Guide, for direct instruction and extra practice in Short *e*

Meeting Individual Needs for Phonics

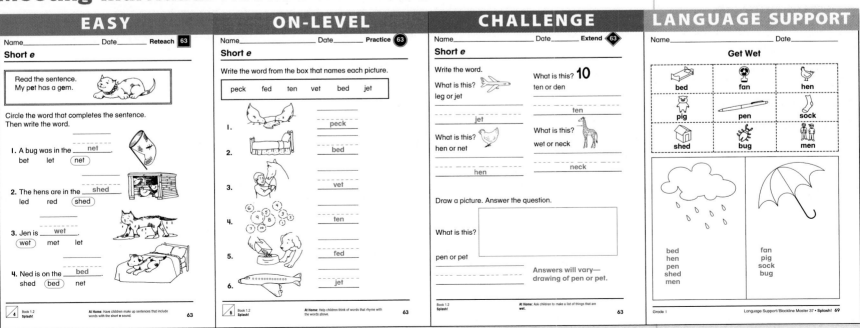

Reteach, 63   **Practice, 63**   **Extend, 63**   Language Support, 69

OBJECTIVES

Children will:

- review /e/e, /o/o, /u/u, /a/a, /i/i; th.
- blend and read short e, o, u, a, i words.
- cumulative review: initial and final consonants.

MATERIALS

- **Teaching Chart 47**
- **Phonics Practice Reader, Volume 1**

Skills Finder

Short e	
Introduce	B2: 66I-J
Review	B2: 95E-F, 95G-H, 124I-J
Test	Book 2
Maintain	B4: 105

ALTERNATE TEACHING STRATEGY

SHORT VOWELS, DIGRAPH *th*

For a different approach to teaching these skills, see pages T64, T65, T69, T70, T71, and T72.

Review Short e, o, u, i, a; th

PREPARE

Identify the Letters for Short Vowel Sounds and *th* for /th/

Review the letters that stand for /e/, /o/, /u/, /i/, /a/, and /th/. Write the short vowel letters and the digraph *th* on the chalkboard and have children repeat each sound after you.

TEACH

BLENDING Model and Guide Practice with Short-Vowel Words and *th* Words

- Display **Teaching Chart 47**. Tell children that each set of letters can be filled in with one letter or digraph that makes a word.

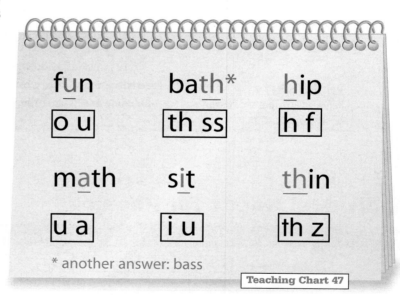

- Blend the first example on the chart with children.
- Ask children which group of letters is a word. *(fun)*
- Have a volunteer write the letter *u* in the blank and read the word.

Use the Word in Context

Ask a volunteer to use the word *fun* in a sentence to reinforce its meaning. Example: *It is not fun to be wet.*

Repeat the Procedure

Continue with **Teaching Chart 47**. Have children blend sounds together to determine which groups of letters make words.

PRACTICE

BLENDING
Build, Write, and Read Words with Short Vowels and _th_

Have children work in small groups. Have each group build and list three or more words with short _e_. Repeat with the remaining short vowels and the digraph _th_. ▶ **Linguistic/Kinesthetic**

ASSESS/CLOSE

Create a Short Vowel and _th_ Art Gallery

Use your observations from the Practice activity to determine if children need more reinforcement with short vowel and _th_ words. Have them build a sentence using at least two words on the list they built. Encourage them to illustrate their sentences. On a class bulletin board, create a "Short Vowel and _th_ Gallery." Have children hang their drawings in this gallery.

Read a Decodable Story

For additional practice reading words with short vowels and the digraph _th,_ and to develop fluency, direct children to read the story _In the Hot Sun_ from the **Phonics Practice Reader, Volume 1.**

ADDITIONAL PHONICS RESOURCES

Phonics/Phonemic Awareness Practice Book,
pages 103–106

PHONICS KIT
Hands-on Activities and Practice

McGraw-Hill School
TECHNOLOGY
Phonics CD-ROM
activities for practice with
Blending and Segmenting

DAY **5** **Letter Substitution**
Using the CVC flip chart, have pairs of children build _hen._ Taking turns, one child changes a letter to build a new word, asking the partner to read it.

Phonics CD-ROM

ℹ **Intervention** ▶ **Skills**
Intervention Guide, for direct instruction and extra practice in Short _e, o, u, i, a; th_

Meeting Individual Needs for Phonics

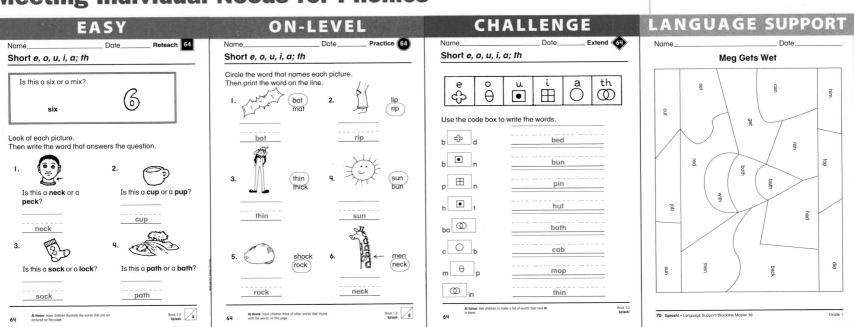

EASY	**ON-LEVEL**	**CHALLENGE**	**LANGUAGE SUPPORT**
Reteach, 64	Practice, 64	Extend, 64	Language Support, 70

OBJECTIVES

Children will:

- **learn how to recognize main idea and supporting details.**
- **understand beginning, middle, and end in a story.**

Skills Finder

Main Idea

Introduce	B2: 95I–J
Review	B2: 123I–J, 137G–H
Test	Book 2
Maintain	B3: 31; B4: 59; B5: 89

SELECTION
Connection

Children may choose from the following titles for independent reading.

ANTHOLOGY

- *Splash!*

LEVELED READERS

- *The Box*
- *A Big, Big Pig*
- *Picnic Farm*

Bibliography, pages T98–T99

Introduce Main Idea

PREPARE

Introduce the Concept of Main Idea

Tell children that every story has a main idea. Explain that the main idea is the most important idea in the story, and that the supporting details give more information about the main idea.

TEACH

Model Main Idea

Display **Teaching Chart 48**. Allow children to discuss the picture. Have volunteers read the sentences aloud.

The boy has a sunburn.
His neck is hot.
His back is red.
His legs are hot.

Teaching Chart 48

MODEL From this picture, I know that the boy is in the sun. He is at the beach. I can imagine that it is hot outside. Then I can see that the boy is not happy. He is too hot. I can see that his body has a sunburn.

Have children refer to the sentences and the picture from the **Teaching Chart** to help create a Main Idea web. Ask volunteers to circle the main idea and underline the supporting details on the **Teaching Chart**. Then, on the chalkboard, write in big letters: *The boy has a sunburn.* Around it, write sentences in smaller letters to illustrate the supporting details. *His neck is hot. His back is red. His legs are hot.*

PRACTICE

Add to Main Idea Web

Tell children they are going to add more details to the story in the **Teaching Chart**. Explain that it is helpful to think about the beginning, middle, and ending as they remember the story so they can add more details. Prompt them with these questions:

- In the beginning, why do you think the boy went to the beach? Where is he sitting?
- In the middle of the story, how do you think he feels? Why do you think he stayed in the sun so long?
- In the end, what will he decide to do?

▶ **Linguistic/Auditory**

ASSESS/CLOSE

Create a New Main Idea Web

Invite children to reread *Splash!* Create a new Main Idea web based on the one from the **Teaching Chart,** listing the main idea of the story and three supporting details. Have a volunteer give a sentence that tells the main idea, and then write it in the center of the web. As children volunteer details from the beginning, middle, and end of the story, add them to the web.

ALTERNATE TEACHING STRATEGY

MAIN IDEA

For a different approach to teaching this skill, see page T73.

**Intervention** **Skills Intervention Guide,** for direct instruction and extra practice in Main Idea

---

Meeting Individual Needs for Comprehension

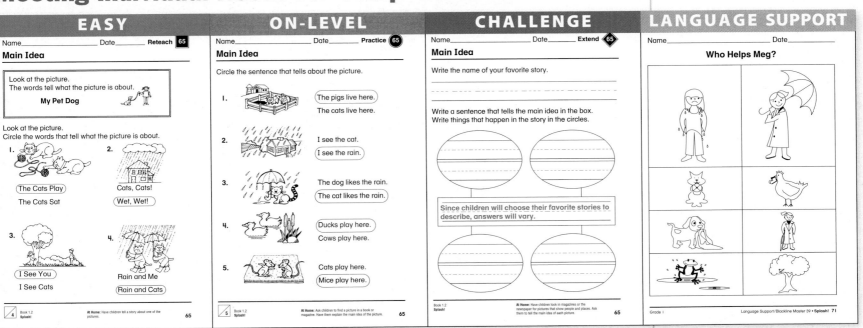

EASY	ON-LEVEL	CHALLENGE	LANGUAGE SUPPORT
Reteach, 65	Practice, 65	Extend, 65	Language Support, 71

 **OBJECTIVES**

Children will use context clues to read unfamiliar words.

....

MATERIALS
- **Teaching Chart 49**

Skills Finder	
Context Clues	
Introduce	B1: 87K-L
Review	B1: 101K-L; B2: 95K–L, 123K-L, B5: 117K-L,
Test	Bk. 1, Bk. 2, Bk. 5 U.1
Maintain	B2: 21, 107; B4: 75, 101

Review Context Clues

PREPARE

Using Context Clues

On the chalkboard, draw a simple picture of a pair of boots. Write below it: *These are my boots.* Point to the word *boots.* Explain that sometimes we don't recognize a word, but we can use clues to help us read it. Tell children they can use picture and sound clues to figure out the word.

TEACH

Using Pictures and Phonics Clues

First ask children to describe what they see in the first picture in **Teaching Chart 49**. Say: *What is the girl doing?* Then track the first sentence, saying "blank" when you come to the underlined word. Point to the word *coat* on the chart. Then model how using context clues can help the children read unfamiliar words.

She puts on her coat .

He put a hat on his head.

He is in the barn.

Teaching Chart 49

MODEL Sometimes, I see a word that I don't know. But if there's a picture, I might have a good clue. I see a girl putting on her coat. Let me see if I recognize any of the letters in the word I don't know. It begins with -c and ends with -t. The sentence is: *She puts on her coat.*

Repeat the process for the other two sentences.

PRACTICE

Using Picture and Phonics Clues

GROUP

Remind children that sometimes a picture gives them a clue when they want to read a word they don't know. Have them look back at the title page of *Splash!* and write the title of the book on the chalkboard. Then ask volunteers to describe what is happening in the picture on the title page. Have children sound out the letters they recognize. Blend the word with them aloud and have them practice saying it.

▶ **Linguistic/Visual**

ASSESS/CLOSE

Draw and Label a Picture

Remind children that the word *splash* was used in the story about Meg because she got wet in the rain. Ask volunteers to think of other places they might get wet. (the bath, a pool, the lake) Write examples of sentences on the chalkboard: *I splash in the pool. I splash in the rain.* Have children choose one sentence to illustrate. Have them write the sentence underneath the picture. Then have volunteers present their drawings. Invite the class to use picture and phonics clues to figure out the unfamiliar words.

Meeting Individual Needs for Vocabulary

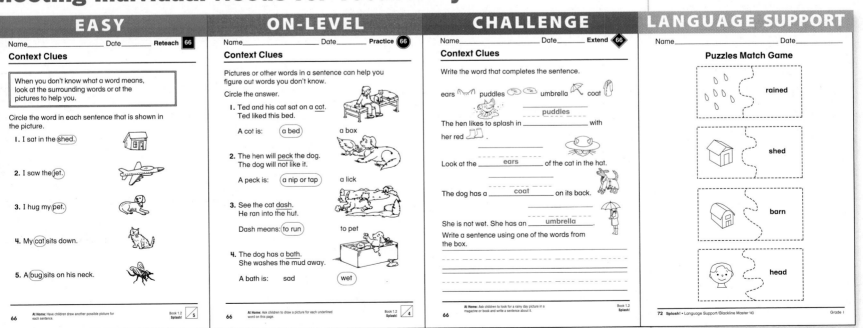

EASY	ON-LEVEL	CHALLENGE	LANGUAGE SUPPORT
Reteach, 66	Practice, 66	Extend, 66	Language Support, 72

Handwriting CD-ROM

GRAMMAR/SPELLING CONNECTIONS

Irregular Plural Nouns: See Grammar and Usage lessons, pages 95O–95P.

Words with Short *e*: See Spelling lessons, pages 95Q–95R.

TEACHING TIP

Technology Word-processing programs allow you to emphasize type with the boldface, underline, and italics features. Encourage children to emphasize the important words in what they write, such as the words in the title, by experimenting with these features.

Handwriting
WRITING Remind children to move their paper up as they near the bottom of the page and continue to keep the paper positioned correctly. For specific instruction see page T78.

Interactive Writing
Make a Weather Chart

Prewrite

LOOK AT THE STORY PATTERN Have children revisit *Splash!* and review with them the language pattern of the story. Then work with them to create a weather chart. The chart will show what Meg's animal pals might bring her to wear while sledding in the snow, while swimming at the beach, while flying a kite in the wind, and so on. Work with children to create a list of different weather conditions and appropriate activities for each.

Draft

WRITE ABOUT CLOTHES AND THE WEATHER Help children choose one weather condition and one activity from their lists and suggest what clothes Meg might wear in that situation.

- For example, begin by saying: *It's hot and sunny at the beach. What might Meg choose to wear on her head? Why would that be a good thing to wear?* As you say words with familiar sounds and patterns, have volunteers write each word on the chalkboard. Write all unfamiliar words yourself.

- Have children pick three articles of clothing for each situation and decide which animal pal should bring that clothing to Meg.

Continue the process until all the weather conditions on the list are covered.

Revise

IRREGULAR PLURAL NOUNS Ask children to reread their sentences about clothing and weather. Have them point out the nouns in the sentences. Then call attention to any irregular plural nouns, such as *children* or *feet*, in their sentences. Have them check and see if the irregular plural nouns are written and spelled correctly.

Publish

CREATE THE CHART Reread the sentences that you've written together. Then ask children to make a chart using those sentences. Discuss different ways of organizing the chart and illustrating it. Instruct children to create illustrations, and to use their sentences as captions for each drawing.

Presentation Ideas

DRAW AN OUTFIT Invite children to draw themselves in an appropriate outfit for the weather and the activity of their choice. Have them display their pictures and talk about what it feels like outside, and why they'd like wearing their outfits in that weather.

▶ **Representing/Speaking**

PUT ON IMAGINARY CLOTHING Invite children to pantomime putting on imaginary clothing while the rest of the class tries to guess what they're wearing and what the weather is. ▶ **Representing/Viewing**

Meeting Individual Needs for Writing

EASY	ON-LEVEL	CHALLENGE
Draw Pictures Children can draw pictures showing what Meg's animal pals might bring her in a different weather condition than the one in the story. Have them use language patterns from *Splash!* as captions for their pictures.	**Write an Invitation** Children can write an invitation to a friend, asking that friend to join them in an activity that they enjoy that requires special clothing. In their invitation, children should tell their friend what kind of clothing to wear and why to wear it for that particular activity.	**New Story** Children can work in groups to write new versions of Meg's story for a different weather condition. Have them refer to the chart they created and the language patterns in *Splash!* as they write their stories.

5 Day Grammar and Usage Plan

DAY 1 — Introduce the Concept

Oral Warm-Up Say the following: *The cats were on the mat.* Ask children which word names more than one thing. (cats)

Introduce Irregular Plural Nouns Remind children that plural nouns name more than one person, place or thing. Ask children how most plural nouns are formed. (By adding *-s* or *-es*.)

Irregular Plural Nouns

- Some nouns that name more than one thing do not end with *-s*.

Display and discuss these singular nouns and their irregular plural forms: *Child/children, goose/geese, foot/feet, man/men, tooth/teeth, mouse/mice.*

✏ **WRITING** Assign the daily Writing Prompt on page 66E.

Daily Language Activity Say the following: *The children have new teeth.* Ask which words name more than one person or thing. (children, teeth)

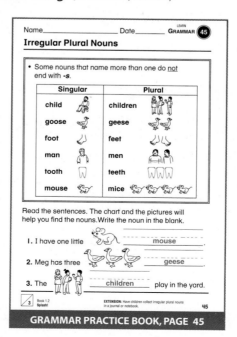

GRAMMAR PRACTICE BOOK, PAGE 45

DAY 2 — Teach the Concept

Review Irregular Nouns Remind children that yesterday they learned about some irregular plural nouns. Write the following on the chalkboard: *I see the mouse. I see the mice.* Read the sentences aloud with children. Ask children which word names more than one, *mouse* or *mice.* (mice)

Daily Language Activity Write the following sentence on the chalkboard: The men have three geese. Ask children to identify the words which name more than one person, place, or thing. (men, geese) Explain that *men* names more than one *man*. Ask children what *geese* names more than one of. (goose)

✏ **WRITING** Assign the daily Writing Prompt on page 66E.

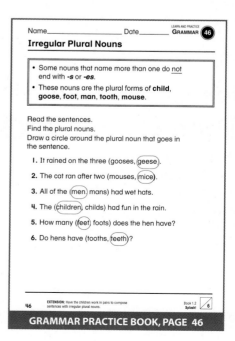

GRAMMAR PRACTICE BOOK, PAGE 46

Irregular Plural Nouns

DAY 3 — Review and Practice

Learn from the Literature Review irregular plural nouns with children. Read the following sentences from *Splash!*

> Then her cat ran up the path.
>
> Then her hen ran up the path.
>
> Then her dog ran up the path.

Write *cat, hen,* and *dog* on the board. Tell children that these are nouns that name animals. Ask children how they would name more than one of each animal. (cats, hens, dogs) Write plural forms.

Daily Language Activity Write *goose* and *mouse* on the board. Ask children how to name more than one of each of these animals. (geese, mice) Write the plurals. Ask children how these plurals are different from the others. (They are not formed by adding -s.)

WRITING Assign the daily Writing Prompt on page 66F.

DAY 4 — Review and Practice

Review Irregular Plural Nouns Say *one mouse.* Then say: *Two .* Raise your voice in question and have the children fill in the correct plural noun. Repeat with *child, foot, goose, man,* and *tooth.*

Daily Language Activity Say a sentence about one thing and ask children to say the same sentence about two things. For example: *I saw one goose in the pond.* (I saw two geese in the pond.) Repeat this exercise with other irregular plural nouns.

Mechanics and Usage Before children begin the daily Writing Prompt on page 66F, review the following:

Sentence Punctuation

- Begin every sentence with a capital letter.
- End an exclamation with an exclamation point.

WRITING Assign the daily Writing Prompt on page 66F.

DAY 5 — Assess and Reteach

Daily Language Activity Write these sentences on the chalkboard and read them aloud with children. Ask children to correct the plural nouns that are wrong.

1. I have two legs and two foots. (feet)

2. How many mans are on the path? (men)

3. Mouses do not like cats. (mice)

4. Do gooses have tooths? (geese, teeth)

Assess Use page 49 of the **Grammar Practice Book** for assessment.

Reteach Have children pick one of the plural nouns they have learned and draw a picture of it. Make sure they draw more than one thing. Then ask them to write a caption for their pictures, and underline the irregular plural noun.

Use page 50 of the **Grammar Practice Book** for additional reteaching.

WRITING Assign the daily Writing Prompt on page 66F.

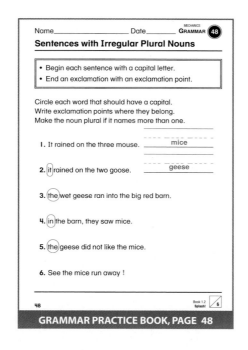

GRAMMAR PRACTICE BOOK, PAGE 47

GRAMMAR PRACTICE BOOK, PAGE 48

GRAMMAR PRACTICE BOOK, PAGE 49

GRAMMAR PRACTICE BOOK, PAGE 50

95P

5 Day Spelling Plan

Assess Prior Knowledge Write the words *shed, hen, wet, red, then, pet* on the chalkboard. Read the words aloud to children. Ask children what vowel sound they hear in each word. (short *e*) Ask children what letter spells this sound. (*e*) Have volunteers circle the letter *e* in each word. Write the words *away, good, into, put* on the chalkboard and read them aloud. Invite children to use these words in sentences to describe things found in the classroom.

Spelling Words		Challenge Words	
1. **shed**	4. **red**	7. **away**	9. **into**
2. **hen**	5. **then**	8. **good**	10. **put**
3. **wet**	6. pet		

*Note: Words in **dark type** are from the story.*

Word Study On page 46 of the **Spelling Practice Book** are word study steps and an at-home activity.

Word Building Write the Spelling Words in random order on the chalkboard. Draw three columns and label them with the spelling patterns *-et, -en, -ed*. Encourage children to read each word and suggest the appropriate column.

Tell children they can build words by using the spelling patterns with other letters. Write the letters *b, l, m, p,* and *w* on the chalkboard. Build words by combining each letter with the spelling pattern *-et*. Repeat the activity with spelling patterns *-en* and *-ed*.

Name_____ Date_____ Spelling **45**

Words with Short *e*

Complete each word by writing the letter that spells the short e sound.

1. sh___**e**___d
2. h___e___n
3. w___e___t
4. r___e___d
5. th___e___n
6. p___e___t

Directions (to teacher)
Review the short e sound by explaining that the letter e stands for /e/ as in the word *shed*. Write *shed* on the chalkboard or form the word with letter cards. Say the word aloud and have children repeat it. Then have children look at the first example on the page. Point out that the letter e has been filled in.

Write the words *hen, wet, red, then,* and *pet* on the chalkboard. Read the words aloud and have children repeat them. Have children listen for the letter that stands for the short e sound in each word. Then have them complete each word.

Book 1.2
Splash!   45

SPELLING PRACTICE BOOK, PAGE 45

WORD STUDY STEPS AND ACTIVITY, PAGE 46

Name_____ Date_____ Spelling **47**

Words with Short *e*

Add the ending **et** or **ed** or **en** to each letter to make a word from the box. Then write the spelling word.

| pet then hen red shed wet |

1. p +___et___= ___pet___
2. w +___et___= ___wet___
3. r +___ed___= ___red___
4. sh +___ed___= ___shed___
5. h +___en___= ___hen___
6. th +___en___= ___then___

Book 1.2
Splash!   47

SPELLING PRACTICE BOOK, PAGE 47

Words with Short e

DAY 3 Practice and Extend	**DAY 4** Practice and Write	**DAY 5** Assess and Reteach

Word Meaning: Endings Write the word *pet* on the chalkboard. Ask children to read it aloud, then ask voluteers to use it in a sentence. Write the words *pets* on the chalkboard. Tell children by adding *s,* you made the word tell about more than one pet. Repeat the process above with the words *hen(s)* and *shed(s)*. Display sentences with pictures to illustrate the plural form of words.

Identify Spelling Patterns Write this story on the chalkboard and read it aloud as you track print:

> *My pet red hen got good and wet.*
> *She went into the shed, I bet!*
> *Put away the dishes—there are no*
> *eggs yet!*

Ask children to cluck when they hear a word with the spelling pattern *-et, -ed,* or *-en,* and to crow like a rooster when they hear a Challenge Word.

Complete Sentences Write the following sentence on the board: *The ___ sleeps.* Read it aloud and invite children to complete it with an *-et* word. Read the completed sentence. Ask children to complete the sentence with an *-en* word. Read the new sentence. Extend the sentences using other Spelling Words. For example: *The pet sleeps in the shed.*

WRITING Have children use as many Spelling Words as possible in the daily Writing Prompt on page 66F. Remind them to check their writing for errors in spelling, grammar, and punctuation.

Optional Spelling Test You may wish to give children a spelling test. You may administer the test in the following manner: (1) Read the word. (2) Give a simple sentence containing the word. (3) Say the word again. Or you may use page 50 of the **Spelling Practice Book** for the post-test. If you wish, you may create additional sentences for the Challenge Words.

Personal Word List Have children **JOURNAL** write any words they still find difficult on their personal troublesome words lists in their journals. Then ask them to write one funny sentence that contains as many of the words as possible. Children should refer to the list during later writing activities.

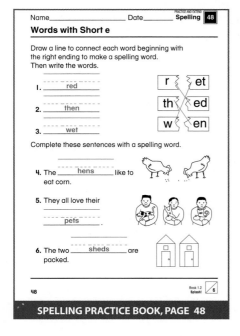

Name_____ Date_____ **Spelling 48**
Words with Short e

Draw a line to connect each word beginning with the right ending to make a spelling word. Then write the words.

r	⟩ et
th	⟩ ed
w	⟩ en

1. ___red___
2. ___then___
3. ___wet___

Complete these sentences with a spelling word.

4. The ___hens___ like to eat corn.
5. They all love their ___pets___
6. The two ___sheds___ are packed.

48

SPELLING PRACTICE BOOK, PAGE 48

Name_____ Date_____ **Spelling 49**
Words with Short e

Look at the picture. Complete each sentence with a spelling word.

1. This cat is my ___pet___
2. Sam fed the ___hen___.
3. The dog is in the ___shed___
4. Stop when it is ___red___
5. Kim got ___wet___ in the rain.
6. It was raining, but ___then___ the sun came out.

49

SPELLING PRACTICE BOOK, PAGE 49

Name_____ Date_____ **Spelling 50**
Words with Short e

Look at the words in each set. One word in each set is spelled correctly. Use a pencil to color in the circle in front of that word. Before you begin, look at the sample sets of words. Sample A has been done for you. Do Sample B by yourself. When you are sure you know what to do, you may go on with the rest of the page.

Sample A
- (A) get ●
- (B) gett
- (C) geet

Sample B
- (D) rok
- (E) roc
- (F) rock ●

1.
- (A) redd
- (B) red
- (C) rede

2.
- (D) wette
- (E) weet
- (F) wet

3.
- (A) pet
- (B) pett
- (C) ppet

4.
- (D) henn
- (E) hen
- (F) henne

5.
- (A) then
- (B) thenn
- (C) theen

6.
- (D) shedd
- (E) shede
- (F) shed

50

SPELLING PRACTICE BOOK, PAGE 50

95R

Concept
- Bugs

Comprehension
- Main Idea

Phonics
- Blends

Vocabulary
- about
- again
- around
- use

Reaching All Learners

Anthology

What Bug Is It?

Selection Summary Children will read about a teacher who takes her class on a field trip. The children learn how to compare and contrast different kinds of bugs based on what they look like, what they do, and the sounds they make.

Snacks

I sniff a great snack,
A snack on a sill.
Let me go and get my fill.

Slip me some bread,
Dip it in jam.
Then pass me a bit of that ham.

Rhyme applies to Phonics

What Bug Is It?
by Pat Cummings

Listening Library

INSTRUCTIONAL pages 98–123

About the Author and Illustrator As a child, Pat Cummings lived in many different places in the United States and in other countries. Living in these places taught her to appreciate many different cultures. Today Ms. Cummings writes and illustrates books that celebrate people of many cultures.

Same Concept, Skills and Vocabulary!

Leveled Books

EASY
on on pages 123A and 123D
`DECODABLE`

INDEPENDENT
Lesson on pages 123B and 123D

🏠 *Take-Home version available*

`DECODABLE`

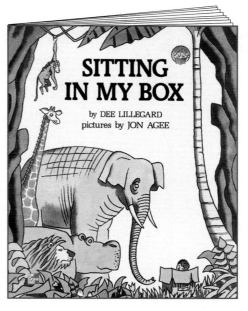

CHALLENGE
Lesson on pages 123C and 123D

Leveled Practice

EASY
Reteach, 67-74 Blackline masters with reteaching opportunities for each assessed skill

INDEPENDENT/ON-LEVEL
Practice, 67-74 Workbook with Take-Home Stories and practice opportunities for each assessed skill and story comprehension

CHALLENGE
Extend, 67-74 Blackline masters that offer challenge activities for each assessed skill

Quizzes Prepared by 📘 Accelerated Reader®

Center Activities

Center Activities

Each of these activities takes 15–20 minutes.

Phonics

Search for Initial Blends

GROUP **Objective:** Identify words with initial and final blends.

◆ Children place the cards in a pile face down.

◆ Each child draws a card and says the blend.

◆ The child then says a word that begins with the blend on the card.

MATERIALS

- *What Bug Is It?* from the Student Anthology
- Index cards with the following blends each written on a card: *sl, sm, sn, fl, fr*

Writing

Describe a Bug

ONE **Objective:** Write a description of a bug photograph.

◆ Have each child choose a favorite bug photograph from *What Bug Is It?*

◆ Children draw a picture of the bug and then write a description of it. Suggest that they include details that tell about color, shape, and size.

MATERIALS

- *What Bug Is It?* from the Student Anthology
- Paper
- Crayons

Reading and Listening

Independent/Self-Selected Reading

ONE **Objective:** Listen and use illustrations to understand a story.

Fill the Center with books and corresponding audiocassettes or CD-ROMs children have read or listened to this week. You can also include books from the Theme Bibliography on pages T98 and T99.

Leveled Readers

◆ *Around Bug Town* by Sherry Tuseth Jackson
◆ *A Box of Bugs* by Clark Maxwell
◆ *Sitting in My Box* by Dee Lillegard

◆ Theme Big Book *My River* by Shari Halpern
◆ *What Bug Is It?* by Pat Cummings
◆ "Cat Kisses" by Bobbi Katz
◆ Phonics Practice Reader, Vol. 1

Working with Words

Concentration

PARTNERS

Objective: Reinforce vocabulary words: *about, again, around, use.*

MATERIALS
- Index cards
- Crayons

◆ Children write each of the words on 2 cards.

◆ Children mix up the cards.

◆ After arranging the cards in 3 rows, partners alternate turning pairs of cards over. If the cards match, that child keeps that pair.

about   around

again   use

Science

A to Z Bugs

PARTNERS

Objective: Generate a list of insect names.

MATERIALS
- Construction paper
- Crayons
- Nature magazines

◆ Have partners write A–Z down the left side of the paper.

◆ Partners write as many bug names as they can that begin with each letter.

◆ You may provide children with nature magazines to help them remember bug names.

Bugs!
A	ant
B	butterfly
C	caterpillar
D	dragonfly

Science

Class Walk

GROUP

Objective: Use the five senses to learn about the environment.

MATERIALS
- Butcher paper
- Crayons

◆ Display a sheet of butcher paper as shown.

◆ Have children examine the materials and resources in and immediately around the Center area.

◆ Encourage children to use their five senses to observe their environment.

◆ Children can write and draw about something they observed with their senses on the chart.

Our Listening Walk.

What Bug Is It? by Pat Cummings

Suggested Lesson Planner

READING AND LANGUAGE ARTS	DAY 1 — *Focus on Reading and Skills*	DAY 2 — *Read the Literature*
● **Phonics Daily Routines**	Daily **Phonics** Routine: Listening, 96J **Phonics**	Daily **Phonics** Routine: Letter Substitution, 98A **Phonics**
● **Phonological Awareness** ● **Phonics** *Blends* ● **Comprehension** ● **Vocabulary** ● **Study Skills** ● **Listening, Speaking, Viewing, Representing**	**Read** **Read Aloud,** 96G *How Spiders Got Eight Legs* ☑ **Develop Phonological Awareness,** 96H ☑ **Introduce Blends,** 96I–96J **Reteach, Practice, Extend,** 67 **Phonics/Phonemic Awareness Practice Book,** 107–110 **Read** **Apply Blends,** 96/97 "Snacks" ⓘ Intervention Program	**Build Background,** 98A Develop Oral Language **Vocabulary,** 98B–98C	*about*	*again*		*around*	*use*	**Word Building Manipulative Cards** **Teaching Chart 50** **Reteach, Practice, Extend,** 68 **Read** **Read the Selection,** 98–119 **Guided Instruction** ☑ Blends ☑ Main Idea **Genre: Informational Story,** 99 **Cultural Perspectives,** 110
● **Curriculum Connections**	**Link** Language Arts, 96G	**Link** Science, 98A
● **Writing**	**Writing Prompt:** What if you had a pet bug? What would you name it? What do you two like to do together?	**Writing Prompt:** Where would you fine interesting bugs in your town? Name the parks, or fields, or streets. **Journal Writing** Quick Write, 119
● **Grammar**	**Introduce the Concept: Proper Nouns,** 123O Daily Language Activity: Identify proper nouns. **Grammar Practice Book,** 51	**Teach the Concept: Proper Nouns,** 123O Daily Language Activity: Identify proper nouns. **Grammar Practice Book,** 52
● **Spelling** *Blends*	**Introduce: Words with Blends,** 123Q **Spelling Practice Book,** 51–52	**Teach the Patterns: Words with Blends,** 123Q **Spelling Practice Book,** 53

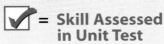

DAY 3 — Read the Literature

Daily Phonics Routine:
Blending, 121

Rereading for Fluency, 118

Story Questions, 120
  Reteach, Practice, Extend, 69

Story Activities, 121

Study Skill, 122
  ☑ Maps

  Teaching Chart 51
  Reteach, Practice, Extend, 70

Test Power, 123

 Read the Leveled Books, 123A–123D
Guided Reading
  ☑ Blends
  ☑ Main Idea
  ☑ High-Frequency Words

 Intervention Program

 **Math,** 106; **Science,** 96D, 104, 108

Writing Prompt: You and your pet bug are going on a trip. Where are you going?

Journal Writing, 123D

Practice and Write: Proper Nouns, 123P
  Daily Language Activity: List proper nouns.

Grammar Practice Book, 53

Practice and Extend: Words with Blends, 123R

Spelling Practice Book, 54

DAY 4 — Build Skills

Daily Phonics Routine:
Writing, 123F

 **Read the Leveled Books and Self-Selected Books**

  ☑ **Review Blends,** 123E–123F
  Teaching Chart 52
  Reteach, Practice, Extend, 71
  Language Support, 78
  Phonics/Phonemic Awareness
  Practice Book, 107–110

  ☑ **Review Blends; sh, th, ck,** 123G–123H
  Teaching Chart 53
  Reteach, Practice, Extend, 72
  Language Support, 79
  Phonics/Phonemic Awareness
  Practice Book, 107–110

  Minilessons, 105, 107, 111, 117

 Intervention Program

 Social Studies, 114

Writing Prompt: What if you were a bug? What would you look like? What would your name be?

Interactive Writing: Write an Article, 123M
  Prewrite, Draft

Meeting Individual Needs for Writing, 123N

Practice and Write: Proper Nouns, 123P
  Daily Language Activity: Write proper nouns.

Grammar Practice Book, 54

Practice and Write: Words with Blends, 123R

Spelling Practice Book, 55

DAY 5 — Build Skills

Daily Phonics Routine:
Fluency, 123H

 **Read Self-Selected Books**

  ☑ **Review Main Idea and Supporting Details,** 123I–123J
  Teaching Chart 54
  Reteach, Practice, Extend, 73
  Language Support, 80

  ☑ **Review Context Clues,** 123K–123L
  Teaching Chart 55
  Reteach, Practice, Extend, 74
  Language Support, 81

  Listening, Speaking, Viewing, Representing, 123N
  Make a Bug Mural
  Perform a Bug Scene

  Minilessons, 105, 107, 111, 117

Intervention Program

Art, 116

Writing Prompt: Imagine that you find a bug you never saw before. Write about it. Tell what it looks like.

Interactive Writing: Write an Article, 123M
  Revise, Publish

Assess and Reteach: Proper Nouns, 123P
  Daily Language Activity: Identify and write proper nouns.

Grammar Practice Book, 55–56

Assess and Reteach: Words with Blends, 123R

Spelling Practice Book, 56

Read Aloud

How Spiders Got Eight Legs
a folktale retold by Katherine Mead

This folktale begins with a very tricky, two-legged spider. He wants to win a race without working hard, and on the day of the race crosses the finish line first. Then he must give credit where it's due!

A Big Problem

Long ago in Africa, spiders had only two legs. There was one spider who was very selfish. He wanted to be better than all the other animals in the jungle. But he did not like to work hard.

Every year, there was a big race in the jungle. All the animals wanted to win. They practiced running every day. Spider thought, "I am much better than the others. I'll think of a way to win this year's race without working hard."

The Plan

Spider watched all the animals run. He thought that Ostrich, Giraffe, or Cheetah could win the race. Spider could not run as fast as any of them. But he did not worry. He had a plan.

Continued on page T4

Oral Comprehension

LISTENING AND SPEAKING After children listen to this folktale, have them explain how it accounts for the fact that spiders have eight legs. Ask children to tell if they like the folktale, and to tell why they do or do not like it. You may also wish to explain to children that good folktales and stories use language that helps the reader see what is being described in the story in his or her head.

Activity Discuss with children what the phrase "winning by a nose" means. Have children draw a picture of the cheetah and spider at the finish line. Can they show the spider "winning by a nose"?

▶ **Visual/Linguistic**

GENRE: FOLKTALE A folktale is a story that comes from a particular culture or geographic area. It is usually passed down from generation to generation through storytelling, meaning that grandparents tell the story to parents, who then tell the story to their children. Ask children what part of the world they think this folktale comes from (Africa). Ask them what clues they used to come to their conclusions. (The animals in the story are found in Africa.)

Develop Phonological Awareness

Blend Sounds

MATERIALS
- colored blocks

Teach Place four colored blocks with spaces between them in front of you. Say: *Listen to these sounds—/s/-/n/-/a/-/p/. I said four sounds.* Have children repeat the sounds. Then move the blocks together and blend these sounds together to say a word. Say *snap.* Have children repeat the word with you.

Practice Have children listen as you say the sounds for the following words. They will blend the sounds together to say the word. Use the following words: *bluff, doll, fill, flash, frog, huff, muff, pass, slam, slick.*

Segment Sounds

MATERIALS
- colored blocks (four per child)

Teach Place four blocks side by side in front of you. Tell children you will say a word and they will repeat it. Then, you will say each sound. Say the word *frog* and then the sounds /f/-/r/-/o/-/g/ and point to a block for each sound. Tell children the word *frog* has four sounds. Have children repeat the word and the sounds with you.

Practice Have children segment the following sounds by saying the complete word, then saying each sound. Ask them to point to a block for each sound: *buzz, snack, frill, frog, flag, slot.*

Delete Sounds

MATERIALS
- puppet

Teach Have the puppet say: *Flap, flat. Now I will say each of these words without its end sound—fla.* Point out that without their end sounds, they sound the same. Repeat the words and have children identify the end sounds. (/p/, /t/)

Practice Say the following word sets. Ask children to repeat the words, then say them without their final sound: *flip, flick; flop, flock; hill, hiss; slam, slap; slid, slim.*

INFORMAL ASSESSMENT Observe children as they blend sounds, segment sounds, and delete final sounds. If children have difficulty, see Alternate Teaching Strategies on page T75.

96H

Introduce Blends

Children will:

- identify initial and final continuant/continuant blends: *sl*, *sm*, *sn*, *fl*, and *fr*; double consonants: *ll*, *ss*, and *ff*.

- blend and read CCVC and CVCC words with initial and final continuant/continuant blends.

- review: final consonants, double consonants, and short vowels.

MATERIALS

- letter cards from the **Word Building Manipulative Cards**

Skills Finder

Blends	
Introduce	B2: 96I-J; B3: 8I-J, 38I-J
Review	B2: 123G-H; B3: 37E-F
Test	Book 2, Book 3
Maintain	B3: 23; B4: 13

SPELLING/PHONICS CONNECTIONS

Words with continuant/continuant blends and double consonants: See the 5-Day Spelling Plan, pages 123Q–123R.

TEACH

Identify Blends and the Corresponding Sounds

Explain to children that some words begin or end with two consonants together. Tell children they can use what they know about blending to blend these sounds together. Point out that they will be able to hear each consonant sound in the blend.

- Display the *s* card and say /s/. Add the *l* card and say /l/.

s **l**

- Blend the sounds together and have children repeat after you.

s **l**   **s** **l**

BLENDING Model and Guide Practice with Continuant/Continuant Blends

- Use letter cards and form the word *slim*.
- Blend the sounds together and read the word. Invite children to repeat after you.

Use the Word in Context

Use the word in context to ask a question. Have children answer the question. Example: *Is there a slim chance it will rain?*

Repeat the Procedure

Use the following words to model and guide practice with continuant/continuant blends and double consonants.

	slam	snap	flat	flag
	smock	slick	frog	smell

PRACTICE

BLENDING
Build Words with Blends Using Letter Banks

JOURNAL GROUP

Write the following letter banks on the chalkboard as shown. Have children work in small groups to build words with blends. They may choose (a) consonant(s) from the first two columns; a vowel from the third column; and (a) consonant(s) from the fourth column. Example: *flap*. Have children write the words in their journals. ▶ Linguistic/Visual

f	l	a, u	p, ff
s	m	e, i	t, ll
d	r	e, u	m, ss

ASSESS/CLOSE

Identify, Read, and Write Sentences with Blends

To assess children's ability to blend and read words with blends, observe them as they build and read their words. Encourage them to write sentences using consonant blends.

ADDITIONAL PHONICS RESOURCES

Phonics/Phonemic Awareness Practice Book, pages107–110

McGraw-Hill School
TECHNOLOGY

Phonics CD-ROM

activities for practice with **Blending and Building Words**

PHONICS KIT
Hands-on Activities and Practice

Meeting Individual Needs for Phonics

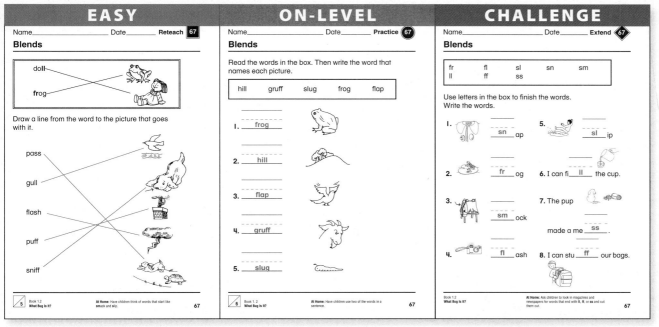

Reteach, 67   Practice, 67   Extend, 67

Daily Routines

DAY 1 Listening Say the sound /fl/. Then read the following words aloud slowly: *flap, slap, flip, flop, frog, fluff.* Have children raise a finger when they hear a word with the /fl/ sound.

DAY 2 Letter Substitution Write the word *slam* on the chalkboard. Emphasize each sound. Replace the *a* with *i*. Say the new word. Continue with *slit/slip* and *snip/snap.*

DAY 3 Blending Write the following words on the chalkboard: *slid, flap, slam,* and *fill.* Have children blend and read each word.

DAY 4 Writing Write the following sentence on the chalkboard: *Fred is a frog.* Ask children to write the sentence and draw a picture to go with it.

DAY 5 Fluency Write a list of words with the initial blends *sl, sn, fl, fr,* that have short vowels. Have children work in pairs, taking turns reading the words.

96J

OBJECTIVES

Children will read a poem with words containing consonant blends and double consonants.

Apply **Blends**

Snacks

I sniff a great snack,
A snack on a sill.
Let me go and get my fill.

Slip me some bread,
Dip it in jam.
Then pass me a bit of that ham.

Anthology pages 96–97

Read and Build Fluency

READ THE POEM Tell children they will read a poem called "Snacks". Have children listen for words with consonant blends as you read the poem. Track print with your finger. Have children read the poem with you.

REREAD FOR FLUENCY Have children work in pairs and take turns rereading the poem. Encourage them to use gestures as they read.

PARTNERS

READ A DECODABLE STORY For additional practice reading and to develop fluency, direct children to read *Let's Go See Bugs* from **Phonics Practice Reader, Volume 1.**

Let's Go See Bugs
written by Michael Lee
illustrated by Andrea Champlin

Dictate and Spell

DICTATE WORDS Segment the word *snack* into its four individual sounds. Repeat the word aloud and use it in a sentence: *I like a snack after school.* Then have children say the word and write the letter that represents each sound until they make the entire word. Repeat with *sniff, fill, slip,* and *pass* from the poem. Then repeat with other words with consonant blends and double consonants, such as *bran, frill, slam, slash, slot, snap,* and *glass.*

JOURNAL

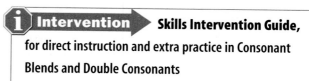
i Intervention **Skills Intervention Guide,** for direct instruction and extra practice in Consonant Blends and Double Consonants

Build Background

Link
Science

Concept: Bugs

Evaluate Prior Knowledge

CONCEPT: BUGS Work together to make a list of insects or bugs that children have seen. Use the following activities if children need more information on how to identify bugs.

MAKE A CHART ABOUT BUGS Display a large picture or photo of an insect. Help children make a chart that describes it.

▶ **Visual**

BUGS
have three body parts
heads have a mouth, eyes, antennae
have legs
some have wings

CREATE AN INSECT Invite children to

ONE   WRITING

draw a picture of a make-believe insect. Have them include characteristics listed on the chart. Encourage them to write a sentence about their insects.

Develop Oral Language

CONNECT WORDS AND ACTIONS

 Invite children to pretend to be bugs. Give directions such as:

- Flutter like a butterfly.
- Buzz like a bee.
- Crawl like an ant.

Prompt children to say what they are doing by asking:

- What are you doing?
- What is that sound I hear?
- Who is crawling?

▶ **Kinesthetic/Linguistic**

DAILY Phonics ROUTINES

DAY 2 **Letter Substitution**
Write the word *slam* on the chalkboard. Emphasize each sound. Replace the *a* with *i*. Say the new word. Continue with *slit/slip* and *snip/snap*.

Phonics CD-ROM

LANGUAGE SUPPORT

To build more background, see pages 73–76, in the **Language Support Book.**

OBJECTIVES

Children will:

- identify high-frequency words *about, again, around,* and *use.*

MATERIALS

- Teaching Chart 50

- Word Building Manipulative Cards *about, again, around, use*

TEACHING TIP

The following chart indicates words from the upcoming story that children have learned to decode and high-frequency words taught in this lesson. As children read, observe any difficulties they may have in reading these words.

Decodable		High-Frequency
buzz	pass	about
flap	slim	again
flat	smack	around
hill	snag	use
Jill	snap	
Miss	will	
Nell		

SPELLING/VOCABULARY CONNECTIONS

The words *about, again, around,* and *use* are Challenge Words. See page 123Q for Day 1 of the 5-Day Spelling Plan.

about

around

again

use

Vocabulary

High-Frequency Words

Bugs

Bugs, bugs go (around) the shed.
(Use) your eyes. You will not miss them.
Two are black and two are red.
Do not kiss them!
Bugs, bugs (again) they run.
We can look. But do not bug them!
Learning (about) the bugs is fun.
But do not hug them!

Teaching Chart 50

Auditory

LISTEN TO WORDS Ask children to think about bugs. How do bugs make them feel? Then, without displaying it, read aloud "Bugs" on **Teaching Chart 50**. After you've read the poem, have children discuss their experiences with bugs.

RHYME HIGH-FREQUENCY WORDS Have children aurally identify each high-frequency word using the following activity:

- Say aloud one of the high-frequency words. Read a line of the poem where that word appears.

- Ask children to think of words that rhyme with that word. Then have them use the high-frequency word and a rhyming word in a sentence about bugs.

- Repeat this activity with each of the high-frequency words.

Visual

DISPLAY WORDS Display "Bugs" on **Teaching Chart 50**. Read the poem, tracking the print with your finger. Next, point to and say the word *about*. Have children say the word with you. Ask them to hold up the vocabulary card for *about* and say it. Repeat with *again, around,* and *use*.

Hold up vocabulary cards for *about, again, around,* and *use* one at a time. Have volunteers read and circle the words on the chart.

Word Building Manipulative Cards

ROUND-ROBIN SENTENCES

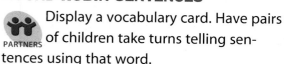

PARTNERS

Display a vocabulary card. Have pairs of children take turns telling sentences using that word.

Word Wall

Finish the Rhyme Tell children you are going to say words that rhyme with the word wall words. Have children finish the rhymes by saying the missing word wall word:

stout, doubt _____ (about)

choose, news _____ (use)

hound, pound _____ (around)

hen, pen, _____ (again)

Bean Letters Give children a tub of dried beans, glue, and construction paper. In groups, have children glue the beans to the paper to spell the word wall words.

LANGUAGE SUPPORT

To help children develop understanding and recognition of high-frequency words, see page 73 in the **Language Support Book.**

Assess

Guess and Write the Word Give a clue about one of the word wall words. Ask children to name which of the words it could be. Then tell children to write the word on a piece of paper. Continue with the rest of the lesson's words.

Meeting Individual Needs for Vocabulary

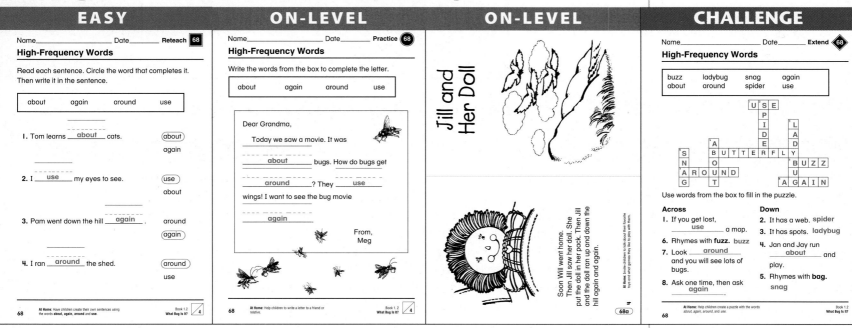

EASY	ON-LEVEL	ON-LEVEL	CHALLENGE
Reteach, 68	Practice, 68	Practice, 68a Take-Home Story	Extend, 68

Comprehension

Prereading Strategies

PREVIEW AND PREDICT Read aloud the book title and the name of the author/illustrator, Pat Cummings. Point out that there are illustrations and photographs. Lead children on a **picture walk** and use words from the story as you discuss the illustrations. Point out one or two high-frequency words as you go. Have children make predictions about the story:

- Who are the characters in the story?
- Will the story be real or make-believe? (real) *Genre*
- What do you think might happen?

Record predictions on a chart.

PREDICTIONS	WHAT HAPPENED
Children look for bugs in this story.	
Someone gets stung by a bug.	

SET PURPOSES Ask children what they want to find out as they read the story. For example:

- What bugs do you want to see?
- What do you want to find out about bugs?

READ TOGETHER

Meet Pat Cummings

When Pat Cummings was a child, she lived in many places in the United States and in other countries. Living in these places taught her to appreciate many different cultures. Today Cummings writes and illustrates books that celebrate people of many cultures.

1

98

Meeting Individual Needs • Grouping Suggestions for Strategic Reading

EASY

Shared Reading Read the story aloud as you model directionality by tracking print. Invite children to chime in with the repetitive words and phrases as you read. Help children use the photographs to read new words and identify the bugs.

ON-LEVEL

Guided Instruction Read the selection with children, using the Comprehension questions. Monitor any difficulties in reading that children may have in order to determine which prompts in the Comprehension section to emphasize. After reading the story with children, have children reread it using the rereading suggestions on page 118.

CHALLENGE

Independent Reading Have children reread the story independently. Remind them to think about the main idea of the story. Encourage them to use the pictures to help them remember the details of the story. After reading, children can use the questions on page 120 for a group discussion.

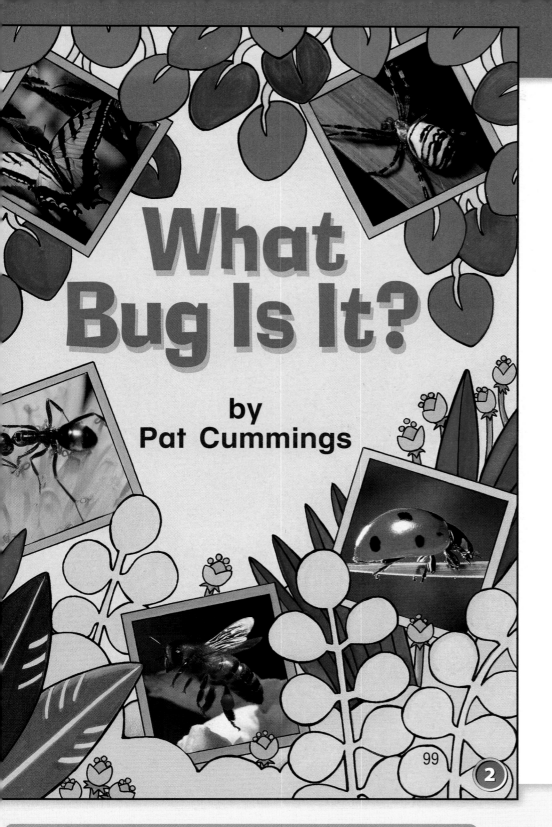

What Bug Is It?

by
Pat Cummings

99

Comprehension

☑ **Phonics** **Blends and Double Consonants**

☑ **Apply Main Idea**

STRATEGIC READING Explain to children that thinking about the main idea will help them understand the story. The illustrations and photographs can give clues about the details. Children will make a bug chart to help them remember the main idea and details.

1 **MAIN IDEA** We are going to read *What Bug Is It?* Let's figure out the main idea and the details of the story.

Let's look at the photograph on page 98. It shows the author/illustrator, Pat Cummings. How do you think she got the idea for this book? *Concept of a Book: Author/Illustrator*

2 Let's look at the picture on page 99. What do you think you will learn in this story? (facts about insects) Why do you think that? (The photographs all show insects.) *Make Predictions/Use Illustrations*

Genre

Informational Story

In an informational story,

• the main purpose is to give information.

• characters and settings are realistic.

Activity Discuss with children that an informational story is real and not make-believe. After reading the story, tell children two statements about an insect. Ask volunteers to tell you if the statement is real or make-believe. For example:

• A bee can buzz. (real)

• A bee has a web. (make-believe)

LANGUAGE SUPPORT

A blackline master for making the bug chart can be found in the **Language Support Book.** Children can color in each bug as it is named in the story. Then have children look back through the pages to list details about each bug. Children can use their notes to help them find out the main idea of the story.

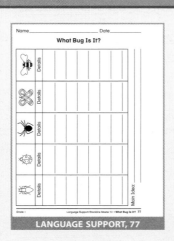

LANGUAGE SUPPORT, 77

Comprehension

TRACKING PRINT Point to the word in the sentence where we will begin reading. Let's read the sentence together. *Syntactic Cues*

3 What is the second word in this sentence? (*around*) Now look around the classroom. What do you see when you look around? *High-Frequency Words*

4 **Phonics** **DOUBLE CONSO-NANTS** Now let's read the second sentence. *"You . . ."* I'm not sure of this word. Let's blend the sounds to read it. w i ll, will Let's reread the sentence. *Fluency*

5 Who do you think Miss Kim is? (the children's teacher) Why do you think that? (She's bigger. She is called Miss Kim.) *Make Inferences*

3
4 "Look around," said Miss Kim.
5 "You will see lots of bugs."

100

P/i **PREVENTION/INTERVENTION**

TRACKING PRINT Write the first sentence on chart paper. Then draw a simple bug on a small paper square. Have children use the bug picture to mark the first word in the sentence. Demonstrate how to place the insect under the first word and then slide it under each word in the sentence. Read the sentence together as the bug moves. *Syntactic Cues*

"I see a bug," said Rick. **6**

"It is a small bug." **7**

101

Comprehension

CONCEPTS OF PRINT What marks do you see before and after the words *"I see a bug"*? (quotation marks) **What do these marks tell you?** (Someone is speaking.) *Syntactic Cues*

6 **What do you notice about the bug?** (It is a photograph; it looks real.) *Use Illustrations*

7 **MAIN IDEA** What are the children looking at? (a bug) **Is it big or small?** (small) **How many legs does it have?** (six)

PREVENTION/INTERVENTION

CONCEPTS OF PRINT Remind children that quotation marks show what a character is saying. Have children use their index fingers to frame the dialogue in the first sentence. Demonstrate how to put your left index finger at the beginning of the sentence and your right index finger after the word *bug*. Ask which character is speaking, and remind them that the word *said* tells who is speaking. *Syntactic Cues*

101

Comprehension

 8 Where is the bug Miss Kim is talking about? (on the ground) *Use Illustrations*

9 What kind of bug do you think Miss Kim is looking at? (an ant) *Make Inferences*

GROUP READING Model tracking print to achieve fluency.

- Point to and read aloud the first word in the sentence.

- Run your finger under each word as you read, stopping at the end of the first line.

- Ask: Where do I go for the next word? (down and left to the beginning of the next line)

- Read the rest of the sentence, tracking each word.

- Reread the sentence with children until they can read it without breaks or pauses.

8 "It runs about on six legs and **9** digs a hill," said Miss Kim.

102

LANGUAGE SUPPORT

ESL Point to the words *It runs about* and read them aloud. Ask children to show you how they run in place. Then ask: Do you think something was actually running in the story? What could the words *runs about* mean, then? Encourage children to come up with a definition similar to *goes along, goes from place to place,* or *moves around.*

"What bug is it?" said Rick. (10)

"It is an ant!" said Jill. (11)

103

Comprehension

(10) **Phonics** **DOUBLE CONSO-NANTS** Point to the last word in the second sentence. Frame the last two letters with your fingers. When you see two *l*'s together, then say /l/. Let's blend the sounds to read the name.

J i ll, Jill

(p/i) **CONCEPTS OF PRINT** Read the first sentence. What is that mark after the word *it*? (a question mark) What does it mean? (Rick is asking a question.) *Syntactic Cues*

(11) **MAIN IDEA** What is the main idea of the story so far? (The children are looking for bugs.) What bug have the children in the story seen? (an ant) Let's color the picture of the ant in our bug chart. What details do you remember about the ant? Let's write them in our bug chart. *Graphic Organizer*

Details	Details	Details	Details	Details
small				
six legs				
digs				

(p/i) PREVENTION/INTERVENTION

CONCEPTS OF PRINT Write the following questions on the chalkboard without question marks. Ask volunteers to write a question mark at the end of each question and then read it aloud. Then invite children to answer each question.

- What is your name(?)
- How old are you(?)
- What bug do you like(?)
Syntactic Cues

Comprehension

12 Look! It's a new bug! What does this bug look like? (It is red with black spots.) Let's read these pages to find out more about it. *Use Illustrations*

"I see a bug," said Jill.
12 "It is red with black spots."

104

Cross Curricular: Science

MIGHTY ANTS Most ants can lift ten times their body weight; some ants can lift as much as fifty times their weight.

- Ask: What is the heaviest thing you have lifted?
- Have children imagine trying to lift a refrigerator (about five times their body weight) or two horses (about fifty times their weight).

Activity Ask children to draw pictures of ants lifting various objects. Encourage children to use their imaginations. ▶ **Visual/Spatial**

"Its wings pop up and snap shut ⑬ again," said Miss Kim. ⑭

105

ESL Pantomime the action of a ladybug's wings by putting your arms above your head, then quickly bringing them to your sides. Have children pantomime the action of the ladybug's wings as you read the text again.

Comprehension

⑬ **Phonics** **BLENDS** *"Its wings pop up and . . ."* I'm not sure I know the next word. Let's blend the sounds of the word together to read it. s n a p, snap *Graphophonic Cues*

⑭ **SUPPORTING DETAILS** What do the wings of this bug do? (pop up and snap shut) Show me how this bug would move its wings. *Pantomime*

Minilesson

REVIEW/MAINTAIN

Short *u*

- Say the word *bug* and emphasize the /u/ sound. Write *u* on the chalkboard and remind children that this letter often makes the /u/ sound.

- Reread the sentence on page 105 slowly. Ask children to stand up and make the /u/ sound when they hear a word with the /u/ sound.

Activity Invite children to make a list of other words with the /u/ sound. Have them draw an outline of a bug and write their words inside it.

Phonics **CD-ROM** Have children use the interactive phonics activities for more reinforcement with short *u*.

105

Comprehension

15 Point to the word *around* in the second sentence. Have we seen this word before? (yes, on page 100) Let's read the word together. *High-Frequency Words*

"Look!" said Jas.
"It is walking around on my hand."

15

106

Cross Curricular: Math

HOW MANY SPOTS? Help children count the number of spots on the ladybug on page 105.

 Cut out circles to use as ladybug bodies.

• On the front side, write an addition problem from 1 to 10.

• On the back side, write the answer.

• Cut out wings and label them with dots. Fasten wings to the body.

▶ **Visual/Kinesthetic**

RESEARCH AND INQUIRY Have children find information about ladybugs.

"What bug is it?" said Jill. **16**
"It is a ladybug!" said Nell. **17**

107

Comprehension

PHONOLOGICAL AWARENESS
Listen to the sentence *"It is a ladybug!" said Nell.* Which word is the longest? *(ladybug)*

16 **MAIN IDEA** What is the story about? (children who are finding bugs) What bugs have they seen so far? (ant, ladybug) Let's add a picture of the ladybug to our bug charts. *Graphic Organizer*

17 What bug do you think the children will see next? (Answers will vary.) *Make Predictions*

Minilesson
REVIEW/MAINTAIN
Context Clues

Point out to children that often they can figure out a new word by the context in which it is used.

- Have children read the second sentence on page 106.
- Then read the sentence omitting the word *walking*.
- Ask children what they think the ladybug might be doing "around (Jas's) hand."
- Have children use what they know about bugs from personal experience, the illustrations, and the sound and letter /w/ *w* to figure out the word.

Activity Help children brainstorm a list of things a ladybug might do on a person's hand. Record children's responses.

PREVENTION/INTERVENTION

PHONOLOGICAL AWARENESS
Have children clap to show the number of syllables in words.

- Have children say the word *ladybug*, clapping once for each syllable. Ask how many syllables there are in the word. (3)
- Repeat with the words *spider* and *ant*.

Comprehension

18 Read the second sentence. What are the marks at the beginning and end of the sentence? (quotation marks) What do they mean? (Someone is saying something.)
Concepts of Print

"I see a bug," said Nell.
18 "I see a bug in a web."

108

Cross Curricular: Science

LADYBUG FACTS Share these facts:

- There are 5,000 kinds of ladybugs.
- Ladybugs help farmers by eating tiny bugs that eat plants.

Activity Have children draw pictures of ladybugs and write a sentence about their pictures. ▶ **Visual/Kinesthetic**

RESEARCH AND INQUIRY Invite children to look in fiction and nonfiction books to find information about ladybugs.

Ladybugs help us.

"It is a bit fat," said Yan.
"But it has thin legs." **19**

109

Comprehension

19 What do you think the children in the story will see? *Make Predictions*

 RHYMING WORDS Listen as I read this sentence: "It is a bit fat." Which two words rhyme? *(it, bit)*

SELF-MONITORING STRATEGY

REREAD Rereading parts of a story can help you understand the main idea and supporting details of the story.

MODEL I don't remember what the children are doing in this story. I'll reread the beginning. Now I remember. Miss Kim has told them to look around at the bugs in the garden. From the pictures I can tell that so far they've seen an ant, a ladybug, and a spider.

P/I PREVENTION/INTERVENTION

RHYMING WORDS Invite children to think of other words that rhyme with *it*. *(fit, hit, lit, pit, sit)* Remind children that words that rhyme end with the same sound.

After children think of rhyming words, challenge them to use the words in sentences such as: *Is the fire lit? Can you sit a bit?*

Comprehension

20 **BLENDS** Let's read this sentence. *"It will use its web to ..."* Hmm. Let's blend the sounds together to read the next word. s n a g, snag

21 How does the spider use its web to snag flies? (The fly gets trapped in the web.) *Make Inferences*

22 Let's look at the picture on this page. Can you tell me how else a spider might *use* its web? *High-Frequency Words*

TEACHING TIP

MANAGEMENT You may find it helpful to pair children from different cultures, or different parts of the United States, for the Cultural Perspectives activities.

21
22 "It will use its web to snag flies," said Miss Kim.
20

110

CULTURAL PERSPECTIVES

ANANSI THE SPIDER Tell children that some regions of the world have folk tales about a spider character named Anansi (or Anancy). Anansi often plays tricks on the other characters in these stories.

Activity Discuss with children the tricks that Anansi played on other characters. Have them imagine what Anansi looks like and draw a picture.
▶ **Visual/Kinesthetic**

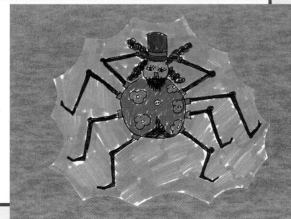

"What bug is it?" said Nell. **23** **24**

"It is a spider!" said Yan. **25**

111

Comprehension

 CONCEPTS OF PRINT What mark do you see after the word *it*? (question mark) What does it tell you? (Nell is asking a question.) What mark do you see after the word *spider*? (exclamation mark) What does it tell you? (Yan is excited.) *Syntactic Cues*

23 What do you think the children in the story will see? *Make Predictions*

24 **MAIN IDEA** What bug did the children see after the ladybug? (spider) What did the spider look like? (fat body with thin legs) Let's color the picture of the spider on our bug charts and write some details about spiders underneath it. *Graphic Organizer*

25 Pretend that you are the spider. How would you move? *Pantomime*

Minilesson

REVIEW/MAINTAIN

Summarizing

Explain to children that when they summarize, they think of the main parts of the story or the *beginning, middle,* and *end.* Prompt discussion with questions such as:

- How did the story begin?
- What kinds of bugs did the children in the story find?
- How did the story end?

Help children summarize the story concept by telling what happens in one sentence. (The children are looking for bugs.)

Activity Model folding a sheet of drawing paper into thirds. Ask children to draw a picture in each section that shows how the story began, what happened next, and how the story ended.

---

p/i **PREVENTION/INTERVENTION**

CONCEPTS OF PRINT Write the following sentences on the chalkboard without punctuation:

- What bug is it (?)
- That is a big bug (.)
- What do you see (?)
- The bug is on my back (!)

Have children write a period, question mark, or an exclamation mark at the end of each sentence. Then have children read the sentences with the appropriate expression. *Syntactic Cues*

Comprehension

26 **Phonics** **BLENDS** Let's read the second sentence. *"I see a bug . . ."* hmm . . . I need to figure out the next word. The *fl* in the word can be blended together to make the /fl/ sound. Let's blend the sounds to read it. f̣ ḷ ạ p̣, flap
Graphophonic Cues

"I see a bug," said Yan.
26 "I see a bug flap its wings."

112

Visual Literacy

VIEWING AND REPRESENTING

Ask children to look at the inset pictures of the ant, ladybug, spider, and butterfly on pages 101, 105, 109, and 113. Ask children questions such as:

- Do you think that ants are really that size?
- Have you ever seen a ladybug that big?
- Why do you think the photographs of those bugs are so big?

Explain that pictures and photographs in books are shown larger than life to provide more detail, so that readers can get a better look at those things.

LANGUAGE SUPPORT

ESL Write the sentence *"I see a bug," said Yan.* on the chalkboard. Ask children how many words are in the sentence. (six) Cut the sentence apart and count the words with the children. Invite volunteers to order the words to make the sentence.

"It flies about and sips from flowers," said Miss Kim. (27)

113

Comprehension

(27) **Phonics** **DOUBLE CONSO-NANTS** Can you find the word that ends with *ss*? We have seen this blend before. Let's blend the sounds of the letters together. M i ss, Miss *Graphophonic Cues*

LANGUAGE SUPPORT

ESL Cut apart the bugs from the bug chart and laminate them to create Bug Cards. Make a stack of the cards and ask a child to choose the top card. Have the child describe how the bug moves. Invite children to pantomime the movements of the bug. Encourage them to identify the bug and share any information that they know about it.

Comprehension

28 **Phonics** **BLENDS** Find the words that come before and after the word *and* in the second sentence. Now read the words with me, using your finger to help you remember to blend the sounds of the letters together. s l i m, slim; f l a t, flat *Graphophonic Cues*

"There it is again!" said Rick.

28 "Now it looks slim and flat."

114

Cross Curricular: Social Studies

BUTTERFLY MIGRATIONS Though they seem delicate, some butterflies travel thousands of miles each year.

Activity On a map, point out Mexico City and have children track the general direction from their state to Mexico City. ▶ **Visual/Spatial**

RESEARCH AND INQUIRY Ask the librarian to help children research other animals or insects that migrate.

*inter***NET** **CONNECTION** Help children log on to **www.mhschool.com/ reading** to find out more about migrating animals.

"What bug is it?" said Yan.
"It is a butterfly!" said Jas. **29**

115

Comprehension

PHONOLOGICAL AWARENESS
Listen to the word *butterfly*. Clap to show each syllable. How many syllables does the word have? (three)

29 **MAIN IDEA** What bug did the children see after the spider? (butterfly) Let's color the picture of the butterfly for our bug charts. Try to make your butterfly look like the photo in the book. Let's add what details we know about butterflies to our charts. *Graphic Organizer*

Details	Details	Details	Details	Details
small	red, black	spins webs	flaps wings	
six legs	spots	fat	sips from	
digs	wings	thin legs	flowers	

PREVENTION/INTERVENTION

PHONOLOGICAL AWARENESS
Have children clap out the number of syllables in words.

- Say *caterpillar*. Have children clap once for each syllable.
- Say *bee*. Have children clap once for each syllable.

Say *caterpillar* and *bee* again. Have children clap out the number of syllables in each word. Ask children which word has more syllables—*ladybug* or *caterpillar*.

115

Comprehension

30 Let's read the first word on this page. What word is it? *(Hush)* What does the last sound in the word remind you of? (someone saying "be quiet".) Sometimes words sound like what they are describing.

31 Why do you think Jas is saying *"hush"*? (She wants everyone to be quiet. She is trying to hear the humming noise.) ***Make Inferences***

32 What do you think will happen next in the story? *Make Predictions*

Fluency

READ WITH EXPRESSION

ONE Have children take turns reading page 116. Point out the exclamation mark. Remind children to:

- think about how Jas is feeling when she sees the bug.
- pause at the end of sentences.
- change their speed of reading, depending on what the character is saying.

30 "Hush!" said Jas.
31 "What is that hum?"
32

116

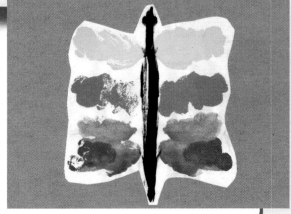

Activity

Cross Curricular: Art

BUTTERFLY PICTURES Give each child a large sheet of construction paper. Demonstrate how to fold it in half, and then lay it out flat. Ask children to choose three colors of paint. Have them put small dollops, lines, or circles of paint on one side. Then have them put a thin line of black paint in the center. Finally, have children fold their papers over and rub from the center outward, then gently rub up and down. When children open their sheets of paper, they will see their butterflies. Suggest that children cut out shapes of butterflies. ▶ **Spatial/Kinesthetic**

"Let that bug pass!" said Jill.
"Do not smack at it."

117

Comprehension

33 **Phonics** **DOUBLE CONSO-NANTS** *"Let that bug . . . "* hmm . . . I need to figure out that word. The two *s*'s at the end of the word make the sound /s/. I can blend the sounds: p a ss, pass
Graphophonic Cues

Comprehension

(34) MAIN IDEA/SUPPORTING DETAILS What is the last bug that the children see? (bee) Let's color the bee in our bug charts and add some details. Now let's think about the main idea of the story. Look at your charts. What can you tell me about bugs? (There are many different kinds of bugs.) Let's write our main idea at the bottom of our charts. *Graphic Organizer*

Details	Details	Details	Details	Details
small	red, black	spins webs	flaps wings	Buzzes
six legs	spots	fat	sips from	can sting
digs	wings	thin legs	flowers	

Retell the Story

Have small groups work together to use their bug charts to retell the story.

(34) "It will buzz," said Miss Kim. "But let it do its job."

118

REREADING FOR *Fluency*

PARTNERS Have partners take turns reading the story aloud. Have them look for exclamation marks and read these sentences in an excited voice.

READING RATE When you evaluate reading rate, have children read aloud from the story for one minute. Place a stick-on note after the last word read. Count words read. To evaluate children's performance, see the Running Record in the **Fluency Assessment** book.

ⓘ Intervention For leveled fluency lessons, passages, and norms charts, see **Skills Intervention Guide**, Part 5, Fluency.

"What bug is it?" said Jas.
"It is a bee, so be careful!" **35**
said Jill.

119

Comprehension

35 **HOMOPHONES** What is Jill's joke?
(She used the words *bee* and *be* in the same sentence.)

Return to Predictions and Purposes

Reread children's predictions about the story. Ask if the story answered the questions they had before they began reading.

Have children discuss the strategy of using the bug charts. Did they feel that the pictures helped them to remember the details about the bugs? Did using the charts help them figure out the main idea of the story?

INFORMAL ASSESSMENT

HOW TO ASSESS

Phonics **BLENDS** Have children turn to page 117 and read the third word in the second sentence. *(smack)*

MAIN IDEA/SUPPORTING DETAILS Ask children to tell the main idea of the story in one or two sentences.

FOLLOW UP

Phonics **BLENDS** Provide word cards for words with blends. Model the blending of the sounds as children read.

MAIN IDEA/SUPPORTING DETAILS
Take a **picture walk** through the book and have children point out details of the story.

LITERARY RESPONSE

QUICK-WRITE Ask children to draw a picture of their favorite bug in the story. Have them write something that they learned about the bug.

ORAL RESPONSE Have children use their journal entries and bug charts to discuss these questions:

• Why did you choose this bug?
• What do you know about this bug?

SENTENCE STRIPS Children can use strips 1–40 to retell the story.

> 1
> "Look around," said Miss Kim.

> 2
> "You will see lots of bugs."

Story Questions

Tell children that now they will read some questions about the story. Help children read the questions. Discuss possible answers.

Answers:

1. Jill saw a ladybug. *Literal/Details*

2. This story takes place outside, perhaps in a park or nature center. *Inferential/Make Inferences*

3. Bees should be left alone because they will sting you. *Inferential/Make Inferences*

4. Answers will vary. Accept appropriate story summaries. *Critical/Summarize*

5. No; *What Bug Is It?* is realistic, and *The Bug Bath* is a fantasy story. *Critical/Reading Across Texts*

Write a Riddle Have children read the directions in their anthologies. You may want to have children brainstorm ideas for riddles before writing one of their own.

Story Questions & Activities

READ TOGETHER

1. Which bug did Jill see?

2. Where does this story take place?

3. Why should bees be left alone?

4. What did you learn from this story?

5. Is this story like "The Bug Bath"?

Write a Riddle

Draw a picture of a bug.
Turn the drawing over.
Write a riddle about the bug.
Share it with the class.

When it bites, I get an itch. What is it?

Meeting Individual Needs

EASY	ON-LEVEL	CHALLENGE

EASY

Name_____ Date_____ Reteach 69

Story Comprehension

Circle the pictures that tell about "What Bug Is It?"

1.
2.
3.
4.
5.
6.

Book 1.2
What Bug Is It?

At Home: Have children describe the bugs in "What Bug Is It?" Which bugs are their favorites?

69

ON-LEVEL

Name_____ Date_____ Practice 69

Story Comprehension

Think about "What Bug Is It?" Then read the sentences. Use the names of bugs to complete the sentences.

| butterfly | ants | ladybug | bee | spider |

BEGINNING

1. Rick can see bugs in a hill. He sees ___ants___

MIDDLE

2. Jill sees a red and black ___ladybug___

3. Nell looks at a ___spider___ in a web.

4. Yan sees a ___butterfly___ flap and flap.

END

5. The last bug they see is a ___bee___.

Book 1.2
What Bug Is It?

At Home: Ask children to draw a picture of one of the bugs from the story.

69

CHALLENGE

Name_____ Date_____ Extend 69

Story Comprehension

| butterfly | ladybug | spider |
| bugs | ant | bee |

What is the story about? Answer the questions

What do the children see?
_____
bugs

What bug is small, has six legs, and digs a hill?
_____
ant

What bug is red with black spots?
_____
ladybug

What bug will use its web to snag?
_____
spider

What bug can flap its wings?
_____
butterfly

What other bug did the children see?
_____
bee

Book 1.2
What Bug Is It?

At Home: Ask children to write a story using the information they have learned.

69

Reteach, 69   Practice, 69   Extend, 69

Sing a Song

Use pipe cleaners to make a spider.
Then sing "Itsy Bitsy Spider."
Move your spider as you sing.

Find Out More

Learn how a caterpillar turns into a butterfly.
Write about it.

121

Story Activities

Sing a Song

Materials: pipe cleaners, construction paper

Read the directions aloud. Help children who have questions. You may wish to have children work with partners to make their spiders and sing the song. Invite volunteers to perform an act for the class: one partner moves the spider while the other partner sings.

Find Out More

RESEARCH AND INQUIRY Read the directions aloud, and help children who have questions. Have them draw pictures to illustrate what they write. Encourage interested children to create posters showing the process of a caterpillar turning into a butterfly. Have them label their posters, and display them for the class.

 Go to **www.mhschool.com/reading** for more information or activities on caterpillars and butterflies.

FORMAL ASSESSMENT

After page 121, see Selection Assessment.

DAILY Phonics ROUTINES

DAY 3 **Blending** Write the following words on the chalkboard: *slid, flap, slam,* and *fill.* Have children blend and read each word.

Phonics CD-ROM

Study Skills

MAPS

BJECTIVES

Students will learn to read a map to gather information.

Remind children that they have just read a story about a class that is studying outside. Most classes usually take place inside a classroom, in a school. Tell them that now they will read a map showing where the school is.

Display **Teaching Chart 39**. Have children read the labels and street names on the map. Discuss the fact that the map shows the neighborhood the school is in, including the streets and houses. Have children point out the school, the firehouse, and the nature center. Point to the compass rose and explain how it works. Then help children read the questions below the map in their books, encouraging them to identify the labels and items that help them answer each question.

STUDY SKILLS

READ TOGETHER

A Street Map
A map helps us find our way.

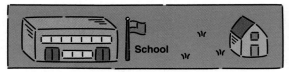

Bug Street

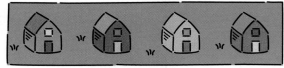

Web Lane

Fire Station

Ant Road

Nature Center

Look at the Map

❶ On what street is the school?

❷ Show how to get from the school to the nature center.

Meeting Individual Needs

EASY	ON-LEVEL	CHALLENGE

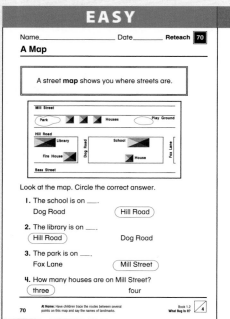

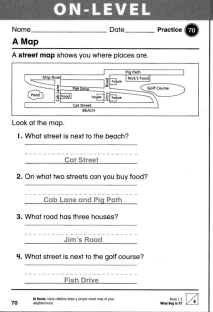

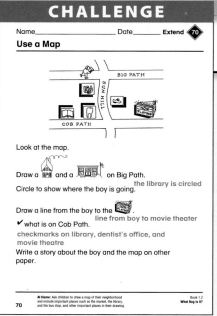

Reteach, 70   **Practice, 70**   **Extend, 70**

TEST POWER

Honey Bees

It is summer.

The bees are buzzing.

They fly from flower to flower.

They get nectar from the flowers.

They make honey from the nectar.

We can eat honey.

It is good on toast.

It is good in tea.

Definition box:
nectar – sugar-water that flowers make

In this story, what makes the honey?

● The bees

○ The tea

Reading the story again can help you answer the question.

123

Test Power

Read the Page

Explain to children that you will be reading this story as a group. You will read the story, and they will follow in their books.

Request that children put pens, pencils, and markers away, since they will not be writing in their books.

Discuss the Question

Children should reread the story and look for the mention of "honey." Then ask them what the word "they" refers to. Point out that the word "they" in this story must mean the bees. Make sure children understand the meaning of "nectar" (sweet water made by plants).

Test-Tip

The answer to the question is always in the story—all you have to do is read carefully to find it.

Leveled Books

EASY

Around Bug Town

☑ **Introduce Blends and Double Consonants**

☑ **Main Idea/Supporting Details**

High-Frequency Words: *about, again, around, use*

written by Sherry Tuseth Jackson
illustrated by James Williamson

Guided Reading

PREVIEW AND PREDICT Discuss each illustration, incorporating the high-frequency words. As you take the **picture walk**, ask children to predict what they think will happen in the story.

SET PURPOSES Ask children to write why they want to read *Around Bug Town*. For example: *I want to know what different types of bugs do.*

READ THE BOOK Use these questions to guide children's reading or after they have read independently.

Page 2: Let's look at the picture. What are the bugs doing? (being busy around town) *Main Idea, Supporting Details*

Page 4: Who can find a vocabulary word on this page? (*again*) Read the sentence that has this word. (second sentence) *High-Frequency Words*

Page 6: Look at the word spelled *f-l-a-p*. Model: I can blend together the sounds of the letters to read it. The sounds /f/-/l/-/a/-/p/ blend together as f l a p. The word is *flap*. *Phonics and Decoding*

Page 7: What words start with /sl/? (slosh, slips) *Phonics and Decoding*

Page 8: Notice the punctuation marks at the end of the sentences. The last sentence ends with an exclamation mark, and it means we should read the sentence with excitement. Let's reread the sentence. Why are the bugs running away from the anteater? (Anteaters eat ants and other bugs.) *Track Print/Make Inferences*

Help children identify the cricket (p. 3), bee (p. 4), grasshopper (p. 5), butterfly (p. 6), caterpillar (p. 7), and anteater (p. 8), as well as ladybugs and ants throughout.

RETURN TO PREDICTIONS AND PURPOSES Reread children's predictions. Explore which were close and why. Ask children to share their purposes for reading. Were their purposes met?

LITERARY RESPONSE Use questions such as the following to engage children in a discussion about the story.

- Do you like bugs? Why or why not? Did this story change your opinion of bugs?

Also see the story questions and activity in *Around Bug Town*.

See the **Phonics** CD-ROM for practice with blends and double consonants.

Intervention **Skills**

Intervention Guide, for direct instruction and extra practice in vocabulary and comprehension

Answers to Story Questions

1. grasshoppers live in grass, spiders live in webs, ants live in an anthill, bees live in flowers
2. Crickets flip about, bees buzz, grasshoppers snack on grass, the butterfly uses its flat wings to pass, and the caterpillar slips and gets wet.
3. buzz, smack, flap, slosh
4. anteater
5. ant, ladybug, butterfly

The Story Questions and Activity below appear in the Easy Book.

Story Questions and Activity

1. Where does each of the bugs live?
2. Tell about what each of the bugs does in the story.
3. What are some sounds bugs make?
4. What scares the bugs?
5. Which of the bugs from this story were also in *What Bug Is It?*

Make a Bug Town

Draw and color a few bugs.

Cut them out.

Paste them on green paper to make your own Bug Town.

from Around Bug Town

Leveled Books

INDEPENDENT

A Box of Bugs

☑ **Introduce Blends and Double Consonants**

☑ **Main Idea/Supporting Details**

High-Frequency Words:
about, again, around, use

by Clark Maxwell
illustrated by Claude Martinot

Guided Reading

PREVIEW AND PREDICT Have children read the title. What do they think the story will be about? Then take a **picture walk** up to page 5, using the high-frequency words. Would children like to change their predictions?

SET PURPOSES Lead children to discuss why they want to read this story. For example: *I want to find out what Nell is going to do with the box.*

READ THE BOOK Use these prompts while the children are reading together or after they have read independently:

Page 2: Which word on this page begins with the *sm?* (smock) What sound do those letters make? (/sm/) *Phonics and Decoding*

Pages 3–4: What is Nell doing? (painting a box with bugs on it) *Main Idea and Supporting Details*

Page 5: Now let's look for words that begin with the sound /sl/. (slick, slugs) How is the sound /sl/ spelled? (sl) *Phonics and Decoding*

Page 6: What does Nell say about the tan bug? (that it is about as snug as a bug in a rug) *High-Frequency Words*

Page 7: Where is Nell putting the ants? (around the box) *High-Frequency Words*

Page 8: Why did Nell make the box? (to give to her Dad) Why do you think she gave him a box with bugs on it? *Main Idea and Supporting Details*

RETURN TO PREDICTIONS AND PURPOSES Have children review their predictions and purposes.

LITERARY RESPONSE: Ask the following questions to help focus children:

• Do you think Nell's present was a good present for her father? Why or why not?

• If you were going to make a box, how would you want to decorate it?

Also see the story questions and activity in *A Box of Bugs.*

See the **Phonics CD-ROM** for practice with blends and double consonants.

Answers to Story Questions

1. Nell painted a ladybug and seven slugs red.
2. Nell painted bugs on the box for her dad.
3. Answers will vary. Nell's dad studies bugs.
4. Nell painted a ladybug, a spider with a web, slugs, a bug, and lots of small ants.
5. an ant

The Story Questions and Activity below appear in the Independent Book.

Story Questions and Activity

1. What red things did Nell paint?
2. Why did Nell paint bugs on the box?
3. Why do you think Nell's dad liked her box so much?
4. Tell what Nell painted first, next, and last.
5. Name a bug from *What Bug Is It?* that Nell painted.

Paint a Box

Use a box with a lid.

Paint the box.

Glue on buttons or other things.

from A Box of Bugs

Leveled Books

SITTING IN MY BOX

by DEE LILLEGARD
pictures by JON AGEE

CHALLENGE

Sitting in My Box

☑ **Introduce Blends and Double Consonants**

☑ **Main Idea and Supporting Details**

Guided Reading

PREVIEW AND PREDICT As you take the **picture walk**, ask children to predict what will happen in the story. Chart their ideas.

SET PURPOSES Have children explain why they want to read the story. For example: *I want to find out about the animals.*

READ THE BOOK Use questions like the following to guide children's reading:

Pages 2–3: What book is the boy reading? (*Wild Animals*) Do you think the name of this book might be important? (Answers will vary.) *Main Idea and Supporting Details/Make Predictions*

Pages 4–5: Look at the word *g-i-r-a-f-f-e*. What sound do the *ff's* make? (/f/) Let's say the word aloud. *Phonics and Decoding*

Pages 6–13: What is the main idea of the story so far? (A lot of animals want to be in the box.) How do we know that? (They all ask to be let into the box.) *Main Idea and Supporting Details*

Pages 14–17: What is the problem? (There are too many animals in the box, and no one will leave.) *Problem and Solution*

Pages 28–29: How do you think the boy is feeling at the end of the story? How can you tell? (He is happy. He is smiling) *Make Inferences*

RETURN TO PREDICTIONS AND PURPOSES Have children review their predictions and purposes.

LITERARY RESPONSE You can use the following questions to engage children in a discussion about the story:

- What is the boy doing at the beginning of the story? Why is the book closed at the end?

- Were you surprised by what the flea caused?

Also see the story questions and activity in the story *Sitting in My Box*.

See the 🔵 **Phonics** **CD-ROM** for practice with blends and double consonants.

Answers to Story Questions

1. giraffe, elephant, baboon
2. A flea bites them.
3. a library
4. A boy sits in a box. He is reading a book about wild animals. Then wild animals climb in the box with him!
5. hippopotamus

The Story Questions and Activity below appear in the Challenge Book.

Story Questions and Activity

1. Name three animals in the box.
2. Why do the animals get out?
3. Name another quiet place to read.
4. Tell what happens in this story.
5. Which animals from *Whose Footprints?* are in this story?

Pretend You Are an Animal

Pretend you are an animal in the box. Draw a picture of how you feel. Write a sentence about your picture.

from *Sitting in My Box*

Bringing Groups Together

Connecting Texts

PLOT CHARTS Write the story titles on a chart. Have children discuss what happens in each story. Write their ideas on the charts. Lead them to see that each story involves bugs. Have them compare the different roles bugs play in each story.

Afterward, use the charts to inspire children to share their own knowledge about bugs.

What Bug Is It?	Around Bug Town	A Box of Bugs	Sitting in My Box
• Children see lots of bugs. • They tell what the bug looks like and what it does. • They teach each other the names of the bugs. • They make a joke about a bee.	• Bugs are busy animals in their habitats. • Each bug has its special job to do.	• Nell paints different kinds of bugs on her box. • She gives the box to her dad for a present. Her dad loves the box.	• A boy sits in a box reading a book about wild animals. • Animals come and sit in the box. It gets too crowded. • A flea goes into the box and makes the animals leave.

Viewing/Representing

GROUP PRESENTATIONS Divide the class into groups, one for each of the four books read in the lesson. (For *What Bug Is It?*, combine children of different reading levels.) Invite each group to make "pop-up" pictures of the main events and to use those pictures to tell what happens in their story. Afterwards they can pass around their "pop-ups" for the other children to examine.

AUDIENCE RESPONSE Ask children to listen carefully, ask questions, and tell what they liked about each group's presentation.

Research and Inquiry

MORE ABOUT BUGS Have children ask themselves: What else would I like to know about bugs? Then invite them to do the following:

- Look at picture books that depict bugs.

- Ask an entomologist to come to class and give a presentation.

- Design a bulletin board to show information and pictures about bugs.

inter NET CONNECTION Have children log on to **www.mhschool.com/reading** for links to web pages about bugs.

  In their journals, children can write and draw what they learned.

Review **Blends**

Children will:

- **read words with initial and final continuant blends and double consonants.**

- **review initial and final consonants and short vowels.**

MATERIALS
- **Teaching Chart 52**

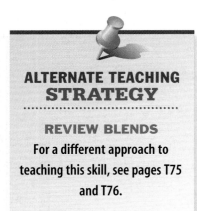

Skills Finder

Blends	
Introduce	B2: 96I–J; B3: 8I–J, 38I–J
Review	B2: 123G–H; B3: 37E–F, 37G–H, 67E–F, 67G–H
Test	Book 2, Book 3
Maintain	B3: 23; B4: 13

ALTERNATE TEACHING STRATEGY

REVIEW BLENDS
For a different approach to teaching this skill, see pages T75 and T76.

PREPARE

Listen for Words with Blends

Read the following sentences aloud. Have children raise their hands when they hear a word that begins with /sl/ or /sn/.

- The <u>slow</u> <u>snail</u> hardly moved.
- The <u>slippery</u> <u>snake</u> <u>slithered</u> away.

TEACH

Review Letters and Symbols

- Write the letters *sl* on the chalkboard, and make the sound. Invite children to say a word that begins with that sound.
- Continue with *sm*, *sn*, and *fl*.

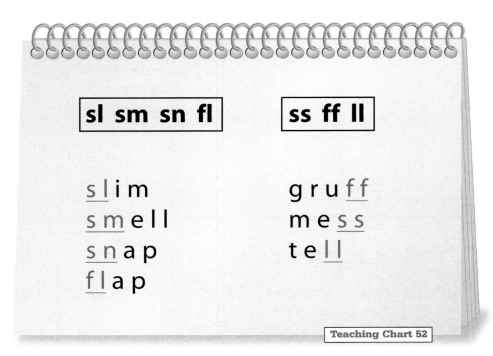

Teaching Chart 52

BLENDING Model and Guide Practice with Blends

- Display **Teaching Chart 52**. Run your hand under the letters *sl* and blend the sounds. s l, sl
- Repeat, having children blend the sounds with you.
- Write the letters to create the word *slim*.
- Run your hand under the letters of *slim*, blending them to read the word. s l i m, slim

Use the Word in Context

Have volunteers use the word in a sentence to reinforce its meaning. Example: *My father is tall and slim.*

PRACTICE

SEGMENTING
Recognize Words
with Blends

GROUP

Give each child a card with a blend written on it and write each blend on the chalkboard. Say a word that has an initial or final blend. Ask children holding the card with that blend to stand. Then ask all children to write the word. Classify the words into groups by having a volunteer write the word under its blend on the chalkboard. Have children switch cards as you continue the activity. ▶ **Auditory/Visual**

ASSESS/CLOSE

Build and Read
Words with
Blends

To assess children's ability to blend and read words with blends, observe them as they do the Practice activity. Ask each child to read aloud three words from his or her list.

ADDITIONAL PHONICS RESOURCES

Phonics/Phonemic Awareness
Practice Book,
pages 107–110

PHONICS KIT
Hands-on Activities and Practice

McGraw-Hill School
TECHNOLOGY
 **CD-ROM**

activities for practice with
Blending and Building Words

DAY 4 **Writing** Write the following sentence on the chalkboard: *Fred is a frog.* Ask children to write the sentence and draw a picture to go with it.

 **CD-ROM**

◈◈◈

SPELLING/PHONICS
CONNECTIONS

Words with blends: See 5-Day Spelling Plan, pages 123Q–123R.

ℹ **Intervention** ▶ **Skills**
Intervention Guide, for direct instruction and extra practice in Blends

Meeting Individual Needs for Phonics

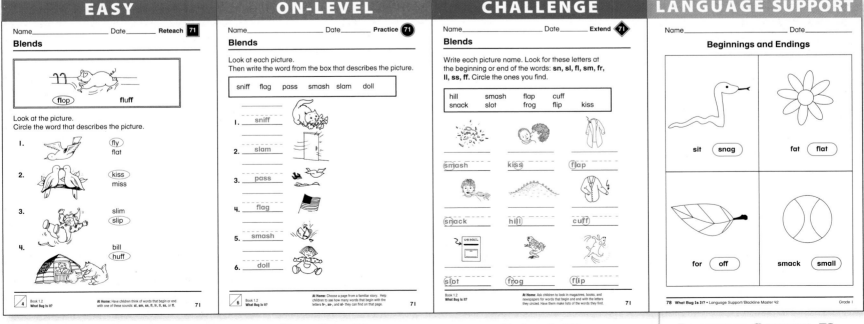

EASY	ON-LEVEL	CHALLENGE	LANGUAGE SUPPORT
Reteach, 71	Practice, 71	Extend, 71	Language Support, 78

Review Blends; sh, th, ck

OBJECTIVES

Children will:

- review blends; *sh, th, ck;* double consonants.
- cumulative review: initial and final consonants; short vowels.

. . . .

MATERIALS

- **Teaching Chart 53**
- letter cards from the **Word Building Manipulative Cards**
- **Phonics Practice Reader, Volume 1**

Skills Finder

Digraphs *sh, th*

Introduce	B1: 68I-J
Review	B1: 87E-F, 87G-H, 88I-J; B2: 35G-H, 123G-H
Test	Book 1
Maintain	B2: 19, 45; B5: 23, 269

ALTERNATE TEACHING STRATEGY

BLENDS AND DIGRAPHS

For a different approach to teaching this skill, see pages T75 and T76.

PREPARE

Identify Letters and Symbols in Blends, Digraphs, and Double Consonants

Remind children that the letters *s* and *l* blend together to form the sound /sl/. Write the letters *sl* on the chalkboard and say the sound. Continue with the letters *sm, sn, fl, fr, ff, ll,* and *ss.*

Write the digraphs *sh, th,* and *ck* on the chalkboard. Remind children that *sh, th,* and *ck* consist of two letters that when together make one sound. Ask volunteers to say words that begin or end with these sounds.

TEACH

BLENDING
Model and Guide Practice with Blends, Digraphs, and Double Consonants

- Display **Teaching Chart 53**. Tell children that they can make words by writing letters in the blank spaces.

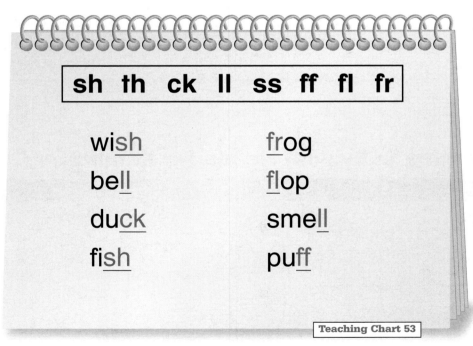

| sh th ck ll ss ff fl fr |

wi<u>sh</u>   <u>fr</u>og

be<u>ll</u>   <u>fl</u>op

du<u>ck</u>   sme<u>ll</u>

fi<u>sh</u>   pu<u>ff</u>

Teaching Chart 53

- Create the word *wish* and blend. w i sh, wish
- Repeat the process with *with, wick* and other words.

Use the Words in Context

After the **Teaching Chart** is completed, say a sentence with a word omitted. Ask volunteers to choose a word that makes sense in the sentence. Example: *Before blowing out the candles, I make a _____.*

Repeat the Procedure

- Continue with **Teaching Chart 53**. Have children say the sounds aloud and create words.

PRACTICE

SEGMENTING
Read Words with Blends and Digraphs

GROUP

Divide children into two groups. Give each child in one group a letter card with a digraph or letter cards for blends. Give children in the other group cards with the words that contain these blends and digraphs. Children look for and find the letters and words that match. Children say each sound and then say the whole word.

▶ **Linguistic/Visual**

ASSESS/CLOSE

Recognize and Write Blends and Digraphs

Observe children during the Practice activity. Show a card and write the word on the chalkboard, omitting the blend or digraph. Invite the children to write the missing blend or digraph.

Read A Decodable Story

For additional practice reading words with blends, double consonants, and digraphs, and to develop fluency, direct children to read the story *Bee and Duck* from the **Phonics Practice Reader, Volume 1.**

ADDITIONAL PHONICS RESOURCES

Phonics/Phonemic Awareness Practice Book,
pages 107–110

PHONICS KIT
Hands-on Activities and Practice

McGraw-Hill School
TECHNOLOGY
Phonics CD-ROM
activities for practice with
Blending and Building Words

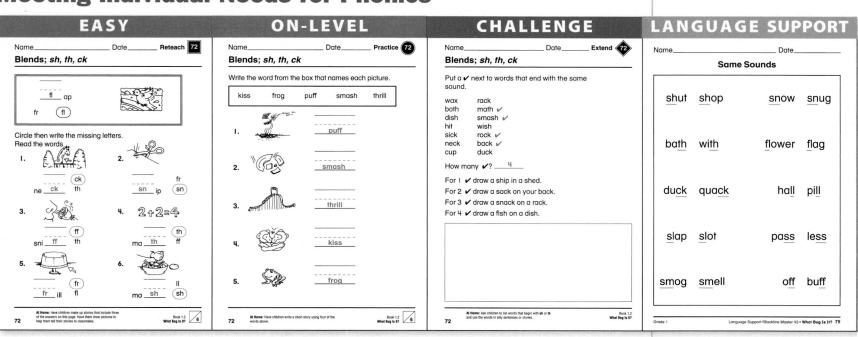

DAILY Phonics ROUTINES

DAY 5
Fluency Write a list of words with the initial blend: *sl, sn, fl, fr,* that have short vowels. Have children work in pairs, taking turns reading the words.

Phonics CD-ROM

i Intervention **Skills Intervention Guide,** for direct instruction and extra practice in Blends, Double Consonants, and Digraphs

Meeting Individual Needs for Phonics

EASY	ON-LEVEL	CHALLENGE	LANGUAGE SUPPORT
Reteach, 72	Practice, 72	Extend, 72	Language Support, 79

123H

OBJECTIVES

Children will identify main idea and supporting details.

MATERIALS
• Teaching Chart 54

Skills Finder

Main Idea

Introduce	B2: 95I-J
Review	B2: 123I-J, 137G-H
Test	Book 2
Maintain	B3: 61, 91; B4: 89

TEACHING TIP

IMPORTANT AND UNIMPORTANT INFORMATION Read the following sentences. Ask children to identify the sentences that give information about bugs: *Bugs are small. Bees make honey. I like honey. Spiders have eight legs.* Learning to differentiate between important and unimportant information will help children recognize the main idea more easily.

SELECTION CONNECTION

Children may choose from the following titles.

ANTHOLOGY
• *What Bug Is It?*

LEVELED BOOKS
• *Around Bug Town*
• *A Box of Bugs*
• *Sitting in My Box*

Bibliography, pages T98–T99

Review Main Idea and Supporting Details

PREPARE

Review the Concept   Remind children that the main idea tells what the story is about. Recognizing the main idea helps us understand the story. Supporting details help tell more about the main idea.

TEACH

Model Main Idea and Details   Display **Teaching Chart 54**. Discuss the picture and read the sentences aloud.

What Is the Bee Doing?

The bee has stripes.
Bees find pollen to make honey.
Honey is good to eat.

Teaching Chart 54

MODEL I want to find out what the picture is mainly about. The stripes tell me something about the bee. Honey is good to eat, but that doesn't tell me what the picture is about. The main idea is about the bee finding pollen to make honey.

Have children underline the sentence on the **Teaching Chart** that identifies the main idea. Then have them tell in their own words why this sentence tells the main idea of the pictures. Ask them to circle the supporting details.

PRACTICE

Add Details

ONE

Have children refer to the picture on **Teaching Chart 54**. Ask them if they can think of more details to add about the picture. Help them write their sentences on the chalkboard. ▶ **Visual/Linguistic**

ASSESS/CLOSE

Identify the Main Idea

Read a short informational article from a children's magazine or book. Work together to write a sentence that tells the main idea of the story. Ask questions such as: What is the article mainly about? What are some details that tell us more about the main idea?

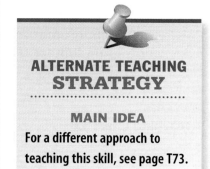

ALTERNATE TEACHING
STRATEGY
· · · · · · · · · · · · · · · · ·
MAIN IDEA
For a different approach to teaching this skill, see page T73.

> **Intervention** ▶ **Skills**
> **Intervention Guide,** for direct instruction and extra practice in Main Idea

Meeting Individual Needs for Comprehension

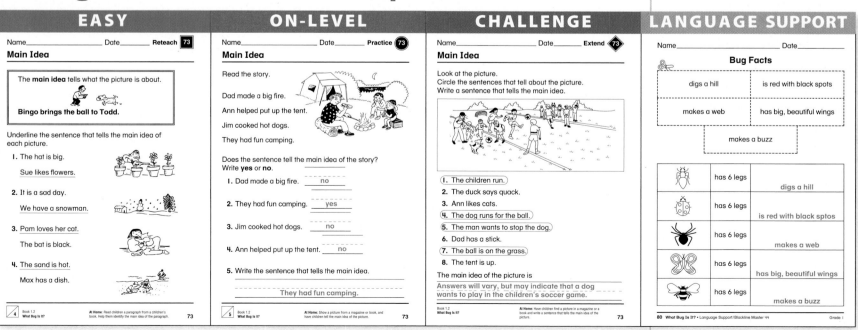

| Reteach, 73 | Practice, 73 | Extend, 73 | Language Support, 80 |

123J

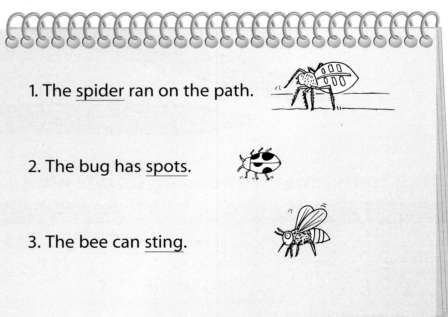

Review **Context Clues**

TESTED

OBJECTIVES

Children will identify unfamiliar words using context clues.

....

MATERIALS
• **Teaching Chart 55**

Skills Finder

Context Clues	
Introduce	B1: 87K-L
Review	B2: 123K-L, 137K-L; B5: 141 K-L
Test	Bk. 1, Bk. 2, Bk. 5 U. 1
Maintain	B2: 21, 87; B4: 75

TEACHING **TIP**

PHONICS CLUES Some children may be jumping to conclusions based on pictures alone, and not looking for phonics clues. To encourage them to keep using phonics clues, point out that a picture can represent two words. *Hand* and *fingers* could be represented by the same picture. Using picture *and* phonics clues will ensure that children figure out the word in question.

PREPARE

Be a Word Detective   On the chalkboard, draw a simple picture of two flowers. Write below it: *I like flowers a lot.* Point to the word *flowers*. Say: *This is a big word and I don't know how to read it. But I think the picture helps. What does it show?* (flowers) Have them identify any familiar sounds (/fl/ at the beginning) to "prove" that they're correct.

TEACH

Pictures Give Clues   Display **Teaching Chart 55.** Have children look at the first sentence while you read it, saying "blank" when you come to the underlined word.

1. The <u>spider</u> ran on the path.

2. The bug has <u>spots</u>.

3. The bee can <u>sting</u>.

Teaching Chart 55

MODEL I know something ran on the path. I count eight legs on the creature. Maybe it's an octopus. But this word starts with *s* and *p*. That makes the sound /sp/. What do I know that has eight legs and starts with /sp/? Can anybody tell me? (spider) What's the last sound in this word? (/ər/) What's the last sound in *spider*? (/ər/) What do you think this word is? (spider) You're very good word detectives!

Have a volunteer read the sentence. Repeat with the second and third sentences, having children do the sounding out themselves.

PRACTICE

Discover Words from Picture Clues and Phonics Clues

GROUP

Remind children that when they see an unfamiliar word, they can often figure it out from picture clues and "sound clues" in the word itself. Tell the class that you are going to write sentences with three unfamiliar words. For each sentence, you'll draw a picture to help them figure out the unfamiliar word. You will also give them a "sound clue."

1. This is my <u>hand</u>. (It begins with the same sound as *hen*.)

2. Here is a bug with two <u>wings</u>. (It begins with the same sound as *winter*.)

3. Ken saw <u>spots</u>. (It begins with the same sound as *spin*.)

ASSESS/CLOSE

Read Unfamiliar Words

Invite volunteers to go back and read aloud page 111 or 113 from *What Bug Is It?* Remind them that the pictures give clues to the unfamiliar words. Also encourage them to use the letter sounds they know to prove they've figured the word out correctly.

ALTERNATE TEACHING STRATEGY

CONTEXT CLUES

For a different approach to teaching this skill, see page T74.

Intervention ▶ Skills Intervention Guide, for direct instruction and extra practice in Context Clues

Meeting Individual Needs for Vocabulary

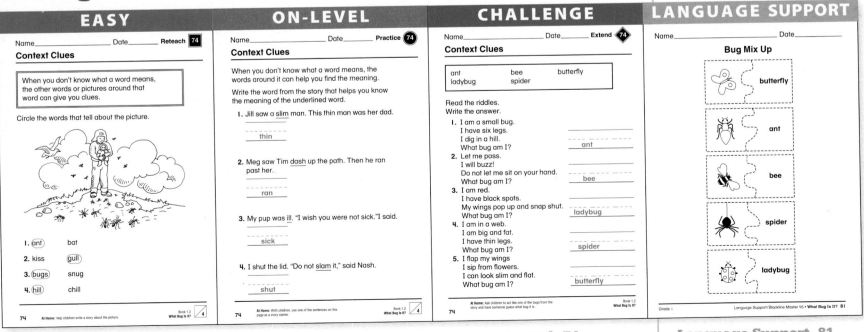

Reteach, 74

Practice, 74

Extend, 74

Language Support, 81

Handwriting CD-ROM

GRAMMAR/SPELLING
CONNECTIONS

Proper Nouns: See the 5-Day Grammar and Usage Plan, pages 123O–123P.

Words with Continuant/ Continuant Blends (initial/final) *sn, fl, ll, ss, ff*: See 5-Day Spelling Plan, pages 123Q–123R.

TEACHING TIP

Technology
Remind children who use the computer to include a heading on each page of their work. Computer-savvy children may use the "header" in their word-processing programs. Others can simply type a new heading on each page.

Interactive Writing
Write an Article

Prewrite

LOOK AT THE STORY PATTERN Have children revisit *What Bug Is It?*, and guide them to notice again the language pattern of the story. Then tell them that the class will create an article about bugs. The article will explain where to find bugs, and how to identify them. List children's ideas for bugs they'd like to include. Then have them explain how they know which bugs are which, following the language pattern of the story.

Draft

WRITE BUG DESCRIPTIONS Help children decide what to write about each bug. Guide them to explain where they might find that bug, and how they can tell which one it is. Suggest a sentence sequence using the language pattern from *What Bug Is It?*

- Begin by saying, for example, *I see a bug. It is yellow and black. It goes "buzz buzz." What bug is it?* (a bee). As you say a word with familiar sounds and patterns, challenge children to come up and write the word. Write all unfamiliar words yourself.

- Help children write sentences explaining how they know which bug it is. For example, *A bug that buzzes is a bee.* Urge them to explain where they might see such a bug. Continue this process for the other bugs suggested by the children.

Revise

CAPITALIZATION Ask children to reread their bug descriptions. Have them check to see that each sentence begins with a capital letter. Then have children find all the nouns in their descriptions. For each noun, ask: *Is this a proper noun? If it is, it should start with a capital letter. Does it?*

Publish

CREATE A BOOK Reread the article together. Then ask children to make a book using the article. Discuss different ways of illustrating it. Have children create illustrations, then copy the appropriate text onto each page. They can number the pages and create a table of contents.

A mosquito bites you. The bite itches.

Presentation Ideas

MAKE A BUG MURAL Invite children to create a class mural showing the different kinds of places they might find bugs: a flower, the grass, the side of a house, a beehive, and so on. Then have them draw pictures of their favorite bugs and paste them onto the appropriate place on the mural. ▶ **Representing/Viewing**

PERFORM A BUG SCENE Guide groups of children to invent a scene where they play the roles of bugs describing humans. Have them explain how they know what kinds of humans they're seeing (Examples: a doctor, a teacher, a schoolchild, a baby).
▶ **Speaking/Listening**

Listening and Viewing

LISTENING STRATEGIES
Have classmates listen attentively to the actors so they can ask any questions they have to elicit more detailed descriptions from the "bugs."

VIEWING STRATEGIES
Ask children to use the pictures on the mural as a guide while drawing their own bugs.

LANGUAGE SUPPORT

ESL If children need help writing, have them refer to *What Bug Is It?* and look closely at the language pattern. Have them work together with fluent partners to draw a bug and write simple identifying labels (*It has six legs, It digs a hill,* and so on.) Have them exchange pictures and figure out from the labels what bug they each drew.

PORTFOLIO Invite children to include their articles or another writing project in their portfolio.

Meeting Individual Needs for Writing

EASY

Draw Pictures Children can draw pictures showing themselves looking at bugs. Encourage them to represent their feelings about bugs on the drawing of their face. Are they afraid? Do they think bugs are disgusting? Do they think bugs are fascinating? Have them label each picture with one fact about the bug.

ON-LEVEL

New Story Children can work in pairs to write a new story about bugs. Have them write the story making believe that they are the bugs. (Example: *I have six legs. I dig a hill. I am an ant.*)

CHALLENGE

Journal Entry Children can imagine that they are on a field trip to find bugs. Have them explain where they would look and why, and describe what they find.

5 Day Grammar and Usage Plan

LANGUAGE SUPPORT

For children who have difficulty with proper nouns, write sentences on the chalkboard that contain vocabulary familiar to your second-language learners. Have children complete sentences with nouns.

Example:

My name is _____.

I live in _____.

DAY 1 — Introduce the Concept

Oral Warm-Up Ask children the names of people they know. Write a brief list on the chalkboard and emphasize each capital letter.

Introduce Proper Nouns Remind children that a *noun* is a word that names a person, a place, or a thing. Discuss:

> **Proper Nouns**
> - Some nouns name a special person or place.
> - This kind of noun is called a **proper noun**.
> - A proper noun begins with a capital letter.

Daily Language Activity Write the following on the board and read aloud: *Did you see Max?* Ask children which word names a special person and what kind of letter it starts with. (*Max;* capital letter)

WRITING — Assign the daily Writing Prompt on page 96E.

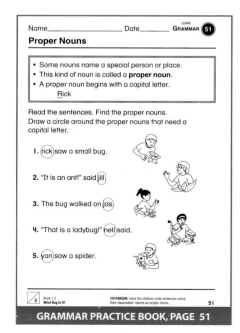

GRAMMAR PRACTICE BOOK, PAGE 51

DAY 2 — Teach the Concept

Review Proper Nouns Remind children that the names of special people begin with capital letters. Write the following on the board: *Where is Jack? Jack went to Dallas.* Ask children which word names a special person. (*Jack*) Tell children that the name of a special place begins with a capital letter, too. Point to the capital *D* in *Dallas.*

Daily Language Activity Write the following on the board and read aloud: *Did Pam have a hat? I live on Hill Street.* Ask children to identify the words that name a special place and person. (*Pam; Hill Street*) Then have children identify the words that should begin with capital letters in the following sentences: *I can see sam. We go to pine Lake.* (*Sam; Pine Lake*)

WRITING — Assign the daily Writing Prompt on page 96E.

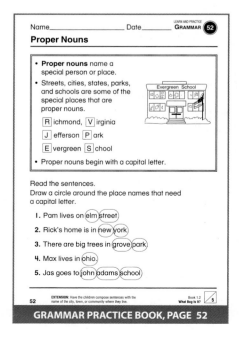

GRAMMAR PRACTICE BOOK, PAGE 52

Proper Nouns

DAY 3 — Review and Practice

Learn from the Literature Discuss with children what proper nouns are. Write the following sentences from *What Bug Is It?* on the chalkboard:

> "Look around," said <u>Miss Kim</u>.
>
> "I see a bug," said <u>Rick</u>.

Ask children to identify the words that name special people. Then ask children what kind of letters begin the names of special people or places. (capital letters)

Daily Language Activity Have children make a list of names of friends, streets, and cities. Then have them write a sentence containing a proper noun.

 WRITING Assign the daily Writing Prompt on page 96F.

DAY 4 — Review and Practice

Review Proper Nouns Write the following sentence on the chalkboard: *My mom's name is jill.* Ask children to tell how to write the sentence correctly. (*Jill* should begin with a capital letter.)

Daily Language Activity Ask children to come to the chalkboard and correct the following proper nouns: *sam; miss smith; pine street; america.* Have children use the proper nouns in sentences orally.

Mechanics and Usage Write the following sentence on the chalkboard. *Jack and Mack live on Red Bug Road.* Review:

> **Proper Nouns**
>
> The special name of a person or place begins with a capital letter.

 WRITING Assign the daily Writing Prompt on page 96F.

DAY 5 — Assess and Reteach

Daily Language Activity Write these sentences on the chalkboard. Read them with children. Have children identify the proper nouns in each sentence, telling how to write each one correctly.

1. Where is miss kim? Miss Kim

2. I saw a bug at brand park. Brand Park

3. I live on black street. Black Street

Assess Use page 55 of the **Grammar Practice Book** for assessment.

Reteach Write the sentences presented on Days 1 through 5 on the chalkboard without capitalizing the proper nouns. Have volunteers identify the special name of a person or place in each sentence and tell how to write it correctly. Have children write the corrected sentences, underlining the special name of a person or place in each sentence.

 WRITING Assign the daily Writing Prompt on page 96F.

Name_____ Date_____ **GRAMMAR** 53
PRACTICE AND WRITE

Proper Nouns

- **Proper nouns** name a special person or place.
- Proper nouns begin with a capital letter.

  [P] am lives on [S] pruce [S] treet.

  [J]ill's address is: [J] ill [M] ason
  124 [P] leasant [S] treet
  [H] amilton, [O] hio 42134

Write proper nouns that name people and places on the lines. Begin the names with capital letters.

My name is ___ Answers will vary.

My address is ___ Answers will vary.

___ Answers will vary.

___ Answers will vary.

Book 1.2
What Bug Is It? EXTENSION: Have the children compose sentences about local place names. 53

GRAMMAR PRACTICE BOOK, PAGE 53

Name_____ Date_____ **GRAMMAR** 54
MECHANICS

Proper Nouns

- A proper noun names a special person or place.
- A proper noun begins with a capital letter.

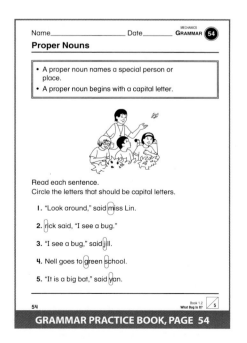

Read each sentence.
Circle the letters that should be capital letters.

1. "Look around," said miss Lin.

2. rick said, "I see a bug."

3. "I see a bug," said jill.

4. Nell goes to green school.

5. "It is a big bat," said yan.

54 Book 1.2
What Bug Is It? 5

GRAMMAR PRACTICE BOOK, PAGE 54

Name_____ Date_____ **GRAMMAR** 55
TEST

Proper Nouns

Read each sentence. Find the proper noun. Mark your answer.

1. We saw a spider at Green School.
   - (A) Green School
   - (B) We
   - (C) saw

2. "It will use its web to snag flies," said Miss Lin.
   - (A) It
   - (B) use
   - (C) Miss Lin

3. "It is a bee," said Jill.
   - (A) Jill
   - (B) a
   - (C) is

4. We saw bugs at Good Park.
   - (A) at
   - (B) We
   - (C) Good Park

5. "Let that bug pass!" said Jill.
   - (A) that
   - (B) Jill
   - (C) Let

5 Book 1.2
What Bug Is It? 55

GRAMMAR PRACTICE BOOK, PAGE 55

5Day Spelling Plan

Assess Prior Knowledge Write *pass, miss, doll,* and *puff* on the chalkboard. Circle the double consonants and have children say the ending sound in each word. (/s/, /l/, /f/) Then write *snap* and *flower.* Ask children to say the sounds the beginning letters make. Repeat with *flip.*

Write the Challenge Words. Read sentences aloud, and have children clap at each Challenge Word. Example: *Tell me again how to use it.*

Spelling Words		Challenge Words
1. **snap**	4. doll	7. **about**
2. **pass**	5. miss	9. **again**
3. **flat**	6. puff	8. **around**
		10. **use**

*Note: Words in **dark type** are from the story.*

Word Study On page 52 of the ***Spelling Practice Book*** are word study steps and an at-home activity.

Match the Pattern Write the words *snap, flat, pass, doll, miss,* and *puff* on the board. Have children find all the words that end with two letters that are the same. Then ask children to find the words that begin with the letters *fl* and *sn.* Have children blend the sounds of each word together to read them aloud.

To extend the activity, introduce other words that rhyme with the Spelling Words, for example: *tap, mat, class, kiss, bluff.*

LANGUAGE SUPPORT

ESL Reinforce the ending sounds *-ss* and *-ff* and beginning sounds *sn-* and *fl-* by leading children in this chant: *puff, puff, flat, flat, miss, miss, snap, snap.* Write the four words on the chalkboard and point to them as you repeat the chant together.

TEACHING TIP

The words in this lesson contain short-vowel sounds and follow the pattern CVCC or CCVC. Some pairs of consonants spell a single sound, while others spell two different sounds. Have children make letter boxes with one box for each sound in the word. Using the Spelling Words, have children fill in the letter or letters that spell each word.

Name_____ Date_____ Spelling **51**

Words with Blends

Complete each word by writing the letters **sn, fl, ss, ll,** or **ff** on the line.

1. ___**sn**___ ap   2. ___fl___ at

3. pa ___ss___   4. mi ___ss___

5. do ___ll___   6. pu ___ff___

Directions (to teacher)
Review the blend *sn* by explaining that the letters *sn* spell the sounds /s/ and /n/, which may come together at the beginning of a word. Write *snap* on the chalkboard or form the word with letter cards. Say the word aloud and have children repeat it. Then have children look at the first example on the page. Point out that the letters *sn* have been filled in.

Display the word *flat.* Say the word aloud and have children repeat it. Have them listen for the two beginning sounds /f/ and /l/. Then have children complete the second example.

Display the word *pass.* Have children listen for the consonant sound at the end of the word (/s/). Tell them it is written with two of the same letter (s). Have them complete the third example.

Write the words *miss, doll,* and *puff* on the chalkboard. Read the words aloud and have children repeat them. Have children listen for the consonant sound at the end of each word. Tell children each is written with two of the same letter. Have children complete each word on the line provided.

Book 1.2
What Bug Is It?   51

SPELLING PRACTICE BOOK, PAGE 51

Name_____ Date_____ Spelling **53**

Words with Blends

Look at the spelling words in the box.

snap pass flat doll miss puff

Write the word that begins with **sn.**

1. ___snap___

Write the word that begins with **fl.**

2. ___flat___

Write the words that end with two letters that are the same.

3. ___pass___   4. ___doll___

5. ___miss___   6. ___puff___

Book 1.2
What Bug Is It?   53

SPELLING PRACTICE BOOK, PAGE 53

WORD STUDY STEPS AND ACTIVITY, PAGE 52

Words with Blends

DAY 3 — Practice and Extend

Word Meaning: Answer Riddles
Write the Spelling Words on the chalkboard. Invite volunteers to use the words to answer riddles. For example:

> **This word means smooth, without bumps.** (flat)
>
> **Lots of children have this kind of toy.** (doll)
>
> **People do this with their fingers.** (snap)
>
> **This is what the wolf did in *The Three Little Pigs*.** (puff)

Identify Spelling Patterns Write this sentence on the chalkboard: *Can you snap your fingers again?* Read it aloud as you track print. Have children read it aloud. Invite volunteers to circle the word with the spelling pattern *sn* and underline the Challenge Word. Repeat with other patterns and words.

DAY 4 — Practice and Write

Match the Pattern Create a concentration game using the Spelling Words and other words that follow the same spelling patterns for a total of ten words. For each word, fold a piece of paper in half and write the word on the inside. Number the folded pieces from 1 to 10 on the outside and display them. Have volunteers choose two numbers, read the words, and determine if the spelling patterns match. Remove the matching pairs. Repeat until all words are matched.

WRITING Have children use as many Spelling Words as possible in the daily Writing Prompt on page 96F. Remind them to check their writing for errors in spelling, grammar, and punctuation.

DAY 5 — Assess and Reteach

Optional Spelling Test You may wish to give children a spelling test. You may administer the test in the following manner: (1) Read the word. (2) Give a simple sentence containing the word. (3) Say the word again. Or you may use page 56 of the **Spelling Practice Book** for the posttest. If you wish, you may create additional sentences for the Challenge Words.

Personal Word List Have children write any words they still find difficult on the personal "troublesome words" lists in their journals. Children should refer to the list during later writing activities.

(Spelling Practice Book, Page 54)

Name_____ Date_____ **Spelling 54**

Words with Blends

Look at the spelling words in the box. Then read the story below. Complete each spelling word.

| snap pass flat doll miss puff |

Jill has a do ___ll___ . She calls it

Mi ___ss___ Nell. The doll is ___fl___ at,

but it has a big pu ___ff___ of hair. It has a hat.

The hat can ___sn___ ap on. Jill said to Max,

"Pa ___ss___ me Miss Nell."

54

SPELLING PRACTICE BOOK, PAGE 54

(Spelling Practice Book, Page 55)

Name_____ Date_____ **Spelling 55**

Words with Blends

Look at the picture. Complete each sentence with a spelling word.

1. Can you ___snap___ your fingers?

2. The tire is ___flat___ .

3. My ___doll___ has a red dress.

4. Please ___pass___ me the dish.

5. "I will huff and ___puff___ !" said the big bad wolf.

6. Hit the ball! Do not ___miss___ that ball!

55

SPELLING PRACTICE BOOK, PAGE 55

(Spelling Practice Book, Page 56)

Name_____ Date_____ **Spelling 56**

Words with Blends

Look at the words in each set. One word in each set is spelled correctly. Use a pencil to color in the circle in front of that word. Before you begin, look at the sample sets of words. Sample A has been done for you. Do Sample B by yourself. When you are sure you know what to do, you may go on with the rest of the page.

Sample A
- (A) bell
- (B) bel
- (C) bbel

Sample B
- (D) cat
- (E) catt
- (F) kat

1.
- (A) mis
- (B) misse
- (C) miss

2.
- (D) doll
- (E) dol
- (F) dolle

3.
- (A) snape
- (B) snapp
- (C) snap

4.
- (D) pas
- (E) pass
- (F) passe

5.
- (A) filat
- (B) flatt
- (C) flat

6.
- (D) puuf
- (E) puff
- (F) puf

56

SPELLING PRACTICE BOOK, PAGE 56

123R

Cumulative Review with Expository Text

Time to Review

Anthology

A Vet

Selection Summary This week children will be reading about a vet. They will learn that vets take care of pets like dogs, cats, and ducks, and also bigger animals like horses and pigs.

Rhyme applies to Phonics

Listening Library

INSTRUCTIONAL pages 126–137

Time to Reread

Reread Leveled Books

EASY
Lesson on pages 137A and 137D
`DECODABLE`

INDEPENDENT
Lesson on pages 137B and 137D
🏠 *Take-Home version available*
`DECODABLE`

CHALLENGE
Lesson on pages 137C and 137D

Leveled Practice

EASY
Reteach, 75-82 Blackline masters with reteaching opportunities for each assessed skill

INDEPENDENT/ON-LEVEL
Practice, 75-82 Workbook with Take-Home Stories and practice opportunities for each assessed skill and story comprehension

CHALLENGE
Extend, 75-82 Blackline masters that offer challenge activities for each assessed skill

CENTER Activities

Social Studies ... A Veterinarian's Day, *124D*

Science .... A Healthy Pet, *128*
Home Sweet Home, *135*

Math .... Animal Word Patterns, *124D*

Language Arts .. Read Aloud, *124G*

Writing .... A List, *134*

Research and Inquiry ...... Find Out More, *135*

💻 **Internet Activities** .... www.mhschool.com/reading

Quizzes Prepared by Accelerated Reader®

Center Activities

Each of these activities takes 15-20 minutes.

Phonics

Identify Short Vowels

Objective: Sort pictures according to their vowel sounds.

◆ Label each can with a vowel.

◆ Children take turns choosing cards.

◆ The child says the letter on the card, names the picture, and places the card in the appropriate can.

◆ The child then says another word with the vowel sound.

MATERIALS
- Phonics Picture Cards for *cap*, *net*, *bib*, *pot*, and *sun*
- 5 large cans or boxes

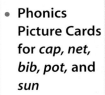

Writing

Pet Stories

Objective: Write a sentence or story about a pet.

◆ Have children draw a picture of a real or imaginary animal they have or would like to have as a pet.

◆ Children can write sentences to tell about their pet and how they care for it.

MATERIALS
- Paper
- Crayons
- Pencil

Reading and Listening

Independent/Self-Selected Reading

Objective: Listen and use illustrations to understand a story.

Fill the Center with books and corresponding audiocassettes or CD-ROMs children have read or listened to this week. You can also include books from the Theme Bibliography on pages T98 and T99.

Leveled Readers

◆ *Cam and Luck* by Gary Apple
◆ *Big?* by Rachel Lear
◆ *The Box* by Constance Andrea Keremes
◆ *Around Bug Town* by Sherry Tuseth Jackson
◆ *The Pup and the Cat* by Elizabeth King

◆ *The Big Sun* by Michael Maia
◆ *A Big, Big Pig* by Andrea Katz
◆ *A Box of Bugs* by Clark Maxwell
◆ *Five Little Ducks* by Jose Aruego
◆ *Whose Footprints?* by Masayuki Yabuuchi
◆ *Picnic Farm* by Christine Morton and Sarah Barringer
◆ *Sitting in My Box* by Dee Lillegard

◆ *A Vet* by *Time for Kids*
◆ "Cat Kisses" by Bobbi Katz

Working with Words

Find a Word

Objective: Reinforce vocabulary words: *small, want, good, out*.

MATERIALS
- *A Vet* in the Student Anthology
- Paper
- Pencil

◆ Children write each word.

◆ Then they look through *A Vet* and find the sentence that contains each word.

◆ Have children write the sentence and draw a square around the word.

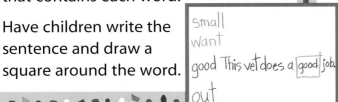

Social Studies

A Veterinarian's Day

Objective: Act out an interview.

MATERIALS
- Microphone

◆ Have one child act as the veterinarian, the other as the interviewer.

◆ The interviewer and "vet" should ask and answer questions about the vet's job.

Math

Animal Word Patterns

Objective: Create a pattern with animal names.

MATERIALS
- Pasta shapes
- Construction paper
- Glue

◆ Provide children with bowls of differently shaped cereal or pasta.

◆ Partners assign an animal from *A Vet* to each shape.

◆ Have them glue repeating patterns to paper and write the animal for each shape.

bird   bird   dog   cat   bird   bird

Suggested Lesson Planner

READING AND LANGUAGE ARTS	DAY 1 — *Focus on Reading and Skills*	DAY 2 — *Read the Literature*
Phonics Daily Routines	Daily Routine: Segmenting, 124J CD-ROM	Daily Routine: Blending, 126A  CD-ROM

Phonological Awareness
 	
 Phonics *Review*
 	
 Comprehension
 	
 Vocabulary
 	
 Study Skills
 	
 Listening, Speaking, Viewing, Representing
	Read Aloud, 124G
	 "Your Friendly Vet"
	
	 ☑ **Develop Phonological Awareness,** 124H
	
	 ☑ **Review Short *a, e, i, o, u*,** 124I–124J
	 Teaching Chart 56
	 Reteach, Practice, Extend, 75
	 Phonics/Phonemic Awareness
	 Practice Book, 111–114
	
	  Apply Review, 124/125
	 "At the Vet"
	
	 ⓘ Intervention Program
		Build Background, 126A
		 Develop Oral Language
		
		 Vocabulary, 126B–126C
		 small want
		 good out
		 Word Building Manipulative Cards
		 Teaching Chart 57
		 Reteach, Practice, Extend, 76
		
		  Read the Selection, 126–133
		 Guided Instruction
		 ☑ Cumulative Review
		 ☑ Main Idea
		
		 Genre: Narrative Nonfiction, 127

Curriculum Connections	Language Arts, 124G	Science, 126A
Writing	**Writing Prompt:** What if you were a dog or a cat? Write about going to the vet, and what you like or dislike about going.	**Writing Prompt:** Write about a pet who visits a vet on a holiday. Who are they? How do they spend the day? **Journal Writing** Quick-Write, 133
Grammar	**Introduce the Concept: Days, Months, and Holidays,** 137O Daily Language Activity: Identify days of the week. **Grammar Practice Book,** 57	**Teach the Concept: Days, Months, and Holidays,** 137O Daily Language Activity: Identify months and holidays. **Grammar Practice Book,** 58
Spelling *Words from Social Studies*	**Introduce: Words from Social Studies,** 137Q **Spelling Practice Book,** 57–58	**Teach the Patterns: Words from Social Studies,** 137Q **Spelling Practice Book,** 59

Meeting Individual Needs

☑ = **Skill Assessed in Unit Test**

ⓘ **Intervention Program Available**

Read EVERY DAY

DAY 3 Read the Literature	**DAY 4** Build Skills	**DAY 5** Build Skills
Daily **Phonics** Routine: **Fluency, 135** **Phonics CD-ROM**	Daily **Phonics** Routine: **Writing, 137F** **Phonics CD-ROM**	Daily **Phonics** Routine: **Letter Substitution, 137H** **Phonics CD-ROM**

Rereading for Fluency, 132
 	
Story Questions, 134
  Reteach, Practice, Extend, 77
 	
Story Activities, 135
 	
Study Skill, 136
  ☑ Maps
  Teaching Chart 58
  Reteach, Practice, Extend, 78
 	
Read the Leveled Books, Guided Reading
  ☑ Cumulative Review
  ☑ Main Idea
  ☑ High-Frequency Words
 	
ⓘ Intervention Program
	Read **Read the Leveled Books and Self-Selected Books**
	
	  ☑ **Review Story Elements, 137E–137F**
	    Teaching Chart 59
	    Reteach, Practice, Extend, 79
	    Language Support, 87
	
	  ☑ **Review Main Idea, 137G–137H**
	    Teaching Chart 60
	    Reteach, Practice, Extend, 80
	    Language Support, 88
	
	  Minilessons, 131
	
	ⓘ Intervention Program
		Read **Read Self-Selected Books**
		
		  ☑ **Review Inflectional Ending -ed, 137I–137J**
		    Teaching Chart 61
		    Reteach, Practice, Extend, 81
		    Language Support, 89
		
		  ☑ **Review Context Clues, 137K–137L**
		    Teaching Chart 62
		    Reteach, Practice, Extend, 82
		    Language Support, 90
		
		  Listening, Speaking, Viewing, Representing, 137N
		  Make Farm Animals
		  Put on Skits
		
		  Minilessons, 131
		
		ⓘ Intervention Program

Activity Science 128		

Writing Prompt: What if you were a vet visiting a farm? What is the biggest animal you see? What is the smallest?
 	
Journal Writing, 137D
	Writing Prompt: What does a vet do every day? Make a calendar for a week that shows what animals the vet visits.
	
	Interactive Writing: Write a Class Story, 137M
	  Prewrite, Draft
	Meeting Individual Needs for Writing, 137N
		Writing Prompt: Write about a vet who has a birthday party for a patient. When will the party be? Who will the guests be?
		
		Interactive Writing: Write a Class Story, 137M
		  Revise, Publish

Practice and Write: Days, Months, and Holidays, 137P
  Daily Language Activity: Identify months, days, and holidays.
 	
Grammar Practice Book, 59
	Practice and Write: Days, Months, and Holidays, 137P
	  Daily Language Activity: Identify months, days, and holidays.
	
	Grammar Practice Book, 60
		Assess and Reteach: Days, Months, and Holidays, 137P
		  Daily Language Activity: Capitalize months, days, and holidays.
		
		Grammar Practice Book, 61–62

Practice and Extend: Words from Social Studies, 137R **Spelling Practice Book,** 60	**Practice and Write: Words from Social Studies,** 137R **Spelling Practice Book,** 61	**Assess and Reteach: Words from Social Studies,** 137R **Spelling Practice Book,** 62

124F

Read Aloud

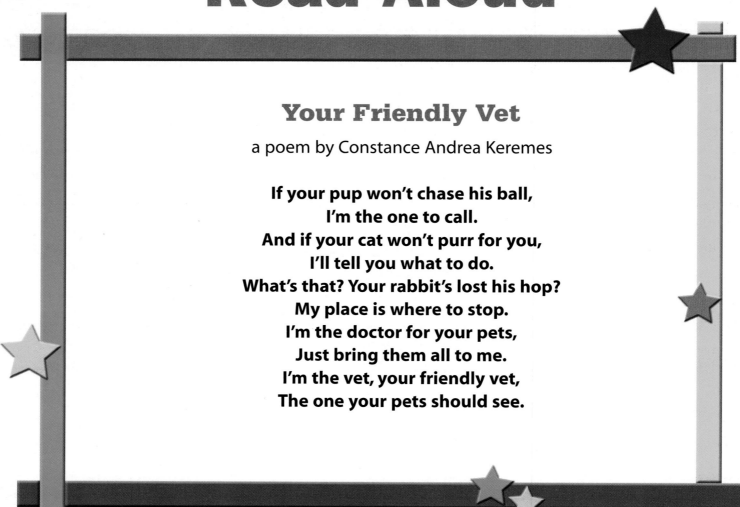

Your Friendly Vet

a poem by Constance Andrea Keremes

**If your pup won't chase his ball,
I'm the one to call.
And if your cat won't purr for you,
I'll tell you what to do.
What's that? Your rabbit's lost his hop?
My place is where to stop.
I'm the doctor for your pets,
Just bring them all to me.
I'm the vet, your friendly vet,
The one your pets should see.**

Oral Comprehension

LISTENING AND SPEAKING Motivate children to think about rhythm by reading them this poem about a veterinarian. As you read each line, have children clap the syllables with you. Point to a pair of lines and ask, "How many times do you clap for the first line? For the second line?" Guide children to see that the first line in each pair has more syllables than the second line.

Activity Have children work in small groups to act out "Your Friendly Vet." Children can act out the parts of the sick pets. They then act the way each pet would behave after being cured. ▶ **Kinesthetic**

GENRE: POEM A poem uses words that rhyme and has a special rhythm, or musical beat. Help children find the rhyming words in the poem. Tell children to listen for the rhythm, or musical beat, as you reread the last four lines of the poem. Clap the beats as you read. Repeat, guiding children to clap with you.

Develop Phonological Awareness

Blend Sounds
Phonemic Awareness

MATERIALS
- puppet

Teach Tell children the puppet is going to think of some words. It will give them a clue by saying the sounds of the word. They will blend them together to figure out the word. Demonstrate by having the puppet say: */p/-/i/-/l/. I take this when I am sick. What is it?* (pill)

Practice Have the puppet say the sounds of the following words, giving clues as needed. Then have children blend the sounds to say each word: *duck, nut, shut, box, lock, rock, legs, pet, vet, buzz, frog, snack, sniff.*

Segment Sounds
Phonemic Awareness

MATERIALS
- Word Building Boxes from Word Building Cards
- colored felt

Teach Tell children you will say a word. They will repeat the word, then say it sound by sound. For each sound they say, they should place a felt square on a box. Demonstrate by saying: *Cut . . . /k/-/u/-/t/.* Place a felt square onto each of the three boxes.

Practice Say the words below and have children repeat after you. Then have them segment the word into sounds, placing a felt square onto a box for each sound: *bun, duck, jug, dot, fog, lock, legs, peck, pets.*

Delete Sounds
Phonemic Awareness

/s/-/l/-/a/-/p/
/l/-/a-/p/

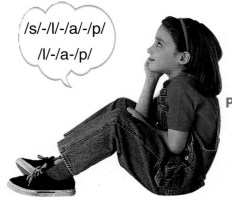

Teach Tell children to listen as you sing the following chant: *Rug without the /r/ sound is /ug/. Thud without the /d/ sound is /thu/. Bus without the /b/ sound is. . . .* Have children fill in the sound /us/.

Practice Sing the chant so children can identify the remaining sounds in a word when you delete either the beginning or end sound. Use the following words: *bud, cup, fun, box, lock, pod, pop, beg, jet, neck, pen, cuff, flap, flick, frock, hiss, sill, slap, slick.*

INFORMAL ASSESSMENT Observe children as they blend sounds, segment sounds, and delete sounds. If children have difficulty, see Alternate Teaching Strategies on pages T64, T69, T71, and T75.

OBJECTIVES

Children will:

- identify short *a, e, i, o,* and *u* in words with blends and digraphs.

- read short *a, e, i, o,* and *u* words with blends and digraphs.

- review: *ck, th, sh; sn, fr, sl, cl; ll; b, g, r, p, m, n, w.*

....

MATERIALS

- letter cards from the **Word Building Manipulative Cards**

- **Teaching Chart 56**

Skills Finder

Short *a, e, i, o,* and *u*

Introduce	B2: 65G-H
Review	B2: 95E-F, 95G-H, 124I-J
Test	Book 2
Maintain	B4: 105

SPELLING/PHONICS CONNECTIONS

Words with short *a, e, i, o,* and *u*: See the 5-Day Spelling Plan, pages 137Q–137R.

TEACHING TIP

RHYMING WORDS Using the words from the Practice activity, have children find a word that rhymes with every word you give them. For example: Can you write down a word that rhymes with *sun?* Have children read their responses to verify that they created real words.

Review Short *a, e, i, o, u*

PREPARE

Identify the Letters *a, e, i, o,* and *u* as Symbols for /a/, /e/, /i/, /o/, and /u/

- Remind children that the letters *a, e, i, o,* and *u* stand for the sounds /a/, /e/, /i/, /o/, and /u/.

- Say the following words and ask children to identify the short vowel sound they hear in each word: *trip, mess, stop, clap, shut.*

TEACH

BLENDING Model and Guide Practice with Short *a, e, i, o,* and *u* Words and Digraphs

- Display **Teaching Chart 56.** Point to the letters *a, e, i, o, u* at the top of the chart.

  Tell children they will use these letters to make words.

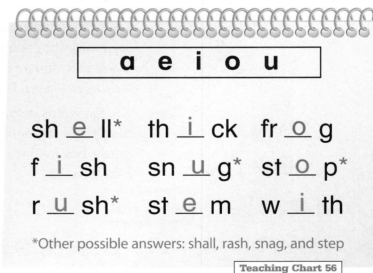

a e i o u

sh <u>e</u> ll*   th <u>i</u> ck   fr <u>o</u> g

f <u>i</u> sh   sn <u>u</u> g*   st <u>o</u> p*

r <u>u</u> sh*   st <u>e</u> m   w <u>i</u> th

*Other possible answers: shall, rash, snag, and step

Teaching Chart 56

- Write the letter *e* to complete the first word.
- Blend the sounds together and have children repeat after you.

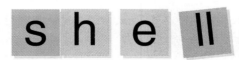

s h e ll

Use the Word in Context

- Replace the *e* with an *a* and repeat the blending.

- Use the word in context. Example: *I found a shell at the beach. I shall go to school today.*

Repeat the Procedure

- Repeat the procedure with the other items on the chart.

- Have children blend the sounds together and read the words aloud.

PRACTICE

LETTER SUBSTITUTION
Build Short *a, e, i, o,* and *u* Words with Letter Cards

GROUP

Build the word *back,* asking children to repeat each sound after you. Change the word to *tack* by replacing the *b* with *t.* Have children repeat after you. Next, ask children to work in small groups to build and write the following words, substituting the appropriate letters: *sick, mist, clap, well, smell, sun.* ▶ **Linguistic/Kinesthetic**

ASSESS/CLOSE

Build and Read Short *a, e, i, o,* and *u* Words

To assess children's ability to blend and read short vowel words, observe children as they build words in the Practice activity. Have children turn to pages 124–125 in their books and read the Phonics Rhyme "At the Vet" aloud with them. Then have them write two short vowel words from the poem.

ADDITIONAL PHONICS RESOURCES

Phonics/Phonemic Awareness Practice Book, pages 111–114

PHONICS KIT
Hands-on Activities and Practice

McGraw-Hill School
TECHNOLOGY

Phonics CD-ROM
activities for practice with Blending and Segmenting

Daily Routines

DAY 1 **Segmenting** Distribute letter boxes. Say a short *e* word aloud. Have children write the spelling of each sound in the appropriate box. (Use *smell, sled,* and *neck.*)

DAY 2 **Blending** Write the spelling of each sound in *duck* as you say it. Have children repeat after you. Ask children to blend the sounds to read the word. Repeat with *up* and *tub.*

DAY 3 **Fluency** Write a list of short *a, e, i, o,* and *u* words. Point to each word, asking children to blend the sounds silently. Ask a volunteer to read each word aloud.

DAY 4 **Writing** Have children choose two short *a, e, i, o,* or *u* words and create a rhyming couplet with the words. Children can illustrate their rhymes.

DAY 5 **Letter Substitution** Using the letter cards, have pairs of children build *rock.* Taking turns, one child changes a letter to build a new word, asking the partner to read it.

Meeting Individual Needs for Phonics

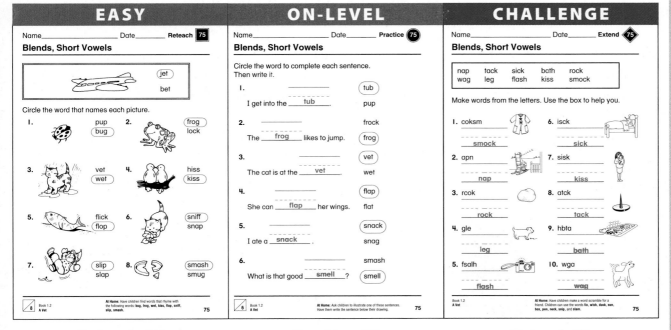

EASY	ON-LEVEL	CHALLENGE
Reteach, 75	Practice, 75	Extend, 75

OBJECTIVES

Children will read a poem with words containing short *a, i, o, u,* and *e,* blends, and double consonants.

Apply Short *a, e, i, o, u*

At the Vet

Muff the pup, Puff the cat,
And Sal the hog are at the vet.
Sal the hog is hot, so hot.
I will see that he drinks a lot.
Muff gets a shot, Puff gets a pill.
Now Muff and Puff will not get ill.

Anthology pages 124–125

Read and Build Fluency

READ THE POEM Tell children they will read a poem called "At the Vet." Provide auditory modeling as you pause at the commas and at the end of sentences. Ask children to read along with you.

REREAD FOR FLUENCY Have children work in small groups to reread the poem. They can sit in a circle, with each child reading a line of the poem.

READ A DECODABLE STORY For additional practice reading and to develop fluency, direct children to one of this week's **Phonics Practice Reader, Vol. 1,** stories.

Dictate and Spell

DICTATE WORDS Segment the word *Muff* into its three individual sounds. Repeat the word aloud and use it in a sentence: *The name of the pup is Muff.* Then have children say the word and write the letter that represents each sound until they make the entire word. Repeat with *vet, pup, cat, hog, drinks, not,* and *ill* from the poem. Then repeat with other words not in the poem, such as *bun, fog, beg, flash, fluff, mass, quill,* and *snip.*

> **ℹ Intervention** **Skills Intervention Guide,** for direct instruction and extra practice in Short *a, e, i o, u,* Consonant Blends, and Double Consonants

Build Background

Link
Science

Concept: Caring for Someone or Something

Evaluate Prior Knowledge

CONCEPT: CARING FOR SOMEONE OR SOMETHING Ask children to share what they know about taking care of someone or something. Use the following activities if children need more information about this concept.

MAKE A WORD WEB ABOUT CARING
Work with children to create a word web to record the different things children take care of, whether they are objects, people, or animals. ▶Linguistic

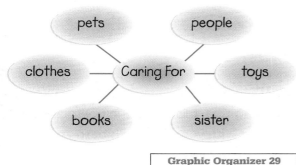

Graphic Organizer 29

MAKE A "CARING FOR" PICTURE

ONE   WRITING   Encourage children to draw a picture illustrating something or someone they take care of at home or school. Suggest that children refer to the word web for ideas.

Develop Oral Language

CONNECT WORDS AND ACTIONS Have
ESL children act out how they take care of something and follow simple instructions, such as:

- *Feed your pet.*
- *Brush your teeth.*
- *Pick up your toys.*
- *Sharpen your pencil.*

Prompt children to say what they are doing by asking:

- *Who are you feeding?*
- *What are you doing?*
- *Why do you take care of that?*
- *Why must you do that?*
  ▶ Linguistic/Kinesthetic

TEACHING TIP

MANAGEMENT To create a quick and easy transparency, place a plastic roll over the easel on the overhead projector. Write on the plastic with permanent felt-tip pens. Pull out more plastic as you need it.

DAILY Phonics ROUTINES

DAY 2 **Blending** Write the spelling of each sound in *duck* as you say it. Have children repeat after you. Ask children to blend the sounds to read the word. Repeat with *up* and *tub*.

Phonics CD-ROM

LANGUAGE SUPPORT

To build more background, see pages 82–85 in the **Language Support Book**.

OBJECTIVES

Children will:

- identify high-frequency words *out, want, good,* and *small.*

MATERIALS

- Teaching Chart 57
- Word Building Manipulative Cards *out, want, good, small*

TEACHING TIP

The following chart indicates words from the upcoming story that children have learned to decode and high-frequency words from the story. As children read, observe any difficulties they may have in reading these words.

Decodable		High-Frequency
and	job	out
pet	well	good
pets	at	want
vet	cat	small
can	sick	
it	pig	
big	this	
dog		

SPELLING/VOCABULARY CONNECTIONS

These words are Challenge Words. See page 137Q for Day 1 of the 5-Day Spelling Plan.

---

out

good

want

small

Vocabulary

High-Frequency Words

A Pet and a Vet

I have a ⟨small⟩ dog that is very sick.

She will not go ⟨out⟩

She does not ⟨want⟩ to run or lick.

What is this about?

I go with my dog and we see the vet.

"What's wrong? Can you tell?"

The vet has ⟨good⟩ pills I can give my pet.

They will get her well.

Teaching Chart 57

Auditory

LISTEN TO WORDS Without displaying it, read aloud "A Pet and a Vet" on **Teaching Chart 57.** Ask children if they've ever had a pet that they had to bring to the vet. How did they feel? How do they think the pet felt? How do they think the vet felt?

SAY "HELP!" FOR HIGH-FREQUENCY WORDS Have children aurally identify each high-frequency word using the following activity:

- Say aloud one of the high-frequency words. Tell children that every time they hear that word, they should say "Help!" and then say the word.

- Read a line from the poem that contains the high-frequency word. Pause at the word to allow children to say "Help!" and the word.

- Repeat this activity with each of the high-frequency words.

Visual

READ WORDS Display "A Pet and a Vet" on **Teaching Chart 57.** Read the poem, tracking the print with your finger. Point to and say the word *out.* Have children say the word with you. Ask them to hold up the vocabulary card for *out* and say the word. Repeat for *want, good,* and *small.*

Hold up vocabulary cards for *out, want, good,* and *small* one at a time. Have volunteers read the words and then circle them on the chart. Pairs of children may also alternate reading lines of the poem.

small   out
good   want

Word Building Manipulative Cards

CHANGE THE POEM Have groups pick different pets. Have them follow the language patterns of "A Pet and a Vet" and recite new poems about their animals using the high-frequency words.

Activities

Word Wall

Word Parts Tell children you are going to say a series of words. Say that each word contains one of the word wall words in it. Encourage children to identify the word wall word.

> outside, without, outing (out)
> goodness, goodbye, goods (good)
> smaller, smallest (small)
> wants, wanted, wanting, (want)

March and Spell Line up a small group of children to march around the classroom. Ask another group of children to call out a word wall word to the marchers. As they march, tell children to say, spell, then say each word again.

LANGUAGE SUPPORT

To help children develop understanding and recognition of high-frequency words, see page 73 in the **Language Support Book**.

Assess

Pass the Word Divide children into groups of three or four. Have groups take turns using each high-frequency word in a sentence. Have one child spell the word aloud and use it in a sentence. Then have that child "pass the word" to the next child. Each child will have a chance to use and spell the words.

TEACHING TIP

PHONICS TEACHING TIP Display the word card for *small*. Cover up the letters *sm* and point to the word *all* as you say it. Emphasize the /ô/ sound. Tell children that the letter *a* in *all* stands for the /ô/ sound. Then have children blend together the sounds of the letters *sm* with *all* to read *small*. Write the words *tall*, *wall*, and *ball* on the chalkboard. Read each word as you point to it. Then ask children to read each word.

Meeting Individual Needs for Vocabulary

EASY	ON-LEVEL	ON-LEVEL	CHALLENGE
Name_____ Date_____ Reteach **76**	Name_____ Date_____ Practice **76**		Name_____ Date_____ Extend **76**
High-Frequency Words	**High-Frequency Words**		**High-Frequency Words**
Circle the word that completes each sentence.	Circle the word to finish each sentence.		The words are mixed up. Make sentences. Write the sentences on the line.
small good want out	small out good want	**My Dog Mack**	1. went out We fish to.
1. The dog sees the — flap. (small) want	1. I will go _out_ to play. (out) small		_We went out to fish._
2. Will he go — ? (out) good	2. This is a _good_ book. (good) out		2. dog is good My.
3. Does he — to play? small (want)	3. My sisters _want_ a pup. good (want)		_My dog is good._
4. The — dog stays in. (good) want	4. Some pets are _small_ want (small)		3. sack small has a rip His.
			His sack has a small rip.
			4. wants The to out cat go.
			The cat wants to go out.
			5. Sam dad has fun with his.
			Sam has fun with his dad.
		"Bark! Bark!" That is Mack. He can swim. He can get my hat for me. He swims to the rock. He comes back with my hat. "Thank you, Mack!" I say. "Now let us go back home!"	Write a mixed up sentence. Give it to a friend to unscramble.
At Home: Have children write a sentence that describes the picture using one of the high-frequency words from the box.	At Home: Ask children to create their own sentences using the words small, out, good, and want.	76a	_Answers will vary._
76 Book 1.2 A Vet 4	76 Book 1.2 A Vet 4		At Home: Have children write a story about one of the sentences. 76 Book 1.2 A Vet
Reteach, 76	**Practice, 76**	**Practice, 76a Take-Home Story**	**Extend, 76**

Comprehension

Prereading Strategies

PREVIEW AND PREDICT Have children read the title and preview the article, looking at the photos for clues about the setting and the people.

- Where do you think the events in this article are taking place?
- What do you know about the people in the article from the title and pictures?
- What will the article most likely be about?

Have children record their predictions about the article as well as the main character.

PREDICTIONS	WHAT HAPPENED
The article will be about a vet.	
The vet will care for different animals.	

SET PURPOSES What do children want to find out by reading the article? For example:

- What is a vet?
- What does she do?
- Who does she take care of?

TIME FOR KIDS
SPECIAL REPORT

A Vet

①

126

Meeting Individual Needs · Grouping Suggestions for Strategic Reading

EASY	ON-LEVEL	CHALLENGE
Shared Reading Read the article aloud as you track print and model directionality. Invite children to chime in with any repetitive words and phrases as you read the article aloud. As you read with children, model using the strategy of paying attention to the main idea and the details to help understand what is happening.	**Guided Instruction** Ask children to read the article with you. Monitor any difficulties in reading that children may have to determine which numbered prompts from the Comprehension section to use. After reading the article with children, have them reread it. See rereading options on page 132.	**Independent Reading** Have children set purposes before they read. Remind them as they read that they should note all the details in the article to help them understand the story. After reading, have children summarize the article and suggest a main idea. They can also use the questions on page 134 for a group discussion.

Do you have a pet? **2**
A vet can care for it. **3**

127

Comprehension

☑ **Phonics** **Short Vowels; Blends; Double Consonants**

☑ **Apply Main Idea**

STRATEGIC READING Tell children that stopping every few pages to think about the main idea and details in *A Vet* is a strategy that will help them understand the story.

1 **MAIN IDEA** Let's look at the picture on page 126. Who do you think that is? (a vet)

2 **Phonics** **SHORT** *e* "Do you have a pet? A . . ." Hmm, I'm not sure what this word is. Let's blend the sounds of the letters together to read it. V e t, Vet *Graphophonic Cues*

3 Let's look at the photographs on this page. What kinds of pets do you see? (a dog, a cat, a bird) *Use Illustrations*

Genre

Narrative Nonfiction

Explain to children that narrative nonfiction

- gives facts about a topic.
- presents information as if it is a story.
- may include photographs, illustrations, and other graphics such as charts.

Activity After reading *A Vet*, have children retell as many facts about a vet as they can recall from the story. Then ask them to look at each of the pictures. Ask volunteers to tell what facts they can learn from each of the pictures.

LANGUAGE SUPPORT

A blackline master of the Main Idea chart can be found in the **Language Support Book.** Work with children to write in the details of the story and then use the details on their charts to determine and write the main idea of *A Vet*.

Name_____ Date_____
What's The Main Idea?

Details

Details

Details

Main Idea

LANGUAGE SUPPORT, 86

127

Comprehension

4 **Phonics** SHORT *e* "*This vet helps big and small …*" Hmm, I'm not sure what this word is. Let's blend the sounds together to read it. p e t s pets *Graphophonic Cues*

5 "*She can give the dog a …*" Hmm, I'm not sure what this word is. But I can look at the picture and the sounds I know to figure it out. I see a word I know: *up.* I also know how to say these letters, too: *check.* Based on what's going on in the picture, and the sounds I know in the word, I think I know that the word is *checkup.* *Context Clues*

6 Let's write this detail on our chart: *A vet can give a dog a checkup. Graphic Organizer*

7 What do you think a "checkup" is? (It means the vet will check to make sure the dog is healthy.) *Make Inferences/ Semantic Cues*

4
6 This vet helps big and small pets.
7 She can give a dog a checkup.
5

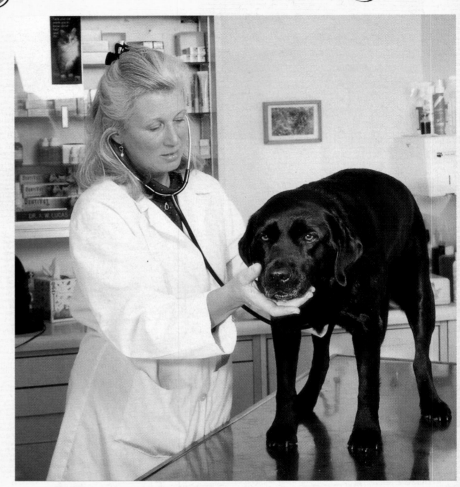

128

Activity

Cross Curricular: Science

A HEALTHY PET Ask children if any of them have taken a pet to a vet. Create a word web with Pet Care at the center. Ask children to think of reasons why a pet would need to visit a vet. (to get shots, to fix broken bones, to have an operation) ▶ **Linguistic/Visual**

RESEARCH AND INQUIRY Invite a vet to class to speak about his or her profession. Before the visit, have children brainstorm a list of questions.

*inter***NET** **CONNECTION** Have children log on to ***www.mhschool.com/ reading*** to access sites about animals.

She can look at a duck. ⑧
She can look at a cat. ⑨

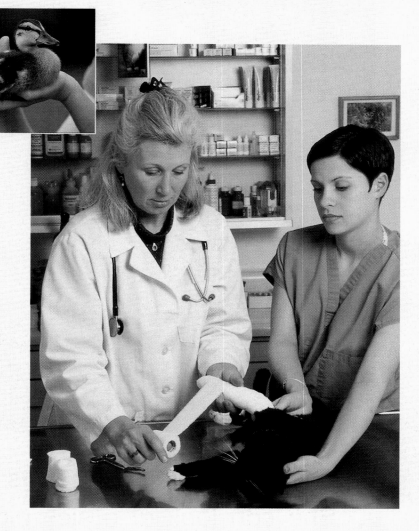

129

Comprehension

⑧ Look at the photographs on page 129 and name what you see the vet doing. (taking care of a duck and a cat) Let's add this detail to our chart. What kind of person do you think would want to take care of animals? (a kind person who loves animals) **Make Inferences/Graphic Organizer**

⑨ **Phonics** SHORT *u* "She can look at a ..." Hmm, I'm not sure what this word is. Let's blend the sounds together to read it. d u ck duck **Graphophonic Cues**

PHONOLOGICAL AWARENESS
Listen to these two sentences: *She can look at a duck. She can look at a cat.* What do you notice? (Many words in each sentence are the same.) How many words are the same? (five) Which words are different? (*duck, cat*)

SELF-MONITORING STRATEGY

REREADING Rereading a part of the story can help a reader to understand why the characters behave as they do.

MODEL I'm not sure I understand what a vet does. I'll reread the story aloud. Now I see that a vet is like a doctor for animals. She helps keep animals healthy and strong.

PREVENTION/INTERVENTION

PHONOLOGICAL AWARENESS
Say the two sentences from page 129 slowly and clearly, so that children hear that the first five words are the same in each sentence.

• Have children chant the sentences, clapping out the words.

• Say the sentence again, leaving out the last word. Have children volunteer words to fill in the "blank." (hamster, parakeet, rabbit)

Comprehension

10 Let's read the first sentence on page 130: *The vet can visit big pets.* What do you think the writer means by "big pets"? (pets that are probably too big to live with you, such as farm animals) *Make Inferences*

11  **SHORT** *i* "She can look at a …" Hmm, I'm not sure what this word is. Let's blend the sounds of the letters together to read it. s i ck sick *Graphophonic Cues*

12 Now let's read the full sentence: *She can look at a sick pig. Fluency*

Fluency

GROUP READING

 Model tracking print and rereading to achieve fluency.

- Point to and read aloud the first word in the sentence.

- Run your finger under each word as you read the rest of the sentence without pausing.

- Then have children repeat this process, pointing to each word as they read. Repeat until children achieve fluency.

130 *A Vet*

10 The vet can visit big pets.
11 She can look at a sick pig.
12

130

LANGUAGE SUPPORT

ESL Restate the verbs *look at,* *visit,* and *help out* using more familiar vocabulary if possible. For example, restate the text on pages 130–131 by saying *The vet goes to see big pets. She can see a sick pig, too. See,* here the vet is looking at the horse. She can help him.

She can help out a horse. **13**
14

131

Comprehension

13 **MAIN IDEA** Who did the vet just help? (a pig) Who is the vet helping now? (a horse) Let's add this detail to our chart: *A vet can take care of a pig and a horse. Graphic Organizer*

Details
A vet can give a dog a checkup.

Details
A vet can take care of a duck and a cat.

Details
A vet can take care of a pig and a horse.

Main Idea

14 Where do you think this vet works? (in the country) How do you know? (She's working with some farm animals.) *Make Inferences*

Minilesson
REVIEW

Fantasy and Reality

Remind children that a make-believe story— one in which animals talk, for instance— could not happen in real life. Ask children:

• Is *A Vet* a real-life story? Why? (Yes, it tells about a real person who takes care of animals.)

• How could you rewrite the story as make-believe? (You could have the animals talk to the vet and tell her where it hurts.)

Activity Brainstorm with children a list of real stories and a list of make-believe stories that they have read or know about. Create a two-column chart with children's responses, headed REAL and MAKE-BELIEVE.

Comprehension

15 Turn to page 132. Look at the picture that goes across both pages. What is happening? *(The vet has done a good job. The people are happy and the pets are, too.)* *Use Illustrations*

16 Let's stand up and pretend to be vets. What are you doing? How are you feeling? How can you show it? *Pantomime*

17 **MAIN IDEA** Let's use our Main Idea chart. Let's read over our details to figure out what the main idea of the article is. I think the main idea is: A vet is a doctor who takes care of big and small animals. *Graphic Organizer*

> **Details**
> *A vet can give a dog a checkup.*

> **Details**
> *A vet can take care of a duck and a cat.*

> **Details**
> *A vet can take care of a pig and a horse.*

> **Main Idea**
> *A vet is a doctor who takes care of big and small animals.*

ORGANIZE INFORMATION Ask children to work with partners to talk about what they learned in the story. Have them discuss the details in the article by referring to their charts. *Summarize*

15

This vet does a good job.

132

REREADING FOR *Fluency*

GROUP Children who need fluency practice can read along silently or aloud as they listen to the story on the recording.

READING RATE When you evaluate reading rate, have children read aloud from the story for one minute. Place a stick-on note after the last word read. Count words read. To evaluate children's performance, see the Running Record in the **Fluency Assessment** book.

> **i Intervention** For leveled fluency lessons, passages, and norms charts, see **Skills Intervention Guide**, Part 5, Fluency.

She wants to keep our pets well.

A story from the editors of *TIME FOR KIDS*.

133

LITERARY RESPONSE

QUICK-WRITE Have children draw a picture of a vet in their journals, and write what they liked or didn't like about the story.

ORAL RESPONSE Have children use their journal entries to discuss these questions:

- Did you like the vet in this story?
- If you were a vet, what kind of animals would you help? Why?

SENTENCE STRIPS Children can use strips 1–11 to retell *A Vet*.

> 1
> Do you have a pet?

> 2
> A vet can care for it.

Comprehension

Return to Predictions and Purposes

Reread children's predictions about the story. Discuss the predictions, noting which needed to be revised. Then ask children if the story answered the questions they had before they read it. Help children complete the Prediction chart.

PREDICTIONS	WHAT HAPPENED
The story will be about a vet.	The vet cares for different animals.
The vet will care for different animals.	This vet cares for cats, dogs, birds, pigs, and horses.

INFORMAL ASSESSMENT

HOW TO ASSESS

Phonics SHORT *u, o, e* Have children turn to page 128. Have them read the page and listen carefully for the short *e* and short *u* in *checkup*. Then have children turn to page 132, read the page, and listen for the short *o* in *job*.

MAIN IDEA Remind children of the first detail in the article: *A vet can give a dog a checkup*. Have them illustrate each detail of the story in their journals, writing a word or two under each picture.

FOLLOW UP

Phonics SHORT *u, o, e* Continue to model the blending of sounds of short *u, o,* and *e* words for children who are having difficulty.

MAIN IDEA Children who are having difficulty can use pictures from the story to help them think about the character of a vet and to remember the details of the story.

Story Questions

Tell children that now they will read some questions about the story. Help children read the questions. Discuss possible answers.

Answers:

1. She helps small and big animals, such as ducks, cats, pigs, and horses. *Literal/Details*

2. in the country *Inferential/Make Inferences*

3. to help them stay healthy *Make Inferences*

4. Answers will vary. Accept appropriate story summaries. Possible answer: The vet takes care of animals. *Critical/Summarize*

5. yes, the dog and the cat *Critical/Reading Across Texts*

Make a List Help children read the directions in their anthologies. You may want to have children brainstorm different kinds of pets and pet names before they begin the activity.

Story Questions & Activities

READ TOGETHER

1 What pets does the vet help?

2 Where does this vet work at times?

3 Why do pets need a vet?

4 Tell what vets do.

5 Do any of these pets look like Meg's pets in "Splash"?

Make a List

Pretend you are a vet.
List pets you need to help.
Name each pet and tell each one which day to come.

Monday	Tuesday	Wednesday	Thursday	Friday	Saturday	Sunday
Tim Cat	Dan Dog	Pat Pig	Pam Pup	Ron Rabbit		

Meeting Individual Needs

EASY

Name_____ Date_____ Reteach 77

Story Comprehension

Complete the word web by writing the names of the animals from "A Vet."

help
dogs

help
horses

help
pigs

VETS

help
cats

help
ducks

Book 1.2
A Vet

At Home: Have children list some of the other animals they think a vet might take care of.

77

Reteach, 77

ON-LEVEL

Name_____ Date_____ Practice 77

Story Comprehension

Write **X** next to each sentence that describes "A Vet."

1. __X__ Vets help hogs.

2. _____ Vets help people get well.

3. __X__ Vets see sick cats.

4. __X__ A vet can help a sick duck.

5. _____ A vet will not go to a farm.

6. __X__ We take pets to the vet.

Book 1.2
A Vet

At Home: Help children to use these sentences to write a summary of "A Vet."

77

Practice, 77

CHALLENGE

Name_____ Date_____ Extend 77

Story Comprehension

Think of a pet that needs a vet.
Write a letter to the vet to tell what the problem is.
A sample answer is shown.
Dear Vet,

I think my guinea pig has a cold. His name is

Marty. He sneezes. He does not want to eat.

Can you help Marty?

Your friend,

Beth

Book 1.2
A Vet

At Home: Ask children to cut pictures from magazines of pets that a vet can care for. Children can use the pictures to create a pet care book.

77

Extend, 77

Story Activities

Home Sweet Home

Use a shoebox.
Make a home for an animal.
Use things like twigs, leaves, and newspaper.

Find Out More

Find out one thing about vets who work in zoos.

135

Home Sweet Home

Materials: shoe box, twigs, leaves, newspaper shreds

GROUP Read the directions aloud. Help children who have questions. Invite children to talk about the kinds of homes their own pets, or other animals, have. Where do dogs live? How about birds?

You may wish to have children work together in small groups to create the pet home. Encourage them to work together cooperatively.

Find Out More

Read the directions aloud again and help children who have questions. Then have them work in pairs.

RESEARCH AND INQUIRY Partners can work together and look through **PARTNERS** books about zoos and the people who work there to learn about what a zoo vet does.

 Go to **www.mhschool.com/reading** to access sites about vets and zoos.

FORMAL ASSESSMENT

After page 135, see the Selection Assessment.

DAILY **Phonics** ROUTINES

DAY 3 **Fluency** Write a list of short *a, e, i, o,* and *u* words. Point to each word, asking children to blend the sounds silently. Ask a volunteer to read each word.

Phonics CD-ROM

Study Skills

MAPS

OBJECTIVES

Children will learn to read a map to gather information.

Remind children that they have just read a story about a vet. Tell them that now they will look at a map that shows a vet's office. Write the word *map* on the chalkboard. Ask children if they know what a map shows. (A map shows streets, towns, rivers, oceans, states, and countries.)

Display **Teaching Chart 58.** Have children describe what they notice on the map, such as the various kinds of stores and offices. Invite them to name places and point to them. Ask children to trace the two different paths with their fingers. Then help them read the questions below the diagram. Encourage them to identify the name of each path and the answer to each question.

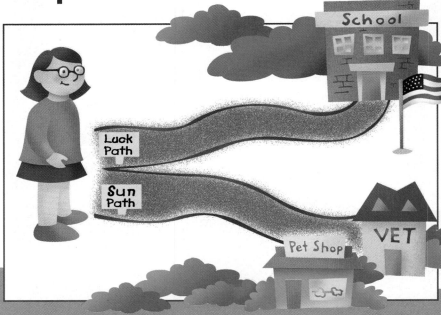

READ TOGETHER

STUDY SKILLS

Map

Look at the Map

❶ What path will the girl take to get to the vet?

❷ What is next to the vet's office?

Meeting Individual Needs

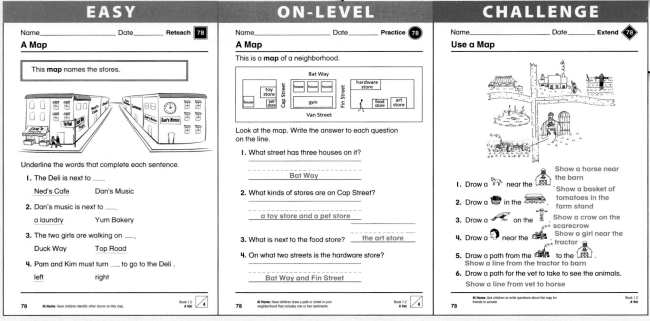

Reteach, 78   **Practice, 78**   **Extend, 78**

Kim's Cat

Kim has a cat.

It is a very round cat.

Her vet says that it is like a ball.

Kim's cat rolls off the vet's table.

It rolls out the door.

Then, Kim's cat rolls all the way home.

What a silly cat!

In this story, what does the cat do?

○ Purrs when the vet holds it

● Rolls off the vet's table

Think about what the story tells you.

137

Test Power

THE PRINCETON REVIEW

Read the Page

Explain to children that you will be reading this story as a group. You will read the story, and they will follow in their books.

Request that children put pens, pencils, and markers away, since they will not be writing in their books.

Discuss the Question

Children should reread the story and look for something that the cat does. Have the children point to and read those lines. The cat rolls off the table, out the door, and all the way home.

Test-Tip

The answer to the question is always in the story—all you have to do is read carefully to find it.

Intervention ▶ Skills

Intervention Guide, for direct instruction and extra practice in vocabulary and comprehension

☑ **Phonics**

- Review continuant/continuant blends *sl,sm,sn,fl,fr* and double consonants *ll, ss,* and *ff.*

- Review short vowels *a, e, i, o,* and *u.*

☑ **Comprehension**

- Review analyze character and plot.

- Review main idea and supporting details.

Answers will vary. Have children cite examples from the story to support their answers.

EASY

Story Questions for Selected Reading

1. What happened in the story?

2. Did the story surprise you? How?

3. What were the characters like?

4. What other title could the story have?

5. Which drawings did you like the best? Why?

Draw a Picture

Draw a picture for the selected story.

Self-Selected Reading
Leveled Books

EASY

UNIT SKILLS REVIEW

☑ **Phonics**

☑ **Comprehension**

Help children self-select an Easy Book to read and apply phonics and comprehension skills.

Guided Reading

PREVIEW AND PREDICT Discuss the illustrations in the beginning of the book. As you take the **picture walk**, have children predict what the story will be about. List their ideas.

SET PURPOSES Have children write or draw why they want to read the book. Have them share their purposes.

READ THE BOOK Use the following items to guide children's reading, or to discuss after they have read the story independently. Model blending and other phonics and decoding strategies for children who need help.

Let's look at the pictures. Can you tell me where this story takes place? *Use Illustrations*

Can you find words in the story that have the short *a*? The short *u*? The short *e*? *Phonics and Decoding*

Can you find the words in the story that have the *sl* blend? the *fr* blend? the *sm* blend? other blends that we learned about? *Phonics and Decoding*

RETURN TO PREDICTIONS AND PURPOSES Discuss children's predictions. Ask which were close to the book's contents and why. Have children review their purposes for reading. Did they find out what they wanted to know?

LITERARY RESPONSE Have children discuss questions such as:

- What parts of the book were most interesting?

- What might be another good title for the book?

 **CD-ROM**

Self-Selected Reading
Leveled Books

INDEPENDENT

UNIT SKILLS REVIEW

  Phonics

☑ Comprehension

Help children self-select an Independent Book to read and apply phonics and comprehension skills.

Guided Reading

PREVIEW AND PREDICT Discuss the illustrations in the beginning of the book. As you take the **picture walk**, have children predict what the story will be about. List their ideas.

SET PURPOSES Have children write or draw why they want to read the book. Have them share their purposes.

READ THE BOOK Use the following items to guide children's reading, or to discuss after they have read the story independently. Model blending and other phonics and decoding strategies for children who need help.

Do you think the story is real or make-believe? Why? *Distinguish Fantasy and Reality*

Was the ending of the story a surprise? Did it end as you thought it would? *Make Predictions*

Can you describe the events of the story as they happened? *Summarize*

RETURN TO PREDICTIONS AND PURPOSES Discuss children's predictions. Ask which were close to the book's contents and why. Have children review their purposes for reading. Did they find out what they wanted to know?

LITERARY RESPONSE Have children discuss questions such as:

- What parts of the book were most interesting?

- What might be another good title for the book?

 **CD-ROM**

☑ Phonics

- Review continuant/continuant blends *sl, sm, sn, fl, fr* and double consonants *ll, ss,* and *ff.*

- Review short vowels *a, e, i, o,* and *u.*

☑ **Comprehension**

- Review analyze character and plot.

- Review main idea and supporting details.

Answers will vary. Have children cite examples from the story to support their answers.

INDEPENDENT

Story Questions for Selected Reading

1. Where does the story take place?

2. Is the story real or make-believe?

3. If you could be a character in the story, who would you be? Why?

4. What is your favorite part of the story? Why?

5. What would make the story better?

Draw a Picture

Draw a picture for the selected story.

CHALLENGE

- Review continuant/continuant blends *sl, sm, sn, fl, fr* and double consonants *ll, ss,* and *ff.*

- Review short vowels *a, e, i, o,* and *u.*

☑ **Comprehension**

- Review analyze character and plot.

- Review main idea and supporting details.

Answers will vary. Have children cite examples from the story to support their answers.

CHALLENGE

Story Questions for Selected Reading

1. Could this story happen in real life? Why or why not?

2. If the story continued, what do you think would happen next?

3. What might be a new title for the story?

4. How would you describe the characters?

5. Which story character would you like to be? Why?

Draw a Picture

Draw a picture for the selected story.

Self-Selected Reading
Leveled Books

CHALLENGE

UNIT SKILLS REVIEW

 Comprehension

Help children self-select a Challenge Book to read and apply phonics and comprehension skills.

Guided Reading

PREVIEW AND PREDICT Discuss the illustrations in the beginning of the book. As you take the **picture walk**, have children predict what the story will be about. List their ideas.

SET PURPOSES Have children write or draw why they want to read the book. Have them share their purposes.

READ THE BOOK Use the following items to guide children's reading, or to discuss after they have read the story independently. Model blending and other phonics and decoding strategies for children who need help.

Do you think this story is real or make-believe? Has anything in the story ever happened in your own life? *Distinguish Fantasy and Reality*

What happens at the end of the story? *Summarize*

What parts of the story did you find most interesting? Why? Has anything similar happened to you? *Analyze Character and Plot*

RETURN TO PREDICTIONS AND PURPOSES Discuss children's predictions. Ask which were close to the book's contents and why. Have children review their purposes for reading. Did they find out what they wanted to know?

LITERARY RESPONSE Have children discuss questions such as:

- What parts of the book were most interesting?

- What might be another good title for the book?

 **CD-ROM**

Bringing Groups Together

Anthology and Leveled Books

Connecting Texts

CLASS DISCUSSION

Lead a discussion of how the unit theme Together Is Better applies to each of the stories:

- What do you think was the most interesting thing the characters experienced? Were they with someone at the time?

- Can you think of something you recently experienced with someone that was different or interesting?

CHARACTER WEB

Have children choose a favorite from the Leveled Books or Anthology selections in this unit. Have them create a web to compare the main characters from their stories. Who are they? What did they experience? A sample web is shown here.

Sitting in My Box
A boy shares his box with several wild animals of the jungle.

Cam and Luck
Cam and his dog, Luck, spend the day playing together.

Together Is Better

The Box
Ken and his sister, Meg, play with a box, imagining it to be a ship, an animal pen, and a plane.

Around Bug Town
The bugs around Bug Town are busy doing their jobs.

Viewing/Representing

GROUP PRESENTATIONS Ask children to choose their favorite book. Divide the children into four groups, one for each story. Have them create skits for a scene from the story. Ask a narrator to introduce each scene.

AUDIENCE RESPONSE Have children tell what they found interesting about each performance. Suggest that audience members ask questions about any parts of the story they would like to learn more about.

Research and Inquiry

SHOW AND TELL Tell children to choose objects that could represent them or an experience they once had. Ask children to present the item to the class and offer a brief description.

interNET CONNECTION Have children log on to **www.mhschool.com/reading** to access links to various sites about sharing or group games.

JOURNAL

Children can write and draw what they learned in their journals.

OBJECTIVES

Children will:

* analyze character and plot.
* identify problem and solution.

MATERIALS

* **Teaching Chart 59**

Skills Finder

Story Elements

Introduce	B2: 35I-J
Review	B2: 65I-J, 137E-F; B3: 37I-J, 125I-J, 139G-H
Test	Book 2, Book 3
Maintain	B3: 89; B4: 107, 109

Review Story Elements

PREPARE

Review the Concept of Character and Plot

Remind children that they can learn how to analyze characters in a story by thinking about how the characters act when things happen. This will also help them understand the plot.

TEACH

Model Analyze Character and Plot

Display **Teaching Chart 59**. Allow children to comment on the picture of the vet. Then read the chart aloud.

The Vet

The vet (cares) for a pet.
The vet is (smart.) He knows what to do.
He is also (kind.)

Teaching Chart 59

Identify Problem and Solution

Remind children that characters in a story usually face a problem—a situation that is causing them trouble. Help children determine a problem and a solution for the text on the chart.

Ask volunteers to circle words on **Teaching Chart 59** that give clues about the vet's character.

MODEL When I look at the picture, I see a vet and a tiny bird. I think the bird is injured. That is the problem. The sentences say the vet cares for a pet. He is also smart and kind. It is a vet's job to help animals that are hurt. I think the solution to the problem will be that the vet will cure the bird.

PRACTICE

Add to Character List

GROUP

Have children use the story, *A Vet,* and **Teaching Chart 59** to add to the character list. As children list qualities, ask them for plot details to reinforce the understanding that character and plot go together. What happens to the character in the plot and how that character reacts to it tells us about what kind of person the character is. Example: The vet in the story took care of a big hog. She knows a lot about many animals. The hog got well because the vet knew what to do. ▶ **Linguistic**

ASSESS/CLOSE

Make Other Lists

Invite children to verbally create character lists for other characters in stories they have read in this unit, such as *The Bug Bath*. Create a character list to record children's observations. Then have children write one sentence about a character they especially liked.

ALTERNATE TEACHING STRATEGY

STORY ELEMENTS

For a different approach to teaching this skill, see page T67.

Intervention ▶ **Skills Intervention Guide,** for direct instruction and extra practice in Story Elements

DAILY Phonics ROUTINES

DAY 4 **Writing** Have children choose two short *a, e, i, o,* or *u* words and create a rhyming couplet with the words. Children can illustrate their rhymes.

 Phonics CD-ROM

Meeting Individual Needs for Comprehension

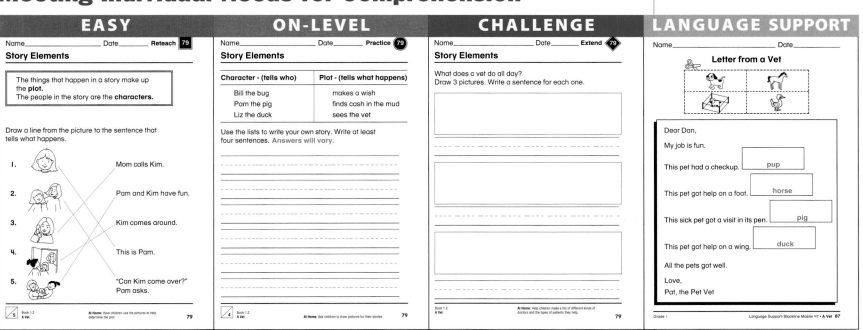

EASY	ON-LEVEL	CHALLENGE	LANGUAGE SUPPORT

Reteach, 79   Practice, 79   Extend, 79   Language Support, 87

OBJECTIVES

Children will:

• understand main idea and supporting details.

• identify beginning, middle, and end in a story.

MATERIALS:

• Teaching Chart 60

Skills Finder

Main Idea

Introduce	B2: 95I-J
Review	B2: 123I-J, 137G-H
Test	Book 2
Maintain	B3: 31, 61, 91, 133

TEACHING TIP

MAIN IDEA Have children create a story line about *A Vet* on the classroom wall. Divide children into eight groups and assign each group a page number in the story. Have individuals in each group draw pictures illustrating their page. Then hang the illustrations in order on the wall to make a picture story.

Review Main Idea

PREPARE

Review Main Idea, Supporting Details

Remind children that they can learn how to find the main idea in a story by remembering to stop and think about the beginning, middle, and end in the story. Tell children they can also think about the details in the story that support the main idea.

TEACH

Model Main Idea, Supporting Details

Display **Teaching Chart 60.** Allow children to comment on the pictures of the vet. Then read the chart aloud.

A Vet Can Help

The vet cares for animals.
They can be big or small.
They can be cats, dogs, or fish.
She helps them get well and stay well.

Teaching Chart 60

Identify Beginning, Middle, End in Story

MODEL I can see a vet's office in this picture. The beginning sentence tells me a vet takes care of animals. The middle sentences are talking about the animals. These sentences give me details about the animals that go to the vet's office. The end tells me that the vet helps the animals get well and stay that way.

Ask volunteers to circle the main idea of **Teaching Chart 60** and underline the supporting details.

PRACTICE

Add to Details and Main Idea List; Tell a Story

GROUP

Have children use the story and **Teaching Chart 60** to add to the list showing supporting details and main idea. As children list further details, ask them to use their own experience to add to the detail list. Examples: The vet helped deliver a calf on my grandfather's farm. The vet helped my dog when she broke her leg. Suggest that they use one of their ideas to tell a story focusing on its beginning, middle, and end. ▶ **Linguistic**

ASSESS/CLOSE

Create Details Lists; Identify Beginning, Middle, End

Invite children to verbally create detail lists for other stories they have read in this unit. Create a detail list to record children's observations, for example, of *Splash!*, in which a girl gets wet in the rain. Tell children to identify the beginning, middle, and end of their stories. Then have children write one sentence explaining the main idea of that story.

ALTERNATE TEACHING STRATEGY

STORY ELEMENTS

For a different approach to teaching this skill, see page T67.

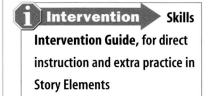

Intervention ▶ **Skills Intervention Guide,** for direct instruction and extra practice in Story Elements

DAILY Phonics ROUTINES

DAY 5 Letter Substitution

Using the letter cards, have pairs of children build *rock*. Taking turns, one child is to change a letter to build a new word, asking the partner to read it.

Phonics **CD-ROM**

Meeting Individual Needs for Comprehension

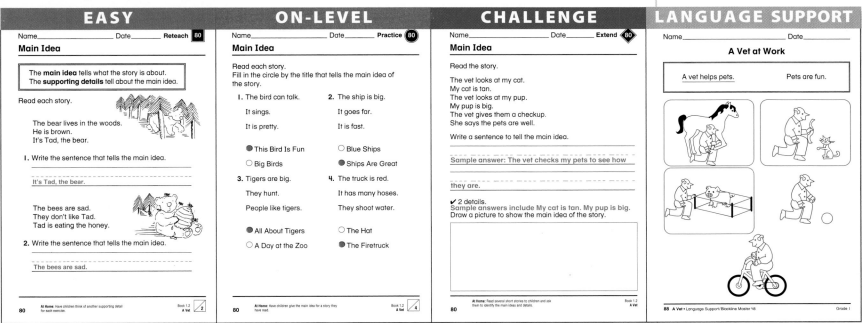

Reteach, 80   Practice, 80   Extend, 80   Language Support, 88

Review Inflectional Ending -ed

MATERIALS

- **Teaching Chart 61**
- blank word cards from the **Word Building Manipulative Cards**

Skills Finder

Inflectional Ending -ed

Introduce	B2: 35K-L
Review	B2: 137I-J; B4: 65K-L
Test	Book 2, Book 4

LANGUAGE SUPPORT

ESL If children are having trouble with the -ed ending, explain that when it appears at the end of an action word, it means that the action happened in the past. Give children a list of present-tense sentences. Then ask children to convert them into past-tense sentences by adding -ed to the verb. Examples of verbs to use: *help, look, visit,* and *walk.*

PREPARE

Act It Out Write the word *kick* on the chalkboard. Have children stand up and pretend to kick a ball. As they tell what they just did, add -ed. Have volunteers tell why you added -ed. Then explain that we often add -ed to words to show that something has already happened.

TEACH

Identify Base or Root Words Track the sentence on **Teaching Chart 61** as you read it with children: *I kicked the ball.* Then point to the word *kicked* on the chart. Ask children if they recognize part of the word. *(kick)* Point out that *kick* is called the base or root word. Model for children how understanding inflectional endings can help them read.

I kicked the ball.

I picked up my book.

I helped my dad.

Teaching Chart 61

MODEL I can use what I already know to help me read words I don't recognize. I know the word *kick.* I can see that the last two letters of the word are -ed. I know that sometimes when these two letters appear together at the end of a word, it means that someone did something in the past. The word is *kicked.*

Repeat for the other two sentences. Then call on children to come up and draw a line under the base or root word in each sentence.

PRACTICE

Add -ed Distribute index cards to children. Then write *packed, tossed,* and *dashed* on the chalkboard. Have children read each word, identifying the part of the word they know first. Then ask children to write each word on a card so that the ending *-ed* appears after a dotted line. Invite volunteers to write the words and use them in sentences.

▶ **Kinesthetic/Linguistic**

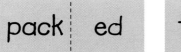

ASSESS/CLOSE

Show Past and Present Invite children to use their word cards from the Practice activity. Say some sentences aloud, repeating the verb after the sentence is read. Tell children to hold up the card for that word. Point out that they may only need to show part of the word by folding the card back along the dotted line, or they may need to show the whole word. Use the following sentences:

- I can pack a bag. (*pack*)
- Have you tossed out the garbage? (*tossed*)
- We dashed across the yard. (*dashed*)

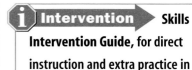

ALTERNATE TEACHING
STRATEGY
....
INFLECTIONAL ENDING
-ed

For a different approach to teaching this skill, see page T68.

i **Intervention** ▶ **Skills Intervention Guide,** for direct instruction and extra practice in **Inflectional Ending** *-ed*

Meeting Individual Needs for Vocabulary

EASY	ON-LEVEL	CHALLENGE	LANGUAGE SUPPORT

EASY

Name_____ Date_____ Reteach **81**

Inflectional Ending *-ed*

> Read the word.
> look + **ed** = look**ed**
> The girl look**ed** at the flower.

Add **-ed** to each of the words.

1. sniff + ed = ____sniffed____
2. pack + ed = ____packed____
3. lick + ed = ____licked____

Using the words from above, complete each sentence.

4. The hog ____licked____ the grass.
5. We ____packed____ our bags.
6. My pup ____sniffed____ at the hen.

Book 1.2 A Vet — **At Home:** Encourage children to write a new sentence for each word. 81

ON-LEVEL

Name_____ Date_____ Practice **81**

Inflectional Ending *-ed*

Draw a line to the word that completes the sentence.

1. The hen _____ at the mud. — pecked
2. Ned _____ in the pond. — jumped
3. Jan _____ the cat. — fished
4. Nell _____ out of bed. — kissed

Book 1.2 A Vet — **At Home:** Ask children to use one of these sentences as the first line in a poem. 81

CHALLENGE

Name_____ Date_____ Extend **81**

Inflectional Ending *-ed*

Write the word that completes the sentence.

1. The vet ____picked____ up the pup.
   pick picked
2. Will the pup ____lick____ her hand?
   lick licked
3. The vet ____filled____ the cat's dish.
   fill filled
4. Will the cat ____hiss____ at her?
   hiss hissed

Choose one of the words. Write a sentence.

_____
_____Sentences will vary._____

Book 1.2 A Vet — **At Home:** Have children look in a magazine or a book for words that end with **ed** and make a list of them. 81

LANGUAGE SUPPORT

Name_____ Date_____

Word Strip

look

help

walk   ed

buzz

pass

Grade 1 — Language Support/Blackline Master 49 • A Vet **89**

OBJECTIVES

Children will read unfamiliar words using context clues.

....

MATERIALS

• **Teaching Chart 62**

• index cards

Skills Finder

Context Clues

Introduce	B1: 87K-L
Review	B1: 101K-L; B2: 137K-L; B5: 117K-L
Test	Bk. 1, Bk. 2, Bk, 5 U. 1
Maintain	B2: 55, 107; B4: 101

TEACHING TIP

HOMOPHONES Point out to children that there is a word that is very close to *our*, but it is spelled differently and has another meaning. Write the words *our* and *hour* on the chalkboard. Explain that the *h* in *hour* is silent.

Review Context Clues

PREPARE

Act It Out Write the word *horse*. Have children stand up and pretend to be riding a horse. Read the word with children, and explain that we often come across words we've never seen when we're reading.

TEACH

Identify Unfamiliar Words Track the sentence on **Teaching Chart 62** as you read it with children: *She can "blank" for it.* Then point to the word *care* on the chart. Ask children if they recognize part of the word. *(c)* Model for children how looking for letters they know, looking at the picture, and reading the rest of the sentence can help them read words they don't know.

She can care for it.

This is our horse.

Our pal has big boots.

Teaching Chart 62

MODEL I can use what I already know to help me read words I don't recognize. What is the girl doing in this picture? She is feeding the little horse. Then I look at the sentence. I can read all these words: *She can _____ for it.* So I think: What is the girl doing? She is taking care of her horse. I see that the word is *care*. She can care for it. The word is *care*.

Repeat this process with *our* and *boots*.

Review Unfamiliar Words

GROUP

Provide two blank index cards to each child. On the chalkboard, write the following sentences: *The horse is in the* <u>*barn*</u>. *The man put on his* <u>*coat*</u>. Call attention to the unfamiliar words *barn* and *coat*. Have children first identify which part of the word they know and then use context clues to help them read each word. Then ask children to write each word on an index card. Invite volunteers to practice reading the words and using them in sentences. ▶ **Kinesthetic/Linguistic**

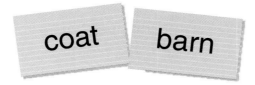

ASSESS/CLOSE

Use Context Clues

Write the following sentences containing the unfamiliar words *ladybug* and *bee* on the chalkboard: *This bug is a* <u>*ladybug*</u>. *Look out! There is a* <u>*bee!*</u> Have children first identify which part of the word they know and then use context clues to help them read each word. For additional informal assessment, use the following sentences:

• My hat is on my <u>head</u>.

• Will the butterfly fly <u>away</u>?

• I can grow pretty <u>flowers</u>.

ALTERNATE TEACHING STRATEGY

··

CONTEXT CLUES

For a different approach to teaching this skill, see page T74.

ℹ Intervention ▶ Skills Intervention Guide, for direct instruction and extra practice in Context Clues

Meeting Individual Needs for Vocabulary

EASY	ON-LEVEL	CHALLENGE	LANGUAGE SUPPORT

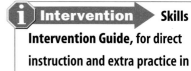

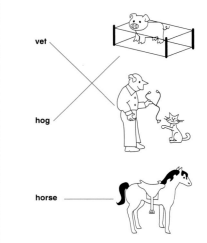

Reteach, 82   Practice, 82   Extend, 82   Language Support, 90

Handwriting CD-ROM

GRAMMAR/SPELLING CONNECTIONS

See 5-Day Grammar Plan on Days, Months, and Holidays, pages 1370–137P.

See the 5-Day Spelling Plan for a Cumulative Review, pages 137Q–137R.

Interactive Writing
Write a Class Story

Prewrite

BRAINSTORM Have children revisit *A Vet*, looking carefully at the pictures and words to see what a vet does. Then tell them that the class will create a new story about a vet. Ask them to pretend they're vets. Have them make suggestions for a list of farm animals that they might help. Then have them make suggestions for a list of things that might be wrong with each animal, and how they (the vet) might help it. After you've listed their suggestions, have them vote on the animal they'd like to write about.

Draft

WRITE ABOUT A VET AND A FARM ANIMAL Help children compose sentences for the class story. Guide them to use familiar words, sounds, and language patterns.

- Begin by saying, for example: *We're going to pretend that we're a vet telling a story about a sick animal on a farm. Let's start by saying something that tells the reader: This story is being told by the vet. Does anybody have any suggestions for sentences?* (I am a vet. My name is Dr. Bicks.)

- As you say a word with familiar sounds and patterns, challenge children to come up and write it. Write all unfamiliar words yourself.

- Guide children to explain what's wrong with the animal, and how they help it.

- Let children decide when they've written

enough.

Revise

PROPER NOUNS Reread the class story together. Check to see that each sentence begins with a capital letter. Remind children that proper nouns must always be capitalized. Have children find all the proper nouns in the class story and make sure they all begin with a capital letter.

Publish

CREATE THE STORY Reread the story together. Discuss different ways of illustrating it. What part of the story should go on each page? Have children create illustrations and label the characters and objects. Then encourage children to copy the story onto their pages.

TEACHING TIP

Technology
Children who use the computer should be encouraged to name their documents in a way that will make them easy to recognize and remember. Ask, "In a month, will you be able to remember what is in this document just by looking at its name?"

Presentation Ideas

MAKE FARM ANIMALS Have children use construction paper to make a collection of farm animals. Have them draw the animals and then cut them out. Help children think about what farm animals look like. Ask: *How big is a pig compared to a rooster? Is the pig skinny or fat? Does the rooster have anything unusual on the top of its head?* Then make a board display of their animals.

▶ **Representing/Viewing**

PUT ON SKITS Help children put on skits about a trip to the vet. One child can be the vet, the other children can be animals or their owners. Children may use the farm animals they made, or pretend that they are bringing animals. Remind the vets to ask questions about the animal's symptoms, and the owners to ask questions about how they can help their animals get well.

▶ **Speaking/Listening**

Listening and Speaking

LISTENING STRATEGIES Remind children of appropriate audience behavior. Remind them to sit quietly, look at the actors, and listen carefully to what the actors are saying.

SPEAKING STRATEGIES Remind children of the correct way to speak at school. They should not interrupt each other, and they should speak slowly and clearly so that the audience can hear them.

LANGUAGE SUPPORT

ESL Include children acquiring English in skits by preparing them in advance to ask questions of the vet. You may wish to pair a more fluent child with a beginner to bring one animal to the vet and take turns asking and answering questions.

Meeting Individual Needs for Writing

EASY

Draw Pictures Children can draw pictures illustrating a trip to the vet with a real or imaginary pet. Have them label drawings with simple sentences, following the patterns of *A Vet.*

ON-LEVEL

New Story Children can work in groups to write a new story about a cat who goes to a vet. Have them imagine that they're the cat, and tell what happens.

CHALLENGE

Journal Entry Children can write a journal entry, telling a story about a sick pet (real or imaginary). Have them explain what they noticed at home that made them decide to take the animal to the vet, what happened at the vet's office, and what happened afterwards.

5 Day Grammar and Usage Plan

LANGUAGE SUPPORT

ESL The capitalization of days, months, and holidays in other languages may differ from English. If children have difficulty with this concept in English, write sentences such as the following on the chalkboard and have children copy them down and repeat them aloud:

- Today is Monday.
- It is the month of December.
- I like Valentine's Day.

Non-native speakers may not be familiar with U.S. holidays. Use pictures to illustrate and explain each holiday.

DAY 1 — Introduce the Concept

Oral Warm-Up Have volunteers recite the days of the week. Write them on the chalkboard and circle the capital letters.

Introduce Days, Months, Holidays Remind children that special names of people and places begin with capital letters. Tell children that the names of days also begin with capital letters. Present and discuss:

Days, Months, Holidays

- Some proper nouns name days of the week.
- Some proper nouns name months.
- Some proper nouns name holidays.

Daily Language Activity Write these sentences and read aloud: *Today is monday. Yesterday was sunday. Tomorrow is tuesday.* Ask children which word in each sentence names a special day and needs a capital letter. (*Mon*day; *Sun*day; *Tues*day)

 Assign the daily writing activity on page 124E.

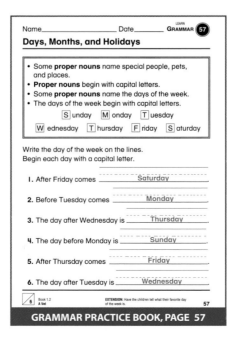

GRAMMAR PRACTICE BOOK, PAGE 57

DAY 2 — Teach the Concept

Review Days, Months, Holidays Remind children names of days, months, and holidays all begin with capital letters. Have children name months of the year. Write them on the chalkboard and point out that each begins with a capital letter. Then, write the holidays for each month on the chalkboard. Help children to read them aloud.

Daily Language Activity Write the following sentences on the chalkboard and read them aloud: *Today is Tuesday. My birthday is in November. We will have a party for Thanksgiving.* Ask children which words name a day, month, and holiday and with what kind of letter each begins. (*Tuesday, November, Thanksgiving*; capital letter)

 Assign the daily writing activity on page 124E.

GRAMMAR PRACTICE BOOK, PAGE 58

Days, Months, Holidays

DAY 3 — Practice and Write

Learn from the Literature Review the names of days, months, and holidays. Remind children that these words begin with a capital letter. Write the following sentences on the board and read them aloud: *The class will visit the vet on Friday. My cat was sick in April.* Ask children to identify which word in each sentence names a day or month.

Daily Language Activity Write the following sentences on the chalkboard and read aloud: *The vet is open on new year's day. Can the vet see my pet on friday? I gave my father a dog for father's day. In april the vet sees many rabbits.* Ask children to identify the special word in each sentence that needs a capital letter. (*New Year's Day, Friday, Father's Day, April*)

 WRITING Assign the daily writing activity on page 124F.

DAY 4 — Practice and Write

Review Days, Months, Holidays Have volunteers say the names of the days and the months. Write them on the board and ask children where to use capital letters.

Daily Language Activity Write the following sentences on the chalkboard and read aloud: *We have a class trip wednesday. Tim will visit in june. I like flag day.* Have children identify the special word in each sentence that needs a capital letter. (*Wednesday; June; Flag Day*)

Mechanics and Usage Remind children:

> ### Days, Months, Holidays
>
> - The name of each day begins with a capital letter.
> - The name of each month begins with a capital letter.
> - The name of a holiday begins with a capital letter.

 WRITING Assign the daily writing activity on page 124F.

DAY 5 — Assess and Reteach

Daily Language Activity Write these sentences on the chalkboard. Read them with children. Have children tell which words should be capitalized in each sentence:

1. We celebrate mother's day on monday. (Mother's Day, Monday)

2. The party is wednesday, the last day of july. (Wednesday, July)

Assess Use page 61 of the **Grammar Practice Book** for assessment.

Reteach Prepare word cards for each day, month, and holiday. Give each group one set. Have them use days, months, and holidays correctly to make a giant calendar in a classroom wall. Have children emphasize the capital letter in each word by writing it in a different color.

Use page 62 of the **Grammar Practice Book** for additional reteaching.

 WRITING Assign the daily writing activity on page 124F.

Grammar Practice Book, Page 59

Name_____ Date_____ **PRACTICE AND WRITE GRAMMAR 59**

Days, Months, and Holidays

- Some proper nouns name holidays.
- The names of holidays begin with capital letters.
  Some of the holidays are:
  **Thanksgiving   Christmas   New Year's Day
  Independence Day   Valentine's Day**

Read the sentences.
Draw a circle around the holidays that need a capital letter.
Write the name of the holiday with a capital letter.

1. When is (christmas)?
   _____ Christmas _____

2. We celebrate (independence day) on the fourth of July.
   _____ Independence Day _____

3. We are thankful on (thanksgiving)
   _____ Thanksgiving _____

4. We send cards on (valentine's day)
   _____ Valentine's Day _____

Book 1.2 A Vet **EXTENSION:** Have the children tell how their family celebrates a holiday. Then they can write a sentence about the holiday. **59**

GRAMMAR PRACTICE BOOK, PAGE 59

Grammar Practice Book, Page 60

Name_____ Date_____ **MECHANICS GRAMMAR 60**

Days, Months, and Holidays

- The name of each day begins with a capital letter.
- Monday, Tuesday, Wednesday
- The name of each month begins with a capital letter.
- March, April, May, June
- The name of a holiday begins with a capital letter.
- Mother's Day, Thanksgiving, Independence Day

Read the sentences. Write the days, months, and holidays. Give the days, months, and holidays capital letters.

1. It rains in april. _____ April _____

2. Summer begins in june. _____ June _____

3. thanksgiving is for giving thanks.
   _____ Thanksgiving _____

4. monday is the first day in the week. _____ Monday _____

5. On independence day, we have fun.
   _____ Independence Day _____

60 Book 1.2 A Vet **EXTENSION:** Have children write a sentence with a day and a month in it.

GRAMMAR PRACTICE BOOK, PAGE 60

Grammar Practice Book, Page 61

Name_____ Date_____ **TEST GRAMMAR 61**

Days, Months, and Holidays

Read the sentences. Write the word that is correct.

I. We give thanks on _____ Thanksgiving _____
   thanksgiving   Thanksgiving

2. I go to school on _____ Monday _____
   Monday   monday

3. We give cards on _____ Valentine's Day _____
   valentine's day   Valentine's Day

4. My birthday is in _____ May _____
   may   May

5. I help Dad on _____ Saturday _____
   Saturday   saturday

Book 1.2 A Vet **61**

GRAMMAR PRACTICE BOOK, PAGE 61

5 Day Spelling Plan

DAY 1 — Introduce Spelling Words

Assess Prior Knowledge Write the Spelling Words on the board and read aloud with children, stressing the vowel sounds in each word. Ask: What letter spells /e/ in *vet* and *help*? (*e*) What letter spells /o/ in *hog* and *job*? (*o*) What letter spells /a/ in *cat* and *pat*? (*a*)

Write the words *small*, *out*, *good*, and *wants* on the chalkboard and read them aloud. Invite children to use each word in a sentence. Read the words again, and then have children read them with you.

Spelling Words		Challenge Words
vet	help	small
hog	job	out
cat	pat	good
		wants

*Note: Words in **dark type** are from the story.*

Word Study On page 58 of the **Spelling Practice Book** are word study steps and an at-home activity.

DAY 2 — Teach the Pattern

Sort the Words Write the words *vet, hog, cat, help, job,* and *pat* in random order on the chalkboard. Draw three columns and label them with spelling patterns short *a*, short *e*, and short *o*. Encourage children to read each word and suggest its appropriate column.

To extend the activity, have children create new words using the spelling patterns *-at, -et, -ob,* and *-og* with the consonants *j, l, m,* and *s.* Have children tell if each new word is a real word or a nonsense word.

Name_____ Date_____ **Spelling** 57

Words from Social Studies

1. vet
2. hog
3. cat
4. help
5. job
6. pat

Directions (to teacher)
Write the words *vet, hog, cat, help, job,* and *pat* on the chalkboard. Have children find the word *vet* filled in on this page. Read the word aloud and have them repeat it.

Tell children they will be writing the other five words on this page. Read each word aloud. Have children repeat it and write it in the blank provided.

You may also wish to present the challenge words *small, out, good,* and *wants.*

Book 1.2
A Vet

57

SPELLING PRACTICE BOOK, PAGE 57

WORD STUDY STEPS AND ACTIVITY, PAGE 58

Name_____ Date_____ **Spelling** 59

Words from Social Studies

Write each spelling word on the line where it belongs.
Look at the spelling words in the box.

> vet hog cat help job pat

Write the spelling words that have short **a** spelled **a**.

1. cat   2. pat

Write the spelling words that have short **e** spelled **e**.

3. vet   4. help

Write the spelling words that have short **o** spelled **o**.

5. hog   6. job

Book 1.2
A Vet

59

SPELLING PRACTICE BOOK, PAGE 59

Words from Social Studies

Word Meaning: Definitions Write the Spelling Words on the chalkboard. Have volunteers find answers to clues using the words. For example:

> **This is a big pig. (hog)**
>
> **This is not a kitten, but a grown up (cat).**
>
> **This is another word for work. (job)**
>
> **This means doing something for someone. (help)**
>
> **This is a doctor for animals. (vet)**
>
> **This means to touch lightly. (pat)**

Identify Spelling Patterns Write this sentence on the chalkboard: *The vet does good things for pets.* Have a volunteer read it aloud. Ask children to tell which words have the spelling pattern *-et* and which is the Challenge Word. (*vet, pets, good*) Repeat with the spelling pattern *-at*, using this sentence: *I gave my cat a small pat.* (*cat, pat, small*)

Complete Sentences Write the following sentence on the chalkboard: *The _____ is a doctor.* Read it aloud and invite children to complete it with an *-et* word. (*vet*) Read the completed sentence. Then ask children to complete this sentence, using an *-at* word: *I took my _____ to the vet.* (*cat*)

WRITING Have children use as many Spelling Words as possible in the daily writing activity on page 124F. Remind them to check their writing for errors in spelling, grammar, and punctuation.

Optional Spelling Test You may wish to give children a spelling test. You may administer the test in the following manner. (1) Read the word. (2) Give a simple sentence containing the word. (3) Say the word again. Or you may use page 62 of the **Spelling Practice Book** for the posttest. If you wish, you may create additional sentences for the Challenge Words.

Personal Word List If children **JOURNAL** are still having trouble with any words in the lesson, have them write the words in their personal "troublesome words" lists in their journals. Have children write a context sentence or draw and label an illustration for each word. Children should refer to their word lists during later writing activities.

Name_____ Date_____ PRACTICE AND EXTEND **Spelling 60**
Words from Social Studies

Find the spelling words in the puzzle. Circle the words you find. Then write them on the lines below.

> vet hog cat help job pat

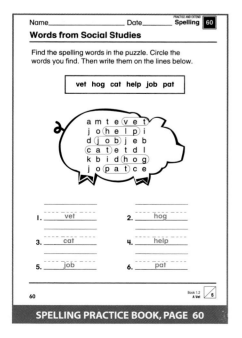

a m t e v e t
j o h e l p i
d j o b j e b
c a t e t d l
k b i d h o g
j o p a t c e

1. _____ vet
2. _____ hog
3. _____ cat
4. _____ help
5. _____ job
6. _____ pat

60   Book 1.2 / 6

SPELLING PRACTICE BOOK, PAGE 60

Name_____ Date_____ PRACTICE AND WRITE **Spelling 61**
Words from Social Studies

Look at the pictures. Complete each spelling word.

1. The v___et___ takes care of pets.

2. His j___ob___ is to care for sick pets.

3. The vet can ___hel___p big pets and small pets.

4. He likes to ___p___at the horse.

5. He can look at a sick h___og___.

6. He helped this c___at___ get well.

6 / Book 1.2
A Vet   61

SPELLING PRACTICE BOOK, PAGE 61

Name_____ Date_____ SPELLING TEST **Spelling 62**
Words from Social Studies

Look at the words in each set. One word in each set is spelled correctly. Use a pencil to color in the circle in front of that word. Before you begin, look at the sample sets of words. Sample A has been done for you. Do Sample B by yourself. When you are sure you know what to do, you may go on with the rest of the page.

Sample A
(A) then
(B) thenn
(C) tenn

Sample B
(D) flatt
(E) flat
(F) flatte

1. (A) catt
   (B) kat
   (C) cat

2. (D) hog
   (E) hogg
   (F) hoog

3. (A) jobb
   (B) jorb
   (C) job

4. (D) helb
   (E) help
   (F) hellp

5. (A) vett
   (B) vete
   (C) vet

6. (D) pat
   (E) patte
   (F) patt

62   Book 1.2 / 6
                                       A Vet

SPELLING PRACTICE BOOK, PAGE 62

137R

Wrap Up the Theme

Together Is Better

We like to share ideas and experiences with others.

REVIEW THE THEME Remind children that all the selections in this unit relate to the theme Together Is Better. Which stories were about children with pets or animal friends? What experiences did the children and animals share? How did the children and animals help each other? Ask children to name other stories or movies they know that also fit the theme Together Is Better.

READ THE POEM Read "Isn't It Strange?" by Leroy F. Jackson aloud to children. Point out that this poem has many plays on words, such as, *Shoes have tongues, But cannot talk*. Explain that this type of language is one way of describing something.

Reread the last line of the poem. Ask: Who do you like to hug? How are the arms of a chair different from the arms of a person? Discuss how the poem connects to the theme Together Is Better. Do you think the poet prefers a person to a chair? Why or why not?

LISTENING LIBRARY The poem is available on **audiocassette** and on **compact disc.**

MAKE CONNECTIONS Have children work in small groups to brainstorm a list of ways that the stories, poems, and the *Time for Kids* magazine article relate to the theme Together Is Better.

GROUP

Groups can then compare their lists as they share them with the class.

138

LOOKING AT GENRE

Have children review *One Good Pup* and *A Bug Bath*. What makes *One Good Pup* realistic fiction? What makes *A Bug Bath* a fantasy?

Help children list the key characteristics of each literary form or genre. Encourage children to give other examples of realistic and fantasy stories.

REALISTIC FICTION *One Good Pup*	FANTASY *A Bug Bath*
• Characters are made up. • Events seem like things that could happen in real life.	• Characters are made up. • Events tell about things that could not happen in real life.

Isn't It Strange?

Shoes have tongues,
But cannot talk;
Tables have legs,
But cannot walk;
Needles have eyes,
But cannot see;
Chairs have arms,
But they can't hug me!

by Leroy F. Jackson

139

LEARNING ABOUT POETRY

Literary Devices Rhyme: Write "Isn't It Strange?" on the chalkboard. Read the poem aloud, asking children to listen for words that rhyme. Reread the poem, having children echo the last words in each line. Have volunteers give pairs of rhyming words from the poem *(talk, walk; see, me)*. Ask volunteers to underline the lines that rhyme on the chalkboard.

 Response Activity. Have **PARTNERS** children work together to create a riddle, such as, *I have legs, but cannot walk. What am I?* (table) Have children share how working together is better!

Research *and* Inquiry

Complete the Theme Project
GROUP Have children work in teams to complete their group project. Remind children that the information they have gathered on their animal can be presented in any creative way. If children choose to report on their own pets, they may enjoy showing photographs of the animal to the class as well as anecdotes on how they care for it. Encourage children to share tasks such as drawing pictures and making charts so that each member of the team can contribute to the project.

Make a Classroom Presentation
Have teams take turns presenting their projects. Be sure to include time for questions from the audience.

Draw Conclusions Have children draw conclusions about what they learned from preparing and sharing their projects. Was the Resource chart they made helpful? What other resources did they use? Were they able to find information they needed on the Internet? What conclusions have children reached about their topic? Finally, ask children if doing the project has changed their opinion of different kinds of pets.

Ask More Questions What are some other things that children would like to learn about animals that are kept as pets? You might encourage the teams to continue their research and prepare another presentation.

Reading the Computer

BUILD BACKGROUND Have children share what they already know about computers. Encourage them to think of the things they already can do on the computer (play games, send e-mail). Ask children what they do at the computer to perform these everyday activities. How do they get to the game they want to play, for instance?

INTRODUCE Ask children to **preview** pages 140–141 by looking carefully at the pictures. Then **set purposes**. **Say:**

- What part of using the computer is this lesson about?
- Do the pictures make you think of any questions you would like answers to?

Explain that the lesson is about recognizing and using the little pictures, called icons, that we see when we turn on the computer. We use these icons to perform everyday tasks like looking up information, typing and printing out class assignments, sending e-mails, and playing games. Some icons, like the one for *Send,* have labels. Others, like the one for *Print,* do not. Together, the picture clues and labels help us understand what each icon does. Be sure to mention that different computers have slightly different-looking icons for the various tasks, or functions, they perform.

PRACTICE Read pages 140–141 aloud with children. **Say:**

- Can anyone tell us what these six icons do?
- Why do you think there is an icon of a printer? (because clicking on the printer allows us to print something)
- Look at the icon of the scissors. What is the word with the scissors? *(Cut)* Why do you think the word *Cut* is with the scissors? When do you use this icon? (when you want to cut, or remove, something from your work)

APPLY **Model** typing in text on a word-processing program for children. Point out and use the icons *Cut, Copy,* and *Paste* to demonstrate their functions. Then use the *Print* icon to print the sentence. As you model typing and using the icons, ask children to explain which computer icon you are using and why.

READ TOGETHER

Reading the Computer

We click on words and pictures to use the computer.

The Bug Bath

File Cut Copy Print Delete Paste

The Bug Bath
I liked it when the duck fell in!

140 *Reading for Information*

Computer Words and Pictures

Can you read these words and pictures?

 = File   = Cut

 = Print   = Copy

 = Delete   = Paste

Questions

❶ What does mean?

❷ What does let you do?

Reading the Computer   141

Anthology pages 140–141

ANSWERS TO QUESTIONS

1. This is the *Delete* Icon. It lets you remove things from your work.

2. This is the *Print* Icon. It lets you print your work.

TRANSFER THE STRATEGY Explain to children that knowing how to use the picture clues and labels will increase the number of things they can do on the computer. Discuss with children possible everyday uses for the computer. These can include both home and school activities. Ask children why learning to use the information on the computer is important to them. Ask them how these computer functions can make certain jobs easier.

Design Your Own Icons

Have children draw their own computer screen with some of their favorite icons. Encourage them to use crayons to design icons for their favorite computer game or other functions they think might be useful to have on a computer. Ask children to share the functions of the icons on their computer screen with a partner.

VOCABULARY

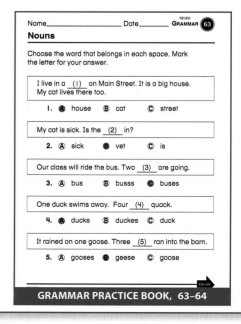

Assign selection vocabulary words to partners. Partner A acts out the meaning of a word. Partner B writes the word. Have them take turns acting out and writing their assigned words.

Unit Review

One Good Pup

no	small
ride	out

The Bug Bath

saw	want
very	two

Splash!

away	into
good	put

What Bug Is It?

about	around
again	use

A Vet

small	good
want	out

Name_____ Date_____ Practice **83**
High-Frequency Words Review

Write a word from the box to complete each sentence.

want	away	put	use	about	very

1. I ___want___ to go to bed.

2. She wants to ___use___ the big cup.

3. Could you ___put___ the cat out?

4. The frog is ___very___ wet.

5. Can you put your toys ___away___ ?

6. What is the book ___about___ ?

PRACTICE BOOK, 83–84

GRAMMAR

Divide the class into groups and assign a different kind of noun to each group. Have each group make a picture card that shows an example of its assigned noun. Have them label the pictures with the correct nouns.

Unit Review

One Good Pup
Nouns

The Bug Bath
Plural Nouns

Splash!
Irregular Plural Nouns

What Bug Is It?
Proper Nouns

A Vet
Days, Months, and Holidays

Name_____ Date_____ REVIEW GRAMMAR **63**
Nouns

Choose the word that belongs in each space. Mark the letter for your answer.

I live in a __(1)__ on Main Street. It is a big house. My cat lives there too.

1. Ⓐ house Ⓑ cat Ⓒ street

My cat is sick. Is the __(2)__ in?

2. Ⓐ sick ⬤ vet Ⓒ is

Our class will ride the bus. Two __(3)__ are going.

3. Ⓐ bus Ⓑ busss ⬤ buses

One duck swims away. Four __(4)__ quack.

4. ⬤ ducks Ⓑ duckes Ⓒ duck

It rained on one goose. Three __(5)__ ran into the barn.

5. Ⓐ gooses ⬤ geese Ⓒ goose

Go on →

GRAMMAR PRACTICE BOOK, 63–64

SPELLING

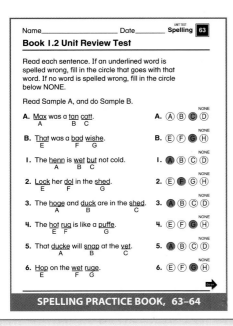

GROUP Divide the class into two teams. Have children write the spelling words on index cards. Have a member from Team A read aloud the word on the first card, for a member of Team B to spell and write on the chalkboard. Each correctly spelled word scores a point.

Unit Review

Short *u*
but
rug
duck

Blends
snap
doll
puff

Short *o*
hot
lock
hop

Social Studies Words
vet
cat
hog

Short *e*
shed
hen
wet

☑ SKILLS & STRATEGIES

Phonics and Decoding
☑ Short *u*
☑ Short *o*
☑ Short *e*
☑ Blends

Comprehension
☑ Story Elements
☑ Main Idea

Vocabulary Strategies
☑ Inflectional Ending *-ed*
☑ Context Clues

Study Skills
☑ Maps

Writing
Interactive Writing

Name_____ Date_____ **Spelling** UNIT TEST **63**

Book 1.2 Unit Review Test

Read each sentence. If an underlined word is spelled wrong, fill in the circle that goes with that word. If no word is spelled wrong, fill in the circle below NONE.

Read Sample A, and do Sample B.

A. <u>Max</u> was a <u>tan</u> <u>catt</u>.
　　A　　　B　　C
A. Ⓐ Ⓑ Ⓒ Ⓓ NONE

B. <u>That</u> was a <u>bad</u> <u>wishe</u>.
　　E　　　F　　G
B. Ⓔ Ⓕ **Ⓖ** Ⓗ NONE

1. The <u>henn</u> is <u>wet</u> <u>but</u> not cold.
　　　A　　　B　　C
1. **Ⓐ** Ⓑ Ⓒ Ⓓ NONE

2. <u>Lock</u> her <u>dol</u> in the <u>shed</u>.
　　E　　　F　　　G
2. Ⓔ **Ⓕ** Ⓖ Ⓗ NONE

3. The <u>hoge</u> and <u>duck</u> are in the <u>shed</u>.
　　　A　　　B　　　C
3. **Ⓐ** Ⓑ Ⓒ Ⓓ NONE

4. The <u>hot</u> <u>rug</u> is like a <u>puffe</u>.
　　E　　F　　　G
4. Ⓔ Ⓕ **Ⓖ** Ⓗ NONE

5. That <u>ducke</u> will <u>snap</u> at the <u>vet</u>.
　　　A　　　B　　　C
5. **Ⓐ** Ⓑ Ⓒ Ⓓ NONE

6. <u>Hop</u> on the <u>wet</u> <u>ruge</u>.
　E　　　F　　　G
6. Ⓔ Ⓕ **Ⓖ** Ⓗ NONE

SPELLING PRACTICE BOOK, 63–64

McGRAW-HILL READING

Unit Test

Student Name: _____

Date: _____

Grade 1 • Book 2

Mc Graw Hill

BOOK 2 TEST

142B

Assessment
Follow-Up

Use the results of the informal and formal assessment opportunities in the unit to help you make decisions about future instruction.

SKILLS AND STRATEGIES	Reteaching Blackline Masters	Alternate Teaching Strategies	Skills Intervention Guide
Phonics and Decoding			ⓘ
Short *u*	43, 47, 48, 56, 64, 75	T64, T65	✓
Short *o*	51, 55, 56, 64, 75	T69, T70	✓
Short *e*	59, 63, 64, 75	T71, T72	✓
Blends	67, 71, 72, 75	T75, T76	✓
Comprehension			
Story Elements	49, 57, 79	T67	✓
Main Idea	65, 73, 80	T73	✓
Vocabulary Strategies			
Inflectional Ending *-ed*	50, 58, 81	T68	✓
Context Clues	66, 74, 82	T74	✓
Study Skills			
Maps	46, 54, 62, 70, 78	T66	✓

Writing	Alternate Writing Project–Easy	
Interactive Writing	35N, 65N, 95N, 123N, 137N	

McGraw-Hill School
TECHNOLOGY

 CD-ROM provides extra phonics support.

 Research & Inquiry ideas. Visit **www.mhschool.com/reading**

Glossary

Introduce children to the Glossary by inviting them to look through the pages, describing and discussing what they see there.

Explain that the Glossary will help them find out the meanings of words. Explain that the **Glossary** is a special kind of dictionary just for words from the selections in this book. You will probably want to give a simple definition of *dictionary*, such as: "a book that shows how words are spelled and what they mean."

Point out that words in a glossary, like words in a dictionary, are listed in **alphabetical order.** Explain that in this glossary, not all the letters of the alphabet are represented.

Point out the **entry words.** Ask children to note that each entry word is printed in heavy black type and that it appears on a line by itself. Also point out that each entry word is used in a sentence and is illustrated in a picture. Mention that there are two sentences for some of the words; in such cases, the second sentence includes a word that has the same meaning as the entry word. Also mention that each picture helps to make the meaning of the accompanying word clearer.

Give children time to study the Glossary and discover what information it includes.

Glossary

This glossary can help you to find out the meanings of words in this book that you may not know.

The words are listed in alphabetical order. There is a picture and a simple sentence for each word. You can use the picture and sentence to help you understand the meaning of each word.

Sample Entry

Main Entry   Sample Sentence

Butterfly
This is a beautiful **butterfly.**

Sample Picture

Boots
Jan's **boots** keep her feet dry.

Boy
There is one **boy** in the picture.
Another word for **boy** is *lad.*

Butterfly
This is a beautiful **butterfly.**

Cat
The **cat** likes to play with yarn.

Coat
My **coat** keeps me warm.

Dog
The **dog** is asleep.

146

Head
I put the hat on my **head.**

Hill
My house is on a **hill.**

147

Legs
A dog has four **legs.**

Nap
The baby is taking a **nap.**
Another word for **nap** is *rest*.

148

Pig
The **pig** stands on the grass.

Sit
The children **sit** and play.

149

Spider

The **spider** lives in a web.

Tub

I give my dog a bath in the **tub.**

150

Vet

The **vet** will help the dog get well.

Wet

I got very **wet** in the rain.

151

Cover Illustration: Mary GrandPré

The publisher gratefully acknowledges permission to reprint the following copyrighted material:

"Hey, Bug!" from I FEEL THE SAME WAY by Lilian Moore. Copyright © 1967 by Lilian Moore. Reprinted by permission of Atheneum.

"How Spiders Got Eight Legs" retold by Katherine Mead. Text copyright © 1998 by Katherine Mead. Illustrations copyright © 1998 by Carol O'Malia. Used by permission of Raintree Steck-Vaughn.

"The Mitten" by Alvin Tresselt. Copyright © 1964 by Lothrop, Lee & Shepard Books. Used by permission.

ZB Font Method Copyright © 1996 Zaner-Bloser. Manuscript handwriting models. Used by permission.

Art/Illustrations
Jennifer Emery, 96H; Steve Sullivan, 124D

Photography
All photographs are by Macmillan/McGraw-Hill (MMH); Clara Aich for MMH; Ken Karp for MMH; Dave Mager for MMH; Mike Provost for MMH; and John Serafin for MMH.

The publisher gratefully acknowledges permission to reprint the following copyrighted material:

"Cat Kisses" by Bobbi Katz. Copyright © 1974. Reprinted with permission of author, who controls all rights.

"Isn't It Strange?" by Leroy F. Jackson from POEMS TO SHARE. Copyright © 1990, 1937 Checkerboard Press. Reprinted by permission of Checkerboard Press.

Illustration
Annie Lunsford, 6–7; Katie O'Leary, 8–9; Frank Asch, 10–32; Daniel Del Valle, 33tr, 62br, 63t, 63cr, 92br, 120br, 121tr; Rita Lascaro, 34, 94, 122; Eldon Doty, 35, 123; Jason Wolff, 36–37; Bernard Adnet, 38–61, 62tl, 62cr, 95; Doug Roy, 64; Ken Bowser, 65, 137; Loretta Krupinski, 66–67; Ken Spengler, 68–91, 93tr; Kim Fernandez, 96–97; Pat Cummings, 98–119; Esther Szedegy, 124–125; Nancy Tobin, 136; Richard Hull, 138–139; Felipe Galindo, 145, 151; Holly Jones, 144, 147; John Carozza, 148, 150.

Photography
10: t. Jan Asch. 33: b.l. PhotoDisc. 38: b. Courtesy of Bernard Adnet. t. courtesy of Kirchoff/Wohlberg , Incl; 68: t.r. Photo by Kent Lacin. 68: t.l. Courtesy of the author. 93: b.c. Richard Hamilton Smith/Corbis. 93: b.r. Richard Hamilton Smith/Corbis-Bettman. 98: t. Photo by Percidia. 99: r. Nuridsany et Perennou/Photo Researchers. 99: l. L. West/Photo Researchers. 99: m. Stephen Dalton/Photo Researchers. 99: t.r. Corbis-Bettman. 99: t.l. PhotoDisc. 101: L. West/Photo Researchers. 105: Nuridsany et Perennou/Photo Researchers. 109: b.r. Corbis-Bettman. 113: b.r. PhotoDisc. 117: b.r. Stephen Dalton/Photo Researchers. 121: b.r. PhotoDisc. 135: b.r. Ken Cavanagh. 143: Pete Turner/Image Bank. 144: b. Karl Weatherly/Corbis. 145: Pete Turner/Image Bank. 146: Francis Westfield. 146: b. Steve Grubman/The Image Works. 147: Berenholtz/The Stock Market. 148: b. Jaime Villaseca/Image Bank. 149: t. Renee Lynn/Tony Stone. 150: b. Stock Market. Spengler Creations/Kent Lacin. 151: Mike Malyszko/PNI/Stock Boston.

READING FOR INFORMATION
All photographs are by Macmillan/McGraw-Hill (MMH); and Ken Cavanagh for MMH except as noted below.
Photography
140: Ariel Skelley/The Stock Market.

Backmatter Contents

The Emerald Tree
a story from Africa retold by Janet Palazzo-Craig

There once was a princess with long, beautiful hair. Each day, the princess marched about, so all could admire her. One day a bird appeared. "Good morning, princess," it said. "May I have a bit of your hair for my nest?"

"Never!" said the princess.

"You will be sorry," said the bird. Then it flew away.

▶ Muoma, a beggar boy, had seen all this. That night, Muoma had a dream. In it, he chased the bird. But it flew far away before he could catch it.

Time passed. A dry spell fell upon the land. Streams and rivers dried up. Leaves died and fell from the trees. One day, a giant dust cloud swirled about the princess. When it passed, the princess's beautiful hair was gone!

That night, Muoma had another dream. In it, he again saw the bird. As it flew, it dropped seeds. From the seeds grew trees full of fruit. From the fruit grew beautiful hair. When Muoma awoke, he knew what he must do. The boy went to the king. "If you give me food and water for a journey, I will make your daughter's hair grow again." But the king would not listen.

Although he had only a bit of water and food, Muoma set off on his journey. He walked and walked until morning. At last, he stopped to eat.

Suddenly, many ants came up to him. "Can you feed us?" they asked. The boy had little food, but he fed the ants.

Next, a flower spoke to him. "I am so dry."

"Here," said the boy, watering the flower.

Then a mouse appeared. "Please help me find my children," it said. "They are lost on the mountain." Muoma was very tired, but he agreed to help.

At last, Muoma reached the mountaintop. Three beautiful trees stood before him. One was gold, one was silver, and one was emerald green. With a flash, the golden tree changed into the bird from Muoma's dream. "Eat," said the bird. A feast was spread below the silver tree.

Muoma was about to eat when he remembered the mouse. "First, I must keep my promise," he said.

"Do not worry," said the bird. "I was the mouse, the ants, and the flower. I wanted to see if you were ready for a special gift." The gift was a seed from the emerald tree. A seed to grow hair! The bird told the boy to plant the seed in the princess's garden. Muoma did so. Each night he watered the seed. It began to grow into a tree. All this time the princess hid away in her room. One night, she looked out and saw Muoma by the tree.

The next night, Muoma was surprised to find that the plant had already been watered. He hid. Soon he heard the princess speak. "I will take care of you, beautiful tree," she said.

Muoma stepped out of the shadows. "You will soon be just as beautiful," he said. Suddenly, a gust of wind blew the princess's veil from her head. The princess's hair had grown back! Happily, Muoma and the princess danced and laughed. By morning, the tree had grown tall. Birds sang and flew about it.

"I'll give them some of my hair for their nests!" said the princess. As she did so, rain began to fall!

The king and his people were full of joy. There was a great celebration to thank Muoma. It came to pass that Muoma and the princess were married. And for many years, they lived very happily, taking care of the singing birds and the emerald tree.

Hey, Bug!

Lilian Moore

Hey, bug, stay!
Don't run away.
I know a game that we can play.

I'll hold my fingers very still
and you can climb a finger-hill.

No, no.
Don't go.

Here's a wall—a tower, too,
a tiny bug town, just for you.
I've a cookie. You have some.

Take this oatmeal cookie crumb.

Hey, bug, stay!
Hey, bug!
Hey!

The Mitten
Alvin Tresselt

It was the coldest day of the winter, and a little boy was trudging through the forest gathering firewood for his grandmother.

"Bring back all you can find," the old woman had said as she sat knitting a pair of mittens. "The north wind blows cold, and we must have a good fire to keep us warm."

All morning the boy worked, picking up sticks, until his sled was well loaded. Then a very strange thing happened. Just as he picked up the last stick he dropped one of his mittens in the snow.

Now, how a boy could do this on the coldest day of winter I'll never know, but that's the way my grandfather tells the story.

Off he went with his load of wood, and the mitten was left lying on a snowdrift.

As soon as he was out of sight a little mouse came scurrying through the woods. She was very cold, and when she spied the little boy's mitten with its feathery fur cuff, she popped right in to get warm. It was just the right size for a tiny mouse.

Presently a green frog came hip-hopping over the snow.

"Anybody home?" she asked when she saw the mitten.

"Only me," said the mouse, "and come in quickly before you freeze."

They had no sooner settled themselves snugly in the red wool lining when an owl flew down.

"May I join you in that lovely mitten?" he asked.

"If you mind your manners," replied the mouse, for owls always made her nervous.

"And don't wiggle around too much," added the frog, "because it's a bit tight in here."

It wasn't long before a rabbit came down the forest path.

"Is there room for me in that nice warm mitten?" asked the rabbit. "It's awfully cold out here."

"Not much space left," said the mouse and the frog and the owl. "But come in. We'll see what we can do."

Even before the rabbit had gotten herself tucked in, a fox trotted up to the mitten, and after a good deal of trouble she got herself in with the others. The mouse was beginning to think maybe she shouldn't have been so generous, but with the bitter wind outside, what else could she do?

And now, as if things weren't bad enough, the next visitor was a big gray wolf who wanted to come in, too. "I don't know how we'll manage it," said the mouse. "But we'll try."

Everyone moved around a bit, and finally the wolf was squeezed into the mitten. It was very crowded by now, but at least it was warm.

Things had just gotten arranged nicely when the animals heard a great snorting. It was a wild boar, and he was very anxious to get in out of the wind.

"Oh, dear!" cried the mouse, for the mitten was already beginning to stretch a little. "We just don't have any more room!"

"I'll be very careful," said the boar. With that he squinched himself into the mitten along with the mouse and the frog, the owl, the rabbit, the fox, and the wolf. I know this is so because my grandfather told me.

But the worst was yet to come, for who should appear now but a bear! He was very big and very cold.

"No room! No room!" cried the animals even before the bear had a chance to speak.

"Nonsense!" said the bear. "There's always room for one more."

And, without so much as a please or thank you, he began crawling into the mitten. He put his paw in first, and the mitten creaked and groaned. He put his other paw in, and one of the seams popped. Then he took a big breath and pushed himself in.

Now while all this was going on, along came a little black cricket. She was very old, and her creaky legs ached with the cold. When she saw the mitten she said to herself, "Now that looks like a nice warm place. I'll just hop over and see if I can squeeze in too!"

But, ah me, that's all that was needed to finish off the poor old mitten. The cricket had no more than put her first scratchy foot inside when, with a rip and a snap, the stitches came apart, the old leather cracked, and the soft red lining split in half, popping all the animals into the snow!

Well, at this very moment the little boy discovered that he had only one mitten, so back he went to see where he might have dropped the other one. But all he could find were the ripped-apart pieces. And he thought he saw a little mouse scurrying away with a bit of red wool perched on her head.

It looked very much like the lining from the thumb of his missing mitten.

"Oh, well," said the boy as he snuggled his cold hand inside his coat, "my grandmother will surely have my new mittens finished by now."

Then he hurried home, with the north wind nipping at his cheeks.

And my grandfather says he never did know what *really* happened to his mitten.

How Spiders Got Eight Legs

A Big Problem

Long ago in Africa, spiders had only two legs. There was one spider who was very selfish. He wanted to be better than all the other animals in the jungle. But he did not like to work hard.

Every year, there was a big race in the jungle. All the animals wanted to win. They practiced running every day. Spider thought, "I am much better than the others. I'll think of a way to win this year's race without working hard."

The Plan

Spider watched all the animals run. He thought that Ostrich, Giraffe, or Cheetah could win the race. Spider could not run as fast as any of them. But he did not worry. He had a plan.

▶ Spider thought, "Ostrich has such strong legs. If I had legs like his, I could win the race." Spider went to the river to see Great Hippo, the hippopotamus. He was the wisest animal. He could grant wishes.

Spider called out, "Great Hippo, I wish to have strong legs like Ostrich."

"Why do you wish to have legs like Ostrich?" Great Hippo asked.

"I have to win the race!" said Spider.

The Promise

Great Hippo said, "I will give you strong legs, but you must promise me something. One day, I will ask you a question. You must answer honestly."

Spider said, "That will be easy." So his wish was granted.

Spider tried to run on his new legs, but it was too hard. He asked Ostrich for help.

Ostrich said, "Watch, my friend. I'll show you how to run with those legs."

Spider watched, but still he could not run.

Spider was mad. He went back to see Great Hippo. He said, "I cannot run with these legs. I wish to have four long legs like Giraffe."

Great Hippo asked, "Why do you wish to have legs like Giraffe?"

Spider said, "I want to take long steps like Giraffe. I have to win the race!"

Great Hippo said, "I will give you four long legs, but you must promise me something. One day, I will ask you a question. You must answer honestly."

Spider said, "That will be easy." So his wish was granted.

Spider tried to run on his long legs, but it was too hard. He asked Giraffe for help.

Read Aloud   ▶ Continue reading here.

Giraffe said, "Watch, my friend. I'll show you how to run with those legs."

Spider watched, but still he could not run.

Spider was really mad. He went back to see Great Hippo. He said, "I cannot run on these long legs. I wish for eight legs."

Great Hippo asked, "Why do you wish for eight legs?"

Spider said, "Cheetah is the fastest four-legged animal. I could run twice as fast as Cheetah if I had eight legs."

Another Promise

Great Hippo said, "I will give you eight legs, but you must promise me something. One day, I will ask you a question. You must answer honestly."

Spider said, "That will be easy." So his wish was granted.

Spider tried hard to run with eight legs, but it was too hard. He asked Cheetah for help.

Cheetah said, "I don't know how to run with eight legs. I could only show you if you had four legs like me."

Spider was madder than ever. He went back to see Great Hippo again. He yelled, "These eight legs don't work! How am I going to win the race?"

Great Hippo did not answer. He just walked into the river to swim.

Spider made his way home. He was still angry. He sat down and thought very hard. How could he win the race with eight legs? Suddenly, he had an idea! He laughed and went to sleep.

On the day of the race, Cheetah could hear someone yelling for help. He said, "That sounds like Spider, I'll go check on him."

Cheetah ran off to Spider's house. Spider was lying down and crying out with pain.

"Spider, what's wrong?" Cheetah asked.

Spider said, "I am very sick. Take me to see Great Hippo. He'll know what to do."

Cheetah said, "Great Hippo is waiting at the finish line. I will take you to him."

Spider could see the finish line. He climbed onto the tip of Cheetah's nose. Everyone cheered as Cheetah crossed the finish line. Great Hippo announced, "Cheetah's the winner!"

Spider yelled, "Wait! Cheetah didn't win. I DID! I crossed the finish line first. I won by a nose!

Great Hippo looked at Spider. He said, "I have a question. Remember that you promised to answer it honestly. Who REALLY won the race?"

A Lesson Learned

Spider was worried. He knew he had to be honest. He said, "I tried to trick all of you. Cheetah is the real winner."

Great Hippo smiled. He said, "Thank you for being honest. Now I will make those eight legs work just right for you."

From then on, spiders everywhere have had eight legs. And they work just right.

Your Friendly Vet
Constance Andrea Keremes

If your pup won't chase his ball,
I'm the one to call.

And if your cat won't purr for you,
I'll tell you what to do.

What's that? Your rabbit's lost his hop?
My place is where to stop.

I'm the doctor for your pets,
Just bring them all to me.

I'm the vet, your friendly vet,
The one your pets should see.

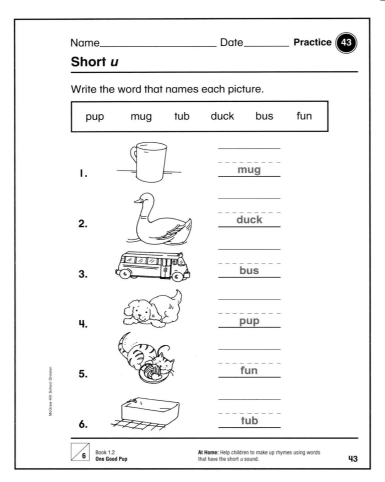

Name_____ Date_____ Practice **43**

Short *u*

Write the word that names each picture.

| pup | mug | tub | duck | bus | fun |

1.   mug

2.   duck

3.   bus

4.   pup

5.   fun

6.   tub

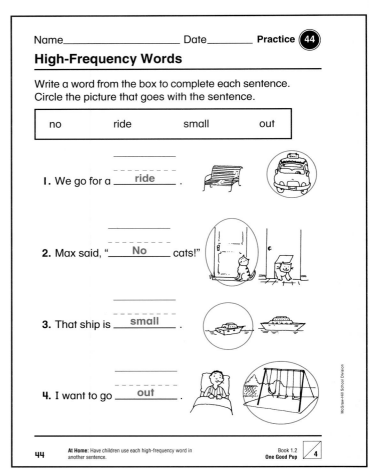

Name_____ Date_____ Practice **44**

High-Frequency Words

Write a word from the box to complete each sentence.
Circle the picture that goes with the sentence.

| no | ride | small | out |

1. We go for a ___ride___ .

2. Max said, "___No___ cats!"

3. That ship is ___small___ .

4. I want to go ___out___ .

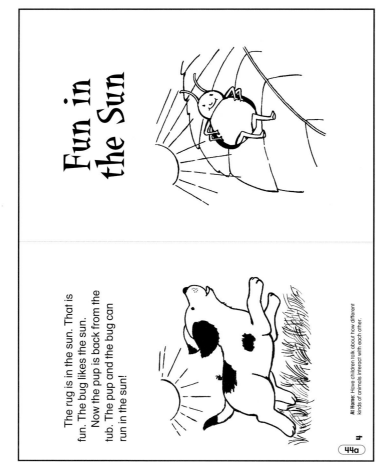

Fun in the Sun

The rug is in the sun. That is fun. The bug likes the sun. Now the pup is back from the tub. The pup and the bug can run in the sun!

At Home: Have children talk about how different kinds of animals interact with each other.

4   44a

A pup dug in the mud. It was fun.
A small bug was in the mud. She got on the pup to go for a ride.
"This pup can be my bus," said the bug.

The pup ran out of the mud.
The pup ran to a tub.
No, the bug will not go to the tub. The bug will go in the rug.
The pup will get a scrub.
Then he will get a hug.

One Good Pup McGraw-Hill School Division

2   3   44b

One Good Pup • PRACTICE

Name_____ Date_____ Practice **45**

Story Comprehension

Circle the sentences that tell what happened in "One Good Pup."

1. (The pup wants to go out.)

2. (It is a wet day.)

3. The boy and the pup run in the sun.

4. (The boy and the pup sit in a ship.)

5. They go with dad in the van.

6. (The boy and the pup play tug.)

7. (They fish in the tub.)

8. (The pup is good.)

Name_____ Date_____ Practice **46**

A Map

This **picture map** shows the inside of a school.

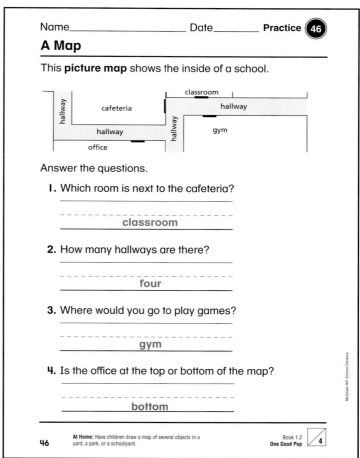

Answer the questions.

1. Which room is next to the cafeteria?
   _____
   classroom

2. How many hallways are there?
   _____
   four

3. Where would you go to play games?
   _____
   gym

4. Is the office at the top or bottom of the map?
   _____
   bottom

Name_____ Date_____ Practice **47**

Short *u*

Look at the pictures.
Read the words.
Then write the two words that tell about the picture.

1. bug   hug   jug
   _____
   bug in a **jug**

2. cut   nut   hut
   _____
   cut the **nut**

3. duck   muck   tuck
   _____
   duck in the **muck**

4. bun   run   sun
   _____
   bun on the **run**

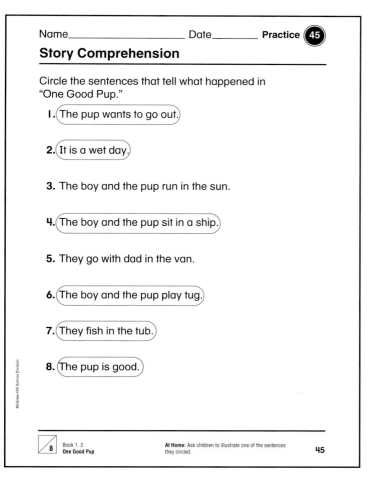

Name_____ Date_____ Practice **48**

Short *u, i, a; sh, th*

Choose the word that completes the sentence.
Use the picture as a clue.
Then write the word.

| ship | duck | bath | thick | pig | rush |

1. The ____ **pig** is in the mud.

2. This is a ____ **thick** sandwich.

3. The ____ **duck** said "quack."

4. I can see a ____ **ship**.

5. The kids ____ **rush** back.

6. The cat sits in the ____ **bath**.

T7

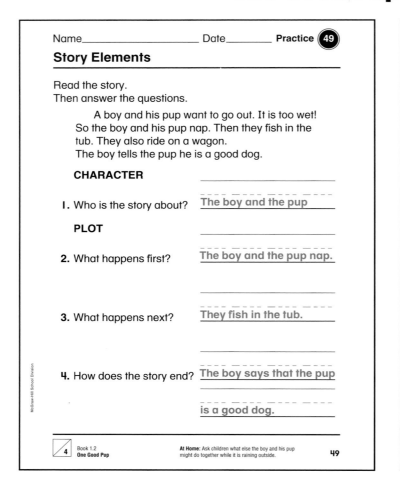

Name_____ Date_____ Practice **49**

Story Elements

Read the story.
Then answer the questions.

> A boy and his pup want to go out. It is too wet! So the boy and his pup nap. Then they fish in the tub. They also ride on a wagon.
> The boy tells the pup he is a good dog.

CHARACTER

1. Who is the story about? _The boy and the pup_

PLOT

2. What happens first? _The boy and the pup nap._

3. What happens next? _They fish in the tub._

4. How does the story end? _The boy says that the pup_

is a good dog.

Book 1.2
One Good Pup

At Home: Ask children what else the boy and his pup might do together while it is raining outside.

49

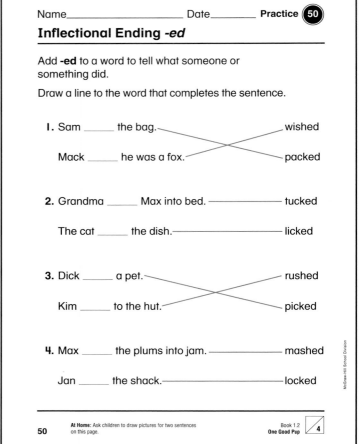

Name_____ Date_____ Practice **50**

Inflectional Ending -ed

Add **-ed** to a word to tell what someone or something did.

Draw a line to the word that completes the sentence.

1. Sam _____ the bag.   wished

   Mack _____ he was a fox.   packed

2. Grandma _____ Max into bed. ——— tucked

   The cat _____ the dish.——————— licked

3. Dick _____ a pet.   rushed

   Kim _____ to the hut.   picked

4. Max _____ the plums into jam.——— mashed

   Jan _____ the shack.——————— locked

50

At Home: Ask children to draw pictures for two sentences on this page.

Book 1.2
One Good Pup

Short *u*

Say the name of the picture.
Listen to the sound the letter **u** makes.

bug

Write the letter **u** to complete the word.
Then circle the picture that the word names.

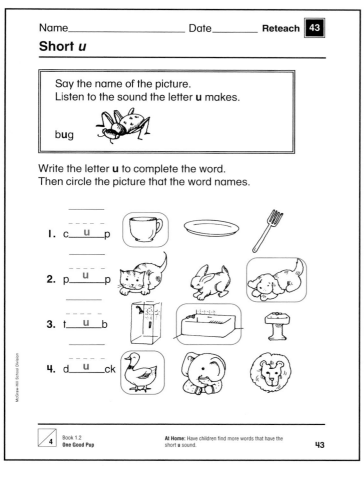

1. c__u__p

2. p__u__p

3. t__u__b

4. d__u__ck

Book 1.2
One Good Pup
4
At Home: Have children find more words that have the
short u sound.
43

High-Frequency Words

Draw a line to the word that completes each
sentence.

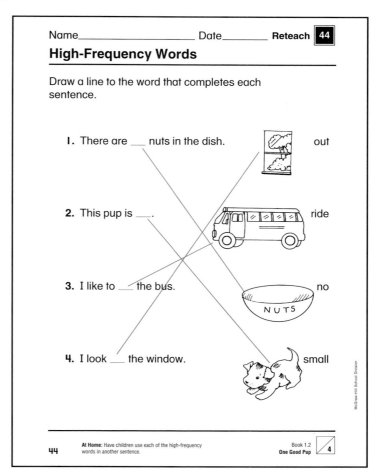

1. There are ___ nuts in the dish.

2. This pup is ___.

3. I like to ___ the bus.

4. I look ___ the window.

out

ride

no

small

44
At Home: Have children use each of the high-frequency
words in another sentence.
Book 1.2
One Good Pup
4

Story Comprehension

Circle the pictures that show what happened in
"One Good Pup."
Then color the picture.

1.
2.
3.
4.
5.
6.

Book 1.2
One Good Pup
6
At Home: Have children use the pictures to talk about
some of the things that happened in the story.
45

A Map

This **picture map** shows the things
you might find on a playground.

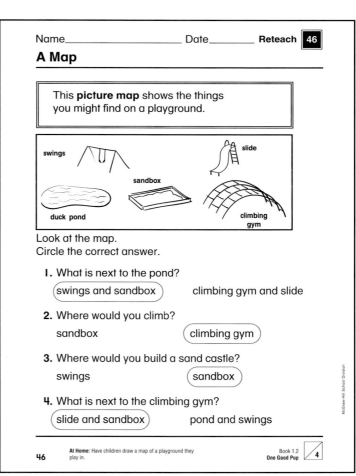

swings

slide

sandbox

duck pond

climbing
gym

Look at the map.
Circle the correct answer.

1. What is next to the pond?

swings and sandbox   climbing gym and slide

2. Where would you climb?

sandbox   climbing gym

3. Where would you build a sand castle?

swings   sandbox

4. What is next to the climbing gym?

slide and sandbox   pond and swings

One Good Pup • RETEACH

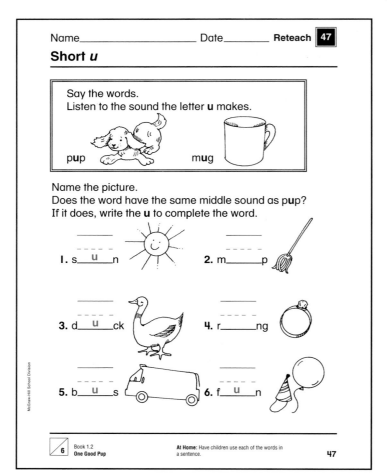

Name_____ Date_____ Reteach **47**

Short u

Say the words.
Listen to the sound the letter **u** makes.

p**u**p   m**u**g

Name the picture.
Does the word have the same middle sound as p**u**p?
If it does, write the **u** to complete the word.

I. s__u__n

2. m____p

3. d__u__ck

4. r____ng

5. b__u__s

6. f__u__n

6 Book 1.2 **One Good Pup**   **At Home:** Have children use each of the words in a sentence.   **47**

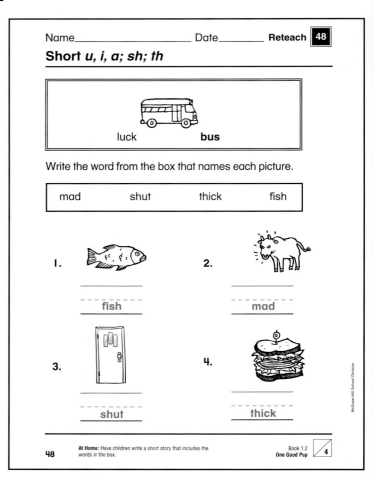

Name_____ Date_____ Reteach **48**

Short u, i, a; sh; th

luck   **bus**

Write the word from the box that names each picture.

| mad | shut | thick | fish |

I. ____ fish

2. ____ mad

3. ____ shut

4. ____ thick

48   **At Home:** Have children write a short story that includes the words in the box.   Book 1.2 **One Good Pup** 4

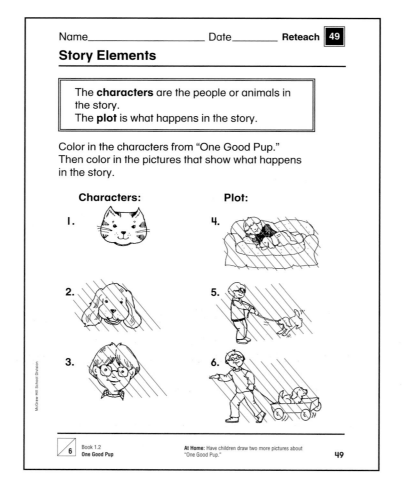

Name_____ Date_____ Reteach **49**

Story Elements

The **characters** are the people or animals in the story.
The **plot** is what happens in the story.

Color in the characters from "One Good Pup."
Then color in the pictures that show what happens in the story.

Characters: **Plot:**

I.   4.

2.   5.

3.   6.

6 Book 1.2 **One Good Pup**   **At Home:** Have children draw two more pictures about "One Good Pup."   **49**

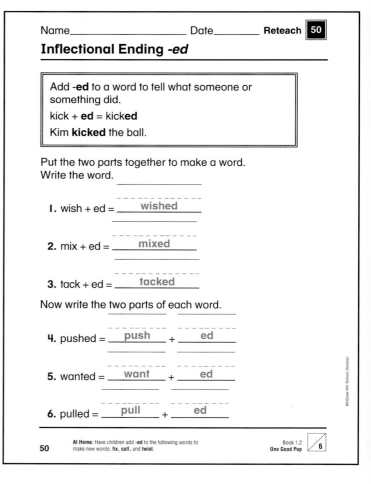

Name_____ Date_____ Reteach **50**

Inflectional Ending -ed

Add **-ed** to a word to tell what someone or something did.
kick + **ed** = kick**ed**
Kim **kicked** the ball.

Put the two parts together to make a word.
Write the word. _____

I. wish + ed = ____ wished ____

2. mix + ed = ____ mixed ____

3. tack + ed = ____ tacked ____

Now write the two parts of each word.

4. pushed = ____ push ____ + ____ ed ____

5. wanted = ____ want ____ + ____ ed ____

6. pulled = ____ pull ____ + ____ ed ____

50   **At Home:** Have children add **-ed** to the following words to make new words: **fix, call,** and **twist.**   Book 1.2 **One Good Pup** 6

T10   *Annotated Workbooks*

One Good Pup • EXTEND

Short *u*

| cub | jug | bun | rut | pup | sun |

Write a rhyming word on each line.
Use words from the box.

Answers will vary; possibilities are shown.

run _____ **bun or sun**

fun _____ **bun or sun**

hug _____ **jug**

rub _____ **cub**

cut _____ **rut**

cup _____ **pup**

Write a sentence using two rhyming words.

_____

Answers will vary.

Book 1.2
One Good Pup

At Home: Look through magazines and newspapers for
pictures of words with the short **u** sound.

43

High-Frequency Words

| no | ride | small | out |

Use a word from the box to finish each sentence.
Answers may vary.

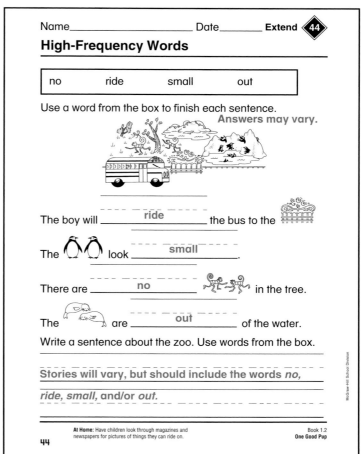

The boy will _____ **ride** _____ the bus to the

The look _____ **small** _____.

There are _____ **no** _____ in the tree.

The _____ are _____ **out** _____ of the water.

Write a sentence about the zoo. Use words from the box.

_____

Stories will vary, but should include the words *no*,

ride, small, and/or out.

At Home: Have children look through magazines and
newspapers for pictures of things they can ride on.

44

Book 1.2
One Good Pup

Story Comprehension

What can Pup do inside?
What can Pup do outside?
Fill in the chart.
Sample answers are shown.

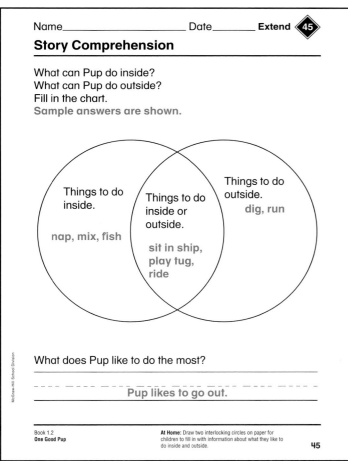

Things to do inside.

nap, mix, fish

Things to do inside or outside.

sit in ship, play tug, ride

Things to do outside.

dig, run

What does Pup like to do the most?

_____

Pup likes to go out.

Book 1.2
One Good Pup

At Home: Draw two interlocking circles on paper for
children to fill in with information about what they like to
do inside and outside.

45

Use a Map

Read the directions. Make a map.

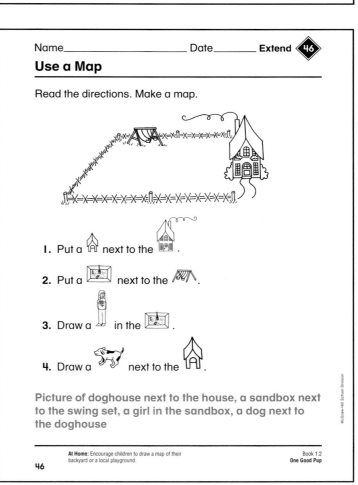

1. Put a 🏠 next to the 🏫 .

2. Put a 🖼 next to the ⛓ .

3. Draw a 🧍 in the 🖼 .

4. Draw a 🐕 next to the ⛺ .

**Picture of doghouse next to the house, a sandbox next
to the swing set, a girl in the sandbox, a dog next to
the doghouse**

At Home: Encourage children to draw a map of their
backyard or a local playground.

46

Book 1.2
One Good Pup

One Good Pup • EXTEND

Short *u*

Put the letters in order to make words.
Write a sentence with one of the words.

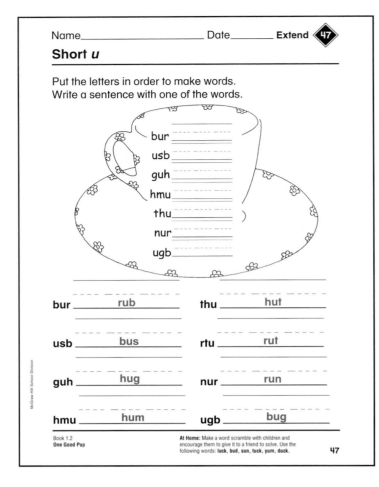

bur _____
usb _____
guh _____
hmu _____
thu _____
nur _____
ugb _____

bur ___rub___   thu ___hut___

usb ___bus___   rtu ___rut___

guh ___hug___   nur ___run___

hmu ___hum___   ugb ___bug___

Book 1.2
One Good Pup

At Home: Make a word scramble with children and encourage them to give it to a friend to solve. Use the following words: **luck, bud, sun, tuck, yum, duck.**

47

Short *u, i, a; sh, th*

u	III
i	II
a	I
sh	IV
th	V

Use the code box to write the words.
The first one is done for you.

t [III] ck ___tuck___   [V] at ___that___

qu [I] ck ___quack___   h [II] d ___hid___

ba [V] ___bath___   k [II] d ___kid___

[IV] ip ___ship___   wi [IV] ___wish___

At Home: Have children write a note to a friend using some of the words from the exercise.

Book 1.2
One Good Pup

48

Story Elements

If Pup could talk, what would he say?

_____
_____
_____
_____
_____

Book 1.2
One Good Pup

At Home: Ask children to draw a picture of something they like to do outside.

49

Inflectional Ending *-ed*

Write the word that completes each sentence.

pack   packed

He ___packed___ his bag.

fish   fished

I can ___fish___ in a tub.

kick   kicked

She ___kicked___ it out.

dash   dashed

Can he ___dash___ to the bus?

wish   wished

She ___wished___ she had a pup.

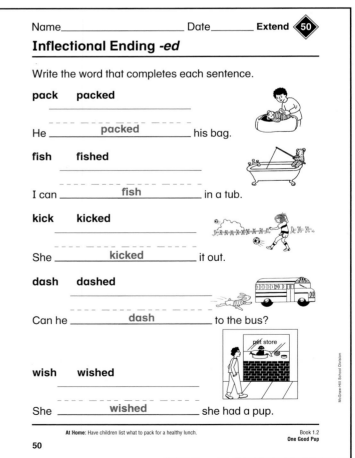

At Home: Have children list what to pack for a healthy lunch.

Book 1.2
One Good Pup

50

One Good Pup • GRAMMAR

Nouns

> • A **noun** is a word that names a person, place, or thing.
>   The **dog** is big.   **Dog** is a noun.

Circle the nouns that name a person, an animal, or a thing.

1. The (cat) is black.

2. The (boy) has a (toy).

3. The (apple) is red.

4. The (mouse) eats (corn).

Match Nouns with Pictures

> • A **noun** is a word that names a person, place, or thing.
>   A **man** is a person.   **Man** is a noun.
>   A **home** is a place.   **Home** is a noun.
>   A **ship** is a thing.   **Ship** is a noun.

Draw a line from the sentence to the noun named in the sentence.

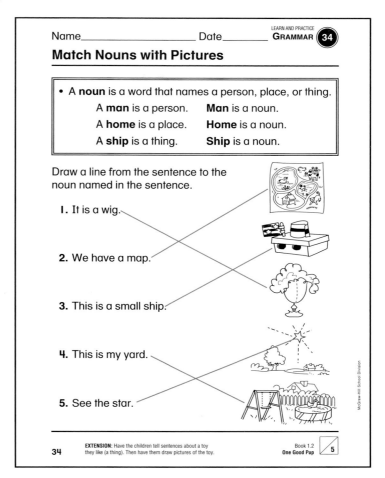

1. It is a wig.

2. We have a map.

3. This is a small ship.

4. This is my yard.

5. See the star.

Nouns in Sentences

> • A **noun** is a word that names a person, place, or thing.
> • A **noun** can name a place.
>   I will play at **home**.

Write the name of a place from the word box in the sentence.

| home | sky | hill | bank | yard |

1. I go _____ home _____ after school.

2. The _____ sky _____ is blue.

3. The tree is on top of a _____ hill _____.

4. I plant flowers in our _____ yard _____.

5. I keep money in a _____ bank _____.

Sentences

> • Begin each sentence with a capital letter.
> • End every sentence with a special mark.

Circle the sentences that are correct.

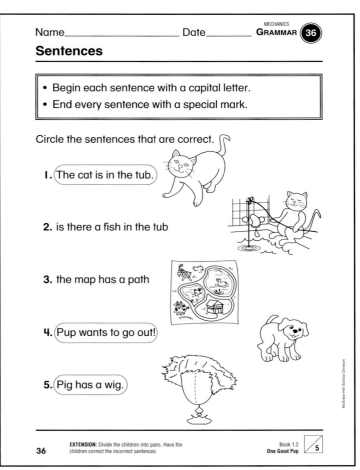

1. (The cat is in the tub.)

2. is there a fish in the tub

3. the map has a path

4. (Pup wants to go out!)

5. (Pig has a wig.)

One Good Pup • GRAMMAR

Nouns

Circle each noun that names the picture.

1. The (dog) is playing.

2. A (girl) is reading.

3. The (owl) hoots.

4. The (kite) flies.

5. Go to the top of the (hill.)

6. It is a big (house.)

Nouns

- A **noun** is a word that names a person, place, or thing.
- A **noun** can name a place.

Mechanics:
- Begin each sentence with a capital letter.
- End every sentence with a special mark.

Circle the nouns. Write the sentence correctly.

1. see the (toy) in the (tub)

   _____

   See the toy in the tub.

2. i have a big (cat)

   _____

   I have a big cat.

3. the (dog) is in the (yard)

   _____

   The dog is in the yard.

4. find the (path) on the (map)

   _____

   Find the path on the map.

5. look at the (duck)

   _____

   Look at the duck.

One Good Pup • SPELLING

Words with Short *u*

Complete each word by writing the letter that spells
the short *u* sound.

1. b_____**u**_____t

2. t_____u_____g

3. d_____u_____ck

4. r_____u_____g

5. c_____u_____t

6. b_____u_____ck

Directions (to teacher)

Review the short *u* sound by explaining that the letter *u* stands for /u/ as in the word *but*. Write *but* on the chalkboard or form the word with letter cards. Say the word aloud and have children repeat it. Then have children look at the first example on the page. Point out that the letter *u* has been filled in.

Write the words *cut, tug, rug, duck,* and *buck* on the chalkboard. Read each word aloud and have children repeat it. Have them listen for the short u sound in each word. Then have them complete each word in the blank provided.

Words with Short u

Using the Word Study Steps

1. LOOK at the word.
2. SAY the word aloud.
3. STUDY the letters in the word.
4. WRITE the word.
5. CHECK the word.
   Did you spell the word right? If not,
   go back to step 1.

Spelling Tip
Use beginnings and
endings of words
you can spell to
help you spell new
words.
but + ba**ck** = **buck**

Find and Circle
Where are the spelling words?

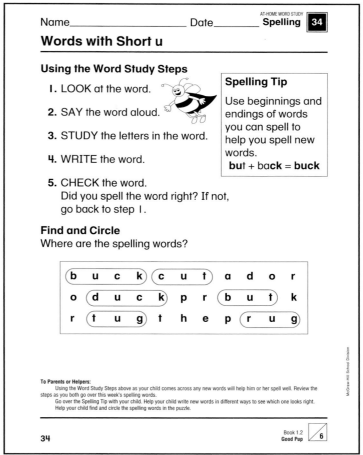

To Parents or Helpers:
Using the Word Study Steps above as your child comes across any new words will help him or her spell well. Review the steps as you both go over this week's spelling words.
Go over the Spelling Tip with your child. Help your child write new words in different ways to see which one looks right.
Help your child find and circle the spelling words in the puzzle.

Words with Short *u*

Complete the spelling words inside each dog bone.
Put the words with the same endings in the same box.

but tug duck rug cut buck

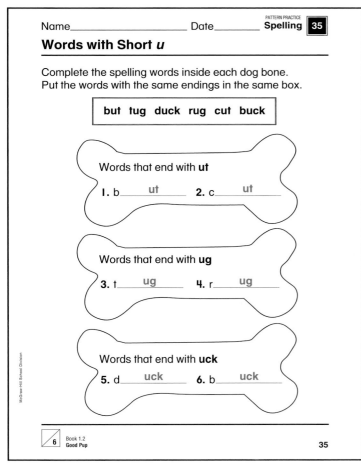

Words that end with **ut**

1. b___ut___   2. c___ut___

Words that end with **ug**

3. t___ug___   4. r___ug___

Words that end with **uck**

5. d___uck___   6. b___uck___

Words with Short *u*

Read the words in the box. Circle the words in the
puzzle. Then write the words on the lines.

but tug duck rug cut buck

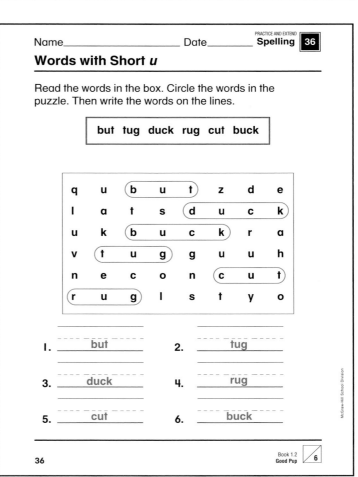

1. ___but___   2. ___tug___

3. ___duck___   4. ___rug___

5. ___cut___   6. ___buck___

One Good Pup • SPELLING

Words with Short *u*

Look at the picture. Complete each sentence with a spelling word.

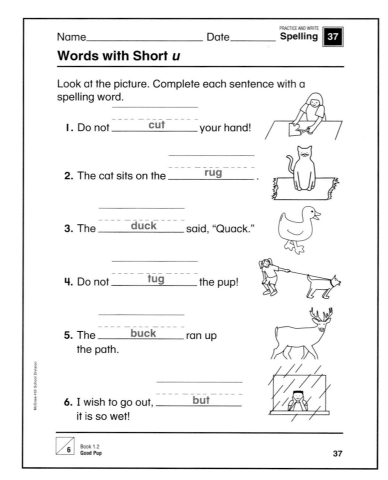

1. Do not _____**cut**_____ your hand!

2. The cat sits on the _____**rug**_____.

3. The _____**duck**_____ said, "Quack."

4. Do not _____**tug**_____ the pup!

5. The _____**buck**_____ ran up the path.

6. I wish to go out, _____**but**_____ it is so wet!

Words with Short u

Look at the words in each set. One word in each set is spelled correctly. Use a pencil to color in the circle in front of that word. Before you begin, look at the sample sets of words. Sample A has been done for you. Do Sample B by yourself. When you are sure you know what to do, you may go on with the rest of the page.

Sample A
- Ⓐ bug
- Ⓑ bugg
- Ⓒ buug

Sample B
- Ⓓ diss
- Ⓔ dish
- Ⓕ dihs

1.
- Ⓐ rugg
- Ⓑ rug
- Ⓒ ruug

4.
- Ⓓ dukk
- Ⓔ duc
- Ⓕ duck

2.
- Ⓓ buck
- Ⓔ buk
- Ⓕ buc

5.
- Ⓐ bot
- Ⓑ buut
- Ⓒ but

3.
- Ⓐ cut
- Ⓑ kut
- Ⓒ kutt

6.
- Ⓓ tugg
- Ⓔ tug
- Ⓕ tuug

The Bug Bath • PRACTICE

Short o

Sound out and say each word.
Print the word on the line.
Then circle the picture it names.

1. h o t   _____ hot

2. r o c k   _____ rock

3. b o x   _____ box

4. h o p   _____ hop

At Home: Have children use the words they wrote in sentences.
51

High-Frequency Words

Write a word from the box to complete each sentence.

want	saw	two	very

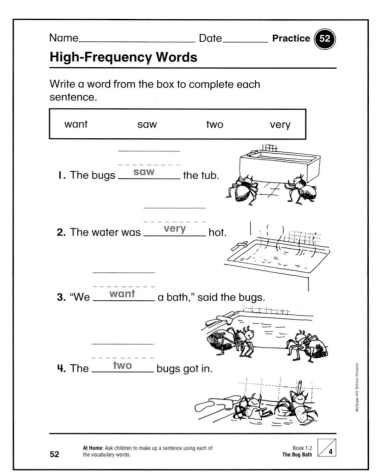

1. The bugs _____ saw _____ the tub.

2. The water was _____ very _____ hot.

3. "We _____ want _____ a bath," said the bugs.

4. The _____ two _____ bugs got in.

52
At Home: Ask children to make up a sentence using each of the vocabulary words.

Hot Pot

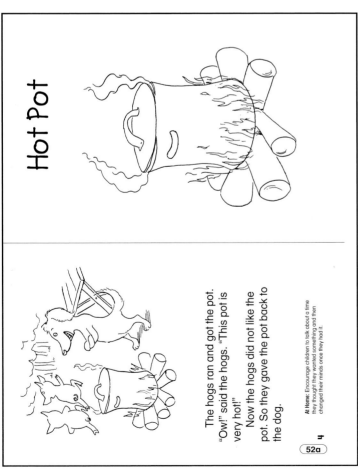

The hogs ran and got the pot. "Ow!" said the hogs. "This pot is very hot!"
Now the hogs did not like the pot. So they gave the pot back to the dog.

At Home: Encourage children to talk about a time they thought they wanted something and then changed their minds once they had it.

4
52a

2

A dog had a pot. The dog put two rocks in the pot. He put a box in the pot. He put a log in the pot. The pot was very hot.

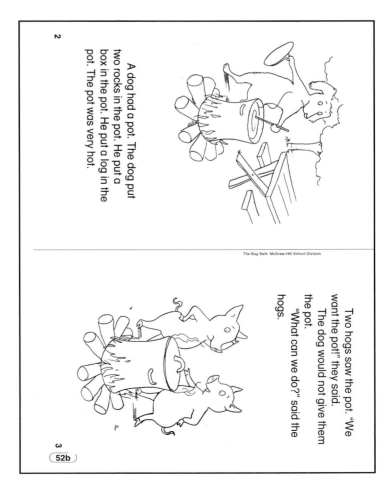

The Bug Bath McGraw-Hill School Division

Two hogs saw the pot. "We want the pot!" they said. The dog would not give them the pot. "What can we do?" said the hogs.

3
52b

T17

The Bug Bath • PRACTICE

Story Comprehension

What happened in "The Bug Bath"?
Read the sentences below.
Write **T** next to the things that happened.
Write **F** next to the things that didn't happen.

1. __T__ Al and Bob wish to have a bath.

2. __F__ Al hops into the small van.

3. __T__ A duck falls into the tub.

4. __F__ Bob and Al give the duck a hat.

5. __T__ A fish falls into the tub.

6. __T__ The boy picks up the fish.

7. __T__ Bob and Al run.

8. __T__ Bob and Al take a bath in a flower.

Book 1.2
The Bug Bath
8

At Home: Have children draw a picture that describes one of the sentences they marked **T**.

53

A Map

This is a hippity-hop **map**.
It shows where the frog goes.

Look at the map.
Write the correct answer on the line.

1. Start at the lily pad. How
   many hops to the boat? __3__

2. How many hops from
   the boat to the dock? __1__

3. How many hops from
   the dock to the rock? __4__

4. How many hops from
   the boat to the rock? __5__

54

At Home: Have children draw a hippity-hop map of a room in their house.

Book 1.2
The Bug Bath
4

Short *o*

dot	log	dog	jog	rod	fog

Use the words in the box to answer the riddles.

1. I wag my tail. What am I? __dog__

2. I come from a tree. What am I? __log__

3. You catch fish with me. What am I? __rod__

4. You do this when you run. What is it? __jog__

5. You can not see if I am here. What am I? __fog__

6. I am a small spot. What am I? __dot__

Book 1.2
The Bug Bath
6

At Home: Make up a simple sentence using a short **o** word. Say the sentence, omitting the word, and ask children to guess the word. Then reverse roles.

55

Short *o, u, i, a; ck*

Look at the pictures.
Use the words in the box to complete the rhymes.

sack	dig	fox	rug	bat

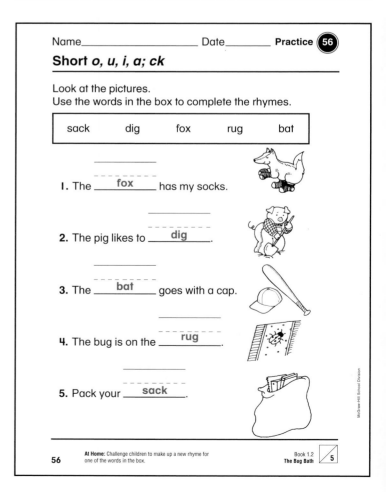

1. The __fox__ has my socks.

2. The pig likes to __dig__.

3. The __bat__ goes with a cap.

4. The bug is on the __rug__.

5. Pack your __sack__.

56

At Home: Challenge children to make up a new rhyme for one of the words in the box.

Book 1.2
The Bug Bath
5

The Bug Bath • PRACTICE

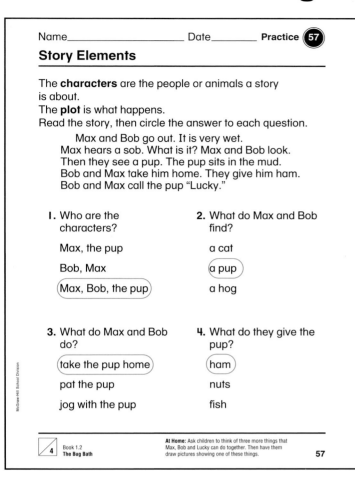

Story Elements

The **characters** are the people or animals a story is about.
The **plot** is what happens.
Read the story, then circle the answer to each question.

> Max and Bob go out. It is very wet.
> Max hears a sob. What is it? Max and Bob look.
> Then they see a pup. The pup sits in the mud.
> Bob and Max take him home. They give him ham.
> Bob and Max call the pup "Lucky."

1. Who are the characters?

Max, the pup

Bob, Max

(Max, Bob, the pup)

2. What do Max and Bob find?

a cat

(a pup)

a hog

3. What do Max and Bob do?

(take the pup home)

pat the pup

jog with the pup

4. What do they give the pup?

(ham)

nuts

fish

At Home: Ask children to think of three more things that Max, Bob and Lucky can do together. Then have them draw pictures showing one of these things.

57

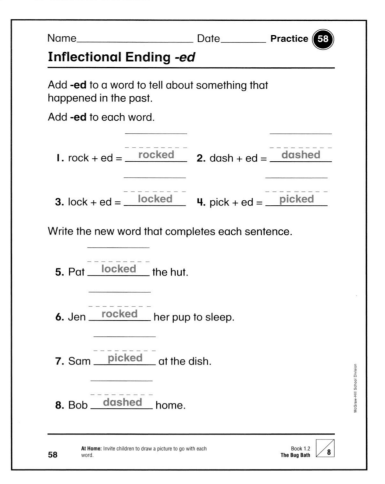

Inflectional Ending -ed

Add **-ed** to a word to tell about something that happened in the past.

Add **-ed** to each word.

1. rock + ed = ___rocked___   **2.** dash + ed = ___dashed___

3. lock + ed = ___locked___   **4.** pick + ed = ___picked___

Write the new word that completes each sentence.

5. Pat ___locked___ the hut.

6. Jen ___rocked___ her pup to sleep.

7. Sam ___picked___ at the dish.

8. Bob ___dashed___ home.

At Home: Invite children to draw a picture to go with each word.

Book 1.2
The Bug Bath 8

T19

The Bug Bath • RETEACH

Short *o*

Pop has a _____.   nod   (top)   jog

Circle the word that completes the sentence.
Then write the word.

1. The pot is ___hot___.
   (hot)   cot   tot

2. Bob likes to ___hop___.
   top   (hop)   sock

3. Max got a ___lot___ of socks.
   tot   (lot)   not

4. I nod at the ___hog___.
   not   jog   (hog)

5. The ham is in the ___pot___.
   job   lock   (pot)

High-Frequency Words

Choose a word to complete each sentence.
Then write the words in the boxes.

| saw | two | very | want |

1. The sun is ___very___ hot. | v | e | r | y |

2. Do you ___want___ a nut? | w | a | n | t |

3. I ___saw___ you on the bus. | s | a | w |

4. There were ___two___ bugs. | t | w | o |

Story Comprehension

Circle the pictures that tell about "The Bug Bath."

A Map

This is a "hippity-hop" **map**.
It shows where the rabbit goes.

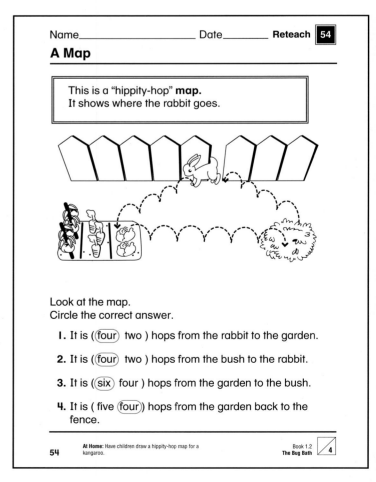

Look at the map.
Circle the correct answer.

1. It is ((four) two) hops from the rabbit to the garden.

2. It is ((four) two) hops from the bush to the rabbit.

3. It is ((six) four) hops from the garden to the bush.

4. It is (five (four)) hops from the garden back to the fence.

Short o

Read these words.
What sound do you hear in each word?
cot   top   lock

Write the word from the box that completes the sentence.

| box | jog | fox | top |

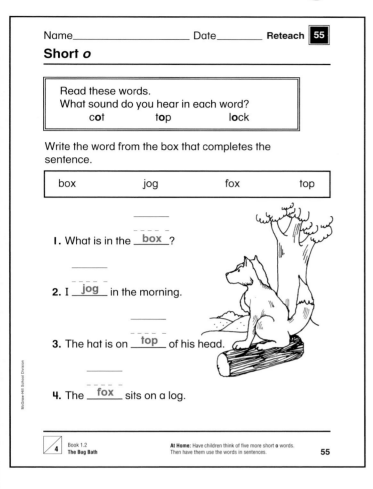

1. What is in the __box__?

2. I __jog__ in the morning.

3. The hat is on __top__ of his head.

4. The __fox__ sits on a log.

Book 1.2
The Bug Bath
At Home: Have children think of five more short o words.
Then have them use the words in sentences.
55

Short o, u, i, a; ck

The tot naps in the ___cot___.
(cot)   got

Circle the word that completes each sentence.
Then write the word on the line.

1. I __shut__ the door.
(shut)   shack

2. I __sip__ the drink.
lip   (sip)

3. I like __ham__ .
(ham)   ran

4. I __pick__ up the box.
luck   (pick)

5. I can not see in this __fog__ .
hog   (fog)

6. A __duck__ quacks.
(duck)   cat

56
At Home: Have children write sentences using some of the
other word choices listed on this page.
Book 1.2
The Bug Bath 6

Story Elements

The **characters** are the people or animals in a story.
The **plot** is what happens.

Read the story. Then complete the chart.

Jan likes to run. She runs with her dog, Lulu. They run down the path. They run to the park. Then they sit down and look at the sky. Jan looks at Lulu. She is asleep!

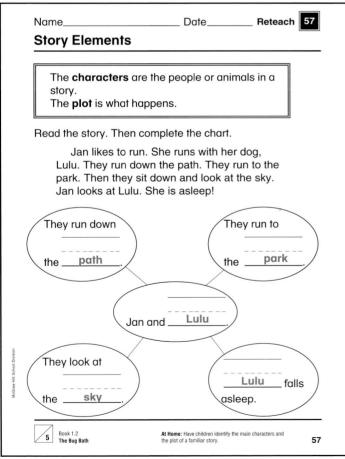

They run down the __path__.

They run to the __park__.

Jan and __Lulu__.

They look at the __sky__.

__Lulu__ falls asleep.

Book 1.2
The Bug Bath
At Home: Have children identify the main characters and
the plot of a familiar story.
57

Inflectional Ending -ed

land + **ed** = land**ed**

The kite **landed** in the tree.

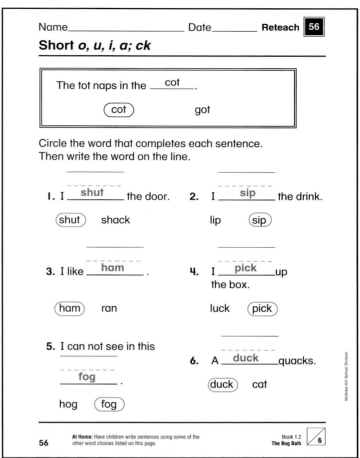

Add -**ed** to each word in the box.
Then write the new word from the box that tells about each picture.

| back__ed__ | tack__ed__ | lick__ed__ | hush__ed__ |

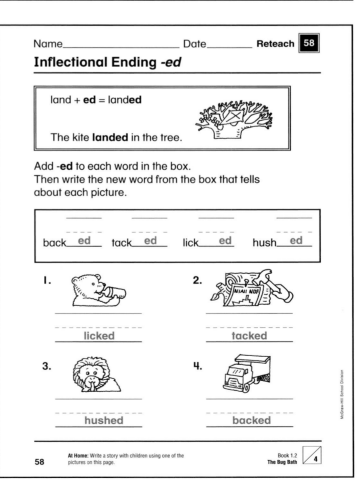

1. __licked__

2. __tacked__

3. __hushed__

4. __backed__

58
At Home: Write a story with children using one of the
pictures on this page.
Book 1.2
The Bug Bath 4

The Bug Bath • EXTEND

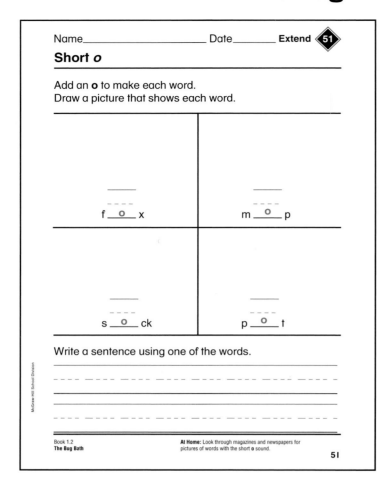

Name_____ Date_____ **Extend** 51

Short *o*

Add an **o** to make each word.
Draw a picture that shows each word.

f __o__ x

m __o__ p

s __o__ ck

p __o__ t

Write a sentence using one of the words.

_____
_____
_____

Book 1.2
The Bug Bath

At Home: Look through magazines and newspapers for
pictures of words with the short o sound.

51

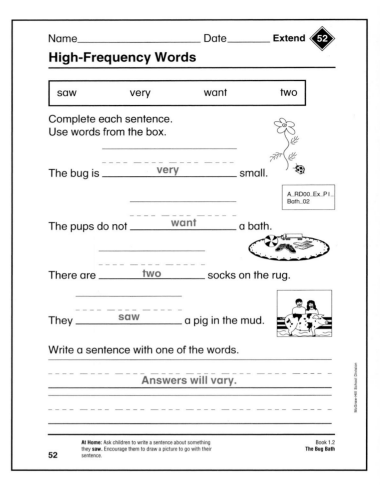

Name_____ Date_____ **Extend** 52

High-Frequency Words

saw	very	want	two

Complete each sentence.
Use words from the box.

The bug is _____ **very** _____ small.

The pups do not _____ **want** _____ a bath.

There are _____ **two** _____ socks on the rug.

They _____ **saw** _____ a pig in the mud.

Write a sentence with one of the words.

Answers will vary.

A_RD00_Ex_P I_
Bath_02

52

At Home: Ask children to write a sentence about something
they **saw**. Encourage them to draw a picture to go with their
sentence.

Book 1.2
The Bug Bath

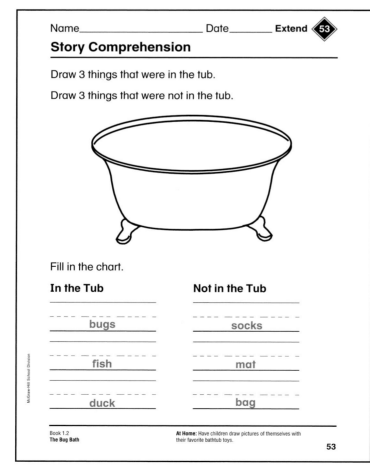

Name_____ Date_____ **Extend** 53

Story Comprehension

Draw 3 things that were in the tub.

Draw 3 things that were not in the tub.

Fill in the chart.

In the Tub	**Not in the Tub**
bugs	socks
fish	mat
duck	bag

Book 1.2
The Bug Bath

At Home: Have children draw pictures of themselves with
their favorite bathtub toys.

53

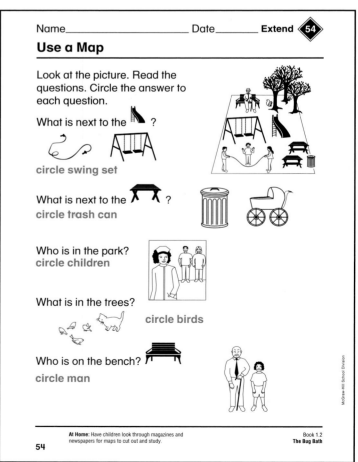

Name_____ Date_____ **Extend** 54

Use a Map

Look at the picture. Read the
questions. Circle the answer to
each question.

What is next to the ?

circle swing set

What is next to the ?
circle trash can

Who is in the park?
circle children

What is in the trees?

circle birds

Who is on the bench?

circle man

54

At Home: Have children look through magazines and
newspapers for maps to cut out and study.

Book 1.2
The Bug Bath

The Bug Bath • EXTEND

Short *o*

Look at the picture. Read the question.
Write the answer.

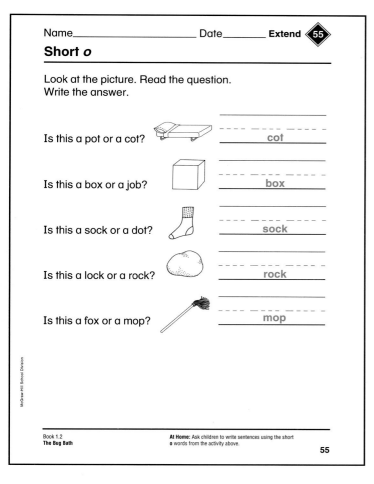

Is this a pot or a cot?   cot

Is this a box or a job?   box

Is this a sock or a dot?   sock

Is this a lock or a rock?   rock

Is this a fox or a mop?   mop

Book 1.2
The Bug Bath

At Home: Ask children to write sentences using the short
o words from the activity above.

55

Short *o, u, i, a; ck*

Circle a word.
Write the word on the line.

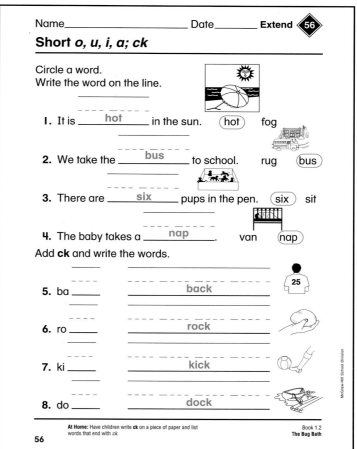

1. It is ___hot___ in the sun.   (hot)   fog

2. We take the ___bus___ to school.   rug   (bus)

3. There are ___six___ pups in the pen.   (six)   sit

4. The baby takes a ___nap___.   van   (nap)

Add **ck** and write the words.

5. ba ___   back

6. ro ___   rock

7. ki ___   kick

8. do ___   dock

56

At Home: Have children write **ck** on a piece of paper and list
words that end with *ck*.

Book 1.2
The Bug Bath

Story Elements

Read about the bugs Bob and Al.
Circle the answer that tells about them.

Al and Bob saw a big tub.
The two bugs got in.
Why did they get in the tub?

Bob and Al were dirty.
Bob and Al were hungry.   *circle the first choice*
Bob and Al were wet.

A big duck fell in the tub.
It landed on top of the bugs.
Did the duck quack? No. Why not?

                                    circle the second choice
The duck was big.
The duck was a toy.
The duck was bad.

Write what Bob and Al do when they get out of the tub.

_____
_____
_____
_____
Answers will vary.

Book 1.2
The Bug Bath

At Home: Ask children to tell a story from an insect's
point of view.

57

Inflectional Ending *-ed*

Circle the word that completes each sentence.
Write the word.

1. She ___tucked___ him into bed.   (tucked)   looked

2. The dog ___licked___ me.   mushed   (licked)

3. We ___picked___ apples.   (picked)   wished

4. They ___rushed___ for the bus.   (rushed)   hushed

Choose one sentence.
Write other sentences to tell more about what happened.
Draw a picture to go with your story.

_____
_____
_____
_____
_____

58

At Home: Help children make a list of things they are doing
today. Help them make a list of things they did yesterday.
Point out the **ed** ending on words on their lists.

Book 1.2
The Bug Bath

T23

The Bug Bath • GRAMMAR

Plural Nouns

- Some nouns name **more than one person, place, or thing**.
- This kind of noun is called a **plural noun**.
- Add **-s** to make most nouns name more than one.
  one bug ➔ two bugs

Circle the plural nouns.

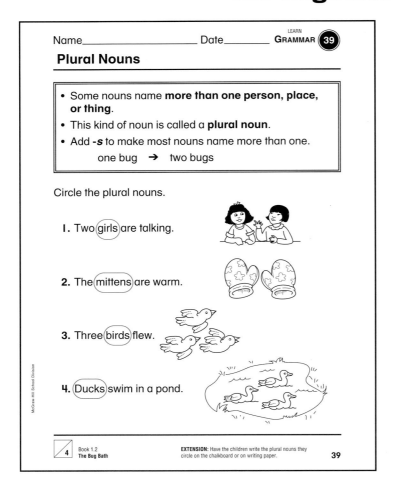

1. Two (girls) are talking.

2. The (mittens) are warm.

3. Three (birds) flew.

4. (Ducks) swim in a pond.

Plural Nouns

- Add **-es** to form the plural of nouns that end with **s**, **sh**, **ch**, or **x**.

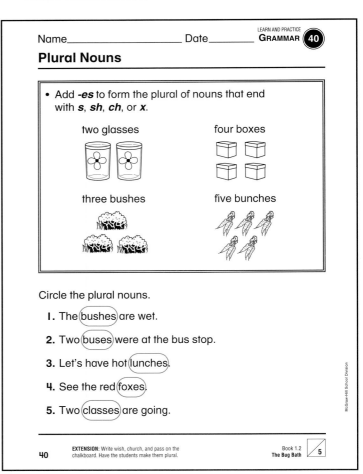

two glasses   four boxes

three bushes   five bunches

Circle the plural nouns.

1. The (bushes) are wet.

2. Two (buses) were at the bus stop.

3. Let's have hot (lunches).

4. See the red (foxes).

5. Two (classes) are going.

Match Plural Nouns with Pictures

- Add **-s** to make most nouns name more than one.
  The bugs fell in the tub.
- Add **-es** to form the plural of nouns that end with **s**, **sh**, **ch**, or **x**.

Read the sentences. Find the plural nouns.
Draw a line from each sentence to the picture of the noun that added **-s** or **-es**.

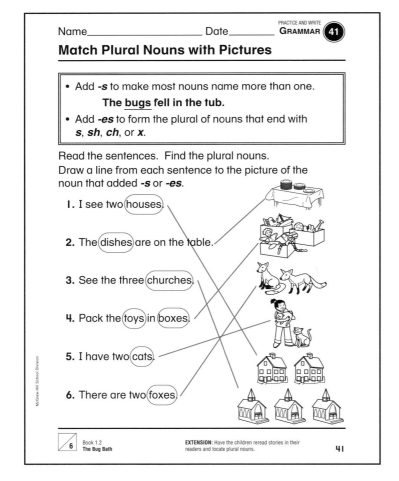

1. I see two (houses).

2. The (dishes) are on the table.

3. See the three (churches).

4. Pack the (toys) in (boxes).

5. I have two (cats).

6. There are two (foxes).

Sentences with Plural Nouns

- Begin every sentence with a capital letter.
- End a question with a question mark.

Read the sentences.
Circle each word that should have a capital letter.
End a question with a question mark.
Add **-s** or **-es** to the noun if it names more than one thing.

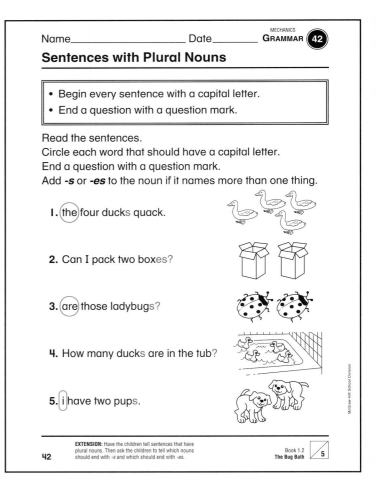

1. (the) four ducks quack.

2. Can I pack two boxes?

3. (are) those ladybugs?

4. How many ducks are in the tub?

5. (i) have two pups.

T24   Annotated Workbooks

The Bug Bath • GRAMMAR

Test

Read the sentences.
Find the plural nouns.
Mark the letter next to each plural noun.

1. The two _____ got in.

   Ⓐ bugs   Ⓑ cat   Ⓒ the

2. Three big _____ fell in the tub.

   Ⓐ a   🅑 ducks   Ⓒ not

3. Jack has four big _____ .

   Ⓐ car   Ⓑ can   🅒 glasses

4. Mack packs two _____ .

   🅐 boxes   Ⓑ the   Ⓒ one

5. The _____ are big.

   Ⓐ saw   🅑 churches   Ⓒ in

Plural Nouns

- Add **-s** to make most nouns name more than one.
- Add **-es** to form the plural of nouns that end with **s**, **sh**, **ch**, or **x**.

Read each sentence aloud. Write the plural noun.

1. The four ducks quack.

   _____ ducks _____

2. I can pack two boxes.

   _____ boxes _____

3. The bugs are in the tub.

   _____ bugs _____

4. I see three foxes.

   _____ foxes _____

5. Do you have two glasses?

   _____ glasses _____

EXTENSION: Have the children tell sentences that have plural nouns. Then ask the children to tell which nouns should end with -s and which should end with -es.

The Bug Bath • SPELLING

Name_____ Date_____

Words with Short *o*

Complete each word by writing the letter that spells the short o sound.

1. h___**O**___t

2. t___o___p

3. n___o___t

4. l___o___ck

5. h___o___p

6. r___o___ck

Directions (to teacher)
Review the short *o* sound by explaining that the letter *o* stands for /o/ as in the word *hot*. Write *hot* on the chalkboard or form the word with letter cards. Say the word aloud and have children repeat it. Then have children look at the first example on the page. Point out that the letter *o* has been filled in.

Write the words *top, not, lock, hop,* and *rock* on the chalkboard. Read the words aloud and have children repeat them. Have children listen for the short o sound in each word. Then, have them complete each word in the space provided.

5 | Book 1.2
The Bug Bath

39

Name_____ Date_____

Words with Short *o*

Using the Word Study Steps

1. LOOK at the word.

2. SAY the word aloud.

3. STUDY the letters in the word.

4. WRITE the word.

5. CHECK the word.
   Did you spell the word right? If not, go back to step 1.

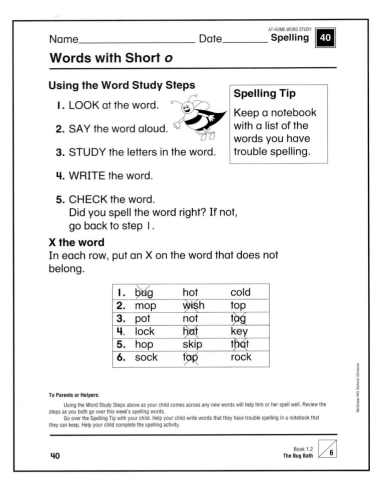

Spelling Tip

Keep a notebook with a list of the words you have trouble spelling.

X the word
In each row, put an X on the word that does not belong.

1.	~~bug~~	hot	cold
2.	mop	~~wish~~	top
3.	pot	not	~~tag~~
4.	lock	~~hat~~	key
5.	hop	skip	~~that~~
6.	sock	~~tap~~	rock

To Parents or Helpers:
Using the Word Study Steps above as your child comes across any new words will help him or her spell well. Review the steps as you both go over this week's spelling words.
Go over the Spelling Tip with your child. Help your child write words that they have trouble spelling in a notebook that they can keep. Help your child complete the spelling activity.

40

Book 1.2
The Bug Bath | 6

Name_____ Date_____

Words with Short *o*

Put each bug in the right tub. Write the words with the same endings in the same tub.

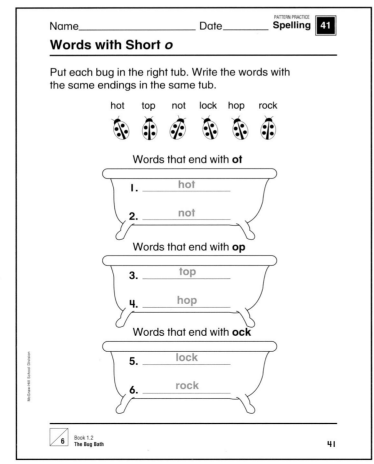

hot   top   not   lock   hop   rock

Words that end with **ot**

1. hot

2. not

Words that end with **op**

3. top

4. hop

Words that end with **ock**

5. lock

6. rock

6 | Book 1.2
The Bug Bath

41

Name_____ Date_____

Words with Short o

Look at the picture. Add **ot** or **op** or **ock** to complete the word.

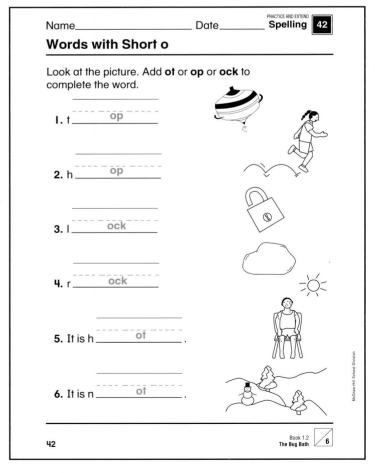

1. t___op___

2. h___op___

3. l___ock___

4. r___ock___

5. It is h___ot___.

6. It is n___ot___.

42

Book 1.2
The Bug Bath | 6

The Bug Bath • SPELLING

Words with Short o

Look at the picture. Complete the sentence with a
spelling word. _____

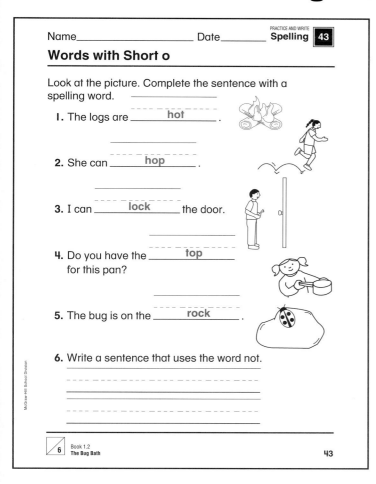

1. The logs are _____ hot _____.

2. She can _____ hop _____.

3. I can _____ lock _____ the door.

4. Do you have the _____ top _____
   for this pan?

5. The bug is on the _____ rock _____.

6. Write a sentence that uses the word not.

_____

_____

_____

Words with Short o

Look at the words in each set. One word in each
set is spelled correctly. Use a pencil to color in the
circle in front of that word. Before you begin, look at
the sample sets of words. Sample A has been done
for you. Do Sample B by yourself. When you are
sure you know what to do, you may go on with the
rest of the page.

Sample A
- (A) pot
- (B) pott
- (C) ppot

Sample B
- (D) duck
- (E) duc
- (F) duk

1.
- (A) hop
- (B) hopp
- (C) hoppe

2.
- (D) locke
- (E) lok
- (F) lock

3.
- (A) hott
- (B) hot
- (C) hote

4.
- (D) top
- (E) topp
- (F) toppe

5.
- (A) nott
- (B) not
- (C) noot

6.
- (D) roc
- (E) rok
- (F) rock

T27

Short e

Name_____ Date_____ Practice **59**

Circle the word that names the picture.
Then write the word on the line.

1. (hen) / deck — **hen**

2. (leg) / beg — **leg**

3. (bed) / met — **bed**

4. net / (shed) — **shed**

5. vet / (neck) — **neck**

6. gem / (pen) — **pen**

6 · Book 1.2 **Splash!**

At Home: Have children make flash cards of words that have the short **e** sound.

59

High-Frequency Words

Name_____ Date_____ Practice **60**

| good | into | put | away |

Write the word from the box that completes each sentence.

1. That dish was ___**good**___!

2. Sam went far ___**away**___.

3. The dog ran ___**into**___ the shed.

4. She ___**put**___ the hat in a box.

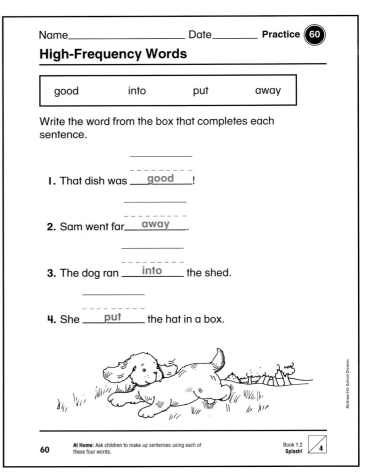

60

At Home: Ask children to make up sentences using each of these four words.

Book 1.2 **Splash!** · 4

Ben the Gem

Ben's red rag is wet. What is this? There is a gem in the hem. It is good the man did not get the gem. It is good I have my pet. Ben is my gem.

At Home: Invite children to talk about what they would do if they lost a pet or something else of value to them.

4

60a

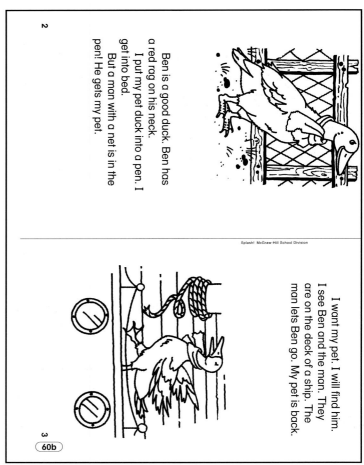

2

Ben is a good duck. Ben has a red rag on his neck. I put my pet duck into a pen. I get into bed. But a man with a net is in the pen! He gets my pet.

I want my pet. I will find him. I see Ben and the man. They are on the deck of a ship. The man lets Ben go. My pet is back.

3

60b

Splash! • PRACTICE

Story Comprehension

Read these sentences.
Circle the sentences that describe what happened in "Splash!"

1. (Meg puts on her hat.)

2. (The hen gets the boots.)

3. The cat gets a box.

4. The pets sit in the shed.

5. (Meg puts on her coat.)

6. (Meg sees her wet pets.)

7. Meg runs away.

8. (The bus comes.)

A Map

This is Pam's footprint **map**.
It shows where Pam goes.

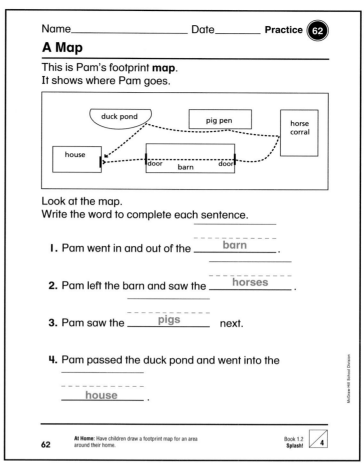

Look at the map.
Write the word to complete each sentence.

1. Pam went in and out of the ___**barn**___.

2. Pam left the barn and saw the ___**horses**___.

3. Pam saw the ___**pigs**___ next.

4. Pam passed the duck pond and went into the ___**house**___.

Short *e*

Write the word from the box that names each picture.

| peck | fed | ten | vet | bed | jet |

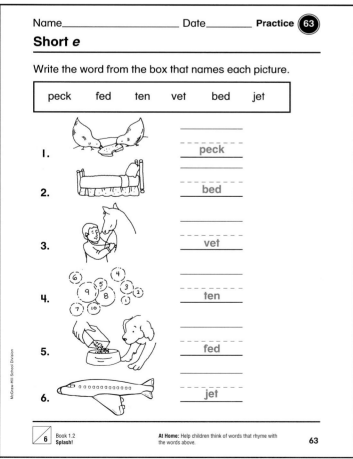

1. ___peck___

2. ___bed___

3. ___vet___

4. ___ten___

5. ___fed___

6. ___jet___

Short *e, o, u, i, a; th*

Circle the word that names each picture.
Then print the word on the line.

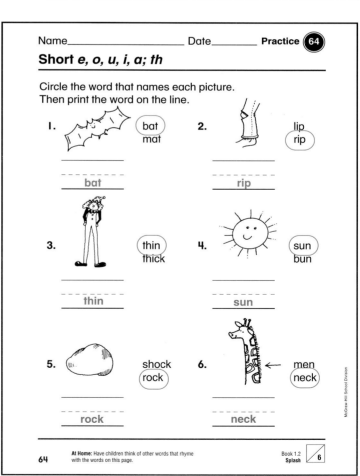

1. bat / mat — ___bat___

2. lip / rip — ___rip___

3. thin / thick — ___thin___

4. sun / bun — ___sun___

5. shock / rock — ___rock___

6. men / neck — ___neck___

Splash! • PRACTICE

Name_____ Date_____ **Practice** **65**

Main Idea

Circle the sentence that tells about the picture.

1. (The pigs live here.)
   The cats live here.

2. I see the cat.
   (I see the rain.)

3. The dog likes the rain.
   (The cat likes the rain.)

4. (Ducks play here.)
   Cows play here.

5. Cats play here.
   (Mice play here.)

5 Book 1.2
Splash!

At Home: Ask children to find a picture in a book or magazine. Have them explain the main idea of the picture.   65

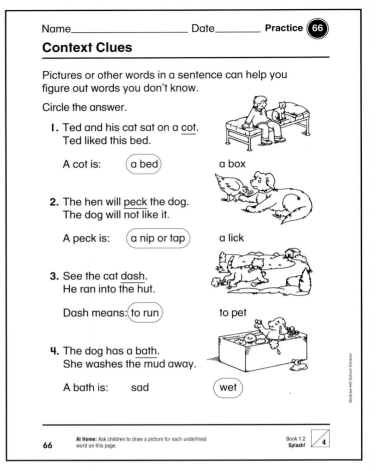

Name_____ Date_____ **Practice** **66**

Context Clues

Pictures or other words in a sentence can help you figure out words you don't know.

Circle the answer.

1. Ted and his cat sat on a <u>cot</u>.
   Ted liked this bed.

   A cot is: (a bed)   a box

2. The hen will <u>peck</u> the dog.
   The dog will not like it.

   A peck is: (a nip or tap)   a lick

3. See the cat <u>dash</u>.
   He ran into the hut.

   Dash means: (to run)   to pet

4. The dog has a <u>bath</u>.
   She washes the mud away.

   A bath is: sad   (wet)

66   **At Home:** Ask children to draw a picture for each underlined word on this page.

Book 1.2
Splash!   4

Splash! • RETEACH

Short *e*

> Read the words.
> What sound do you hear in each word?
>
> w**e**t   sh**e**d

Circle the word that completes each sentence.
Then write the word.

1. This is a ____hen____ .
  (hen)   men

2. She was fed in ____bed____ .
  led   (bed)

3. We met on a ____jet____ .
  net   (jet)

4. Do not peck my____neck____ !
  (neck)   deck

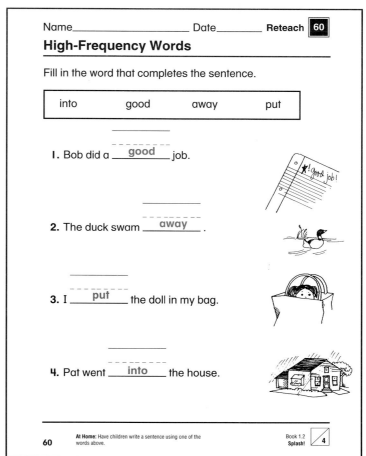

High-Frequency Words

Fill in the word that completes the sentence.

into	good	away	put

1. Bob did a ____good____ job.

2. The duck swam ____away____ .

3. I ____put____ the doll in my bag.

4. Pat went ____into____ the house.

Story Comprehension

Circle the pictures that tell about "Splash!"

1.   **2.**

3.   **4.**

5.   **6.**

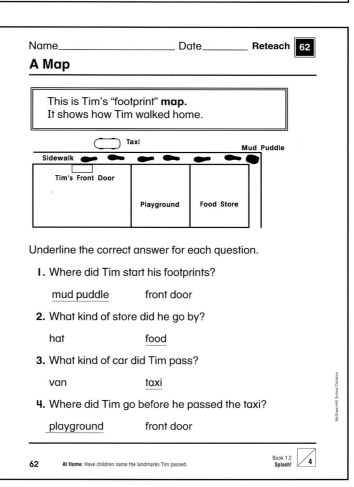

A Map

> This is Tim's "footprint" **map.**
> It shows how Tim walked home.

Taxi
Sidewalk   Mud Puddle
Tim's Front Door   Playground   Food Store

Underline the correct answer for each question.

1. Where did Tim start his footprints?
  mud puddle   front door

2. What kind of store did he go by?
  hat   food

3. What kind of car did Tim pass?
  van   taxi

4. Where did Tim go before he passed the taxi?
  playground   front door

Splash! • RETEACH

Short e

Read the sentence.
My p**e**t has a g**e**m.

Circle the word that completes the sentence.
Then write the word.

1. A bug was in the _____ net _____.
   bet   let   (net)

2. The hens are in the _____ shed _____.
   led   red   (shed)

3. Jen is _____ wet _____.
   (wet)   met   let

4. Ned is on the _____ bed _____.
   shed   (bed)   net

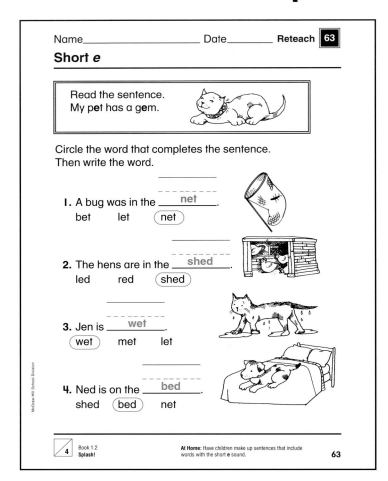

Short e, o, u, i, a; th

Is this a six or a mix?

six   6

Look at each picture.
Then write the word that answers the question.

1. Is this a **neck** or a **peck**?
   _____ neck _____

2. Is this a **cup** or a **pup**?
   _____ cup _____

3. Is this a **sock** or a **lock**?
   _____ sock _____

4. Is this a **path** or a **bath**?
   _____ path _____

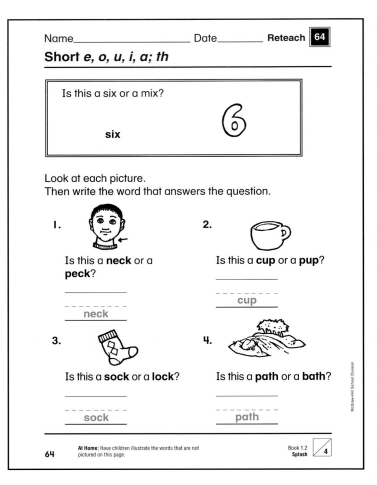

Main Idea

Look at the picture.
The words tell what the picture is about.

My Pet Dog

Look at the picture.
Circle the words that tell what the picture is about.

1. (The Cats Play)
   The Cats Sat

2. Cats, Cats!
   (Wet, Wet!)

3. (I See You)
   I See Cats

4. Rain and Me
   (Rain and Cats)

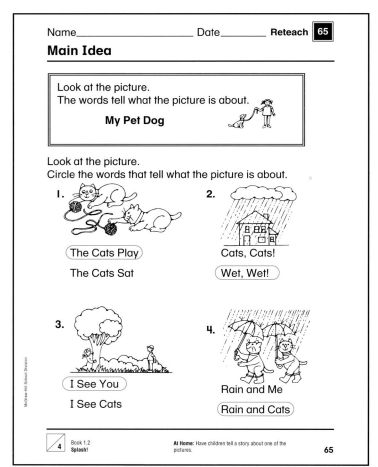

Context Clues

When you don't know what a word means, look at the surrounding words or at the pictures to help you.

Circle the word in each sentence that is shown in the picture.

1. I sat in the (shed.)

2. I saw the (jet.)

3. I hug my (pet.)

4. My (cat) sits down.

5. A (bug) sits on his neck.

T32   *Annotated Workbooks*

Splash! • EXTEND

Short *e*

Change the last letter to make a new word.
Sample answers are shown.

led
_____

le _____ **let** _____

bed
_____

be _____ **bet** _____

men
_____

me _____ **met** _____

pet
_____

pe _____ **peg** _____

Choose one word that you made.
Write a sentence.

_____
Answers will vary.
_____
_____

Book 1.2
Splash!

At Home: Write **bed, leg, led, Meg, red, peg** on paper. Help children identify the pattern in the spelling of the words. Encourage children to use this pattern to create more words.

59

High-Frequency Words

| away | good | into | put |

Write a word from the box to complete each sentence.
Draw a line to the picture that goes with the sentence.

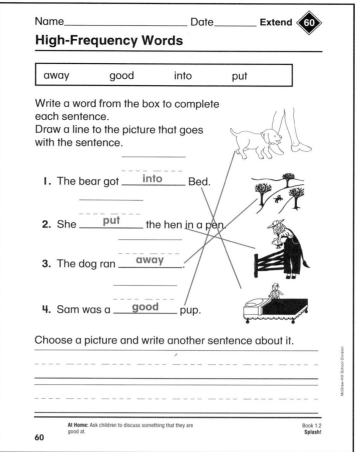

_____

1. The bear got _____ **into** _____ Bed.

_____

2. She _____ **put** _____ the hen in a pen.

_____

3. The dog ran _____ **away** _____.

_____

4. Sam was a _____ **good** _____ pup.

Choose a picture and write another sentence about it.

_____
_____
_____

60

At Home: Ask children to discuss something that they are good at.

Book 1.2
Splash!

Story Comprehension

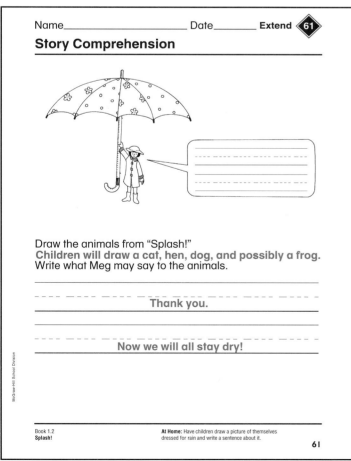

Draw the animals from "Splash!"
Children will draw a cat, hen, dog, and possibly a frog.
Write what Meg may say to the animals.

_____
_____
Thank you.
_____
_____
Now we will all stay dry!

Book 1.2
Splash!

At Home: Have children draw a picture of themselves dressed for rain and write a sentence about it.

61

Use a Map

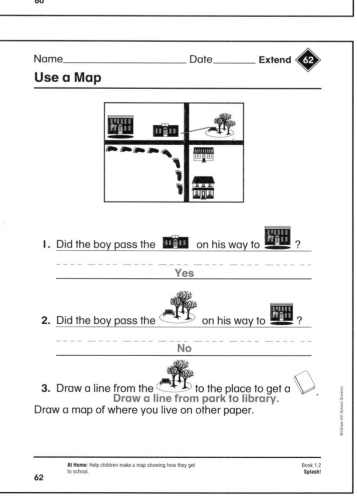

1. Did the boy pass the 🏫 on his way to 🏛 ?
_____
Yes

2. Did the boy pass the 🌳 on his way to 🏫 ?
_____
No

3. Draw a line from the 🌳 to the place to get a 📖 .
Draw a line from park to library.
Draw a map of where you live on other paper.

62

At Home: Help children make a map showing how they get to school.

Book 1.2
Splash!

T33

Splash! • EXTEND

Name_____ Date_____ **Extend** ◆63◆

Short e

Write the word.

What is this?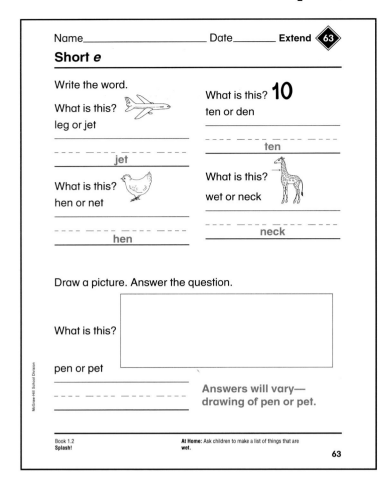
leg or jet

_____

- - - jet - - -
_____

What is this? 🐔
hen or net

_____

- - - hen - - -
_____

What is this? **10**
ten or den

_____

- - - ten - - -
_____

What is this? 🦒
wet or neck

_____

- - - neck - - -
_____

Draw a picture. Answer the question.

What is this?

pen or pet

- - - - - - - - - - - -
_____

*Answers will vary—
drawing of pen or pet.*

Book 1.2
Splash!

At Home: Ask children to make a list of things that are
wet.

63

Name_____ Date_____ **Extend** ◆64◆

Short e, o, u, i, a; th

e 🍀	o θ̄	u ⊡	i ⊞	a ◯	th ⊗

Use the code box to write the words.

b 🍀 d   **bed**

b ⊡ n   **bun**

p ⊞ n   **pin**

h ⊡ t   **hut**

ba ⊗   **bath**

c ◯ b   **cab**

m θ̄ p   **mop**

⊗ in   **thin**

Book 1.2
Splash!

At Home: Ask children to make a list of words that have **th**
in them.

64

Name_____ Date_____ **Extend** ◆65◆

Main Idea

Write the name of your favorite story.

_____
_____

Write a sentence that tells the main idea in the box.
Write things that happen in the story in the circles.

**Since children will choose their favorite stories to
describe, answers will vary.**

Book 1.2
Splash!

At Home: Have children look in magazines or the
newspaper for pictures that show people and places. Ask
them to tell the main idea of each picture.

65

Name_____ Date_____ **Extend** ◆66◆

Context Clues

Write the word that completes the sentence.

ears ᴖᴖ   puddles 🌊🌊   umbrella ☂   coat 🧥

_____
puddles

The hen likes to splash in _____ with

her red 👢 .

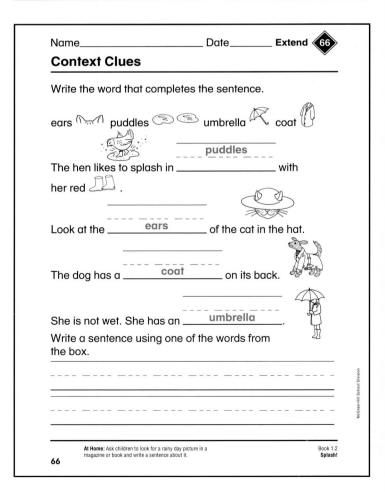

Look at the ___**ears**___ of the cat in the hat.

The dog has a ___**coat**___ on its back.

She is not wet. She has an ___**umbrella**___ .

Write a sentence using one of the words from
the box.

- - - - - - - - - - - - - - -
_____
_____

At Home: Ask children to look for a rainy day picture in a
magazine or book and write a sentence about it.

Book 1.2
Splash!

66

Splash! • GRAMMAR

Irregular Plural Nouns

- Some nouns that name more than one do not end with **-s**.

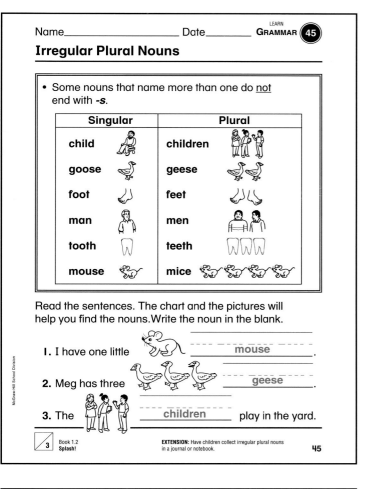

Singular	Plural
child	children
goose	geese
foot	feet
man	men
tooth	teeth
mouse	mice

Read the sentences. The chart and the pictures will help you find the nouns. Write the noun in the blank.

1. I have one little ____mouse____ .

2. Meg has three ____geese____ .

3. The ____children____ play in the yard.

Irregular Plural Nouns

- Some nouns that name more than one do not end with **-s** or **-es**.
- These nouns are the plural forms of **child**, **goose**, **foot**, **man**, **tooth**, **mouse**.

Read the sentences.
Find the plural nouns.
Draw a circle around the plural noun that goes in the sentence.

1. It rained on the three (gooses, (geese)).

2. The cat ran after two (mouses, (mice)).

3. All of the ((men) mans) had wet hats.

4. The ((children), childs) had fun in the rain.

5. How many ((feet), foots) does the hen have?

6. Do hens have (tooths, (teeth))?

Irregular Plural Nouns

- Some nouns that name more than one do not end with **-s** or **-es**.

  The nouns child, goose, foot, man, tooth, and mouse tell about more than one with a new word. These words are **children**, **geese**, **feet**, **men**, **teeth**, and **mice**.

Read the nouns.
Write the plural for each noun.

child	children
goose	geese
foot	feet
man	men
tooth	teeth
mouse	mice

Sentences with Irregular Plural Nouns

- Begin each sentence with a capital letter.
- End an exclamation with an exclamation point.

Circle each word that should have a capital.
Write exclamation points where they belong.
Make the noun plural if it names more than one.

1. It rained on the three mouse. ____mice____

2. (it) rained on the two goose. ____geese____

3. (the) wet geese ran into the big red barn.

4. (in) the barn, they saw mice.

5. (the) geese did not like the mice.

6. See the mice run away !

Splash! • GRAMMAR

Plural Nouns

Circle the plural noun that should go in the sentence.

1. The three (goose, (geese)) had a bath.

2. Many (child, (children)) like to play.

3. Jack lost two (tooth, (teeth)).

4. The five (mouse, (mice)) like to nap.

5. Al has two (foot, (feet)).

6. The four (man, (men)) will make lunch.

Irregular Plural Nouns

- Some nouns that name more than one do not end with **-s** or **-es**.

Look at the picture. Read the words next to it. Draw a circle around the plural noun.

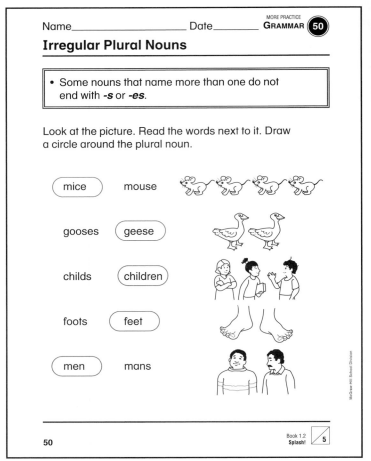

(mice)   mouse

gooses   (geese)

childs   (children)

foots   (feet)

(men)   mans

Splash! • SPELLING

Words with Short *e*

Complete each word by writing the letter that spells the short e sound.

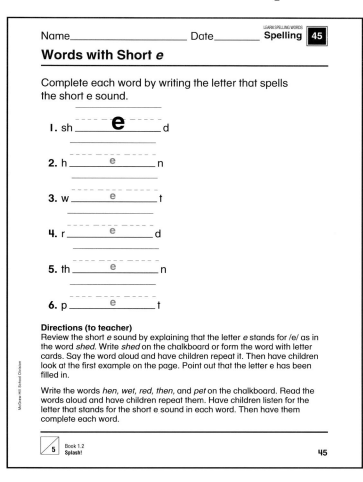

1. sh __**e**__ d

2. h __e__ n

3. w __e__ t

4. r __e__ d

5. th __e__ n

6. p __e__ t

Directions (to teacher)

Review the short e sound by explaining that the letter e stands for /e/ as in the word *shed*. Write *shed* on the chalkboard or form the word with letter cards. Say the word aloud and have children repeat it. Then have children look at the first example on the page. Point out that the letter e has been filled in.

Write the words *hen, wet, red, then*, and *pet* on the chalkboard. Read the words aloud and have children repeat them. Have children listen for the letter that stands for the short e sound in each word. Then have them complete each word.

Words with Short *e*

Using the Word Study Steps

1. LOOK at the word.

2. SAY the word aloud.

3. STUDY the letters in the word.

4. WRITE the word.

5. CHECK the word.
   Did you spell the word right? If not, go back to step 1.

Spelling Tip

Rhyming words are often spelled alike. A word you know can help you spell new words.

w + et = wet
p + et = pet

Find and Circle

Where are the spelling words?

```
u  t (s  h  e  d) t  a (h  e  n)
o  d  u  c (w  e  t) l (r  e  d)
r (t  h  e  n) h  e (p  e  t) g
```

Words with Short e

Add the ending **et** or **ed** or **en** to each letter to make a word from the box. Then write the spelling word.

pet then hen red shed wet

1. p + __et__ = __pet__

2. w + __et__ = __wet__

3. r + __ed__ = __red__

4. sh + __ed__ = __shed__

5. h + __en__ = __hen__

6. th + __en__ = __then__

Words with Short e

Draw a line to connect each word beginning with the right ending to make a spelling word. Then write the words.

1. __red__

2. __then__

3. __wet__

```
r    et
th   ed
w    en
```

Complete these sentences with a spelling word.

4. The __hens__ like to eat corn.

5. They all love their __pets__ .

6. The two __sheds__ are packed.

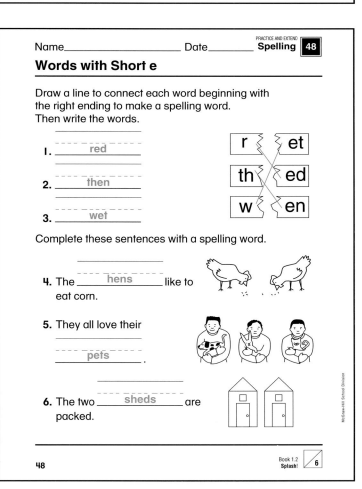

T37

Splash! • SPELLING

Words with Short *e*

Look at the picture. Complete each sentence with a spelling word. _____

1. This cat is my _____ **pet** _____ .

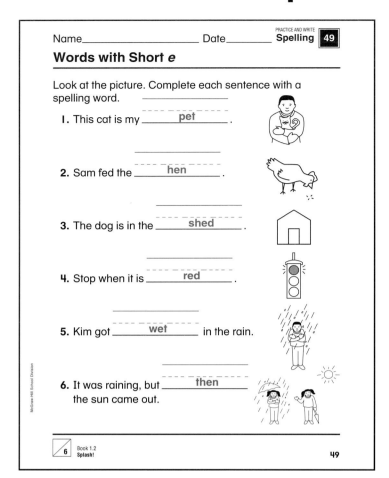

2. Sam fed the _____ **hen** _____ .

3. The dog is in the _____ **shed** _____ .

4. Stop when it is _____ **red** _____ .

5. Kim got _____ **wet** _____ in the rain.

6. It was raining, but _____ **then** _____ the sun came out.

Words with Short e

Look at the words in each set. One word in each set is spelled correctly. Use a pencil to color in the circle in front of that word. Before you begin, look at the sample sets of words. Sample A has been done for you. Do Sample B by yourself. When you are sure you know what to do, you may go on with the rest of the page.

Sample A
- (A) get
- (B) gett
- (C) geet

Sample B
- (D) rok
- (E) roc
- (F) rock

1.
- (A) redd
- (B) red
- (C) rede

4.
- (D) henn
- (E) hen
- (F) henne

2.
- (D) wette
- (E) weet
- (F) wet

5.
- (A) then
- (B) thenn
- (C) theen

3.
- (A) pet
- (B) pett
- (C) ppet

6.
- (D) shedd
- (E) shede
- (F) shed

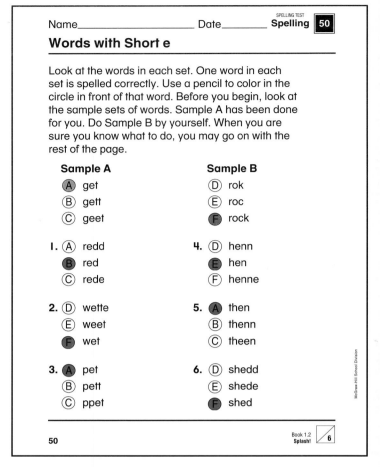

What Bug Is It? • PRACTICE

Blends

Read the words in the box. Then write the word that names each picture.

| hill | gruff | slug | frog | flap |

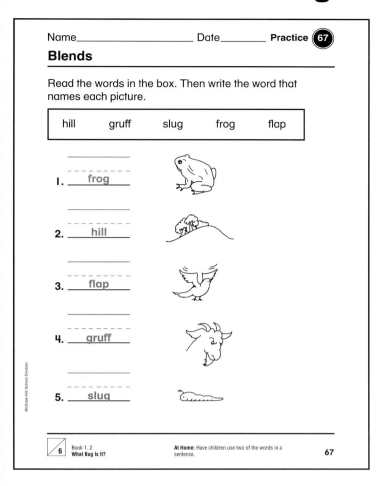

1. _frog_

2. _hill_

3. _flap_

4. _gruff_

5. _slug_

High-Frequency Words

Write the words from the box to complete the letter.

| about | again | around | use |

Dear Grandma,

Today we saw a movie. It was

about bugs. How do bugs get

around? They _use_

wings! I want to see the bug movie

again.

From,
Meg

68
At Home: Help children to write a letter to a friend or relative.

Book 1. 2
What Bug Is It?
4

Jill and Her Doll

Soon Will went home. Then Jill saw her doll. She put the doll in her pack. Then Jill and the doll ran up and down the hill again and again.

At Home: Invite children to talk about their favorite toys and what games they like to play with them.

4

68a

2

Jill sat by a hill with a doll. Will asked Jill to go with him. What about the doll? Will did not want to use it.
Jill left her doll. She and Will ran down the hill again and again.

A slug slid around the doll. The slug told the doll she could go with him. The doll sat there. The slug went away. A gull saw the doll. The gull told the doll she could go with him. The doll sat there. The gull went away.

What Bug Is It? McGraw-Hill School Division

3

68b

T39

What Bug Is It? • PRACTICE

Practice 69

Name_____ Date_____ **Practice** 69

Story Comprehension

Think about "What Bug Is It?" Then read the sentences. Use the names of bugs to complete the sentences.

butterfly	ants	ladybug	bee	spider

BEGINNING _____

1. Rick can see bugs in a hill. He sees ___ants___.

↓

MIDDLE _____

2. Jill sees a red and black ___ladybug___.

3. Nell looks at a ___spider___ in a web.

4. Yan sees a ___butterfly___ flap and flap.

↓

END _____

5. The last bug they see is a ___bee___.

5 Book 1.2 **What Bug Is It?**   At Home: Ask children to draw a picture of one of the bugs from the story.   69

Practice 70

Name_____ Date_____ **Practice** 70

A Map

A **street map** shows you where places are.

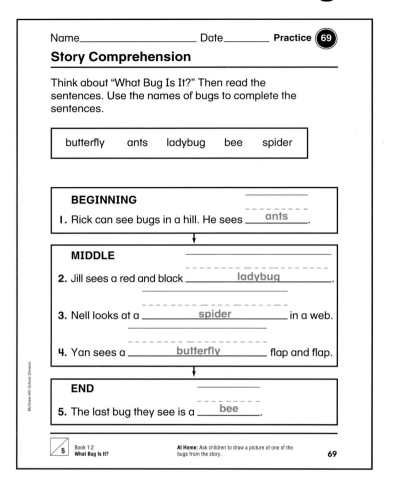

Look at the map.

1. What street is next to the beach?
   _____
   ___Cat Street___

2. On what two streets can you buy food?
   _____
   ___Cab Lane and Pig Path___

3. What road has three houses?
   _____
   ___Jim's Road___

4. What street is next to the golf course?
   _____
   ___Fish Drive___

70   At Home: Have children draw a simple street map of your neighborhood.   Book 1.2 **What Bug Is It?** 4

Practice 71

Name_____ Date_____ **Practice** 71

Blends

Look at each picture.
Then write the word from the box that describes the picture.

sniff	flag	pass	smash	slam	doll

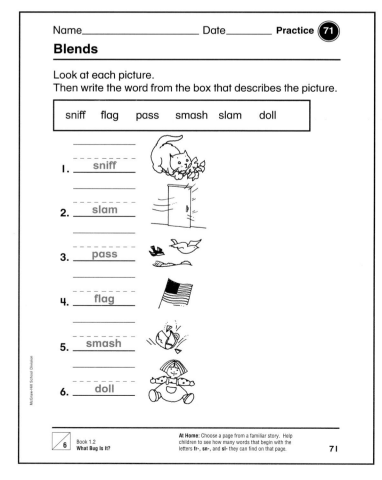

1. ___sniff___

2. ___slam___

3. ___pass___

4. ___flag___

5. ___smash___

6. ___doll___

6 Book 1.2 **What Bug Is It?**   At Home: Choose a page from a familiar story. Help children to see how many words that begin with the letters fr-, sn-, and sl- they can find on that page.   71

Practice 72

Name_____ Date_____ **Practice** 72

Blends; *sh, th, ck*

Write the word from the box that names each picture.

kiss	frog	puff	smash	thrill

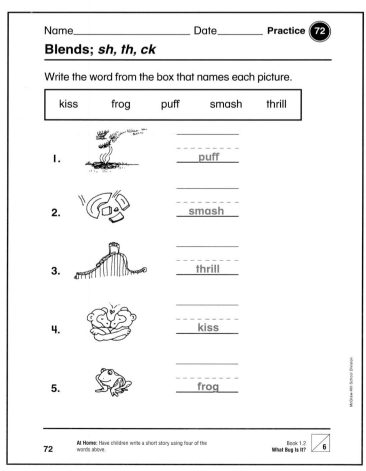

1. ___puff___

2. ___smash___

3. ___thrill___

4. ___kiss___

5. ___frog___

72   At Home: Have children write a short story using four of the words above.   Book 1.2 **What Bug Is It?** 6

Main Idea

Name_____ Date_____ Practice **73**

Read the story.

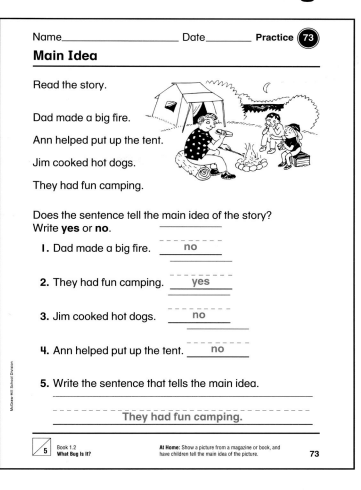

Dad made a big fire.

Ann helped put up the tent.

Jim cooked hot dogs.

They had fun camping.

Does the sentence tell the main idea of the story?
Write **yes** or **no**. _____

1. Dad made a big fire. _____ no _____

2. They had fun camping. _____ yes _____

3. Jim cooked hot dogs. _____ no _____

4. Ann helped put up the tent. _____ no _____

5. Write the sentence that tells the main idea.

_____

_____ They had fun camping. _____

5 / Book 1.2
What Bug Is It?

At Home: Show a picture from a magazine or book, and
have children tell the main idea of the picture.

73

Context Clues

Name_____ Date_____ Practice **74**

When you don't know what a word means, the
words around it can help you find the meaning.

Write the word from the story that helps you know
the meaning of the underlined word.

1. Jill saw a <u>slim</u> man. This thin man was her dad.

_____

_____ thin

2. Meg saw Tim <u>dash</u> up the path. Then he ran
past her.

_____

_____ ran

3. My pup was <u>ill</u>. "I wish you were not sick." I said.

_____

_____ sick

4. I shut the lid. "Do not <u>slam</u> it," said Nash.

_____

_____ shut

74

At Home: With children, use one of the sentences on this
page as a story starter.

Book 1.2
What Bug Is It? / 4

What Bug Is It? • RETEACH

Blends

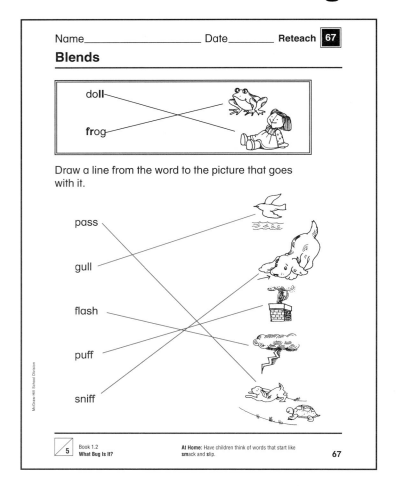

Draw a line from the word to the picture that goes with it.

pass

gull

flash

puff

sniff

High-Frequency Words

Read each sentence. Circle the word that completes it. Then write it in the sentence.

about	again	around	use

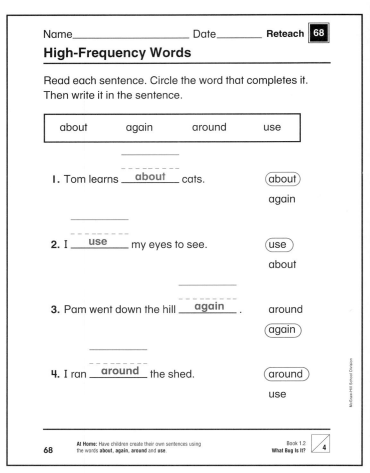

1. Tom learns ___about___ cats.　　(about)　again

2. I ___use___ my eyes to see.　　(use)　about

3. Pam went down the hill ___again___ .　　around　(again)

4. I ran ___around___ the shed.　　(around)　use

Story Comprehension

Circle the pictures that tell about "What Bug Is It?"

1.

2.

3.

4.

5.

6.

A Map

A street **map** shows you where streets are.

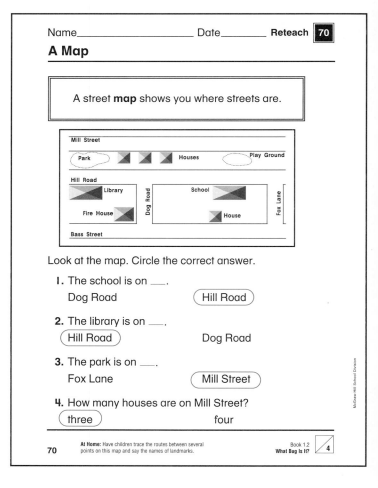

Look at the map. Circle the correct answer.

1. The school is on ___.
   Dog Road　　(Hill Road)

2. The library is on ___.
   (Hill Road)　　Dog Road

3. The park is on ___.
   Fox Lane　　(Mill Street)

4. How many houses are on Mill Street?
   (three)　　four

What Bug Is It? • RETEACH

Reteach 71

Name_____ Date_____ **Reteach** 71

Blends

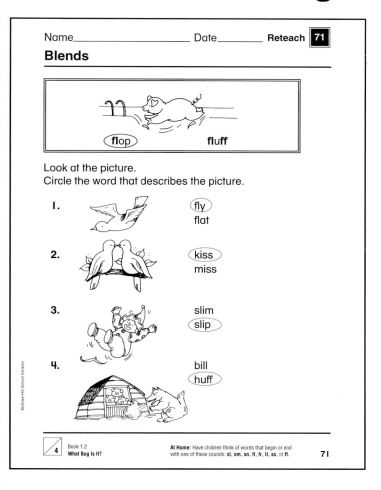

(flop)   fluff

Look at the picture.
Circle the word that describes the picture.

1. (fly)
   flat

2. (kiss)
   miss

3. slim
   (slip)

4. bill
   (huff)

Book 1.2
What Bug Is It?   **At Home:** Have children think of words that begin or end
with one of these sounds: **sl, sm, sn, fl, fr, ll, ss,** or **ff.**   71

Reteach 72

Name_____ Date_____ **Reteach** 72

Blends; *sh, th, ck*

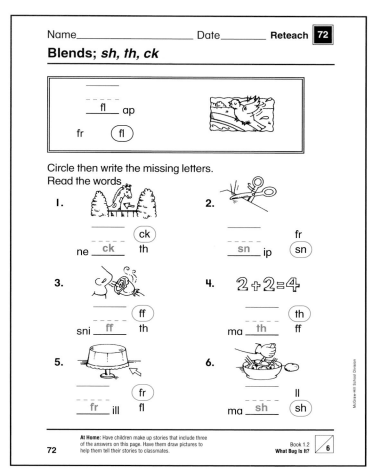

____fl ap

fr   (fl)

Circle then write the missing letters.
Read the words.

1. ne __ck__ (ck)
               th

2. __sn__ ip   fr
               (sn)

3. sni __ff__ (ff)
               th

4. ma __th__   (th)
               ff

5. __fr__ ill (fr)
               fl

6. ma __sh__   ll
               (sh)

At Home: Have children make up stories that include three
of the answers on this page. Have them draw pictures to
help them tell their stories to classmates.   72   Book 1.2
What Bug Is It?   6

Reteach 73

Name_____ Date_____ **Reteach** 73

Main Idea

The **main idea** tells what the picture is about.

Bingo brings the ball to Todd.

Underline the sentence that tells the main idea of
each picture.

1. The hat is big.
   Sue likes flowers.

2. It is a sad day.
   We have a snowman.

3. Pam loves her cat.
   The bat is black.

4. The sand is hot.
   Max has a dish.

Book 1.2
What Bug Is It?   **At Home:** Read children a paragraph from a children's
book. Help them identify the main idea of the paragraph.   73

Reteach 74

Name_____ Date_____ **Reteach** 74

Context Clues

When you don't know what a word means,
the other words or pictures around that
word can give you clues.

Circle the words that tell about the picture.

1. (ant)   bat

2. kiss   (gull)

3. (bugs)   snug

4. (hill)   chill

What Bug Is It? • EXTEND

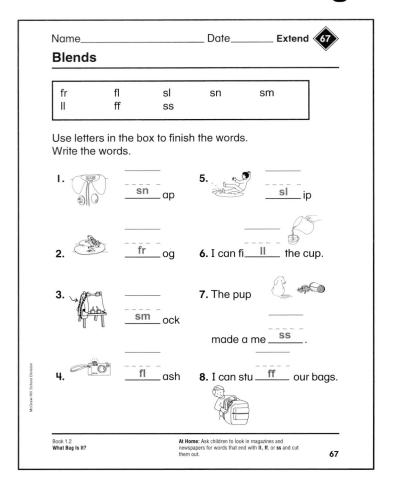

Name_____ Date_____ Extend **67**

Blends

fr	fl	sl	sn	sm
ll	ff	ss		

Use letters in the box to finish the words.
Write the words.

1. _____ **sn** ap

5. _____ **sl** ip

2. _____ **fr** og

6. I can fi___**ll** the cup.

3. _____ **sm** ock

7. The pup _____ made a me ___**ss**.

4. _____ **fl** ash

8. I can stu ___**ff** our bags.

Book 1.2
What Bug Is It?

At Home: Ask children to look in magazines and
newspapers for words that end with **ll**, **ff**, or **ss** and cut
them out.

67

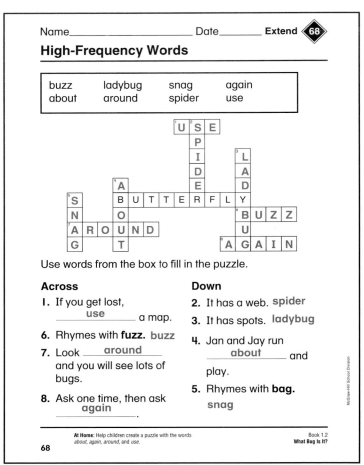

Name_____ Date_____ Extend **68**

High-Frequency Words

buzz	ladybug	snag	again
about	around	spider	use

Use words from the box to fill in the puzzle.

Across

1. If you get lost, _____ **use** a map.
6. Rhymes with **fuzz**. **buzz**
7. Look _____ **around** and you will see lots of bugs.
8. Ask one time, then ask _____ **again** .

Down

2. It has a web. **spider**
3. It has spots. **ladybug**
4. Jan and Jay run _____ **about** and play.
5. Rhymes with **bag**. **snag**

At Home: Help children create a puzzle with the words
about, again, around, and *use.*

68

Book 1.2
What Bug Is It?

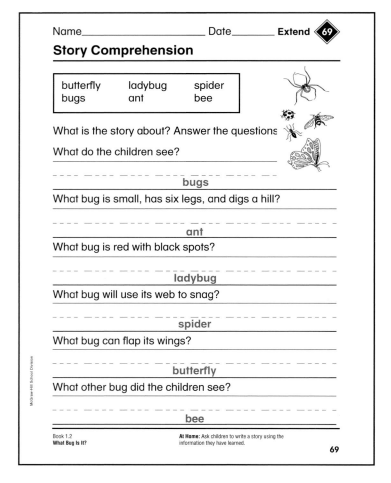

Name_____ Date_____ Extend **69**

Story Comprehension

butterfly	ladybug	spider
bugs	ant	bee

What is the story about? Answer the questions

What do the children see?

_____ **bugs**

What bug is small, has six legs, and digs a hill?

_____ **ant**

What bug is red with black spots?

_____ **ladybug**

What bug will use its web to snag?

_____ **spider**

What bug can flap its wings?

_____ **butterfly**

What other bug did the children see?

_____ **bee**

Book 1.2
What Bug Is It?

At Home: Ask children to write a story using the
information they have learned.

69

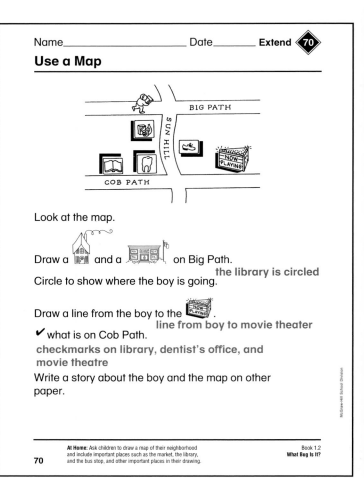

Name_____ Date_____ Extend **70**

Use a Map

Look at the map.

Draw a 🏠 and a 🏢 on Big Path. **the library is circled**
Circle to show where the boy is going.

Draw a line from the boy to the 🎬 . **line from boy to movie theater**
✔ what is on Cob Path.
checkmarks on library, dentist's office, and movie theatre

Write a story about the boy and the map on other paper.

70

At Home: Ask children to draw a map of their neighborhood
and include important places such as the market, the library,
and the bus stop, and other important places in their drawing.

Book 1.2
What Bug Is It?

What Bug Is It? • EXTEND

Blends

Write each picture name. Look for these letters at the beginning or end of the words: **sn, sl, fl, sm, fr, ll, ss, ff.** Circle the ones you find.

hill	smash	flap	cuff
snack	slot	frog	flip	kiss

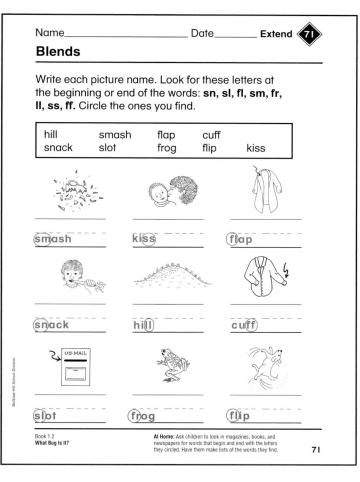

smash   kiss   flap

snack   hill   cuff

slot   frog   flip

Book 1.2
What Bug Is It?

At Home: Ask children to look in magazines, books, and newspapers for words that begin and end with the letters they circled. Have them make lists of the words they find.

71

Blends; *sh, th, ck*

Put a ✔ next to words that end with the same sound.

wax	rack
both	math ✔
dish	smash ✔
hit	wish
sick	rock ✔
neck	back ✔
cup	duck

How many ✔? ___4___

For 1 ✔ draw a ship in a shed.

For 2 ✔ draw a sack on your back.

For 3 ✔ draw a snack on a rack.

For 4 ✔ draw a fish on a dish.

At Home: Ask children to list words that begin with **sh** or **th** and use the words in silly sentences or stories.

72

Book 1.2
What Bug Is It?

Main Idea

Look at the picture.
Circle the sentences that tell about the picture.
Write a sentence that tells the main idea.

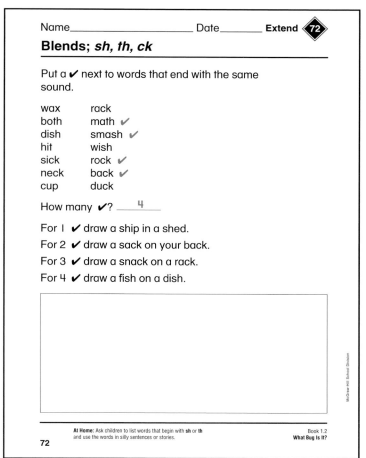

1. The children run.
2. The duck says quack.
3. Ann likes cats.
4. The dog runs for the ball.
5. The man wants to stop the dog.
6. Dad has a stick.
7. The ball is on the grass.
8. The tent is up.

The main idea of the picture is

Answers will vary, but may indicate that a dog wants to play in the children's soccer game.

Book 1.2
What Bug Is It?

At Home: Have children find a picture in a magazine or a book and write a sentence that tells the main idea of the picture.

73

Context Clues

ant	bee	butterfly
ladybug	spider	

Read the riddles.
Write the answer.

1. I am a small bug.
   I have six legs.
   I dig in a hill.
   What bug am I?   ant

2. Let me pass.
   I will buzz!
   Do not let me sit on your hand.
   What bug am I?   bee

3. I am red.
   I have black spots.
   My wings pop up and snap shut.
   What bug am I?   ladybug

4. I am in a web.
   I am big and fat.
   I have thin legs.
   What bug am I?   spider

5. I flap my wings
   I sip from flowers.
   I can look slim and flat.
   What bug am I?   butterfly

At Home: Ask children to act like one of the bugs from the story and have someone guess what bug it is.

74

Book 1.2
What Bug Is It?

What Bug Is It? • GRAMMAR

Page 51

Name_____ Date_____ LEARN GRAMMAR **51**

Proper Nouns

- Some nouns name a special person or place.
- This kind of noun is called a **proper noun**.
- A proper noun begins with a capital letter.
  Rick

Read the sentences. Find the proper nouns.
Draw a circle around the proper nouns that need a
capital letter.

1. (rick) saw a small bug.

2. "It is an ant!" said (jill).

3. The bug walked on (jas).

4. "That is a ladybug!" (nell) said.

5. (yan) saw a spider.

Book 1.2
What Bug Is It?
EXTENSION: Have the children write sentences using
their classmates' names as proper nouns.
51

Page 52

Name_____ Date_____ LEARN AND PRACTICE GRAMMAR **52**

Proper Nouns

- **Proper nouns** name a special person or place.
- Streets, cities, states, parks, and schools are some of the special places that are proper nouns.

  [R]ichmond, [V]irginia
  [J]efferson [P]ark
  [E]vergreen [S]chool

- Proper nouns begin with a capital letter.

Evergreen School

Read the sentences.
Draw a circle around the place names that need
a capital letter.

1. Pam lives on (elm) (street).

2. Rick's home is in (new) (york).

3. There are big trees in (grove) (park).

4. Max lives in (ohio).

5. Jas goes to (john) (adams) (school).

EXTENSION: Have the children compose sentences with the
name of the city, town, or community where they live.
52
Book 1.2
What Bug Is It?

Page 53

Name_____ Date_____ PRACTICE AND WRITE GRAMMAR **53**

Proper Nouns

- **Proper nouns** name a special person or place.
- Proper nouns begin with a capital letter.

  [P]am lives on [S]pruce [S]treet.
  [J]ill's address is: [J]ill [M]ason
  124 [P]leasant [S]treet
  [H]amilton, [O]hio 42134

Write proper nouns that name
people and places on the lines.
Begin the names with capital letters.

My name is _____ *Answers will vary.* .

My address is _____ *Answers will vary.*

_____ *Answers will vary.*

_____ *Answers will vary.*

Book 1.2
What Bug Is It?
EXTENSION: Have the children compose sentences about
local place names.
53

Page 54

Name_____ Date_____ MECHANICS GRAMMAR **54**

Proper Nouns

- A proper noun names a special person or place.
- A proper noun begins with a capital letter.

Read each sentence.
Circle the letters that should be capital letters.

1. "Look around," said (m)iss Lin.

2. (r)ick said, "I see a bug."

3. "I see a bug," said (j)ill.

4. Nell goes to (g)reen (s)chool.

5. "It is a big bat," said (y)an.

54
Book 1.2
What Bug Is It?

What Bug Is It? • GRAMMAR

Proper Nouns

Read each sentence. Find the proper noun. Mark your answer.

1. We saw a spider at Green School.
   - Ⓐ Green School
   - Ⓑ We
   - Ⓒ saw

2. "It will use its web to snag flies," said Miss Lin.
   - Ⓐ It
   - Ⓑ use
   - Ⓒ Miss Lin

3. "It is a bee," said Jill.
   - Ⓐ Jill
   - Ⓑ a
   - Ⓒ is

4. We saw bugs at Good Park.
   - Ⓐ at
   - Ⓑ We
   - Ⓒ Good Park

5. "Let that bug pass!" said Jill.
   - Ⓐ that
   - Ⓑ Jill
   - Ⓒ Let

Book 1.2
What Bug Is It?   55

Proper Nouns

- Some nouns name a special person or place.
- This kind of noun is called a proper noun.
- A proper noun begins with a capital letter.

Read each sentence aloud. Draw a circle around each proper noun.

1. (Rick) has a bug in a box.

2. (Miss Lin) sees a big cat.

3. (Pam) is in the yard.

4. Do you live in (Texas)?

5. Where is (Spring Street)?

6. I go to (West End School).

56

Book 1.2
What Bug Is It?

T47

What Bug Is It? • SPELLING

Name_____ Date_____

Words with Blends

Complete each word by writing the letters **sn**, **fl**, **ss**, **ll**, or **ff** on the line.

1. **sn** ap
2. **fl** at
3. pa **ss**
4. mi **ss**
5. do **ll**
6. pu **ff**

Directions (to teacher)

Review the blend *sn* by explaining that the letters *sn* spell the sounds /s/ and /n/, which may come together at the beginning of a word. Write *snap* on the chalkboard or form the word with letter cards. Say the word aloud and have children repeat it. Then have children look at the first example on the page. Point out that the letters *sn* have been filled in.

Display the word *flat*. Say the word aloud and have children repeat it. Have them listen for the two beginning sounds /f/ and /l/. Then have children complete the second example.

Display the word *pass*. Have children listen for the consonant sound at the end of the word (/s/). Tell them it is written with two of the same letter (s). Have them complete the third example.

Write the words *miss*, *doll*, and *puff* on the chalkboard. Read the words aloud and have children repeat them. Have children listen for the consonant sound at the end of each word. Tell children each is written with two of the same letter. Have children complete each word on the line provided.

Name_____ Date_____

Words with Blends

Using the Word Study Steps

1. LOOK at the word.
2. SAY the word aloud.
3. STUDY the letters in the word.
4. WRITE the word.
5. CHECK the word.
   Did you spell the word right?
   If not, go back to step 1.

> **Spelling Tip**
>
> Think of times when you have seen the word. Maybe you have read it in a book or on a sign. Try to remember how it looked. Write the word in different ways to see which one looks correct.
> ~~dol, dool,~~ doll

Word Scramble

Unscramble each set of letters to make a spelling word.

1. pasn **snap**
2. sims **miss**
3. oldl **doll**
4. alft **flat**
5. sasp **pass**
6. fupf **puff**

To Parents or Helpers:
Using the Word Study Steps above as your child comes across any new words will help him or her spell well. Review the steps as you both go over this week's spelling words.
Go over the Spelling Tip with your child. Help your child write new words in different ways to see which one looks right. Help your child complete the spelling activity.

Name_____ Date_____

Words with Blends

Look at the spelling words in the box.

| snap pass flat doll miss puff |

Write the word that begins with **sn.**

1. **snap**

Write the word that begins with **fl.**

2. **flat**

Write the words that end with two letters that are the same.

3. **pass**
4. **doll**
5. **miss**
6. **puff**

Name_____ Date_____

Words with Blends

Look at the spelling words in the box. Then read the story below. Complete each spelling word.

| snap pass flat doll miss puff |

Jill has a do **ll** . She calls it

Mi **ss** Nell. The doll is **fl** at,

but it has a big pu **ff** of hair. It has a hat.

The hat can **sn** ap on. Jill said to Max,

"Pa **ss** me Miss Nell."

T48 *Annotated Workbooks*

What Bug Is It? • SPELLING

Words with Blends

Look at the picture. Complete each sentence with a spelling word.

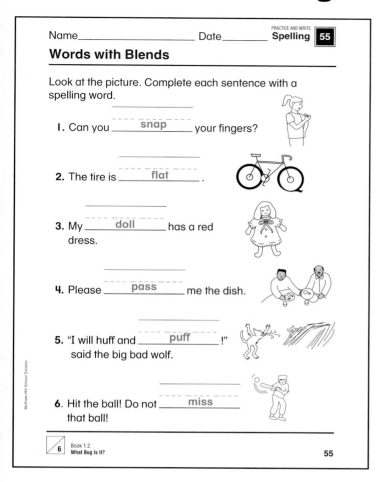

1. Can you ___snap___ your fingers?

2. The tire is ___flat___ .

3. My ___doll___ has a red dress.

4. Please ___pass___ me the dish.

5. "I will huff and ___puff___ !" said the big bad wolf.

6. Hit the ball! Do not ___miss___ that ball!

Words with Blends

Look at the words in each set. One word in each set is spelled correctly. Use a pencil to color in the circle in front of that word. Before you begin, look at the sample sets of words. Sample A has been done for you. Do Sample B by yourself. When you are sure you know what to do, you may go on with the rest of the page.

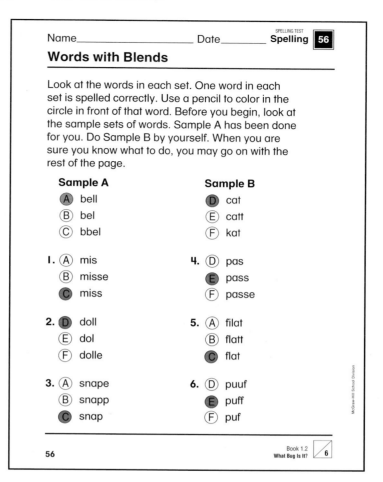

Sample A
- (A) bell
- (B) bel
- (C) bbel

Sample B
- (D) cat
- (E) catt
- (F) kat

1.
- (A) mis
- (B) misse
- (C) miss

4.
- (D) pas
- (E) pass
- (F) passe

2.
- (D) doll
- (E) dol
- (F) dolle

5.
- (A) filat
- (B) flatt
- (C) flat

3.
- (A) snape
- (B) snapp
- (C) snap

6.
- (D) puuf
- (E) puff
- (F) puf

Practice 75

Name_____ Date_____ Practice **75**

Blends, Short Vowels

Circle the word to complete each sentence.
Then write it.

1. _____ (tub)
   I get into the __tub__. pup

2. _____ frock
   The __frog__ likes to jump. (frog)

3. _____ (vet)
   The cat is at the __vet__. wet

4. _____ (flap)
   She can __flap__ her wings. flat

5. _____ (snack)
   I ate a __snack__. snag

6. _____ smash
   What is that good __smell__? (smell)

6 Book 1.2
A Vet

At Home: Ask children to illustrate one of these sentences.
Have them write the sentence below their drawing.

75

Practice 76

Name_____ Date_____ Practice **76**

High-Frequency Words

Circle the word to finish each sentence.

small	out	good	want

1. I will go __out__ to play. (out) / small

2. This is a __good__ book. (good) / out

3. My sisters __want__ a pup. good / (want)

4. Some pets are __small__. want / (small)

76 At Home: Ask children to create their own sentences using
the words **small**, **out**, **good**, and **want**.

Book 1.2 4
A Vet

My Dog Mack

"Bark! Bark!"
That is Mack. He can swim.
He can get my hat for me. He
swims to the rock. He comes
back with my hat.
"Thank you, Mack!" I say.
"Now let us go back home!"

At Home: Have children draw a picture of a windy
day. Encourage them to show what can happen
when it is windy.

4 (76a)

2

My small dog Mack wants to
go out. That is good. I want to
go out, too. It is windy. I take
my hat.
Mack has his ball. I toss the
ball. Mack runs fast and gets the
ball.

A Vet McGraw-Hill School Division

A small gust of wind gets my
hat. It is up in the sky. I run. I
cannot get my hat! Now my hat
is on a rock. The rock is in a
creek. I still cannot get my hat!

3 (76b)

Annotated Workbooks

A Vet • PRACTICE

Story Comprehension

Write **X** next to each sentence that describes "A Vet."

1. __X__ Vets help hogs.

2. _____ Vets help people get well.

3. __X__ Vets see sick cats.

4. __X__ A vet can help a sick duck.

5. _____ A vet will not go to a farm.

6. __X__ We take pets to the vet.

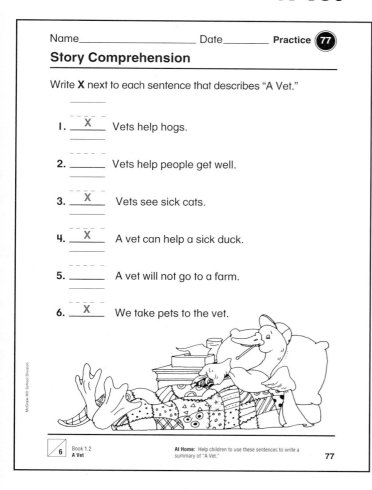

A Map

This is a **map** of a neighborhood.

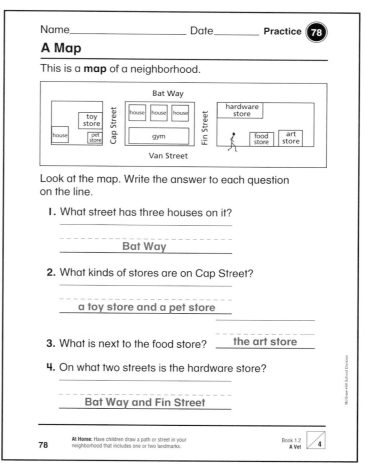

Look at the map. Write the answer to each question on the line.

1. What street has three houses on it?

   _____
   Bat Way

2. What kinds of stores are on Cap Street?

   _____
   a toy store and a pet store

3. What is next to the food store? **the art store**

4. On what two streets is the hardware store?

   Bat Way and Fin Street

Story Elements

Character - (tells who)	Plot - (tells what happens)
Bill the bug	makes a wish
Pam the pig	finds cash in the mud
Liz the duck	sees the vet

Use the lists to write your own story. Write at least four sentences. **Answers will vary.**

Main Idea

Read each story.
Fill in the circle by the title that tells the main idea of the story.

1. The bird can talk.

   It sings.

   It is pretty.

   ● This Bird Is Fun   ○ Blue Ships

   ○ Big Birds   ● Ships Are Great

2. The ship is big.

   It goes far.

   It is fast.

3. Tigers are big.

   They hunt.

   People like tigers.

   ● All About Tigers   ○ The Hat

   ○ A Day at the Zoo   ● The Firetruck

4. The truck is red.

   It has many hoses.

   They shoot water.

A Vet • PRACTICE

Name_____ Date_____ Practice **81**

Inflectional Ending *-ed*

Draw a line to the word that completes the sentence.

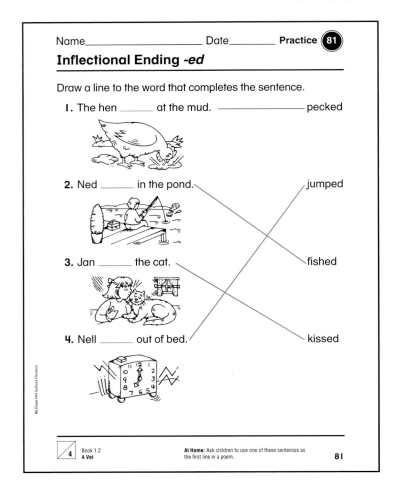

1. The hen _____ at the mud. _____ pecked

2. Ned _____ in the pond. jumped

3. Jan _____ the cat. fished

4. Nell _____ out of bed. kissed

4 | Book 1.2
A Vet

At Home: Ask children to use one of these sentences as the first line in a poem.

81

Name_____ Date_____ Practice **82**

Context Clues

Use the pictures and sentences to help you figure out what the underlined word means. Circle the answer.

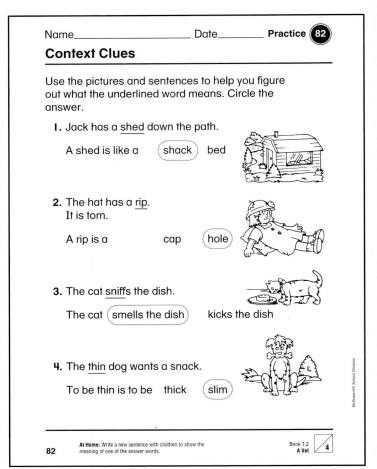

1. Jack has a shed down the path.

   A shed is like a (shack) bed

2. The hat has a rip.
   It is torn.

   A rip is a   cap   (hole)

3. The cat sniffs the dish.

   The cat (smells the dish)   kicks the dish

4. The thin dog wants a snack.

   To be thin is to be   thick   (slim)

82   **At Home:** Write a new sentence with children to show the meaning of one of the answer words.

Book 1.2
A Vet | 4

A Vet • RETEACH

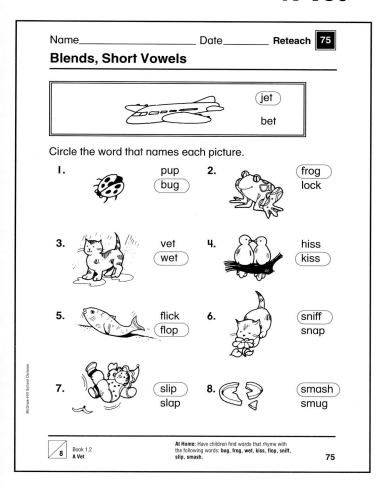

Name_____ Date_____ **Reteach** 75

Blends, Short Vowels

| jet |
| bet |

Circle the word that names each picture.

1. pup
   bug

2. **frog**
   lock

3. vet
   wet

4. hiss
   kiss

5. flick
   flop

6. **sniff**
   snap

7. **slip**
   slap

8. **smash**
   smug

Book 1.2
A Vet   8

At Home: Have children find words that rhyme with
the following words: **bug, frog, wet, kiss, flop, sniff,
slip, smash.**

75

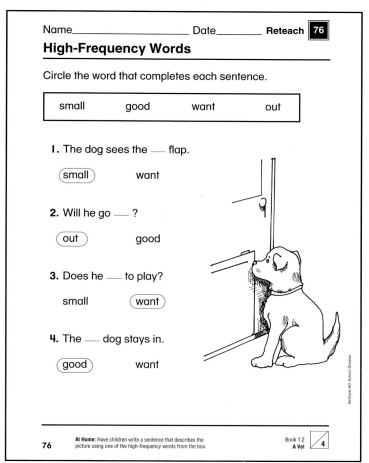

Name_____ Date_____ **Reteach** 76

High-Frequency Words

Circle the word that completes each sentence.

| small   good   want   out |

1. The dog sees the ___ flap.

   small   want

2. Will he go ___ ?

   out   good

3. Does he ___ to play?

   small   **want**

4. The ___ dog stays in.

   good   want

76   At Home: Have children write a sentence that describes the
picture using one of the high-frequency words from the box.

Book 1.2
A Vet   4

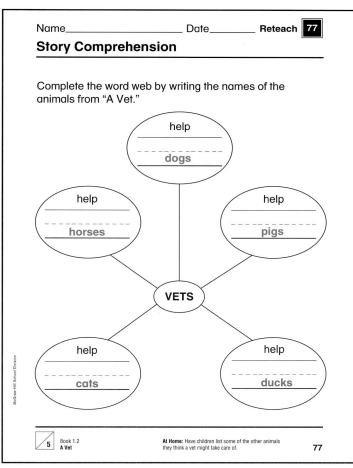

Name_____ Date_____ **Reteach** 77

Story Comprehension

Complete the word web by writing the names of the
animals from "A Vet."

help
_____
dogs

help
_____
horses

help
_____
pigs

VETS

help
_____
cats

help
_____
ducks

Book 1.2
A Vet   5

At Home: Have children list some of the other animals
they think a vet might take care of.

77

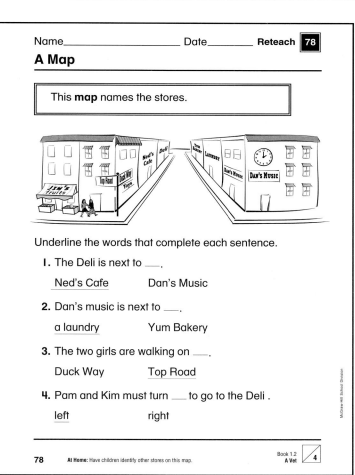

Name_____ Date_____ **Reteach** 78

A Map

| This **map** names the stores. |

Underline the words that complete each sentence.

1. The Deli is next to ___.

   Ned's Cafe   Dan's Music

2. Dan's music is next to ___.

   a laundry   Yum Bakery

3. The two girls are walking on ___.

   Duck Way   Top Road

4. Pam and Kim must turn ___ to go to the Deli .

   left   right

78   At Home: Have children identify other stores on this map.

Book 1.2
A Vet   4

A Vet • RETEACH

Reteach 79

Name_____ Date_____ **Reteach** 79

Story Elements

> The things that happen in a story make up the **plot.**
> The people in the story are the **characters.**

Draw a line from the picture to the sentence that tells what happens.

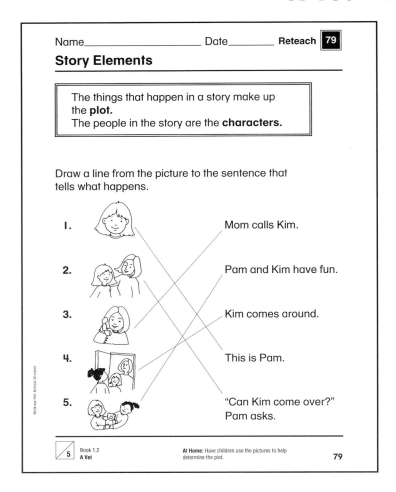

1.   Mom calls Kim.

2.   Pam and Kim have fun.

3.   Kim comes around.

4.   This is Pam.

5.   "Can Kim come over?" Pam asks.

5   Book 1.2   **A Vet**   **At Home:** Have children use the pictures to help determine the plot.   79

Reteach 80

Name_____ Date_____ **Reteach** 80

Main Idea

> The **main idea** tells what the story is about.
> The **supporting details** tell about the main idea.

Read each story.

The bear lives in the woods.
He is brown.
It's Tad, the bear.

1. Write the sentence that tells the main idea.

_____
It's Tad, the bear.

The bees are sad.
They don't like Tad.
Tad is eating the honey.

2. Write the sentence that tells the main idea.

_____
The bees are sad.

80   **At Home:** Have children think of another supporting detail for each exercise.   Book 1.2   **A Vet**   2

Reteach 81

Name_____ Date_____ **Reteach** 81

Inflectional Ending -ed

> Read the word.
> look + **ed** = look**ed**
> The girl **looked** at the flower.

Add -**ed** to each of the words.

1. sniff + ed = ____**sniffed**____

2. pack + ed = ____**packed**____

3. lick + ed = ____**licked**____

Using the words from above, complete each sentence.

4. The hog ____**licked**____ the grass.

5. We ____**packed**____ our bags.

6. My pup ____**sniffed**____ at the hen.

6   Book 1.2   **A Vet**   **At Home:** Encourage children to write a new sentence for each word.   81

Reteach 82

Name_____ Date_____ **Reteach** 82

Context Clues

> When you don't know what a word means, the other words or pictures can help you.

Circle the picture that tells what the underlined word means.

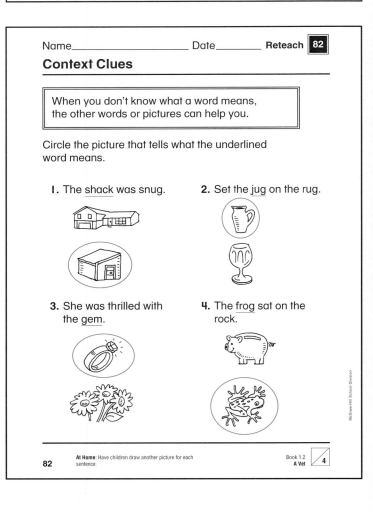

1. The <u>shack</u> was snug.

2. Set the <u>jug</u> on the rug.

3. She was thrilled with the <u>gem</u>.

4. The <u>frog</u> sat on the rock.

82   **At Home:** Have children draw another picture for each sentence.   Book 1.2   **A Vet**   4

T54   *Annotated Workbooks*

A Vet • EXTEND

Blends, Short Vowels

nap	tack	sick	bath	rock
wag	leg	flash	kiss	smock

Make words from the letters. Use the box to help you.

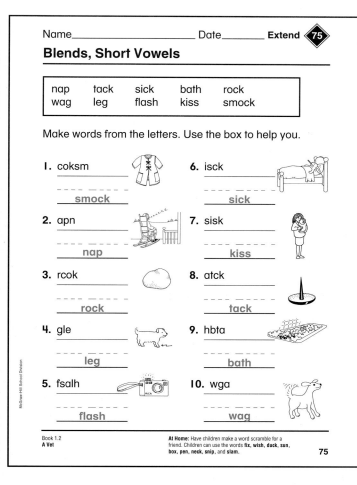

1. coksm

   __smock__

2. apn

   __nap__

3. rcok

   __rock__

4. gle

   __leg__

5. fsalh

   __flash__

6. isck

   __sick__

7. sisk

   __kiss__

8. atck

   __tack__

9. hbta

   __bath__

10. wga

    __wag__

Book 1.2
A Vet

At Home: Have children make a word scramble for a friend. Children can use the words **fix**, **wish**, **duck**, **sun**, **box**, **pen**, **neck**, **snip**, and **slam**.

75

High-Frequency Words

The words are mixed up.
Make sentences.
Write the sentences on the line.

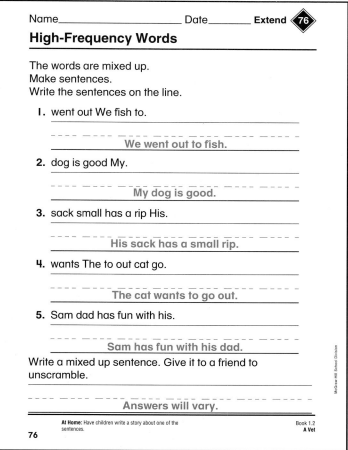

1. went out We fish to.

   __We went out to fish.__

2. dog is good My.

   __My dog is good.__

3. sack small has a rip His.

   __His sack has a small rip.__

4. wants The to out cat go.

   __The cat wants to go out.__

5. Sam dad has fun with his.

   __Sam has fun with his dad.__

Write a mixed up sentence. Give it to a friend to unscramble.

__Answers will vary.__

76

At Home: Have children write a story about one of the sentences.

Book 1.2
A Vet

Story Comprehension

Think of a pet that needs a vet.
Write a letter to the vet to tell what the problem is.
A sample answer is shown.
Dear Vet,

__I think my guinea pig has a cold. His name is__

__Marty. He sneezes. He does not want to eat.__

__Can you help Marty?__

Your friend,

__Beth__

Book 1.2
A Vet

At Home: Ask children to cut pictures from magazines of pets that a vet can care for. Children can use the pictures to create a pet care book.

77

Use a Map

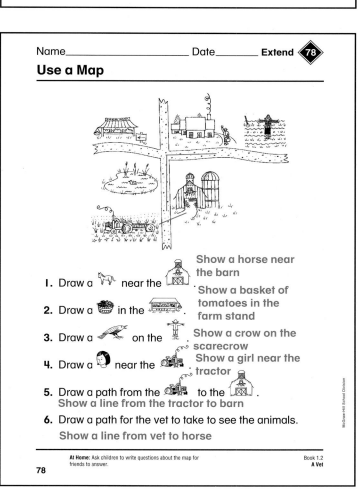

1. Draw a [horse] near the [barn].

   Show a horse near the barn

2. Draw a [basket] in the [farm stand].

   Show a basket of tomatoes in the farm stand

3. Draw a [crow] on the [scarecrow].

   Show a crow on the scarecrow

4. Draw a [girl] near the [tractor].

   Show a girl near the tractor

5. Draw a path from the [tractor] to the [barn].

   Show a line from the tractor to barn

6. Draw a path for the vet to take to see the animals.

   Show a line from vet to horse

78

At Home: Ask children to write questions about the map for friends to answer.

Book 1.2
A Vet

A Vet • EXTEND

Name_____ Date_____ **Extend** 79

Story Elements

What does a vet do all day?
Draw 3 pictures. Write a sentence for each one.

[box]

_____

[box]

_____

[box]

_____

At Home: Help children make a list of different kinds of
doctors and the types of patients they help.
79

Name_____ Date_____ **Extend** 80

Main Idea

Read the story.

The vet looks at my cat.
My cat is tan.
The vet looks at my pup.
My pup is big.
The vet gives them a checkup.
She says the pets are well.

Write a sentence to tell the main idea.

_____

Sample answer: The vet checks my pets to see how

they are.

✔ 2 details.
Sample answers include My cat is tan. My pup is big.
Draw a picture to show the main idea of the story.

[box]

At Home: Read several short stories to children and ask
them to identify the main ideas and details.
Book 1.2
A Vet

Name_____ Date_____ **Extend** 81

Inflectional Ending *-ed*

Write the word that completes the sentence.

_____

1. The vet _____ **picked** _____ up the pup.
   pick   picked

_____

2. Will the pup _____ **lick** _____ her hand?
   lick   licked

_____

3. The vet _____ **filled** _____ the cat's dish.
   fill   filled

_____

4. Will the cat _____ **hiss** _____ at her?
   hiss   hissed

Choose one of the words. Write a sentence.

_____

Sentences will vary.

At Home: Have children look in a magazine or a book for
words that end with **ed** and make a list of them.
81

Name_____ Date_____ **Extend** 82

Context Clues

| fine   help   barn   head   coat   horse |

Write words from the box to finish the story.

_____

The vet will look at our _____ **horse** _____.

_____

She wants to _____ **help** _____.

_____

The vet puts on her _____ **coat** _____.

_____

She goes into the _____ **barn** _____.

_____

She pets the horse's _____ **head** _____
with her hand.
She gives the horse a checkup. The vet says he is
not sick.

_____

He is _____ **fine** _____.

At Home: Have children read the story again with a friend or
family member. Encourage them to use picture clues and context
clues to help them figure out words that they do not know.
Book 1.2
A Vet

T56   *Annotated Workbooks*

A Vet • GRAMMAR

Days, Months, and Holidays

- Some **proper nouns** name special people, pets, and places.
- **Proper nouns** begin with capital letters.
- Some **proper nouns** name the days of the week.
- The days of the week begin with capital letters.

[S]unday   [M]onday   [T]uesday
[W]ednesday   [T]hursday   [F]riday   [S]aturday

Write the day of the week on the lines.
Begin each day with a capital letter.

1. After Friday comes _____ **Saturday** _____.

2. Before Tuesday comes _____ **Monday** _____.

3. The day after Wednesday is _____ **Thursday** _____.

4. The day before Monday is _____ **Sunday** _____.

5. After Thursday comes _____ **Friday** _____.

6. The day after Tuesday is _____ **Wednesday** _____.

Book 1.2 A Vet   **EXTENSION:** Have the children tell what their favorite day of the week is.   57

Days, Months, and Holidays

- Some proper nouns name months.
- These proper nouns begin with capital letters.

[J]anuary, [F]ebruary, [M]arch, [A]pril, [M]ay,
[J]une, [J]uly, [A]ugust, [S]eptember,
[O]ctober, [N]ovember, [D]ecember

Read each sentence.
Draw a circle around the letters that need to be capitals.

1. School starts in ⓐugust or ⓢeptember.

2. The first month is ⓙanuary.

3. My birthday is in ⓙune.

4. Valentine's Day is in ⓕebruary.

5. A hot month is ⓐugust.

EXTENSION: Have the children name their favorite month and explain why it is their favorite. They can write a sentence about this month.   Book 1.2 A Vet   58   5

Days, Months, and Holidays

- Some proper nouns name holidays.
- The names of holidays begin with capital letters.
  Some of the holidays are:
  Thanksgiving   Christmas   New Year's Day
  Independence Day   Valentine's Day

Read the sentences.
Draw a circle around the holidays that need a capital letter.
Write the name of the holiday with a capital letter.

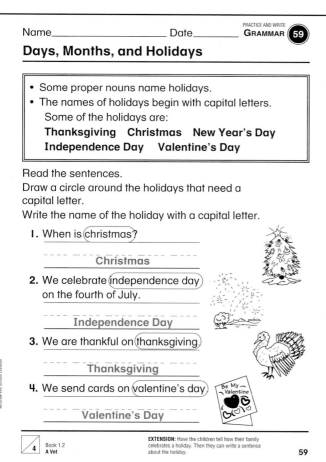

1. When is (christmas)?

_____ **Christmas** _____

2. We celebrate (independence day) on the fourth of July.

_____ **Independence Day** _____

3. We are thankful on (thanksgiving).

_____ **Thanksgiving** _____

4. We send cards on (valentine's day).

_____ **Valentine's Day** _____

Book 1.2 A Vet   **EXTENSION:** Have the children tell how their family celebrates the holiday. Then they can write a sentence about the holiday.   59

Days, Months, and Holidays

- The name of each day begins with a capital letter.
- Monday, Tuesday, Wednesday
- The name of each month begins with a capital letter.
- March, April, May, June
- The name of a holiday begins with a capital letter.
- Mother's Day, Thanksgiving, Independence Day

Read the sentences. Write the days, months, and holidays. Give the days, months, and holidays capital letters.

1. It rains in april. _____ **April** _____

2. Summer begins in june. _____ **June** _____

3. thanksgiving is for giving thanks.

_____ **Thanksgiving** _____

4. monday is the first day in the week. _____ **Monday**

5. On independence day, we have fun.

_____ **Independence Day** _____

60   **EXTENSION:** Have children write a sentence with a day and a month in it.   Book 1.2 A Vet   5

Days, Months, and Holidays

Read the sentences. Write the word that is correct.

1. We give thanks on _____**Thanksgiving**_____.

thanksgiving   Thanksgiving

2. I go to school on _____**Monday**_____.

Monday   monday

3. We give cards on _____**Valentine's Day**_____.

valentine's day   Valentine's Day

4. My birthday is in _____**May**_____.

may   May

5. I help Dad on _____**Saturday**_____.

Saturday   saturday

Days, Months, and Holidays

- Some proper nouns name days of the week.
- Some proper nouns name months.
- Some proper nouns name holidays.
- The name of each day begins with a capital letter.
- The name of each month begins with a capital letter.
- The name of a holiday begins with a capital letter.

Read the sentences. Put a circle on the letters that should be capital letters.

1. Meg has a birthday on ⓦednesday.

2. Who has a birthday in ⓜay?

3. Will Al have a birthday in ⓐpril?

4. Rick has a birthday on ⓥalentine's ⓓay.

5. I do not have a ⓕebruary birthday.

6. The vet gave me a dog in ⓜarch.

A Vet • SPELLING

Words from Social Studies

1. vet
2. hog
3. cat
4. help
5. job
6. pat

Directions (to teacher)

Write the words *vet, hog, cat, help, job,* and *pat* on the chalkboard. Have children find the word *vet* filled in on this page. Read the word aloud and have them repeat it.

Tell children they will be writing the other five words on this page. Read each word aloud. Have children repeat it and write it in the blank provided.

You may also wish to present the challenge words *small, out, good,* and *wants.*

Words from Social Studies

Using the Word Study Steps

1. LOOK at the word.
2. SAY the word aloud.
3. STUDY the letters in the word.
4. WRITE the word.
5. CHECK the word.
   Did you spell the word right? If not, go back to step 1.

Spelling Tip

Study words that do not match spelling patterns or rules. Use your word study steps.

Fill in the Blank

Write the spelling word that best fits each sentence.

1. I have a pet __cat__.
2. I __help__ with the work.
3. I did a good __job__.
4. His dog is at the __vet__.
5. A __hog__ eats a lot.
6. You __pat__ the puppy.

To Parents or Helpers:
Using the Word Study Steps above as your child comes across any new words will help him or her spell well. Review the steps as you both go over this week's spelling words.
Go over the Spelling Tip with your child. Help your child use the word study steps to study words that do not match spelling patterns or rules.
Help your child complete the spelling activity.

Words from Social Studies

Write each spelling word on the line where it belongs.
Look at the spelling words in the box.

| vet hog cat help job pat |

Write the spelling words that have short **a** spelled **a.**

1. cat
2. pat

Write the spelling words that have short **e** spelled **e.**

3. vet
4. help

Write the spelling words that have short **o** spelled **o.**

5. hog
6. job

Words from Social Studies

Find the spelling words in the puzzle. Circle the words you find. Then write them on the lines below.

| vet hog cat help job pat |

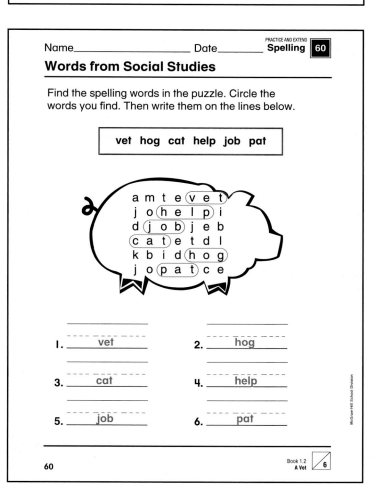

1. vet
2. hog
3. cat
4. help
5. job
6. pat

A Vet • SPELLING

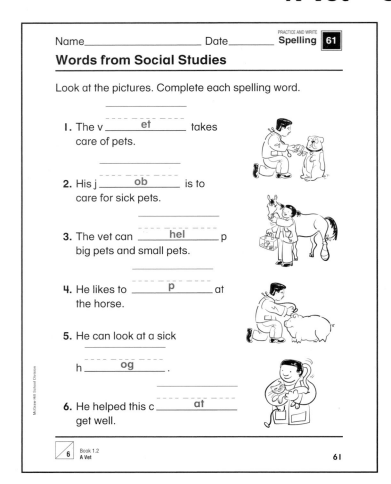

Words from Social Studies

Look at the pictures. Complete each spelling word.

1. The v _____et_____ takes care of pets.

2. His j _____ob_____ is to care for sick pets.

3. The vet can _____hel_____p big pets and small pets.

4. He likes to _____p_____ at the horse.

5. He can look at a sick h _____og_____ .

6. He helped this c _____at_____ get well.

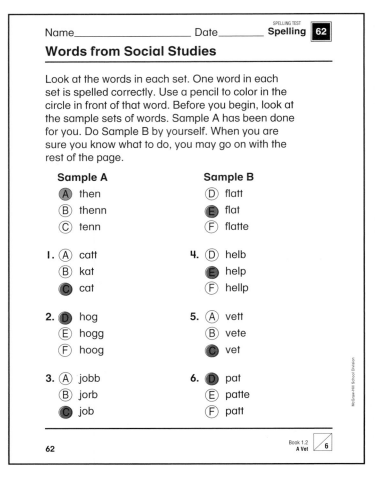

Words from Social Studies

Look at the words in each set. One word in each set is spelled correctly. Use a pencil to color in the circle in front of that word. Before you begin, look at the sample sets of words. Sample A has been done for you. Do Sample B by yourself. When you are sure you know what to do, you may go on with the rest of the page.

Sample A
- Ⓐ then
- Ⓑ thenn
- Ⓒ tenn

Sample B
- Ⓓ flatt
- Ⓔ flat
- Ⓕ flatte

1.
- Ⓐ catt
- Ⓑ kat
- Ⓒ cat

4.
- Ⓓ helb
- Ⓔ help
- Ⓕ hellp

2.
- Ⓓ hog
- Ⓔ hogg
- Ⓕ hoog

5.
- Ⓐ vett
- Ⓑ vete
- Ⓒ vet

3.
- Ⓐ jobb
- Ⓑ jorb
- Ⓒ job

6.
- Ⓓ pat
- Ⓔ patte
- Ⓕ patt

Unit 2 Review • PRACTICE and RETEACH

Name_____ Date_____ Practice **83**

High-Frequency Words Review

Write a word from the box to complete each sentence.

want	away	put	use	about	very

1. I __want__ to go to bed.

2. She wants to __use__ the big cup.

3. Could you __put__ the cat out?

4. The frog is __very__ wet.

5. Can you put your toys __away__ ?

6. What is the book __about__ ?

Name_____ Date_____ Practice **84**

High-Frequency Words Review

Write the word from the box that completes each sentence.

two	ride	saw	around

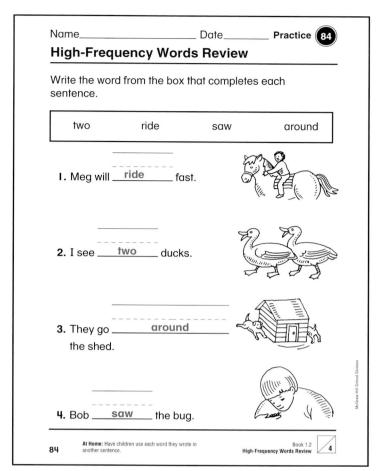

1. Meg will __ride__ fast.

2. I see __two__ ducks.

3. They go __around__ the shed.

4. Bob __saw__ the bug.

Name_____ Date_____ Reteach **83**

High-Frequency Words Review

Circle the word that tells about the picture.

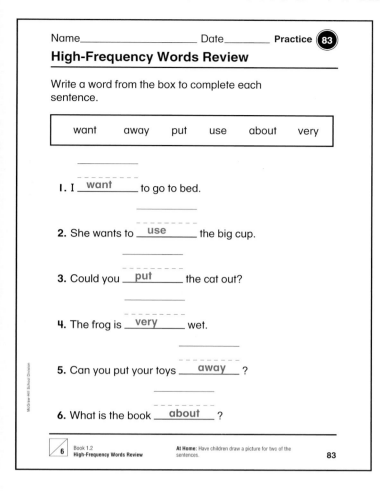

1.
one
(two)

2.
(ride)
bug

3.
small
(big)

4.
mop
(away)

5.
(good)
bad

6.
(no)
yes

Name_____ Date_____ Reteach **84**

High-Frequency Words Review

Write the word that fits the picture.

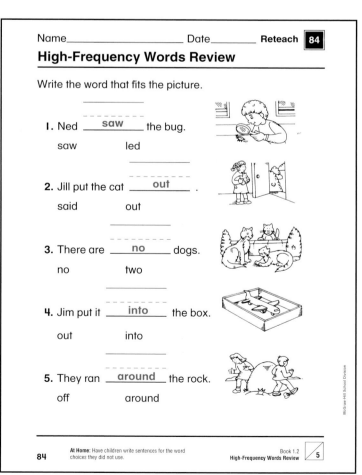

1. Ned __saw__ the bug.
   saw   led

2. Jill put the cat __out__ .
   said   out

3. There are __no__ dogs.
   no   two

4. Jim put it __into__ the box.
   out   into

5. They ran __around__ the rock.
   off   around

Unit 2 Review • EXTEND and GRAMMAR

Name_____ Date_____ **Extend** ◆83◆

High-Frequency Words Review

no	small	put	two	good
into	use	again	away	about

Read each riddle. Write the word.
Circle the picture.

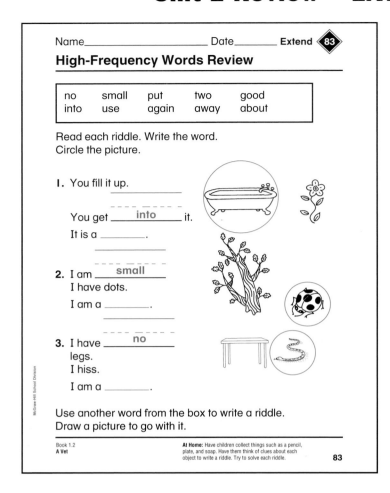

1. You fill it up.
   _____
   You get ___into___ it.
   It is a _____.
   _____

2. I am ___small___
   I have dots.
   I am a _____.
   _____

3. I have ___no___
   legs.
   I hiss.
   I am a _____.

Use another word from the box to write a riddle.
Draw a picture to go with it.

Book 1.2
A Vet

At Home: Have children collect things such as a pencil,
plate, and soap. Have them think of clues about each
object to write a riddle. Try to solve each riddle.

83

Name_____ Date_____ **Extend** ◆84◆

High-Frequency Words Review

very	want	put	saw
out	ride	around	

Finish the sentences. Write words from the box.

1. Max __s__ __a__ __w__ a cat and pet it. ____

2. When Dan jogs, he is __v__ __e__ __r__ __y__ quick.

3. Max lets the dog __o__ __u__ __t__ to run.

4. Jill __p__ __u__ __t__ her hat on her head.

5. I __w__ __a__ __n__ __t__ to have a snack.

6. We __r__ __i__ __d__ __e__ in the cab.

Write the letters from the ☐ on the lines.
Where did the boy see the ball?

__A__ __r__ __o__ __u__ __n__ __d__!

At Home: Help children make up their own sentences using
the words in the box.

Book 1.2
A Vet

84

Name_____ Date_____ REVIEW **GRAMMAR** ●63●

Nouns

Choose the word that belongs in each space. Mark
the letter for your answer.

> I live in a __(1)__ on Main Street. It is a big house.
> My cat lives there too.

1. Ⓐ house   Ⓑ cat   Ⓒ street

> My cat is sick. Is the __(2)__ in?

2. Ⓐ sick   Ⓑ vet   Ⓒ is

> Our class will ride the bus. Two __(3)__ are going.

3. Ⓐ bus   Ⓑ busss   Ⓒ buses

> One duck swims away. Four __(4)__ quack.

4. Ⓐ ducks   Ⓑ duckes   Ⓒ duck

> It rained on one goose. Three __(5)__ ran into the barn.

5. Ⓐ gooses   Ⓑ geese   Ⓒ goose

Go on →

Book 1.2
Together is Better

63

Name_____ Date_____ REVIEW **GRAMMAR** ●64●

> One mouse was in the barn. Three other __(6)__ ran
> in with the geese.

6. Ⓐ mouses   Ⓑ mice   Ⓒ mouse

> The barn is near Deer Park. The park is on Elm
> Street in El Paso, __(7)__ .

7. Ⓐ Texas   Ⓑ park   Ⓒ town

> We had a soccer game last Friday. Are we
> playing on __(8)__ ?

8. Ⓐ Tuesday   Ⓑ game   Ⓒ soccer

> My birthday is in December. When is your birthday?
> Is it in __(9)__ ?

9. Ⓐ party   Ⓑ June   Ⓒ today

> Grandma lives in Topeka, Kansas. She visits us
> every __(10)__ .

10. Ⓐ airplane   Ⓑ far   Ⓒ Thanksgiving

64

Book 1.2
Together is Better ●10●

Unit 2 Review • SPELLING

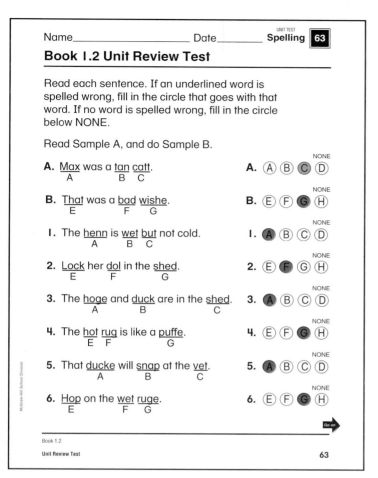

Book 1.2 Unit Review Test

Read each sentence. If an underlined word is spelled wrong, fill in the circle that goes with that word. If no word is spelled wrong, fill in the circle below NONE.

Read Sample A, and do Sample B.

A. <u>Max</u> was a <u>tan</u> <u>catt</u>.
   A   B C

A. Ⓐ Ⓑ **Ⓒ** Ⓓ   NONE

B. <u>That</u> was a <u>bad</u> <u>wishe</u>.
   E   F G

B. Ⓔ Ⓕ **Ⓖ** Ⓗ   NONE

1. The <u>henn</u> is <u>wet</u> <u>but</u> not cold.
   A   B C

1. **Ⓐ** Ⓑ Ⓒ Ⓓ   NONE

2. <u>Lock</u> her <u>dol</u> in the <u>shed</u>.
   E   F   G

2. Ⓔ **Ⓕ** Ⓖ Ⓗ   NONE

3. The <u>hoge</u> and <u>duck</u> are in the <u>shed</u>.
   A   B   C

3. **Ⓐ** Ⓑ Ⓒ Ⓓ   NONE

4. The <u>hot</u> <u>rug</u> is like a <u>puffe</u>.
   E F   G

4. Ⓔ Ⓕ **Ⓖ** Ⓗ   NONE

5. That <u>ducke</u> will <u>snap</u> at the <u>vet</u>.
      A   B   C

5. **Ⓐ** Ⓑ Ⓒ Ⓓ   NONE

6. <u>Hop</u> on the <u>wet</u> <u>ruge</u>.
   E   F G

6. Ⓔ Ⓕ **Ⓖ** Ⓗ   NONE

Go on

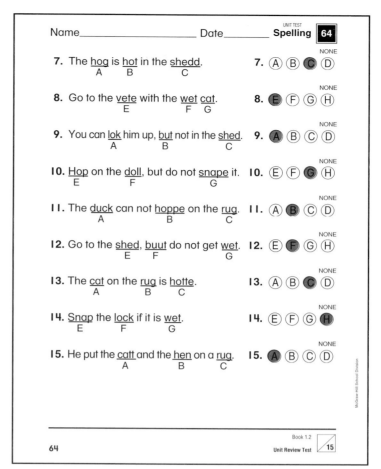

7. The <u>hog</u> is <u>hot</u> in the <u>shedd</u>.
   A   B   C

7. Ⓐ Ⓑ **Ⓒ** Ⓓ   NONE

8. Go to the <u>vete</u> with the <u>wet</u> <u>cat</u>.
         E   F G

8. **Ⓔ** Ⓕ Ⓖ Ⓗ   NONE

9. You can <u>lok</u> him up, <u>but</u> not in the <u>shed</u>.
      A   B   C

9. **Ⓐ** Ⓑ Ⓒ Ⓓ   NONE

10. <u>Hop</u> on the <u>doll</u>, but do not <u>snape</u> it.
    E   F   G

10. Ⓔ Ⓕ **Ⓖ** Ⓗ   NONE

11. The <u>duck</u> can not <u>hoppe</u> on the <u>rug</u>.
    A   B   C

11. Ⓐ **Ⓑ** Ⓒ Ⓓ   NONE

12. Go to the <u>shed</u>, <u>buut</u> do not get <u>wet</u>.
         E   F   G

12. Ⓔ **Ⓕ** Ⓖ Ⓗ   NONE

13. The <u>cat</u> on the <u>rug</u> is <u>hotte</u>.
     A   B   C

13. Ⓐ Ⓑ **Ⓒ** Ⓓ   NONE

14. <u>Snap</u> the <u>lock</u> if it is <u>wet</u>.
    E   F   G

14. Ⓔ Ⓕ Ⓖ **Ⓗ**   NONE

15. He put the <u>catt</u> and the <u>hen</u> on a <u>rug</u>.
       A   B   C

15. **Ⓐ** Ⓑ Ⓒ Ⓓ   NONE

Phonological Awareness

 OBJECTIVES Children will identify rhyming words, blend sounds, and segment sounds.

Alternate  Activities

Identify Rhyming Words

TELL ME A RHYME

 Use this activity to help children identify rhyming words.

- Sing the following song to the tune of "The Wheels on the Bus." *I'm thinking of some words that rhyme with* bug, *rhyme with* bug, *rhyme with* bug. *I know one word that rhymes is* tug. *What other words could there be?*

- Have children name additional rhyming words. *(hug, dug, jug, mug, rug)* Continue the song by using other pairs of rhyming words, such as *sun/fun, shut/nut, back/sack,* or *thick/sick.*

Blend Sounds

BLENDING BLOCKS

 Materials: blocks

This activity will help children blend sounds to form words.

- Give each child three blocks. Say a word containing three sounds, and have children move the blocks to make a horizontal line, one for each sound they hear in the word. For example, the word *hush* can be represented by three blocks: /h/-/u/-/sh/.

- Ask children to sweep their finger over the blocks and blend the sounds to say the word *hush.* Continue with other words.

Segment Sounds

TAKE IT APART

Materials: linking cubes

This activity will help children segment the individual sounds in words.

- Distribute three linking cubes to each child. Say a word with three sounds, such as *duck.* Have the class repeat the word slowly, taking apart a cube as they say each corresponding sound.

- Repeat the activity with the following words: *shack, that, thick, dash, rush,* and *luck.*

Short *u*

 **OBJECTIVES** Children will be introduced to the short *u* sound.

Alternate Activities

Visual

RHYMING SHORT *U* WORDS

ONE Mix up the following words and write them on the chalkboard to introduce children to the short *u* sound: *hut, cut, up, cup, pup, run, sun, fun.*

- Ask children to organize the words by listing groups of three rhyming words.

- Ask children, "What sound do all of these words have in common?" (the short *u* sound)

WRITING Call on volunteers to write each group of three rhyming words on the chalkboard. Then ask for suggestions of other words with the short *u* sound which would rhyme with any of the four groups. (*tuck, nut, bun*) ▶**Linguistic**

Kinesthetic

SHORT *U* CHARADES

GROUP Children will work together as a class to compile a list of words with the short *u* sound.

- After children have finished their lists, write the words on the chalkboard. Have children take turns acting out each of the words.

- Once the class has guessed a word, erase it from the chalkboard and let the next person act out one of the remaining words.

- Some of the words may be harder to act out than others, in which case children may elect to work with a partner to act out a word.
  ▶**Bodily/Kinesthetic**

Auditory

KEEP YOUR EARS OPEN

ONE Use the following activity to develop children's knowledge of words containing the short *u* sound.

- Make up a series of sentences which use words containing the short *u* sound. For example: *The pup would not hush, so Sam picked him up.*

- Read a sentence aloud and ask children to identify the words they hear which contain the short *u* sound. As they mention the words, make a list of them on the chalkboard.

WRITING After you have a good-sized list of words, ask children to create sentences of their own using some of the words included on the list.
▶**Linguistic**

 **Phonics** CD-ROM

See Reteach 43, 47, 48, 56, 64, 75

Using Maps

OBJECTIVES Children will be introduced to various types of maps and will have an opportunity to interpret and create maps of their own.

Alternate Activities

Visual

CLASSROOM MAPS

 Materials: a standard map, large sheets of white paper, pencils, markers, crayons

Give each child a large piece of white paper, pencils, markers and crayons. Ask children to make a map of the classroom. Encourage them to include as many details as possible and to label all of the elements that make up the map.

- Using a standard map, explain what a "key" is —a code which indicates with a color or symbol something which appears on a map.

- Discuss which common elements in the classroom might be appropriate to include in a key.

- Invite children to share their finished maps with the group and ask questions they may have about the maps. ▶**Spatial**

Kinesthetic

TREASURE MAPS

Materials: paper, markers, coin or token In this activity, children will create and interpret "treasure maps."

- Organize the class into four small groups. Give each group materials to draw a treasure map, as well as a coin or token to represent the "treasure."

- Have each group hide their treasure somewhere in the school building, and then create a map showing where the treasure is "buried."

- Each group will decide as a whole where the treasure will be hidden, but only one child will be elected to hide the treasure.

- Have groups exchange maps. Each group will study the map together and choose a member to retrieve the treasure. ▶**Bodily/Kinesthetic**

Auditory

MARK THE ROUTE

Materials: old road maps, markers, cardboard or index cards

Have children bring in old road maps or atlases from home to examine and discuss.

- Tell partners to use a map to plan a trip. Ask them to determine where the trip will begin and end and to circle some of the places of interest where they will stop along the way.

 Have children write postcards describing highlights of their trips and including details from the maps, which will help the class find where they are.

- Read the postcards aloud. Post the maps and cards on a bulletin board for the whole class to view. ▶**Logical/Mathematical**

See Reteach 46, 54, 62, 70, 78

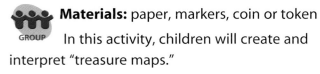

Story Elements
Character and Plot

OBJECTIVES Children will be introduced to analyzing characters and plot in a story.

Alternate Activities

Visual

CAST OF CHARACTERS

ONE **Materials:** paper, crayons or markers

Share a familiar story with the class to introduce story elements: *character* and *plot*. You may want to choose a well-known fairy tale, folktale, or favorite classroom picture book.

* As you read the story aloud, ask children to make a list of all the characters in the book.

* Have children draw pictures of what they imagine the characters look like based on any details given in the story.

* Make a bulletin board showing the names of characters from the story. Under each name, place the drawings children created for that particular character. ▶**Intrapersonal**

Kinesthetic

BE THE CHARACTER

GROUP Children will act out scenes in which they pretend to be characters from a favorite story.

* Have children choose a story for you to read aloud. Make a list of the characters in the story.

* Assign one child to play each character.

* In order to discuss and explore the nature of the characters, create simple scenarios for children. For example, the characters meet to play together at the playground, or they all want to take the same book out of the library.

* Have children discuss and improvise how they think their characters would behave in the situation. For example, a bossy character might want to go on the slide first at the playground, or he might grab the book out of someone else's hands in the library. ▶**Bodily/Kinesthetic**

Auditory

BEGINNING, MIDDLE, AND END

ONE **Materials:** paper, markers or crayons

Choose a favorite book to read to the class. Discuss character and plot. For this activity you will want a story with a clear plot line and several strong characters.

* Map out the plot with children. Write three headings on the chalkboard: BEGINNING, MIDDLE, and END.

* Ask children to come up with simple sentences to organize the plot under the three headings.

* Discuss the characters in the story. Ask the following question: *What is it that each character desires and works for within the story?*

* Have children draw one of the characters with the following caption: *I want _____.*

* Encourage children to use what they know about the character to complete the sentence. ▶**Spatial**

See Reteach 49, 53, 57, 61, 79

Inflected Ending -ed

OBJECTIVES Children will be introduced to the concept of adding -ed to a word to indicate past tense.

Alternate Activities

Visual

WHEN DID IT HAPPEN?

Use the following activity to introduce the concept of adding -ed to the end of a word to indicate past tense.

- Write the following sentences on the chalkboard: *"Let's visit the zoo," said John. "We visit___ the zoo last week," said Jim.*

- Have children identify two letters to add to the word *visit* in the second sentence. (-ed)

- Explain that adding -ed to the end of these words shows that something happened in the past.

- Write more sentences which need to have -ed added. Ask volunteers to fill in the blanks to make words with the -ed ending. ▶**Linguistic**

Kinesthetic

READ MY SHIRT

Materials: slips of white paper, cardboard square, tape

Use the following activity for children to practice making words with the -ed ending.

- Organize the class into two groups.

- Cut out slips of white paper and write one word on each slip to which -ed can be added. (*heat, watch, look, toss, jump, bump, etc.*) Tape the slips of paper to the fronts of the shirts of one group.

- Write ED on a cardboard square. The second group will use the ED card to change the words worn by the first group. They will take turns standing next to a member of the first group and holding up the ED card at the end of the word.

- Ask children wearing the word to use it in a sentence. (*I can* toss *a ball.*) When the ED is added, ask the other child to make a new sentence. (*Fred* tossed *the ball.*) ▶**Bodily/Kinesthetic**

Auditory

WHAT MAKES A MARCH?

Materials: recording of march music

Use the following activity for children to practice reading and hearing words with the -ed ending.

- Tell children that you are going to play a piece of music called a march.

- Write two headings on the board: *We are going to* listen *to music,* and *We have* listened *to music.*

- Ask children to make up sentences to describe the types of sounds they think they will hear. (*The cymbals will crash! The flutes will toot.*) Write the sentences on the chalkboard under the first heading.

- Play the recording. Now rewrite the sentences under the second heading and add -ed to reflect the fact that children have *listened* to the march. (*The cymbals crashed! The flutes tooted.*) ▶**Musical**

See Reteach 50, 58, 81

Phonological Awareness

 OBJECTIVES Children will blend onsets and rimes, blend sounds, and segment sounds.

Alternate

Blend Onsets and Rimes

WHAT'S IN THE SACK

 Materials: paper sack, small items or pictures of items that have three sounds

Use this activity to help children blend onsets and rimes.

- Tell children you have some mystery items to show them, but they have to say the name of the item to see it. Tell them you will give them a clue. Say, *It starts with /f/ and it ends with /ish/. (fish) It starts with /s/ and it ends with /ock/. (sock) It starts with /b/ and it ends with /ox/. (box)*

- Have children blend the sounds and say the word. Then pull the item that they say from the sack.

Blend Sounds

WHISPER IT

This activity will help children blend sounds to form words.

- Whisper the three sounds of a word to children. Have children whisper the blended word in response. For example, whisper /n/-/o/-/d/, and children whisper the word *nod.*

- Continue the activity with the following words: *lock, cot, thin, wish,* and *shop.*

Segment Sounds

SHOULDERS, KNEES, TOES

This activity will help children segment the individual sounds in words.

- Invite children to stand. Say a word with three sounds such as *dog.* Have children repeat the word slowly.

- Then, have children touch their shoulders, knees, and toes as they say each separate sound.

- Repeat the activity with the following words: *hot, dock, dish, mom,* and *luck.*

Short *o*

OBJECTIVES Children will be introduced to sounds containing the short *o* sound.

Alternate

Activities

Visual

MEET SHORT *O*

Materials: white paper, markers or crayons
Children will practice making words that contain the short *o* sound.

- Have children draw a large circle in the middle of a sheet of white paper. Explain that they will be creating a character called "Short O."

- Ask children to imagine that the *o* is the body of the character. Using crayons or markers have them turn the *o* into a "short" person by adding a head and short arms and legs to the body.

- Once the drawing is completed, ask children to add one letter to the left of "Short O" and one letter to the right to make a word. (*hot, pot, won, son, hop, pop*, etc.) Post the drawings.
  ▶**Spatial**

Kinesthetic

SHORT *O* BINGO

Materials: paper, pencils, markers
Use the following game to introduce children to hearing and recognizing words containing the short *o* sound.

- Play a game called Short *o* Bingo. Make up game cards by giving each child a piece of paper with a grid made up of nine squares.

- As a group, come up with as many short *o* words as possible and list them on the chalkboard.

- Ask children to write one of the words in each square on their grids, making sure not to use any word more than once.

- While children are working, write down each word from the list on a slip of paper and put it in a box or bowl.

- Pull out slips, one at a time, and read them aloud. Children will mark off squares as they hear words that match. The winner is the first one to mark off all of the squares. ▶**Logical/Mathematical**

Auditory

WORD TALLY

Materials: paper and pencil
Children will practice making words that contain the short *o* sound.

Have children work with a partner to make a list of short *o* words. After fifteen minutes, ask them to tally their words.

- The pair with the longest list then reads the list aloud. As they read, other children will cross off the same words from their own lists.

- If a word is read that only appears on the longest list, that word is circled and receives one point.

- When all of the words have been read and crossed off, have partners share the words that are left on their lists. For every real word, the pair receives one point. ▶**Interpersonal**

 **CD-ROM**

See Reteach 51, 55, 56, 64

Phonological Awareness

OBJECTIVES Children will blend sounds, segment sounds, and delete sounds.

Alternate

Activities

Blend Sounds

COLOR TIME

ONE

Materials: crayons, paper

This activity will help children blend sounds to form words.

- Have children place several crayons on their desk. Say the individual sounds in a color word, and ask children to hold up the corresponding crayon that names the color word; for example, /r/-/e/-/d/.

- Segment the individual sounds in the name of an object for children to draw with that crayon. For example, say /p/-/e/-/n/ (pen) or /b/-/e/-/l/ (bell), and invite children to blend the sounds and draw the item. Continue with other colors and simpler words.

Segment Sounds

SNAP, CLAP, TAP

GROUP This activity will help children segment the individual sounds in words.

- Say a word that has three sounds, such as *bed*. Have children snap their fingers as they say the beginning sound, clap their hands as they say the middle sound, and tap their feet as they say the ending sound.

- Continue the activity with the following words: *pet, shed, neck,* and *kick.*

Delete Sounds

STEP ASIDE

GROUP This activity will help children delete the beginning sound of a word.

- Invite three children to stand in front of the class. Secretly tell each child one of the sounds in a word.

- Have children say each sound in sequence. For example, /b/-/e/-/g/. Ask the class to identify the word. *(beg)* Ask the first volunteer to step aside, and have the other two children repeat their sounds (/e/-/g/) Ask the class to identify the word part that is left. *(eg)*

- Continue the activity with the following words: *jet, men, neck, box,* and *fed.*

Short *e*

OBJECTIVES Children will be introduced to words containing the short *e* sound.

Alternate Activities

Visual

SHORT *e* MOBILES

 Materials: clothes hangers, paper, scissors, string, markers

Children will create mobiles to display words containing the short *e* sound.

- Have partners make lists of short *e* words.

- Use clothes hangers as the base for the mobiles. Children can make signs to label each hanger, such as "Our Short *e* Mobile."

- On pieces of colored paper, have children write and illustrate each short *e* word.

- Help children use string to attach short *e* words to the mobile. Display the mobiles around the classroom. ▶**Spatial**

Kinesthetic

SHORT *e* GO FISH

 Materials: index cards, markers or colored pencils

Partners will create and play a card game called "Short *e* Go Fish."

- Give each pair an even number of index cards.

- Children must think of a number of short *e* words and write them down twice on two separate cards.

- The cards are then shuffled and each player is dealt three cards.

- The object of the game is to make pairs of words. The first player asks for a word which he or she holds in his or her hand. If the second player holds a card with that word, he or she gives it to the first player. If not, the first player must draw a card from the pile in the middle. The person with the greatest number of pairs in the end is the winner. ▶**Interpersonal**

Auditory

SHORT *e* RAPPERS

 Materials: examples of rap music, paper and pencils

- Play some examples of rap music written specifically for children.

 Have children try to write some rap-type lyrics using short *e* words. You can either have children make their own lists of words or work as a group to contribute words to a general list.

- Point out that rhyme plays a big role in rap lyrics. Suggest that children organize their short *e* words in groups that rhyme before starting to write the lyrics. ▶**Musical**

 **CD-ROM**

See Reteach 59, 63, 64, 75

Main Idea

OBJECTIVES Children are introduced to the concept of main idea and supporting details in a text.

Alternate Activities

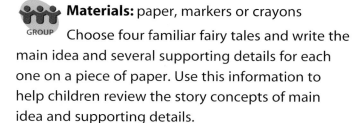

Visual

WHAT'S SUPPORTING IT?

 Materials: photo or drawing of a table, ONE paper, markers

Use this activity to discuss the story concepts: *main idea* and *supporting details.*

- Show a picture of a table, and ask, *What is holding this table up? What is* supporting *it?* (the legs)

- Explain that the *main idea* of a story is like a tabletop and that the *supporting details* are like the legs which hold it up.

- Read a brief story with which children are familiar. Ask, *What is the main idea of this story?* After the class has explored that question, ask, *What details in the story support the main idea?*

Have children draw a table and label the WRITING top with the main idea of the story and the legs with the supporting details. ▶**Spatial**

Kinesthetic

SUNNY IDEAS

Materials: yellow construction paper, PARTNERS scissors

- Read a picture book aloud to the class. Use the story to discuss *main idea* and *supporting details.*

- Organize the class into pairs and give each pair a large circle of yellow construction paper and several long strips of yellow paper. Help children create a sun with its rays.

Tell children to write the main idea of the WRITING story in the sun. Have them write some of the supporting details on the sun's rays. ▶**Spatial**

Auditory

WHAT STORY IS THIS?

Materials: paper, markers or crayons GROUP Choose four familiar fairy tales and write the main idea and several supporting details for each one on a piece of paper. Use this information to help children review the story concepts of main idea and supporting details.

- Organize the class into small groups. Give each group the breakdown sheets for the four fairy tales. Ask them to read and discuss the material and work together to figure out the titles of the fairy tales.

- Once children have figured out what the fairy tales are, have each group create an illustration to go with its breakdown sheet. ▶**Interpersonal**

See Reteach 65, 69, 73, 77, 80

Context Clues

OBJECTIVES Children use context clues to figure out the meanings of unfamiliar words.

Alternate Activities

Visual

WHAT DOES IT MEAN?

 PARTNERS Use the following activity to introduce the concept of using context clues to find the meaning of unfamiliar words.

- Write a passage from a chapter book on the chalkboard, or copy the passage and hand it out to the class. Read the passage aloud and ask children to underline any unfamiliar words.

- Ask children to figure out the meaning of at least one of the unfamiliar words.

- Have children answer the following questions:
  What do you think the sentence is trying to say?
  Are there any words nearby that give you hints about the unfamiliar word?
  Is there another word that you think you could use instead of the unfamiliar word? ▶**Interpersonal**

Kinesthetic

CIRCLE ROUND

Materials: book, newspaper

GROUP Children will practice using context clues to find the meanings of unfamiliar words.

- Ask children to stand and form a circle.
- Read aloud a passage from a book or newspaper article and ask children to crouch when they hear a word that they do not know.

- If everyone crouches for a particular word, write it on the chalkboard to discuss later.

- If some children crouch and others do not, ask one of the children who is still standing to define the word which is unfamiliar to those who are crouching.

- Invite children to share with the class how he or she figured out the meaning of the unfamiliar word. ▶**Bodily/Kinesthetic**

Auditory

WORD LISTS

Materials: picture book or passage from **PARTNERS** a book

Read aloud a picture book or a passage from a book. Have partners work together to use what they know about context clues to find the meanings of unfamiliar words.

- Make sure that one child in each pair is a good reader. Have partners take turns reading the same book or passage aloud to each other.

- When children come across unfamiliar words, encourage them to discuss what they think the words might mean.

- Invite partners to share with the class the methods they used to figure out the meanings of unfamiliar words.
  ▶**Interpersonal**

See Reteach 66, 74, 82

Phonological Awareness

OBJECTIVES Children will blend sounds, segment sounds, and delete sounds.

Alternate

Blend Sounds

I SPY

 This activity will help children blend sounds to form words.

- Play *I Spy* with children, but in this game, your clue will be the segmented sounds in a word. For example, say, *I spy a /f/-/l/-/a/-/g/. (flag)*

- Have children blend the sounds and name the object. Repeat for the following objects: *snack, bell,* and *smock.*

Segment Sounds

SEE THE SOUNDS

 Materials: self-stick notes, counters

This activity will help children separate words into individual sounds.

- Have children place four self-stick notes in a horizontal row on their desk. Give each child four counters, such as raisins or beans.

- Say a word with three or four phonemes, such as *less* or *frog.* Ask children to repeat the word slowly, separating each sound. Have them move a counter onto each self-stick note as they say each phoneme. For words with three phonemes, such as *less* or *bath (/l/-/e/-/s/, /b/-/a/-/th/),* they will place a counter on only three of the notes and leave the last one empty.

- Continue with other words.

Delete Sounds

FORGETFUL EARS

Materials: puppet

This activity will help children delete the ending sound of a word.

- Tell children that your puppet is forgetful. When you say a word, the puppet forgets the last sound. For example, you say *smack* and the puppet says */sma/.*

- Ask children what sound the puppet left off. *(/k/)* Continue with *snap, flat,* and *slip.*

- Then, say a word and have children tell you what the puppet will say. For example, if you say *flop,* children say, */flo/.* If you say bib, children say */bi/.*

Blends

OBJECTIVES Children will be introduced to words containing the blends *sl, sm, sn, fl, fr; and double consonants ll, ss, ff.*

Alternate Activities

Visual

C IS FOR CONSONANT, V IS FOR VOWEL

 Materials: felt board or mounting clay, index cards

Use the following activity to introduce children to words that contain the blends: *sl, sm, sn, fl, fr; and double consonants ll, ss, ff.*

- Make two columns on the chalkboard with the headings: CVCC and CCVC. Explain that C stands for consonant and V for vowel. If necessary, post a list of consonants and vowels.

- Make up cards for the following words, splitting them onto two cards so the blend or double consonant part of the word is on a separate piece. (*ta-ll, wa-ll, hu-ff, pu-ff, sm-og, sn-ag, sn-ip, fl-ip, fl-ag, fr-og, pa-ss, la-ss*)

- Hand each child two halves of a word and have them post it on the chalkboard under the proper column. (*ta-ll* would be placed under CVCC.)

- After the word is posted, have children say the two parts of the word separately and then pronounce the whole word. ▶Linguistic

Kinesthetic

STEPPING STONES

 Materials: gray and brown construction paper, scissors, markers

Use the following exercise to challenge children to read and pronounce words with the blends: *sl, sm,*

sn, fl, fr; and double consonants ll, ss, ff.

- Cut large circles out of sheets of gray and brown paper and print one of the following words on each "stepping stone": *tall, wall, huff, puff, smog, snag, snip, flip, flag, pass, lass.*

- Underline the blend or double consonant in each word with a red marker to highlight it.

- Tape the "stepping stones" to the floor and ask children to "cross the river" by walking on them.

- In order to cross the river without "falling in," children must use each stepping stone. Tell them that before they can step on a stone, they must read aloud the word written on it.
  ▶Bodily/Kinesthetic

Auditory

A TALL WALL

 Write the following blends and double consonants on the board: *sl, sm, sn, fl, fr; and double consonants ll, ss, ff.* Go over the sound each blend or double consonant represents.

- Make up sentences that contain one or more of these words: *tall, wall, huff, puff, smog, snag, snip, flip, flag, pass, lass.* Read them aloud.

- Ask children to identify the word or words with blends or double consonants.

- When each word has been correctly identified, write it on the chalkboard and ask children to underline the blend or double consonants.
  ▶Linguistic

See Reteach 67, 71, 72, 75

Notes

Writing Readiness

Before children begin to write, fine motor skills need to be developed. Here are examples of activities that can be used:

- **Simon Says** Play Simon Says using just finger positions.
- **Finger Plays and Songs** Sing songs such as "Where Is Thumbkin" or "The Eensie, Weensie, Spider" or songs that use Signed English or American Sign Language.
- **Mazes** Use or create mazes, especially ones that require moving the writing instruments from left to right.

The Mechanics of Writing

POSTURE

- Chair height should allow for the feet to rest flat on the floor.
- Desk height should be two inches above the elbows.
- There should be an inch between the child and the desk.
- Children sit erect with the elbows resting on the desk.
- Letter models should be on the desk or at eye level.

PAPER POSITION

- **Right-handed children** should turn the paper so that the lower left-hand corner of the paper points to the abdomen.

- **Left-handed children** should turn the paper so that the lower right-hand corner of the paper points to the abdomen.

- The nondominant hand should anchor the paper near the top so that the paper doesn't slide.

- The paper should be moved up as the child nears the bottom of the paper. Many children won't think of this.

The Writing Instrument Grasp

For handwriting to be functional, the writing instrument must be held in a way that allows for fluid dynamic movement.

FUNCTIONAL GRASP PATTERNS

- **Tripod Grasp** The writing instrument is held with the tip of the thumb and the index finger and rests against the side of the third finger. The thumb and index finger form a circle.

- **Quadrupod Grasp** The writing instrument is held with the tip of the thumb and index finger and rests against the fourth finger. The thumb and index finger form a circle.

INCORRECT GRASP PATTERNS

- **Fisted Grasp** The writing instrument is held in a fisted hand.

- **Pronated Grasp** The instrument is held diagonally within the hand with the tips of the thumb and index finger but with no support from other fingers.

- **Five-Finger Grasp** The writing instrument is held with the tips of all five fingers.

- **Flexed or Hooked Wrist** Flexed or bent wrist is typically seen with left-handed writers but is also present in some right-handed writers.

- To correct wrist position, have children check their writing posture and paper placement.

TO CORRECT GRASPS

- Have children play counting games with an eye dropper and water.
- Have children pick up small objects with a tweezer.
- Do counting games with children picking up small coins using just the thumb and index finger.

Evaluation Checklist

Formation and Strokes

- ☑ Does the child begin letters at the top?
- ☑ Do circles close?
- ☑ Are the horizontal lines straight?
- ☑ Do circular shapes and extender and descender lines touch?
- ☑ Are the heights of all upper-case letters equal?
- ☑ Are the heights of all lower-case letters equal?
- ☑ Are the lengths of the extenders and descenders the same for all letters?

Directionality

- ☑ Do the children form letters starting at the top and moving to the bottom?
- ☑ Are letters formed from left to right?

Spacing

- ☑ Are the spaces between letters equidistant?
- ☑ Are the spaces between words equidistant?
- ☑ Do the letters rest on the line?
- ☑ Are the top, bottom and side margins on the paper even?

Write the Alphabet

Trace and write the letters.

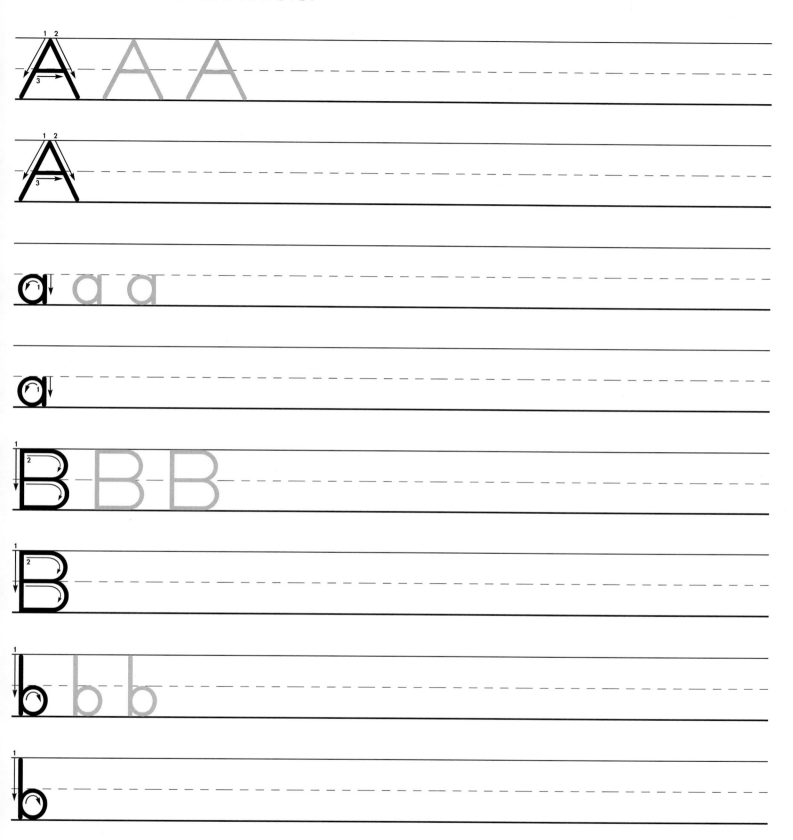

Trace and write the letters.

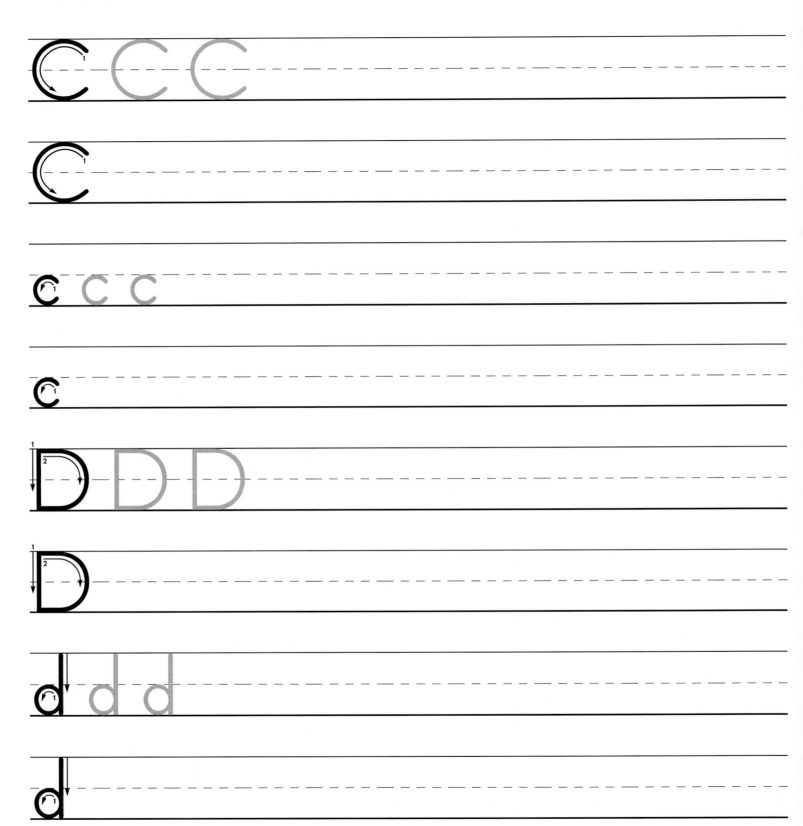

Trace and write the letters.

Trace and write the letters.

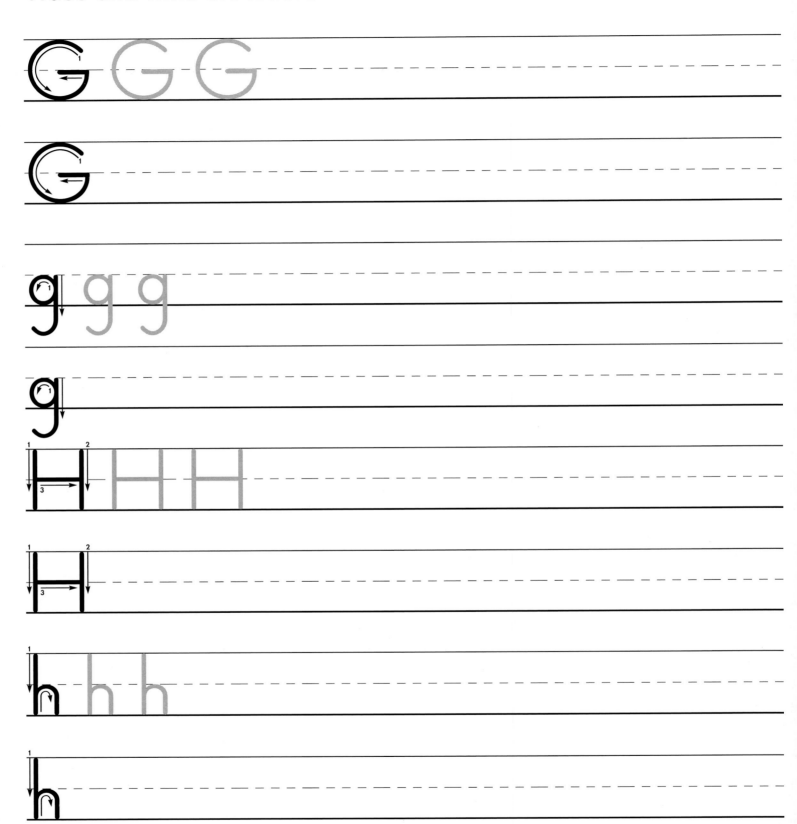

Trace and write the letters.

Trace and write the letters.

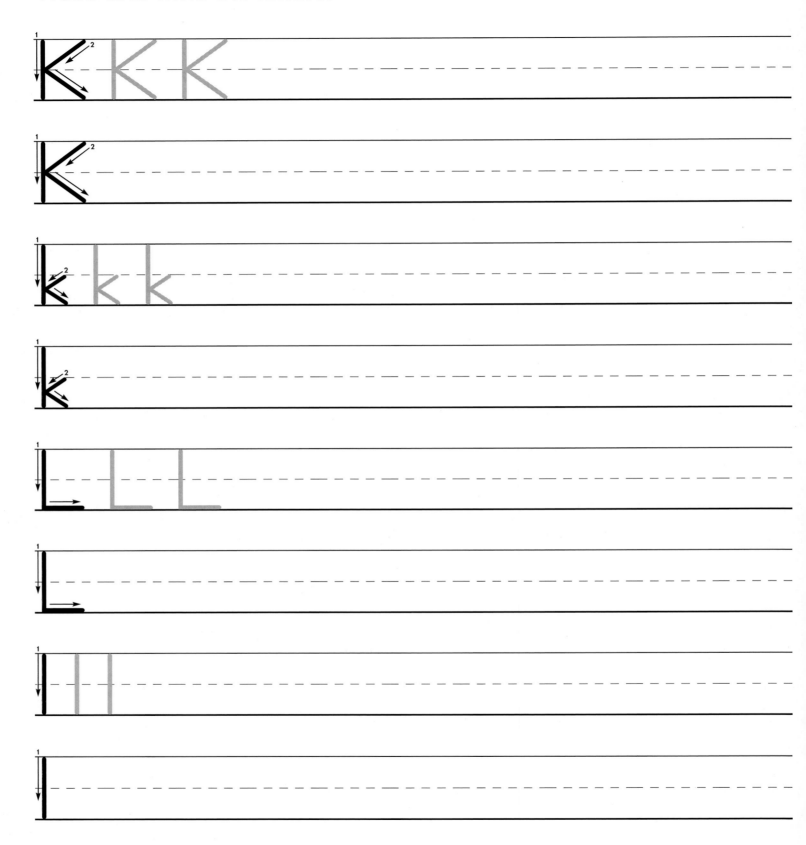

Trace and write the letters.

M M M

M

m m m

m

N N N

N

n n n

n

Trace and write the letters.

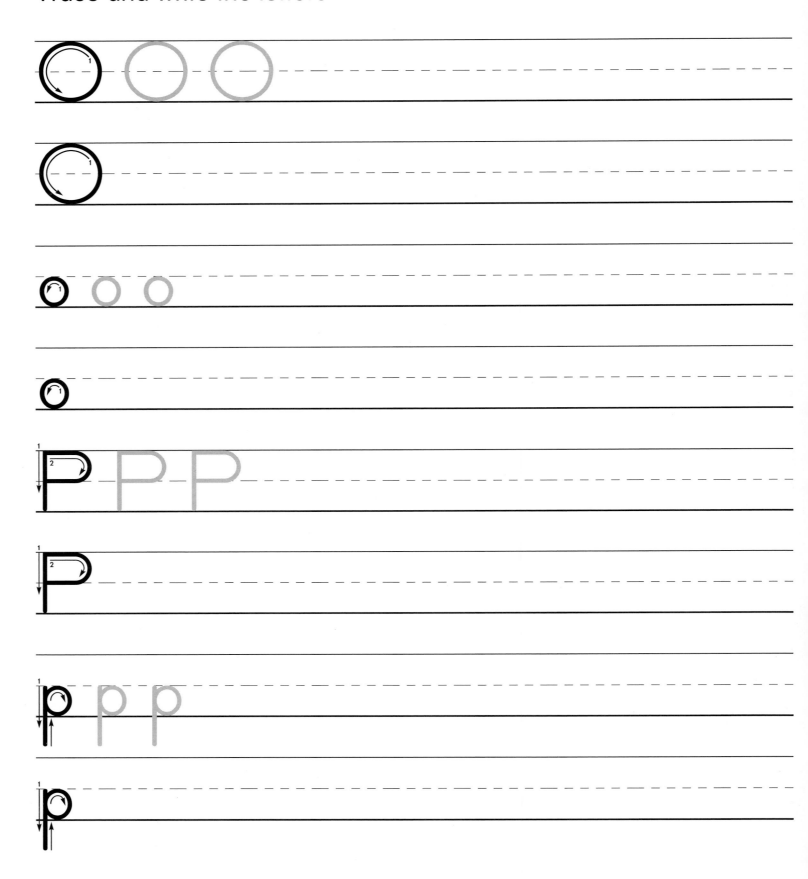

Trace and write the letters.

Q Q Q

Q

q q q

q

R R R

R

r r r

r

Trace and write the letters.

S S S

S

S S S

S

T T T

T

t t t

t

Trace and write the letters.

U U U U

U

u u u

u

V V V V

V

v v v

v

Trace and write the letters.

W W W

W

w w w

w

X X X

X

x x x

x

Trace and write the letters.

Y Y Y Y

Y

y y y

y

Z Z Z

Z

Z Z Z

Z

Handwriting Models—Slant

A B C D E F G H

I J K L M N O P

Q R S T U V W

X Y Z

a b c d e f g h

i j k l m n o p

q r s t u v w

x y z

Handwriting Practice

Selection Titles

Honors, Prizes, and Awards

QUACK
Book 1, p. 30
by *Judy Barrett*

Author/Illustrator: *Judy Barrett*, winner of IRA-CBC Children's Choice Award (1978) for *Cloudy With a Chance of Meatballs*

WHAT DOES PIG DO?
Book 1, p. 50
by *Angela Shelf Medearis*
Illustrated by *Barbara Reid*

Author: *Angela Shelf Medearis*, winner of IRA-Teachers' Choice Award (1995) for *Our People*
Illustrator: *Barbara Reid,* winner of Canada Council Award (1985) for Children's Illustrations for *Have You Seen Birds?*; Ezra Jack Keats Award (1988); Mr. Christie Book Award (1991) for the *Zoe* series; ALA Notable (1994) for *Two By Two*; IBBY Honor List (1996) for *Gifts*; Governor General's Award for Illustration (1997) for *The Party*

A YEAR LATER
Book 1, p. 102
by *Mary Ann Hoberman*

Poet: *Mary Ann Hoberman*, winner of American Book Award Paper Picture Book Award (1983) for *A House Is a House for Me*

ONE GOOD PUP
Book 2, p. 10
by *Frank Asch*

Author/Illustrator: *Frank Asch*, winner of American Book Award Pick of the List Award (1997) for *Barnyard Animals*

WHAT BUG IS IT?
Book 2, p. 98
by *Pat Cummings*

Author/Illustrator: *Pat Cummings*, winner of Coretta Scott King Award (illustration; 1984) for *My Mama Needs Me*; National Council of Teachers of English Orbis Pictus Award, Boston Globe-Horn Book Award (1992), ALA Notable (1993) for *Talking with Artists*; ALA Notable (1996) for *Talking with Artists, Vol. 2*

Selection Titles	Honors, Prizes, and Awards
STAN'S STUNT Book 3, p. 10 by *Lynn Plourde* Illustrated by *Pam Levy*	**Illustrator:** *Pam Levy,* winner of 1996 Society of Children's Book Writers and Illustrators Magazine Merit Award for *Cricket* magazine
GREG'S MASK Book 3, p. 40 by *Ann McGovern*	**Author:** *Ann McGovern,* winner of Boston Globe-Horn Book Honor (1975) for *Scram Kids*
THE SHOPPING LIST Book 4, p. 10 by *Gary Apple* Illustrated by *Shirley Beckes*	**Illustrator:** *Shirley Beckes,* winner of The 39th Annual Book Exhibit, The Chicago Book Clinic Honor Book Certificate Award for *Irwin the Sock*
THE KNEE-HIGH MAN Book 4, p. 68 by *Ellen Dreyer* Illustrated by *Tim Raglin*	**Illustrator:** *Tim Raglin,* winner of Silver Medal by the Society Illustrators, 39th Exhibition

Selection Titles	Honors, Prizes, and Awards

 BABY CHICK
Book 5, p. 8
by *Aileen Fisher*

Poet: *Aileen Fisher*, winner of National Council of Teachers of English Award for Excellence in Poetry for Children (1978)

 SHRINKING MOUSE
Book 5, p. 48
by *Pat Hutchins*

Author/Illustrator: *Pat Hutchins*, winner of Boston Globe-Horn Book Honor (1968) for *Rosie's Walk;* New York Times Best Illustrated (1972) for *You'll Soon Grow Into Them, Titch;* IBBY Honor Award (1974); ALA Notable (1997) for *The Doorbell Rang*

 YOU CAN'T SMELL A FLOWER WITH YOUR EAR!
Book 5, p. 84
by *Joanna Cole*

Author: *Joanna Cole*, winner of ALA Notable (1983) for *Bony-Legs* and *Cars and How They Go;* ALA Notable, Golden Kite Honor Book (1984) for *How You Were Born;* Boston Globe-Horn Book Honor (1987) for *The Magic School at the Waterworks;* Texas Blue Bonnet Master List (1995) for *On the Bus with Joanna Cole;* IRA-CBC Children's Choice (1997) for *The Magic School Bus Blows Its Top: A Book About Volcanos*

 OWL AND THE MOON
Book 5, p. 120
by *Arnold Lobel*

Author/Illustrator: *Arnold Lobel*, Caldecott Honor (1970) for *Frog and Toad Are Friends,* (1972) for *Hildilid's Night;* Christopher Award (1972) for *On the Day Peter Stuyvesant Sailed Into Town;* Newbery Honor (1973) for *Frog and Toad Together;* Christopher Award (1977) for *Frog and Toad All Year;* Caldecott Medal (1981) for *Fables;* ALA Notable, Caldecott Honor (1982), Boston Globe-Horn Book Honor, New York Times Best Illustrated (1981) for *On Market Street;* Boston Globe-Horn Book Honor (1984) for *Rose in My Garden;* ALA Notable (1984) for *Book of Pigericks/Pig Limericks;* ALA Notable (1986) for *Three Day Hat;* Golden Kite Award Book (1987) for *The Devil and Mother Crump*

Selection Titles

Honors, Prizes, and Awards

🎖 **NEW SHOES FOR SILVIA**
Book 5, p. 194
by **Johanna Hurwitz**
Illustrated by **Jerry Pinkney**

Author: *Johanna Hurwitz*, winner of Texas Blue Bonnet Award (1987) for *The Hot and Cold Summer;* ALA Notable (1984) for *Rip-Roaring Russell;* Texas Blue Bonnet Master List (1996–97) for *Birthday Surprises: Ten Great Stories to Unwrap*

Illustrator: *Jerry Pinkney*, winner of Coretta Scott King Award, ALA Notable, Christopher Award (1986) for *Patchwork Quilt;* Newbery Medal, Boston Globe-Horn Book Honor (1977) for *Roll of Thunder, Hear My Cry;* Boston Globe-Horn Book Honor (1980) *Childtimes: A Three Generation Memoir;* Coretta Scott King Award (1987) for *Half a Moon and One Whole Star;* ALA Notable (1988) for *Tales of Uncle Remus: The Adventures of Brer Rabbit;* ALA Notable, Caldecott Honor, Coretta Scott King Award (1989) for *Mirandy and Brother Wind;* ALA Notable, Caldecott Honor, Coretta Scott King Honor (1990) for *Talking Eggs: A Folktale for the American South;* Golden Kite Award Book (1990) for *Home Place;* ALA Notable (1991) for *Further Tales of Uncle Remus: The Misadventures of Brer Rabbit, Brer Fox ...;* ALA Notable (1993) for *Back Home;* ALA Notable, Boston Globe-Horn Book Award, Caldecott Honor (1995) for *John Henry;* ALA Notable, Blue Ribbon (1997) for *Sam and the Tigers;* ALA Notable, Christopher Award, Coretta Scott King Award, Golden Kite Honor Book (1997) for *Minty: A Story of Young Harriet Tubman;* Aesop Prize (1997) for *The Hired Hand;* National Council for Social Studies Notable Children's Book Award (1998) for *The Hired Hand* and *Rikki-Tikki-Tavi;* Rip Van Winkle Award (1998); 1998 Hans Christian Andersen nominee

🎖 **MY MAMI TAKES ME TO THE BAKERY** Book 5, p. 304
by **Charlotte Pomerantz**

Poet: *Charlotte Pomerantz,* winner of Jane Addams Book Award (1975) for *Princess and the Admiral;* ALA Notable (1994) for *Outside Dog*

Theme Bibliography

ONE GOOD PUP
THE BUG BATH

Trade Books

Additional fiction and nonfiction trade books related to each selection can be shared with children throughout the unit.

ONE GOOD PUP

Moonbear's Pet
Frank Asch (Aladdin Paperbacks, 1997)

Bear finds a little fish while playing with his friend Little Bird and Bear decides to keep it for a pet.

Let's Get a Pet
Harriet Ziefert, illustrated by Mavis Smith (Viking, 1993)

All the things that have to be considered when choosing a pet are discussed in an appealing format.

Pet Show
Ezra Jack Keats (Macmillan, 1972)

Archie's cat disappears just as the Pet Show is about to start. The cat reappears in time to win a Blue Ribbon. A classic.

THE BUG BATH

Silly Sally
Audrey Wood (Harcourt Brace Jovanovich, 1992)

Sally makes many friends as she travels to town backward and upside down.

Little Cloud
Eric Carle (Philomel Books, 1996)

A little cloud becomes many different things before it joins the other clouds and ends with rain.

Inspector Hopper
Doug Cushman (HarperCollins, 2000)
An I Can Read *Book*

Inspector Hopper and his friend McBug solve some genuine mysteries, including one involving a ladybug and a boat that have disappeared.

Technology

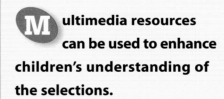

Multimedia resources can be used to enhance children's understanding of the selections.

 The Big Snow (Weston Woods) Filmstrip, 11 min. Animals busily prepare for the long, cold winter.

 Animals A to Z (National Geographic Educational Services) Video, 15 min. Introduces children to familiar and exotic animals in alphabetical order.

 The Wonderful World of Dogs (Direct Cinema Limited) Video, 35 min. A humorous and colorful look at the world of dogs.

 Insects (National Geographic Educational Services) Video, 12 min. Watch metamorphosis and learn the common characteristics of the most numerous creatures on Earth.

 I-Spy (Scholastic New Media) CD-ROM, Macintosh and Windows. Teaches logic, problem solving, and visual memory skills.

 Make a Masterpiece (Crayola) CD-ROM, Macintosh and Windows. Children create artwork using tools that include chalk, paint, pencil, and marker sets; special effects; and photo manipulation.

SPLASH!

Herman the Helper
Robert Kraus, illustrated by Jose Aruego and Ariane Dewey (Simon & Schuster Books for Young Readers, 1987)

Herman is a helpful octopus, always ready to help anyone—friend or enemy.

Matilda the Moocher
Diana C. Bluthenthal (Orchard Books, 1997)

Matilda takes advantage of her friendship with Libby by borrowing one thing after another.

My Brother, Ant
Betsy Byars, illustrated by Marc Simont (Viking Children's Books, 1996)

In four separate stories, Ant's older brother shows compassion and understanding for Ant.

WHAT BUG IS IT?

The Grouchy Ladybug
Eric Carle (HarperCollins, 1977)

A grouchy ladybug challenges everyone she meets to a fight, regardless of their size.

Itsy-Bitsy Spider
Iza Trapini (Whispering Coyote Press, 1993)

The itsy-bitsy spider encounters a fan, a mouse, a cat, and a rocking chair as she makes her way to the top of a tree to spin her web.

Ten Flashing Fireflies
Philemon Sturges, illustrated by Anna Vojtech (North-South Books, 1995)

Two children catch fireflies on a summer night and release them to watch them fly away.

A VET

Veterinarians Help Animals
Carol Greene (The Child's World, Inc., 1997)

With large colorful photographs and simple text, the work of a veterinarian is described.

What Zookeepers Do
Jack Hanna, photographs by Rick A. Preberg (Scholastic, 1998)

Photographs and text describe how zookeepers care for the animals.

If You Were a . . . Veterinarian
Virginia Schomp (Marshall Cavendish, 1998)

The work of veterinarians as they care for various animals is described and shown.

 Alexander and the Terrible, No Good, Very Bad Day (AIMS Media) Video, 14 min. Little things pile up on 7-year-old Alexander until a normal day seems like a catastrophe.

 Noisy Nora (Weston Woods) Video, filmstrip, or cassette, 6 min. In a family too busy to listen, Nora makes her presence known.

 Why Mosquitoes Buzz in People's Ears (Weston Woods) Video, filmstrip, or cassette, 13 min. In this traditional story from Africa, a tall tale sets off a chain of mishaps through the jungle grapevine.

 Backyard Bugs (National Geographic Educational Services) Video, 15 min. Viewers learn to distinguish between insects and spiders and to identify many neighborhood bugs.

 The Magic School Bus Explores the Rainforest (Microsoft) CD-ROM, Windows. Teaches ecology and problem solving as children collect samples from the Costa Rican rainforest.

 Pets and Their Wild Relatives (National Geographic Educational Services) Video, 15 min. Compare pets with their wild relatives.

 Animal Life Spans (National Geographic Educational Services) Video, 15 min. Find out how scientists determine the age of animals and discover some of the factors that affect how long an animal lives.

 Sammy's Science House (Edmark) CD-ROM, Macintosh and Windows. Through interactive activities, children learn how animals live and how the seasons change.

Publishers Directory

Abdo & Daughters
4940 Viking Drive, Suite 622
Edina, MN 55435
(800) 800-1312 • www.abdopub.com

Aladdin Paperbacks
(Imprint of Simon & Schuster Children's
Publishing)

Atheneum
(Imprint of Simon & Schuster Children's
Publishing)

**Bantam Doubleday Dell Books for
Young Readers**
(Imprint of Random House)

Blackbirch Press
260 Amity Road
Woodbridge, CT 06525
(203) 387-7525 • (800) 831-9183 •
www.blackbirch.com

Blue Sky Press
(Imprint of Scholastic)

Boyds Mills Press
815 Church Street
Honesdale, PA 18431
(570) 253-1164 • Fax (570) 253-0179 •
(800) 490-5111 • www.boydsmillspress.com

Bradbury Press
(Imprint of Simon & Schuster Children's
Publishing)

BridgeWater Books
(Distributed by Penguin Putnam)

Candlewick Press
2067 Masssachusetts Avenue
Cambridge, MA 02140
(617) 661-3330 • Fax (617) 661-0565 •
www.candlewick.com

Carolrhoda Books
(Division of Lerner Publications Co.)

Children's Press (Division of Grolier, Inc.)
P.O. Box 1795
Danbury, CT 06816-1333
(800) 621-1115 • www.grolier.com

Child's World
P.O. Box 326
Chanhassen, MN 55317-0326
(612) 906-3939 • (800) 599-READ •
www.childsworld.com

Chronicle Books
85 Second Street, Sixth Floor
San Francisco, CA 94105
(415) 537-3730 • Fax (415) 537-4460 •
(800) 722-6657 • www.chronbooks.com

Clarion Books
(Imprint of Houghton Mifflin, Inc.)
215 Park Avenue South
New York, NY 10003
(212) 420-5800 • (800) 225-3362 •
www.houghtonmifflinbooks.com/clarion

Crowell (Imprint of HarperCollins)

Crown Publishing Group
(Imprint of Random House)

Dial Books
(Imprint of Penguin Putnam Inc.)

Dorling Kindersley (DK Publishing)
95 Madison Avenue
New York, NY 10016
(212) 213-4800 • Fax (212) 213-5240 •
(888) 342-5357 • www.dk.com

Doubleday (Imprint of Random House)

E. P. Dutton Children's Books
(Imprint of Penguin Putnam Inc.)

Farrar Straus & Giroux
19 Union Square West
New York, NY 10003
(212) 741-6900 • Fax (212) 741-6973 •
(888) 330-8477

Four Winds Press
(Imprint of Macmillan, see Simon &
Schuster Children's Publishing)

Greenwillow Books
(Imprint of William Morrow & Co, Inc.)

Grosset & Dunlap
(Imprint of Penguin Putnam, Inc.)

Harcourt Brace & Co.
6277 Sea Harbor Drive
Orlando, FL 32887
(407) 345-2000 • (800) 225-5425 •
www.harcourtbooks.com

Harper & Row (Imprint of HarperCollins)

HarperCollins Children's Books
1350 Avenue of the Americas
New York, NY 10019
(212) 261-6500 • Fax (212) 261-6689 •
(800) 242-7737 •
www.harperchildrens.com

Holiday House
425 Madison Avenue
New York, NY 10017
(212) 688-0085 • Fax (212) 421-6134

Henry Holt and Company
115 West 18th Street
New York, NY 10011
(212) 886-9200 • (212) 633-0748 • (888)
330-8477 • www.henryholt.com/byr/

Houghton Mifflin
222 Berkeley Street
Boston, MA 02116
(617) 351-5000 • Fax (617) 351-1125 •
(800) 225-3362 •
www.houghtonmifflinbooks.com

Hyperion Books
(Division of ABC, Inc.)
77 W. 66th Street, 11th Floor
New York, NY 10023
(212) 456-0100 • (800) 343-4204 •
www.disney.com

Ideals Children's Books
(Imprint of Hambleton-Hill Publishing, Inc.)
1501 County Hospital Road
Nashville, TN 37218
(615) 254-2451 • (800) 327-5113

Joy Street Books
(Imprint of Little, Brown & Co.)

Just Us Books
356 Glenwood Avenue
E. Orange, NJ 07017
(973) 672-7701 • Fax (973) 677-7570 •
www.justusbooks.com

Alfred A. Knopf
(Imprint of Random House)

Lee & Low Books
95 Madison Avenue, Room 606
New York, NY 10016
(212) 779-4400 • Fax (212) 683-1894

Lerner Publications Co.
241 First Avenue North
Minneapolis, MN 55401
(612) 332-3344 • Fax (612) 332-7615 •
(800) 328-4929 • www.lernerbooks.com

Little, Brown & Co.
3 Center Plaza
Boston, MA 02108
(617) 227-0730 • Fax (617) 263-2864 •
(800) 759-0190 • www.littlebrown.com

Lothrop Lee & Shepard
(Imprint of William Morrow & Co.)

Macmillan
(Imprint of Simon & Schuster
Children's Publishing)

Marshall Cavendish
99 White Plains Road
Tarrytown, NY 10591
(914) 332-8888 • Fax (914) 332-1888 •
(800) 821-9881 •
www.marshallcavendish.com

Millbrook Press
2 Old New Milford Road
Brookfield, CT 06804
(203) 740-2220 • (800) 462-4703 •
Fax (203) 740-2526

William Morrow & Co.
(Imprint of HarperCollins)

Morrow Junior Books
(Imprint of HarperCollins)

Mulberry Books
(Imprint of HarperCollins)

National Geographic Society
1145 17th Street, NW
Washington, DC 20036
(202) 857-7345 • (800) 638-4077 •
www.nationalgeographic.com

Northland Publishing
(Division of Justin Industries)
P.O. Box 1389
Flagstaff, AZ 86002
(520) 774-5251 • Fax (800) 744-0592 •
(800) 346-3257 • www.northlandpub.com

North-South Books
1123 Broadway, Suite 800
New York, NY 10010
(212) 463-9736 • Fax (212) 633-1004 •
(800) 722-6657 • www.northsouth.com

Orchard Books (A Grolier Company)
95 Madison Avenue
New York, NY 10016
(212) 951-2600 • Fax (212) 213-6435 •
(800) 433-3411 • www.grolier.com

Owlet (Imprint of Henry Holt & Co.)

Penguin Putnam, Inc.
375 Hudson Street
New York, NY 10014
(212) 366-2000 • Fax (212) 366-2636 •
(800) 631-8571 •
www.penguinputnam.com

Willa Perlman Books
(Imprint of Simon & Schuster
Children's Publishing)

Philomel Books
(Imprint of Penguin Putnam, Inc.)

Puffin Books
(Imprint of Penguin Putnam, Inc.)

G. P. Putnam's Sons Publishing
(Imprint of Penguin Putnam, Inc.)

Random House
1540 Broadway
New York, NY 10036
(212) 782-9000 • Fax (212) 302-7985 •
(800) 200-3552 •
www.randomhouse.com/kids

Scholastic
555 Broadway
New York, NY 10012
(212) 343-7500 • Fax (212) 965-7442 •
(800) SCHOLASTIC • www.scholastic.com

Charles Scribner's Sons
(Imprint of Simon & Schuster Children's
Publishing)

Sierra Club Books for Children
85 Second Street, Second Floor
San Francisco, CA 94105-3441
(415) 977-5500 • Fax (415) 977-5793 •
(800) 935-1056 • www.sierraclub.org

Simon & Schuster Children's Books
1230 Avenue of the Americas
New York, NY 10020
(212) 698-7200 • (800) 223-2336 •
www.simonsayskids.com

Smith & Kraus
177 Lyme Road
Hanover, NH 03755
(603) 643-6431 • Fax (603) 643-1831 •
(800) 895-4331 • www.smithkraus.com

Teacher Ideas Press
(Division of Libraries Unlimited)
P.O. Box 6633
Englewood, CO 80155-6633
(303) 770-1220 • Fax (303) 220-8843 •
(800) 237-6124 • www.lu.com

Ticknor & Fields
(Imprint of Houghton Mifflin, Inc.)

Usborne (Imprint of EDC Publishing)
10302 E. 55th Place, Suite B
Tulsa, OK 74146-6515
(918) 622-4522 • (800) 475-4522 •
www.edcpub.com

Viking Children's Books
(Imprint of Penguin Putnam Inc.)

Walker & Co.
435 Hudson Street
New York, NY 10014
(212) 727-8300 • (212) 727-0984 •
(800) AT-WALKER

Watts Publishing
(Imprint of Grolier Publishing;
see Children's Press)

Whispering Coyote Press
300 Crescent Court, Suite 860
Dallas, TX 75201
(800) 929-6104 • Fax (214) 319-7298

Albert Whitman
6340 Oakton Street
Morton Grove, IL 60053-2723
(847) 581-0033 • Fax (847) 581-0039 •
(800) 255-7675 • www.awhitmanco.com

Workman Publishing Co., Inc.
708 Broadway
New York, NY 10003
(212) 254-5900 • Fax (800) 521-1832 •
(800) 722-7202 • www.workman.com

Multimedia Resources

AGC/United Learning
6633 West Howard Street
Niles, IL 60714-3389
(800) 424-0362 • www.unitedlearning.com

AIMS Multimedia
9710 DeSoto Avenue
Chatsworth, CA 91311-4409
(800) 367-2467 •
www.AIMS-multimedia.com

BFA Educational Media
(see Phoenix Learning Group)

Broderbund
(Parsons Technology;
also see The Learning Company)
500 Redwood Blvd
Novato, CA 94997
(800) 395-0277 • www.broderbund.com

Carousel Film and Video
260 Fifth Avenue, Suite 705
New York, NY 10001
(212) 683-1660 • e-mail:
carousel@pipeline.com

Cloud 9 Interactive
(888) 662-5683 • www.cloud9int.com

Computer Plus (see ESI)

Coronet/MTI
(see Phoenix Learning Group)

Crayola (Binney Smith)
1100 Church Lane
Easton, PA 18042
(800) 272-9652 • www.crayola.com

Davidson (see Knowledge Adventure)

Direct Cinema, Ltd.
P.O. Box 10003
Santa Monica, CA 90410-1003
(310) 636-8200

Disney Interactive
(800) 900-9234 •
www.disneyinteractive.com

DK Multimedia (Dorling Kindersley)
95 Madison Avenue
New York, NY 10016
(212) 213-4800 • Fax: (800) 774-6733 •
(888) 342-5357 • www.dk.com

Edmark Corp.
P.O. Box 97021
Redmond, WA 98073-9721
(800) 362-2890 • www.edmark.com

Encyclopaedia Britannica Educational Corp.
310 South Michigan Avenue
Chicago, IL 60604
(800) 522-8656 • www.eb.com

ESI/Educational Software
4213 S. 94th Street
Omaha, NE 68127
(800) 955-5570 • www.edsoft.com

GPN/Reading Rainbow
University of Nebraska-Lincoln
P.O. Box 80669
Lincoln, NE 68501-0669
(800) 228-4630 • www.gpn.unl.edu

Great Tapes for Kids
P.O. Box 954
Middlebury, VT 05753
(888) 543-8273 •
www.greattapes.com/cart/home.phtml

Hasbro Interactive
(800) 683-5847 • www.hasbro.com

Humongous
13110 NE 177th Pl., Suite B101, Box 180
Woodenville, WA 98072
(800) 499-8386 • www.humongous.com

IBM Corp.
1133 Westchester Ave.
White Plains, NY 10604
(770) 863-1234 • Fax (770) 863-3030 •
(888) 411-1932 •
www.pc.ibm.com/multimedia/crayola

ICE, Inc.
(Distributed by Arch Publishing)
12B W. Main St.
Elmsford, NY 10523
(914) 347-2464 • (800) 843-9497 •
www.educorp.com

Knowledge Adventure
19840 Pioneer Avenue
Torrence, CA 90503
(800) 542-4240 • (800) 545-7677 •
www.knowledgeadventure.com

The Learning Company
6160 Summit Drive North
Minneapolis, MN 55430
(800) 395-0277 • www.learningco.com

Listening Library
One Park Avenue
Greenwich, CT 06870-1727
(800) 733-3000 • www.listeninglib.com

Macmillan/McGraw-Hill
(see SRA/McGraw-Hill)

Maxis
2121 N. California Blvd
Walnut Creek, CA 94596-3572
(925) 933-5630 • Fax (925) 927-3736 •
(800) 245-4525 • www.maxis.com

MECC
(see the Learning Company)

Microsoft
One Microsoft Way
Redmond, WA 98052-6399
(800) 426-9400 • www.microsoft.com/kids

**National Geographic Society
Educational Services**
P.O. Box 1041
Des Moines, IA 50340-0597
(800) 225-5647 •
www.nationalgeographic.com

National School Products
101 East Broadway
Maryville, TN 37804
(800) 251-9124 • www.ierc.com

PBS Video
1320 Braddock Place
Alexandria, VA 22314
(800) 344-3337 • www.pbs.org

Phoenix Films
(see Phoenix Learning Group)

Phoenix Learning Group
2348 Chaffee Drive
St. Louis, MO 63146
(800) 221-1274 • e-mail:
phoenixfilms@worldnet.att.net

Pied Piper (see AIMS Multimedia)

Scholastic New Media
555 Broadway
New York, NY 10003
(800) 724-6527 • www.scholastic.com

Simon & Schuster Interactive
(see Knowledge Adventure)

SRA/McGraw-Hill
220 East Danieldale Road
De Soto, TX 75115
(888) 772-4543 • www.sra4kids.com

SVE/Churchill Media
6677 North Northwest Highway
Chicago, IL 60631
(800) 829-1900 • www.svemedia.com

Tom Snyder Productions (also see ESI)
80 Coolidge Hill Rd.
Watertown, MA 02472
(800) 342-0236 • www.teachtsp.com

Troll Associates
100 Corporate Drive
Mahwah, NJ 07430
(888) 998-7655 • Fax (800) 979-8765 •
www.troll.com

Voyager (see ESI)

Weston Woods
12 Oakwood Avenue
Norwalk, CT 06850
(800) 243-5020 • Fax (203) 845-0498

Zenger Media
10200 Jefferson Blvd., Room 94,
P.O. Box 802
Culver City, CA 90232-0802
(800) 421-4246 • (800) 944-5432 •
www.Zengermedia.com

BOOK 1

	Decodable Words			Spelling	Vocabulary

MAX, THE CAT

Short *a* (Decodable Words)

am	ham	**Pam**
and	**has**	pan
as	hat	pat
at	jam	rag
bad	Jan	ran
bag	lap	**sad**
bat	**mad**	Sam
cab	man	sat
can	map	tag
cap	**mat**	tan
cat	**Max**	tap
dad	nag	van
Dan	Nan	wag
fan	**nap**	wax
fat	pad	yam
had		

Short *a* (Spelling)

bad
can
had
hat
mat
pan

High-Frequency Words (Vocabulary)

give
likes
one
this

QUACK

Digraph *ck* (Decodable Words)

back	**pack**	rack
Jack	**packs**	sack
Mack	**quack**	tack

Digraph *ck* (Spelling)

back
pack
quack
rack
sack
tack

High-Frequency Words (Vocabulary)

on
they
what
your

WHAT DOES PIG DO?

Short *i* (Decodable Words)

bib	is	pin
big	it	pit
bin	jig	quick
bit	Jim	quit
Dick	**kick**	quiz
did	**kicks**	rib
dig	kid	Rick
digs	Kim	rip
dip	kit	sick
fin	lick	Sid
fit	lid	sip
fix	Lin	sit
hid	lip	six
him	mix	tick
hip	Nick	Tim
his	nip	tin
hit	**pick**	tip
if	**picks**	**wig**
in	**pig**	win

Short *i* (Spelling)

dig
kick
pick
pig
pin
win

High-Frequency Words (Vocabulary)

does
her
look
there

Boldfaced words appear in the selection.

BOOK 1

	Decodable Words			Spelling	Vocabulary

A PATH ON THE MAP

Decodable Words — Digraphs *sh, th*

bath	math	that
cash	**path**	thick
dash	rash	thin
dish	**shack**	**this**
finish	shin	thrash
fish	ship	wish
mash	than	with

Spelling — Digraphs *sh, th*

dish
path
shack
that
thin
wish

Vocabulary — High-Frequency Words

be
could
down
see

TIME FOR KIDS: SHIPS

Decodable Words — Phonics Review

Spelling — Words from Social Studies

bus	map
fast	**ship**
go	stop

Vocabulary — Review High-Frequency Words

look	**one**
this	**what**

BOOK 2

ONE GOOD PUP

Decodable Words — Short *u*

buck	hum	shut
bud	hush	sub
bug	hut	suck
bun	jug	sum
bus	luck	sun
but	mud	sup
cub	mug	thud
cup	nut	**tub**
cut	**pup**	tuck
duck	rub	**tug**
dug	rug	up
fun	run	us
gum	rush	yum
hug	rut	

Spelling — Short *u*

buck
but
cut
duck
rug
tug

Vocabulary — High-Frequency Words

no
out
ride
small

THE BUG BATH

Decodable Words — Short *o*

Bob	job	pop
box	jog	pot
cob	jot	rock
cot	lock	**rocked**
dock	log	rod
Don	lot	shock
dot	mom	sob
fog	mop	sock
fox	nod	tock
got	**not**	Tom
hog	**on**	**top**
hop	ox	tot
hot	pod	

Spelling — Short *o*

hop
hot
lock
not
rock
top

Vocabulary — High-Frequency Words

saw
two
very
want

BOOK 2

	Decodable Words	Spelling	Vocabulary

SPLASH!

Decodable Words — Short e

bed	led	**pets**
beg	leg	**red**
Ben	**legs**	Rex
bet	let	set
Beth	**Meg**	**shed**
Deb	men	Ted
deck	met	ten
den	**neck**	**them**
fed	Ned	**then**
get	net	vet
hem	peck	web
hen	peg	**wet**
Jen	pen	yes
jet	pet	yet
Ken		

Spelling — Short e

hen
pet
red
shed
then
wet

Vocabulary — High-Frequency Words

away
good
into
put

WHAT BUG IS IT?

Decodable Words — Blends and Double Consonants

bass	**hill**	**slim**
bell	hiss	slip
Bess	huff	slit
bill	hull	slob
buzz	ill	slop
cuff	**Jill**	slot
doll	kiss	slug
dull	lull	slush
fell	mass	**smack**
fill	mess	smash
flap	mill	smell
flash	**Miss**	smock
flat	muff	smug
flesh	**Nell**	snack
flick	**pass**	**snag**
flip	pill	**snap**
flock	puff	sniff
flop	quill	snip
fluff	ruff	snob
fresh	sell	snug
frill	sill	tell
frock	slam	thrill
frog	slap	till
fuss	slash	well
gill	slick	**will**
gull	slid	yell

Spelling — Blends and Double Consonants

doll
flat
miss
pass
puff
snap

Vocabulary — High-Frequency Words

about
again
around
use

TIME FOR KIDS: A VET

Decodable Words — Phonics Review

Spelling — Words from Social Studies

cat	job
help	pat
hog	**vet**

Vocabulary — Review High-Frequency Words

small	**good**
out	**want**

BOOK 3

Decodable Words	Spelling	Vocabulary

STAN'S STUNT

Blends

asked	melt	spend
bang	mend	spent
belt	milk	spill
bend	mint	spin
bent	mist	splash
best	must	spot
bump	nest	stab
camp	pant	stack
can't	past	staff
damp	pest	stamp
dent	pond	**Stan**
dump	pump	**Stan's**
dust	quilt	stand
end	raft	stem
fang	ramp	step
fast	rang	stick
felt	rent	stiff
fist	rest	still
fling	ring	sting
flung	risk	stomp
gang	rung	**stop**
gasp	rust	stub
gift	sand	stuck
gust	sang	stuff
hang	scab	stump
held	scat	stung
help	scuff	**stunt**
hint	self	**stunts**
hump	send	sung
hung	sent	swift
hunt	shelf	swim
jest	shift	swing
jump	sift	swung
just	silk	task
Kent	sing	tend
king	skid	tent
lamp	skill	test
last	skimp	theft
left	skin	**thing**
lend	skip	thump
lent	skit	tilt
lift	skull	trust
limp	slant	vent
lint	soft	vest
list	span	**went**
loft	spat	west
lump	speck	wilt
lung	sped	wind
mask	spell	wing

Blends

bump
jump
spell
spill
tent
went

High-Frequency Words

fall
their
try
would

T105

BOOK 3

Decodable Words	Spelling	Vocabulary

GREG'S MASK

Blends

black	clasp	drift	plot
blast	**class**	drill	plug
blend	click	**drip**	plum
blimp	cliff	**drop**	plump
blob	cling	drum	plus
block	**clip**	glad	press
blond	clock	glass	print
blot	clog	Glen	prop
bluff	club	**glob**	track
blush	cluck	grab	tramp
Brad	clump	grand	trap
brag	crab	grant	**trash**
brand	crack	grasp	trick
brass	craft	grass	trim
brick	cramp	**Greg**	trip
bring	crash	Greg's	trot
brisk	crib	grill	truck
brush	crisp	grip	trust
clack	crop	gruff	twig
clam	crush	grump	twin
clamp	crust	grunt	**twist**
clang	draft	plan	
clap	drag	plant	
clash	dress	plop	

Blends

clap
class
dress
drop
track
trip

High-Frequency Words

any
grow
new
old

SAM'S SONG

ch, wh, nk

bank	chip	link	stink
bench	chomp	lunch	such
blank	chop	**much**	sunk
branch	**Chuck**	munch	tank
brunch	chunk	pinch	thank
bunch	clank	pink	**think**
Chad	clunk	plank	trunk
champ	crank	**plink**	whack
chant	**crunch**	pluck	**when**
check	drank	**plunk**	which
chess	drink	prank	whip
chest	Frank	punch	**whish**
Chet	French	ranch	whisk
chick	Hank	rank	**wink**
chill	honk	**sank**	yank
chimp	hunk	**sink**	
chin	inch	spank	

ch, wh, nk

chick
chin
sink
think
when
wink

High-Frequency Words

eat
now
together
too

BOOK 3

	Decodable Words			Spelling	Vocabulary

SNAKES

Long *a: a-e*			Long *a: a-e*	High-Frequency Words
bake	gate	save	came	**know**
base	gave	scale	**lake**	**under**
blame	gaze	**scales**	**made**	**where**
brake	grade	shade	name	**why**
brave	grape	shake	shade	
cake	grate	shame	**snake**	
came	hate	shape		
cane	Jake	shave		
cape	Jane	skate		
case	Kate	**snake**		
cave	**lake**	**snake's**		
chase	lane	state		
crate	late	take		
date	**made**	tale		
Dave	**make**	tame		
daze	mane	tape		
drape	name	trade		
fade	pane	vase		
fake	plane	wade		
fame	plate	wake		
flake	rake	wave		
flame	**safe**	whale		
frame	sale			
game	same			

TIME FOR KIDS: LET'S CAMP OUT!

Phonics Review

Words from Science

		Review High-Frequency Words
fire	**sticks**	**old**
mud	**sun**	**eat**
snow	**twigs**	**together**
		under

BOOK 4

Decodable Words	Spelling	Vocabulary

THE SHOPPING LIST

Decodable Words

Long i: i-e

bike	lime	**smile**
bite	line	**smiled**
bribe	live	snipe
bride	**Mike**	spike
chime	**Mike's**	spine
chive	mile	stride
crime	mime	strike
dime	mine	stripe
dine	mite	swine
dive	Nile	swipe
drive	nine	tide
file	pike	tile
fine	pile	**time**
fire	pine	tire
five	pipe	tribe
glide	pride	vile
grime	prime	vine
gripe	prize	while
hide	quite	whine
hike	ride	**white**
hire	**ripe**	**wide**
hive	shine	wife
jive	side	wine
kite	size	wipe
life	slide	wire
like	slime	

Spelling

Long i: i-e

bite
hide
smile
while
white
wide

Vocabulary

High-Frequency Words

after
always
blue
were
who

YASMIN'S DUCKS

Decodable Words

Long o: o-e

bone	home	rose
broke	**hope**	scope
choke	hose	shone
chose	**hoses**	slope
clone	**joke**	smoke
close	mope	spoke
clove	**nope**	stole
code	nose	stone
coke	note	stove
cone	poke	strode
cope	pope	stroke
cove	pose	those
dome	probe	throne
dove	prone	tone
drone	prose	vote
drove	quote	woke
globe	rode	yoke
grove	**Rome's**	zone
hole	rope	

Spelling

Long o: o-e

hole
home
hope
nose
rope
those

Vocabulary

High-Frequency Words

because
buy
found
some
work

BOOK 4

	Decodable Words	Spelling	Vocabulary
THE KNEE-HIGH MAN	**Long _u: u-e_** **brute** dune prune cube flute pure cure fume rude cute fuse **rule** dude **June** tube duke **mule** tune	**Long _u: u-e_** cute flute mule **rule** tube tune	**High-Frequency Words** **been** **carry** **clean** **done** **far**
JOHNNY APPLESEED	**Long _a: ai, ay_** bail **jays** sail bait laid **sailed** bay lay **say** braid maid snail brain mail Spain chain main sprain clay **May** spray **day** nail stain **days** paid stay drain pail strain **explained** pain stray fail pay sway faint plain tail frail play trail Gail praise train gay quail tray grain **quail's** vain **gray** raid wail **hail** rail wait hay **rain** **way** jail raise jay ray	**Long _a: ai, ay_** **day** **rain** say tail **wait** **way**	**High-Frequency Words** **how** **light** **little** **live** **pretty**
TIME FOR KIDS: RING! RING! RING! PUT OUT THE FIRE!	**Phonics Review**	**Words from Social Studies** **bell** **ring** **brave** **smoke** **pole** **truck**	**Review High-Frequency Words** work always done

BOOK 5, UNIT 1

Decodable Words	Spelling	Vocabulary

SEVEN SILLIES

Decodable Words
Long *e*: *e*, *ee*

be	green	**sheep**
bee	greet	sheet
beef	he	sleep
beep	heel	sleet
beet	jeep	speech
bleed	keep	steel
cheek	Lee	steep
cheep	me	steer
creek	meet	street
creep	need	sweep
deed	peek	sweet
deep	peel	tee
deer	peep	teen
fee	queen	**three**
feed	reef	tree
feel	screech	tweet
feet	screen	we
flee	**see**	weed
fleet	seed	week
free	seek	weep
freed	seem	wheel
freeze	seen	
greed	she	

Spelling
Long *e*: *e*, *ee*

bee
she
sheep
three
tree
we

Vocabulary
High-Frequency Words

all
four
many
over
so

SHRINKING MOUSE

Decodable Words
Long *e*: *ie*, *ea*

beach	heal	sneak
bead	heat	speak
beak	Jean	squeak
bean	lead	steal
beast	leak	steam
beat	leap	streak
bleach	least	stream
cheat	meal	tea
chief	mean	teach
clean	meat	team
cream	neat	thief
deal	pea	weak
Dean	peach	yield
dream	peak	
each	reach	
east	**reached**	
eat	read	
feast	scream	
field	sea	
fields	seal	
flea	seat	
grief	shield	

Spelling
Long *e*: *ie*, *ea*

fields
leaf
piece
reached
read
sea

Vocabulary
High-Frequency Words

before
come
off
our
right

BOOK 5, UNIT 1

	Decodable Words	Spelling	Vocabulary

YOU CAN'T SMELL A FLOWER WITH YOUR EAR!

Decodable Words
Long o: o, oa, oe, ow

blow	glow	**opening**
blown	go	**pillow**
boat	goal	road
bold	goat	roast
both	**goes**	roll
bow	groan	row
bowl	grow	scold
coach	grown	show
coal	**hold**	shown
coast	**holding**	slow
coat	Joan	snow
cold	Joe	so
croak	load	soak
crow	loan	sold
don't	low	throat
float	moan	toad
flow	**moment**	toast
flown	most	toe
foal	mow	told
foam	no	toll
fold	oat	won't
follow	old	

Spelling
Long o: o, oa, oe, ow

boat
cold
goes
hold
road
show

Vocabulary
High-Frequency Words

by
find
kind
high
more

OWL AND THE MOON

Decodable Words
Long i: i, y, igh

blind	grind	sigh
bright	high	sight
by	**I**	**sky**
child	**kind**	slight
cry	**light**	sly
dry	might	tight
fight	mild	try
find	mind	why
flight	**my**	wild
fly	**night**	wind
fright	**right**	
fry	shy	

Spelling
Long i: i, y, igh

child
my
night
shy
sky
tight

Vocabulary
High-Frequency Words

everything
eyes
gone
head
room

TIME FOR KIDS: THE NIGHT ANIMALS

Decodable Words
Phonics Review

Spelling
Words from Science

bugs	**owl**
frog	pond
logs	**rat**

Vocabulary
Review High-Frequency Words

many
off
all

BOOK 5, UNIT 2

	Decodable Words			Spelling	Vocabulary

A FRIEND FOR LITTLE BEAR

/ü/oo (Decodable Words)

bloom	fool	pool	spoon
boo	groom	proof	stool
boom	hoop	**roof**	stoop
boot	hoot	**room**	too
booth	loom	root	tool
broom	loop	scoop	tooth
cool	moo	shoot	troop
doom	mood	snoop	zoo
droop	moon	soon	zoom
food	noon	spool	

/ü/oo (Spelling)

cool
fool
moon
roof
soon
zoo

High-Frequency Words (Vocabulary)

called
friend
only
pulled
these

NEW SHOES FOR SILVIA

/ä/ar (Decodable Words)

ark	chart	mark
arm	Clark	park
art	dark	part
bar	dart	shark
bark	**far**	sharp
barn	farm	spark
Bart	hard	star
car	harm	start
Carl	harp	tart
cart	Lark	yard
charm	march	yarn

/ä/ar (Spelling)

bark
car
dark
park
part
star

High-Frequency Words (Vocabulary)

every
morning
once
or
took

THE STORY OF A BLUE BIRD

/ûr/ir, ur, er (Decodable Words)

bird	first	squirt
birds	fur	stir
birth	girl	**surprised**
burn	her	term
churn	herself	third
clerk	hurt	thirst
curb	jerk	turn
curl	shirt	twirl
dirt	sir	verb
fern	skirt	whirl
fir	stern	

/ûr/ir, ur, er (Spelling)

bird
burn
first
girl
hurt
serve

High-Frequency Words (Vocabulary)

brother
from
mother
sister
walked

BOOK 5, UNIT 2

	Decodable Words	Spelling	Vocabulary

YOUNG AMELIA EARHART

Decodable Words

/ou/ou, ow; /oi/oi, oy

boil	fowl	our
bound	frown	out
bow	gown	plow
boy	grouch	point
boys	ground	pound
broil	growl	pout
brow	hound	proud
brown	**how**	prowl
cloud	howl	round
clown	**Howland**	Roy
coin	join	scout
couch	joint	soil
count	joy	sound
cow	loud	sour
crown	moist	south
down	mound	spoil
drown	mount	sprout
flour	mouth	town
foil	now	toy
found	oil	wound

Spelling

/ou/ou, ow; /oi/oi, oy

boys	sound
mouse	town
noise	toy

Vocabulary

High-Frequency Words

father
horse
people
should
woman

TIME FOR KIDS: ON THE GO!

Phonics Review

Words from Math

feet	miles
five	sum
less	**ten**

Review High-Frequency Words

from	**or**
these	**horse**
called	**people**

Listening, Speaking, Viewing, Representing

☑ Tested Skill

Tinted panels show skills, strategies, and other teaching opportunities

	K	1	2	3	4	5	6
LISTENING							
Learn the vocabulary of school (numbers, shapes, colors, directions, and categories)							
Identify the musical elements of literary language, such as rhymes, repetition, onomatopoeia, alliteration, assonance							
Determine purposes for listening (get information, solve problems, enjoy and appreciate)							
Understand and follow directions							
Listen critically and responsively; recognize barriers to effective listening							
Ask and answer relevant questions (for clarification; to follow up on ideas)							
Listen critically to interpret and evaluate							
Listen responsively to stories and other texts read aloud, including selections from classic and contemporary works							
Connect and compare own experiences, feelings, ideas, and traditions with those of others							
Apply comprehension strategies in listening activities							
Understand the major ideas and supporting evidence in spoken messages							
Participate in listening activities related to reading and writing (such as discussions, group activities, conferences)							
Listen to learn by taking notes, organizing, and summarizing spoken ideas							
Know personal listening preferences							
SPEAKING							
Uses repetition, rhyme, and rhythm in oral texts (such as in reciting songs, poems, and stories with repeating patterns)							
Learn the vocabulary of school (numbers, shapes, colors, directions, and categories)							
Use appropriate language, grammar, and vocabulary learned to describe ideas, feelings, and experiences							
Ask and answer relevant questions (for clarification; to follow up on ideas)							
Communicate effectively in everyday situations (such as discussions, group activities, conferences, conversations)							
Demonstrate speaking skills (audience, purpose, occasion, clarity, volume, pitch, intonation, phrasing, rate, fluency)							
Clarify and support spoken messages and ideas with objects, charts, evidence, elaboration, examples							
Use verbal communication in effective ways when, for example, making announcements, giving directions, or making introductions							
Use nonverbal communication in effective ways such as eye contact, facial expressions, gestures							
Retell a story or a spoken message by summarizing or clarifying							
Connect and compare own experiences, ideas, and traditions with those of others							
Determine purposes for speaking (inform, entertain, compare, describe, give directions, persuade, express personal feelings and opinions)							
Recognize differences between formal and informal language							
Demonstrate skills of reporting and providing information							
Demonstrate skills of interviewing, requesting and providing information							
Apply composition strategies in speaking activities							
Monitor own understanding of spoken message and seek clarification as needed							
VIEWING							
Demonstrate viewing skills (focus attention, organize information)							
Understand and use nonverbal cues							
Respond to audiovisual media in a variety of ways							
Participate in viewing activities related to reading and writing							
Apply comprehension strategies in viewing activities, including main idea and details							
Recognize artists' craft and techniques for conveying meaning							
Interpret information from various formats such as maps, charts, graphics, video segments, technology							
Knows various types of mass media (such as film, video, television, billboards, and newspapers)							
Evaluate purposes of various media, including mass media (information, appreciation, entertainment, directions, persuasion)							
Use media, including mass media, to compare ideas, information, and points of view							
REPRESENTING							
Select, organize, or produce visuals to complement or extend meanings							
Produce communication using appropriate media to develop a class paper, multimedia or video reports							
Show how language, medium, and presentation contribute to the message							

Reading: Alphabetic Principle, Sounds/Symbols

☑ Tested Skill

☐ Tinted panels show skills, strategies, and other teaching opportunities

PRINT AWARENESS	K	1	2	3	4	5	6
Know the order of the alphabet							
Recognize that print represents spoken language and conveys meaning							
Understand directionality (tracking print from left to right; return sweep)							
Understand that written words and sentences are separated by spaces							
Know the difference between individual letters and printed words							
Understand that spoken words are represented in written language by specific sequence of letters							
Recognize that there are correct spellings for words							
Know the difference between capital and lowercase letters							
Recognize how readers use capitalization and punctuation to comprehend							
Recognize the distinguishing features of a letter, word, sentence, paragraph							
Understand appropriate book handling							
Recognize that parts of a book (such as cover/title page and table of contents) offer information							

PHONOLOGICAL AWARENESS	K	1	2	3	4	5	6
Listen for environmental sounds							
Identify spoken words and sentences							
Divide spoken sentence into individual words							
Produce rhyming words and distinguish rhyming words from nonrhyming words							
Identify, segment, and combine syllables within spoken words							
Blend and segment onsets and rimes							
Identify and isolate the initial, medial, and final sound of a spoken word							
Add, delete, or substitute sounds to change words (such as *cow* to *how*, *pan* to *fan*)							
Blend sounds to make spoken words							
Segment one-syllable spoken words into individual phonemes							

PHONICS AND DECODING	K	1	2	3	4	5	6
Alphabetic principle: Letter/sound correspondence	☑	☑	☑				
Blending CVC words	☑	☑					
Segmenting CVC words	☑						
Blending CVC, CVCe, CCVC, CVCC, CVVC words	☑	☑	☑				
Segmenting CVC, CVCe, CCVC, CVCC, CVVC words and sounds	☑	☑	☑				
Initial and final consonants: /n/n, /d/d, /s/s, /m/m, /t/t, /k/c, /f/f, /r/r, /p/p, /l/l, /k/k, /g/g, /b/b, /h/h, /w/w, /v/v, /ks/x, /kw/qu, /j/j, /y/y, /z/z	☑	☑					
Initial and medial short vowels: *a, i, u, o, e*	☑	☑	☑				
Long vowels: *a-e, i-e, o-e, u-e* (vowel-consonant-e)		☑	☑				
Long vowels, including *ay, ai; e, ee, ie, ea; o, oa, oe, ow; i, y, igh*		☑	☑				
Consonant Digraphs: *sh, th, ch, wh*		☑					
Consonant Blends: continuant/continuant, including *sl, sm, sn, fl, fr, ll, ss, ff*		☑					
Consonant Blends: continuant/stop, including *st, sk, sp, ng, nt, nd, mp, ft*		☑					
Consonant Blends: stop/continuant, including *tr, pr, pl, cr, tw*		☑					
Variant vowels: including /ù/oo; /ô/a, aw, au; /ü/ue, ew		☑	☑				
Diphthongs, including /ou/ou, ow; /oi/oi, oy		☑	☑				
r-controlled vowels, including /âr/are; /ôr/or, ore; /îr/ear		☑	☑				
Soft *c* and soft *g*			☑				
nk		☑	☑				
Consonant Digraphs: *ck*	☑	☑					
Consonant Digraphs: *ph, tch, ch*			☑				
Short *e: ea*			☑				
Long *e: y, ey*			☑				
/ü/oo			☑				
/är/ar; /ûr/ir, ur, er		☑	☑				
Silent letters: including *l, b, k, w, g, h, gh*			☑				
Schwa: /ər/er; /ən/en; /əl/le;			☑				
Reading/identifying multisyllabic words		☑	☑				
Using graphophonic cues							

Reading: Vocabulary/Word Identification

WORD STRUCTURE	K	1	2	3	4	5	6
Common spelling patterns							
Syllable patterns							
Plurals		☑					
Possessives		☑					
Contractions		☑					
Root, or base, words and inflectional endings (-s, -es, -ed, -ing)		☑	☑	☑		☑	
Compound Words		☑	☑	☑	☑	☑	☑
Prefixes and suffixes (such as un-, re-, dis-, non-; -ly, -y, -ful, -able, -tion)			☑	☑	☑	☑	☑
Root words and derivational endings				☑	☑	☑	☑

WORD MEANING	K	1	2	3	4	5	6
Develop vocabulary through concrete experiences, word walls, other people							
Develop vocabulary through selections read aloud							
Develop vocabulary through reading							
Cueing systems: syntactic, semantic, graphophonic							
Context clues, including semantic clues (word meaning), syntactical clues (word order), and graphophonic clues	☑	☑	☑	☑	☑	☑	☑
High-frequency words (such as the, a, and, said, was, where, is)	☑	☑					
Identify words that name persons, places, things, and actions							
Automatic reading of regular and irregular words							
Use resources and references (dictionary, glossary, thesaurus, synonym finder, technology and software, and context)							
Classify and categorize words							
Synonyms and antonyms			☑	☑	☑	☑	☑
Multiple-meaning words			☑		☑	☑	☑
Figurative language			☑	☑	☑	☑	☑
Decode derivatives (root words, such as like, pay, happy with affixes, such as dis-, pre-, un-)							
Systematic study of words across content areas and in current events							
Locate meanings, pronunciations, and derivations (including dictionaries, glossaries, and other sources)							
Denotation and connotation							☑
Word origins as aid to understanding historical influences on English word meanings							
Homophones, homographs							
Analogies							☑
Idioms							

Reading: Comprehension

PREREADING STRATEGIES	K	1	2	3	4	5	6
Preview and predict							
Use prior knowledge							
Set and adjust purposes for reading							
Build background							

MONITORING STRATEGIES	K	1	2	3	4	5	6
Adjust reading rate							
Reread, search for clues, ask questions, ask for help							
Visualize							
Read a portion aloud, use reference aids							
Use decoding and vocabulary strategies							
Paraphrase							
Create story maps, diagrams, charts, story props to help comprehend, analyze, synthesize and evaluate texts							

(continued on next page)

(Reading: Comprehension continued)

SKILLS AND STRATEGIES	K	1	2	3	4	5	6
Recall story details, including character and setting	☑	☑					
Use illustrations	☑	☑					
Distinguish reality and fantasy	☑	☑	☑				
Classify and categorize	☑						
Make predictions	☑	☑	☑	☑	☑	☑	☑
Recognize sequence of events (tell or act out)	☑	☑	☑	☑	☑	☑	☑
Recognize cause and effect	☑	☑	☑	☑	☑	☑	☑
Compare and contrast	☑	☑	☑	☑	☑	☑	☑
Summarize	☑	☑	☑	☑	☑	☑	☑
Make and explain inferences	☑	☑	☑	☑	☑	☑	☑
Draw conclusions		☑	☑	☑	☑	☑	☑
Distinguish important and unimportant information			☑	☑	☑	☑	☑
Recognize main idea and supporting details			☑	☑	☑	☑	☑
Form conclusions or generalizations and support with evidence from text	☑	☑	☑	☑	☑	☑	☑
Distinguish fact and opinion (including news stories and advertisements)			☑	☑	☑	☑	☑
Recognize problem and solution				☑	☑	☑	☑
Recognize steps in a process			☑	☑	☑	☑	☑
Make judgments and decisions		☑	☑	☑	☑	☑	☑
Distinguish fact and nonfact				☑	☑	☑	☑
Recognize techniques of persuasion and propaganda							☑
Evaluate evidence and sources of information, including checking other sources and asking experts							☑
Identify similarities and differences across texts (including topics, characters, problems, themes, cultural influences, treatment, scope, or organization)							
Practice various questions and tasks (test-like comprehension questions)							
Paraphrase and summarize to recall, inform, and organize							
Answer various types of questions (open-ended, literal, interpretive, test-like such as true-false, multiple choice, short-answer)							
Use study strategies to learn and recall (preview, question, reread, and record)							

LITERARY RESPONSE	K	1	2	3	4	5	6
Listen to stories being read aloud							
React, speculate, join in, read along when predictable and patterned selections are read aloud							
Respond to a variety of stories and poems through talk, movement, music, art, drama, and writing							
Show understanding through writing, illustrating, developing demonstrations, and using technology							
Connect ideas and themes across texts							
Support responses by referring to relevant aspects of text and own experiences							
Offer observations, make connections, speculate, interpret, and raise questions in response to texts							
Interpret text ideas through journal writing, discussion, enactment, and media							

TEXT STRUCTURE/LITERARY CONCEPTS	K	1	2	3	4	5	6
Distinguish forms and functions of texts (lists, newsletters, signs)							
Use text features to aid comprehension							
Understand story structure							
Identify narrative (for entertainment) and expository (for information)							
Distinguish fiction from nonfiction, including fact and fantasy							
Understand literary forms (stories, poems, plays, and informational books)							
Understand literary terms by distinguishing between roles of author and illustrator							
Understand title, author, and illustrator across a variety of texts							
Analyze character, character's motive, character's point of view, plot, setting, style, tone, mood		☑	☑	☑	☑	☑	☑
Compare communication in different forms							
Understand terms such as *title, author, illustrator, playwright, theater, stage, act, dialogue,* and *scene*							
Recognize stories, poems, songs, myths, legends, folktales, fables, tall tales, limericks, plays, biographies, autobiographies							
Judge internal logic of story text							
Recognize that authors organize information in specific ways							
Recognize author's purpose: to inform, influence, express, or entertain							
Describe how author's point of view affects text				☑	☑	☑	☑
Recognize biography, historical fiction, realistic fiction, modern fantasy, informational texts, and poetry				☑	☑	☑	☑
Analyze ways authors present ideas (cause/effect, compare/contrast, inductively, deductively, chronologically)							
Recognize literary techniques such as imagery, repetition, flashback, foreshadowing, symbolism							

(continued on next page)

(Reading: Comprehension continued)

VARIETY OF TEXT	K	1	2	3	4	5	6
Read a variety of genres and understand their distinguishing features							
Use expository and other informational texts to acquire information							
Read for a variety of purposes							
Select varied sources when reading for information or pleasure							
Know preferences for reading literary and nonfiction texts							
FLUENCY							
Read regularly in independent-level and instructional-level materials							
Read orally with fluency from familiar texts							
Self-select independent-level reading							
Read silently for increasing periods of time							
Demonstrate characteristics of fluent and effective reading							
Adjust reading rate to purpose							
Read aloud in selected texts, showing understanding of text and engaging the listener							
CULTURES							
Connect own experience with culture of others							
Compare experiences of characters across cultures							
Articulate and discuss themes and connections that cross cultures							
CRITICAL THINKING							
Experiences (comprehend, apply, analyze, synthesize, evaluate)							
Make connections (comprehend, apply, analyze, synthesize, evaluate)							
Expression (comprehend, apply, analyze, synthesize, evaluate)							
Inquiry (comprehend, apply, analyze, synthesize, evaluate)							
Problem solving (comprehend, apply, analyze, synthesize, evaluate)							
Making decisions (comprehend, apply, analyze, synthesize, evaluate)							

Study Skills

INQUIRY/RESEARCH AND STUDY STRATEGIES	K	1	2	3	4	5	6
Follow and give directions							
Use alphabetical order							
Use text features and formats to help understand text (such as boldface, italic, or highlighted text; captions; headings and subheadings; numbers or symbols)							
Use study strategies to help read text and to learn and recall information from text (such as preview text, set purposes, and ask questions; use SQRRR; adjust reading rate; skim and scan; use KWL)							
Identify/frame and revise questions for research							
Obtain, organize, and summarize information: classify, take notes, outline, web, diagram							
Evaluate research and raise new questions							
Use technology for research and/or to present information in various formats							
Follow accepted formats for writing research, including documenting sources							
Use test-taking strategies							
Use text organizers (book cover; title page—title, author, illustrator; contents; headings; glossary; index)		☑	☑	☑	☑	☑	☑
Use graphic aids, such as maps, diagrams, charts, graphs, schedules, calendars		☑	☑	☑	☑	☑	☑
Read and interpret varied texts, such as environmental print, signs, lists, encyclopedia, dictionary, glossary, newspaper, advertisement, magazine, calendar, directions, floor plans, online resources		☑	☑	☑	☑	☑	☑
Use print and online reference sources, such as glossary, dictionary, encyclopedia, telephone directory, technology resources, nonfiction books		☑	☑	☑	☑	☑	☑
Recognize Library/Media center resources, such as computerized references; catalog search—subject, author, title; encyclopedia index		☑	☑	☑	☑	☑	☑

Writing

MODES AND FORMS

	K	1	2	3	4	5	6
Interactive writing							
Descriptive writing							
Personal narrative			☑				
Writing that compares			☑	☑	☑	☑	☑
Explanatory writing		☑	☑	☑	☑	☑	☑
Persuasive writing			☑	☑	☑	☑	☑
Writing a story				☑	☑	☑	☑
Expository writing; research report		☑	☑	☑	☑	☑	☑
Write using a variety of formats, such as advertisement, autobiography, biography, book report/report, comparison-contrast, critique/review/editorial, description, essay, how-to, interview, invitation, journal/log/notes, message/list, paragraph/multi-paragraph composition, picture book, play (scene), poem/rhyme, story, summary, note, letter		☑	☑	☑	☑	☑	☑

PURPOSES/AUDIENCES

	K	1	2	3	4	5	6
Dictate sentences and messages such as news and stories for others to write							
Write labels, notes, and captions for illustrations, possessions, charts, and centers							
Write to record, to discover and develop ideas, to inform, to influence, to entertain							
Exhibit an identifiable voice							
Use literary devices (suspense, dialogue, and figurative language)							
Produce written texts by organizing ideas, using effective transitions, and choosing precise wording							

PROCESSES

	K	1	2	3	4	5	6
Generate ideas for self-selected and assigned topics using prewriting strategies							
Develop drafts							
Revise drafts for varied purposes, elaborate ideas							
Edit for appropriate grammar, spelling, punctuation, and features of published writings							
Proofread own writing and that of others							
Bring pieces to final form and "publish" them for audiences							
Use technology to compose, revise, and present text							
Select and use reference materials and resources for writing, revising, and editing final drafts							

SPELLING

	K	1	2	3	4	5	6
Spell own name and write high-frequency words							
Words with short vowels (including CVC and one-syllable words with blends CCVC, CVCC, CCVCC)							
Words with long vowels (including CVCe)							
Words with digraphs, blends, consonant clusters, double consonants							
Words with diphthongs							
Words with variant vowels							
Words with r-controlled vowels							
Words with /ər/, /əl/, and /ən/							
Words with silent letters							
Words with soft *c* and soft *g*							
Inflectional endings (including plurals and past tense and words that drop the final *e* and double a consonant when adding *-ing, -ed*)							
Compound words							
Contractions							
Homonyms							
Suffixes such as *-able, -ly, -ful,* or *-less,* and prefixes such as *dis-, re-, pre-,* or *un-*							
Spell words ending in *-tion* and *-sion,* such as *station* and *procession*							
Accurate spelling of root or base words							
Orthographic patterns and rules such as *keep/can; sack/book; out/now; oil/toy; match/speech; ledge/cage;* consonant doubling, dropping *e,* changing *y* to *i*							
Multisyllabic words using regularly spelled phonogram patterns							
Syllable patterns (including closed, open, syllable boundary patterns)							
Synonyms and antonyms							
Words from Social Studies, Science, Math, and Physical Education							
Words derived from other languages and cultures							
Use resources to find correct spellings, synonyms, and replacement words							
Use conventional spelling of familiar words in writing assignments							
Spell accurately in final drafts							

(continued on next page)

(Writing continued)

	K	1	2	3	4	5	6
GRAMMAR AND USAGE							
Understand sentence concepts (word order, statements, questions, exclamations, commands)							
Recognize complete and incomplete sentences							
Nouns (common, proper, singular, plural, irregular plural, possessives)							
Verbs (action, helping, linking, irregular)							
Verb tense (present, past, future, perfect, and progressive)							
Pronouns (possessive, subject and object, pronoun-verb agreement)							
Use objective case pronouns accurately							
Adjectives							
Adverbs that tell how, when, where							
Subjects, predicates							
Subject-verb agreement							
Sentence combining							
Recognize sentence structure (simple, compound, complex)							
Synonyms and antonyms							
Contractions							
Conjunctions							
Prepositions and prepositional phrases							
PENMANSHIP							
Write each letter of alphabet (capital and lowercase) using correct formation, appropriate size and spacing							
Write own name and other important words							
Use phonological knowledge to map sounds to letters to write messages							
Write messages that move left to right, top to bottom							
Gain increasing control of penmanship, pencil grip, paper position, beginning stroke							
Use word and letter spacing and margins to make messages readable							
Write legibly by selecting cursive or manuscript as appropriate							
MECHANICS							
Use capitalization in sentences, proper nouns, titles, abbreviations and the pronoun *I*							
Use end marks correctly (period, question mark, exclamation point)							
Use commas (in dates, in addresses, in a series, in letters, in direct address)							
Use apostrophes in contractions and possessives							
Use quotation marks							
Use hyphens, semicolons, colons							
EVALUATION							
Identify the most effective features of a piece of writing using class/teacher-generated criteria							
Respond constructively to others' writing							
Determine how his/her own writing achieves its purpose							
Use published pieces as models for writing							
Review own written work to monitor growth as writer							